ADROS VERSE I

Learn & Retain

Spanish, Portuguese, Italian, & French

with Spaced Repetition

1,000+ Anki Notes with Comparative Grammar, Vocabulary, Common Phrases, and Audio Pronunciation

Bucharest - 2024

Published by ADROS VERSE EDUCATION S.R.L.

website: https://www.adrosverse.com/

e-mail: info@adrosverse.com

Table of Contents

I. Introduction to Spaced Repetition

Spaced repetition is a method of learning new material and then reviewing and memorizing that material over *spaced* intervals. Spaced repetition is often carried out using *flashcards*. The cards that you memorize successfully (i.e., *easy* material) will be reviewed less often, whereas the cards that you stumble over and struggle to memorize (i.e., *hard* material) will be shown more often.

In essence, spaced repetition is an enhancement of the old technique of learning by flashcards. You review flashcards and choose how *"easy"* or *"hard"* it is to recall what was on the given flashcard. Based on this assessment, the spaced repetition system (SRS) algorithm determines which flashcard to review next time. By applying it regularly, you prime your mind to transfer information from your short-term to long-term memory.

To apply spaced repetition to flashcards, we need to decide on many parameters, such as the interval between reviews and whether the interval is fixed or graduated. Many software programs use algorithms to implement spaced-repetition learning. We will not delve into the details of each software and the algorithms they use. Instead, we will pick the most popular software among students and language learners, and that is *Anki.*

Anki in Japanese means *"memorization"* and that's exactly what the Anki flashcard app is. It is a way to help you memorize specific information, in this case, a foreign language.

Interestingly, Anki was not originally created or even marketed as a language learning app. Nevertheless, it is extremely useful for learning new vocabulary and grammar.

The Anki software can be used on a desktop device (AnkiWeb) or a smartphone using Android (AnkiDroid) or iOS (AnkiMobile). The use of AnkiWeb and AnkiDroid is free. AnkiMobile, unfortunately, is paid and can be purchased from the Apple Store. Alternatively, if you use an iPhone or iPad, you could install AnkiWeb on your computer and test it for a few days. If you like it, you can continue to use AnkiWeb or purchase AnkiMobile—if you deem it worthwhile. If you create an account using your Anki software, you can synchronize your account on different devices, including multiple desktops and mobile phones.

ROMANCE LANGUAGES

The Romance languages, sometimes known as Latin or Neo-Latin, are a group of contemporary languages that emerged from Late Latin-based languages and their spoken forms, Vulgar Latin. They are the sole subgroup of the Indo-European language family's Italic languages branch. It is estimated that there are 485 million native speakers of *Spanish*, 235 million Portuguese, 80 million native speakers of *French*, 65 million native speakers of *Italian*, and 24 million native speakers of *Romanian*. These *five* languages are all national languages of their respective nations of origin. Other examples of Romance languages include Catalan as well as other provincial dialects in Italy, Spain, France, Switzerland, and Austria.

About 900 million people speak Romance languages natively worldwide, mainly in the Americas and Europe. The major Romance languages have many non-native speakers and are widely spoken. Romance languages are a group of closely related languages derived from Vulgar Latin, the vernacular Latin of the Roman people. The Romance languages are derived from the Latin language. The Indo-European family of languages includes these languages.

How to Use This Book

This book is useful for learners of most variations of Spanish, Portuguese, Italian, and French. However, when it comes to regional differences in vocabulary and pronunciation, we generally focus on Latin American Spanish, Brazilian Portuguese, Italian from Italy, and French from France.

The best way to study using this book is to start with reading Level I, Lesson 1 in the book, then go to your Anki app and activate the cards of that lesson. If a card is familiar to you, you will be able to answer it as *easy*. As a result, you will see these cards less often in the future as they *fade away* in the memory of the app.

There may be some lessons that you find useful to return to for further review or reference. We try to point these out throughout the book. The appendix also contains some cheat sheets that summarize some of these rules. You can use those if you find them useful. The Anki app will help you through this process because it will keep repeating the concepts that slip your memory.

The Anki package that accompanies the book contains a vocabulary-building section, in which we cover basic verbs and adjectives; then, we go over nouns from different categories. In addition, you will find a section dedicated for common phrases at each level.

In the appendix, you will find two useful cheat sheets for each language to give you an overall perspective of most moods and verb tenses. The first cheat sheet is the Verb Conjugation Chart, which is structured as a comprehensive reference for the reader. The second sheet dives deeper into the irregular verbs of each tense where necessary.

We recommend that you keep these two sheets handy by printing them out or having them available separately on your desk or electronic device.

Specially designed as a fun, practical, and accessible path to learn and compare the four major Romance languages through spaced repetition, this ultimate package offers readers an engaging and enjoyable way of building their vocabulary and learning comparative grammar faster.

Featuring six levels of difficulty with multiple charts, tables, and examples, inside you will find an intuitive path to effortlessly improving your comprehension, memory, and comparative grammar skills of Spanish, Portuguese, Italian, and French simultaneously.

Instead of studying each language separately, this book allows you to save a great deal of time to study and compare the four main Romance languages at once.

This book can serve as a reference whether you are a multilingual person or just want to get a general knowledge to get started. If you are familiar with one or more of the Romance languages, this book can help you extend that knowledge without starting from scratch.

II. Setting Up Anki

To use the Anki flashcards that accompany the book, which is highly recommended for your maximum benefit, visit:

https://www.adrosverse.com/setting-up-anki/

You will learn how to download the Anki software, import the Spanish/Portuguese/Italian/French Anki package, and activate the cards associated with the lessons in the book as you read through it.

If you prefer video instructions, go to our YouTube page at https://www.youtube.com/watch?v=kLlWwhFmMHM or simply search for **ADROS VERSE EDUCATION** channel on YouTube and look for the title: **Setting up Anki and Importing the ADROS VERSE Package - All Languages**.

To get the Anki App go to https://apps.ankiweb.net/ and download the latest version for Desktop or other mobile devices.

To create an Anki account, click on "**Sync**," then click on "**Sign Up**." This will take you to a web page where you can complete the signup process.

To use the flashcards that accompany the book, go to https://www.adrosverse.com/books-and-flashcards/, and download the "**Spanish/Portuguese/Italian/French: Level I - Basic**" package.

At the check-out, use the discount code provided to you in **Appendix A**. If you purchased the book, you should get the Level I Anki package for FREE for a limited time. Once you download the cards, the cards do not expire.

Go to your Anki app, and in the menu bar, go to "**File**," then select "**Import**" from the list of options and navigate to where the package was downloaded.

Important Notes:

1. All the cards are suspended by default. This is done intentionally because you do not want to be presented with cards from all levels before you even start reading the book.

   You are expected to start reading Level 1, Lesson 1. After you finish, you want to activate or *unsuspend* the cards associated with that lesson.

   To do this, follow the simple steps described here.

- On the main Anki page where decks are presented, click on "**Browse**."

- Highlight Lesson 1 from the menu on the left.

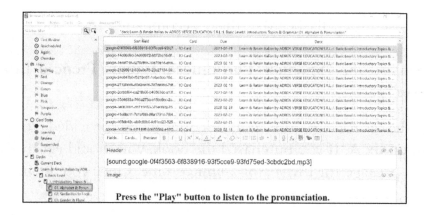

Press the "Play" button to listen to the pronunciation.

- Highlight all the cards (shown on the right) in Lesson 1 using CTRL+A. Alternatively, you can click on **Edit** > **Select All**.

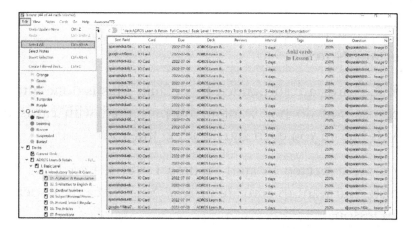

- After highlighting all the cards from Lesson 1, activate them by clicking on **Cards** > **Toggle Suspend** to unsuspend the cards.

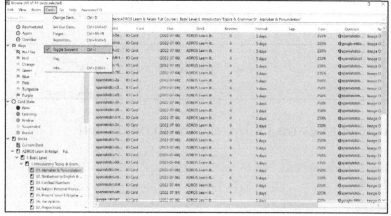

- Go back to the decks page. You will notice now that there are a few cards that are due from Lesson 1.

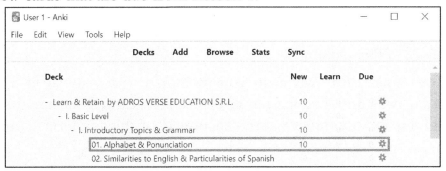

2. Remember to switch off the automatic audio play. These settings can be accessed by clicking on the settings icon on your deck page, as shown below.

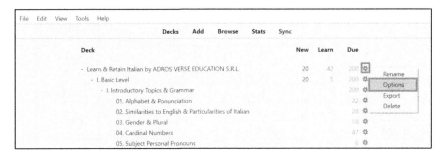

We recommend that you switch off the automatic audio play and keep the other default settings. However, feel free to experiment with the settings for a better personal experience.

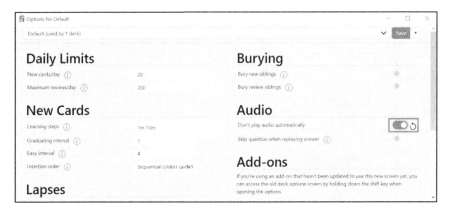

LEVEL I: BASIC

Start your journey by familiarizing yourself with the introductory topics in this section.

Your Anki cards will help you memorize the material in a non-boring way until you master what you have learned. Ensure that you did not skip the introductory Chapter II of this book on setting up Anki.

1. ALPHABET & PRONUNCIATION

Start with the alphabet in the table below, and use your Anki cards to anchor what you learned via spaced-repetition exercises.

	A	B	C	D	E	F	G
SP	ah	be	se	de	e	ef-e	he
PT		be	se	de		ef-e	je
IT		bee	chee	dee		eff-e	jee
FR		be	se	de	ə	ef	je

	H	I	J	K	L	M	N
SP	ach-e	ee	ho-ta	ka	el-e	em-e	en-e
PT	a-**ga**		**jo**-ta				
IT	**ak**-ka	ee	ee **loon**-ga	**kap**-pa	**el**-le	**em**-me	**en**-ne
FR	ash		jee	ka	el	em	en

	O	P	Q	R	S	T	U
SP	o	pe	koo	er-e	es-e	te	oo
PT			ke	eh-e			
IT		pee	koo	er-re	es-se	tee	
FR		pe	kμ	eя	es	te	μ

	V	W	X	Y	Z	RR	Ñ
SP	**oo**-be	**dob**-le oo	**ek**-ees	ee gree-**ye**-ga	**se**-ta	**er**-re	**en**-ye
PT	ve	**dab**-lee-yo	shees	**eep**-see-lõ	ze	-	-
IT	voo	voo **dop**-pia	eeks	ee-psee-lon	**dze**-ta	-	-
FR	ve	doublə ve		ee gяek	zed	-	-

Throughout the book, we will use slash marks "/" to mark the pronunciation of some words, and we will highlight the stressed syllable in bold in case of multi syllable words, e.g., "**casa**" in Italian /**ka**-za/ *(house)*.

In the official Italian alphabet, there are only 21 letters (five vowels and 16 consonants) compared to 26 in the English alphabet. The letters "**j**," "**k**," "**w**," "**x**," and "**y**" are not in the official Italian alphabet, but can still be encountered in some loanwords and acronyms.

Consonants

- The following letters are only found in borrowed foreign words:

SP	"k" and "w"
PT	"k," "w," and "y"
IT	"j," "k," "w," "x," and "y"

- The letter "**b**":

  In Spanish, the letters "**b**" and "**v**" have identical sounds, which are close to the English "**b**" but with less pressure on the lips and with less aspiration. The letter "**v**" is called "**uve**" (pronounced "**oo**-be") or "**ve corta**" (pronounced "**be cor**-ta").

- The letter "**c**":

"**c**" + any letter other than "**e**," "**i**," or "**h**"

  In Spanish, Portuguese, Italian, and French, the letter "**c**" sounds like English "**k**," before any letter other than "**e**," "**i**," or "**h**."

"**c**" + "**e**" or "**i**"

  In Latin American Spanish, Portuguese, and French, the letter "**c**" sounds like English "**s**" only before "**e**" or "**i**." In the Spanish of Spain, the "**c**" before "**e**" or "**i**" sounds like "**th**" in "**three**."

In Italian, if the letter "**c**" is followed by "**e**" or "**i**," it is pronounced like "**ch**" in "**ch**eese."

"**ç**"

In Portuguese and French, if the letter "**c**" is written with a cedilla, i.e., "**ç**," it is pronounced like "**s**" in "**s**ea." The cedilla is always followed by a vowel other than "**e**" or "**i**."

"**c**" + "**h**"

In Spanish, "**ch**" sounds exactly like in English, that is, like "**ch**" in "**ch**eese."

In Portuguese and French, the "**ch**" combination is pronounced like "**sh**" in "**sh**eep."

In Italian, "**ch**" can only sound like "**k**" in "**k**it," and never like "**ch**" in "**ch**eese." The equivalent "**ch**" sound in English is formed only when the "**c**" is followed by an "**i**" or "**e**."

c	+	"**e**" or "**i**"	SP/PT/FR	like English "**s**" in "**s**ea"
			IT	like English "**ch**" in "**ch**eese"
ç	+	"**a**," "**o**," or "**u**"	PT/FR	like English "**s**" in "**s**ea"
c	+	"**h**"	SP	like English "**ch**" in "**ch**eese"
			PT/FR	like English "**sh**" in "**sh**eep"
			IT	like English "**k**" in "**k**it"
c	+	any letter other than "**e**," "**i**," or "**h**"	SP/PT/FR/IT	like English "**k**" in "**k**it"

Here are some examples:

SP	"**c**" + "**e**" or "**i**"	"**cielo**"	/**sye**-lo/	*sky*
	"**c**" + "**h**"	"**China**"	/**chee**-na/	*China*
	"**c**" + other letters	"**casa**"	/**ka**-sa/	*house*
PT	"**c**" + "**e**" or "**i**"	"**céu**"	/**se**-oo/	*sky*
	"**ç**" + "**a**," "**o**," or "**u**"	"**maçã**"	/ma-**sã**/	*apple*
	"**c**" + "**h**"	"**China**"	/**shee**-na/	*China*
	"**c**" + other letters	"**casa**"	/**ka**-za/	*house*
IT	"**c**" + "**e**" or "**i**"	"**cielo**"	/**che**-lo/	*sky*
	"**c**" + other letters	"**casa**"	/**ka**-za/	*house*
FR	"**c**" + "**e**" or "**i**"	"**ciel**"	/syel/	*sky*
	"**ç**" + "**a**," "**o**," or "**u**"	"**ça**"	/sa/	*this*
	"**c**" + "**h**"	"**Chine**"	/sheen /	*China*
	"**c**" + other letters	"**café**"	/ka-**fe**/	*coffee*

- The letter "**d**":

  In Spanish, the letter "**d**" is equivalent to English "**d**" with tongue slightly forward like "**th**" in "**then**."

  In Portuguese, the letter "**d**" is pronounced like an English "**d**," except before "**i**" or an unstressed final "**e**," where it sounds like "**j**" in "**joy**," e.g., "**dia**" /**jee**-ya/ *(day)*, "**sede**" /se-ji/ *(thirst)*, etc.

- The letter "**g**":

"**g**" + "**e**" or "**i**"

  Before "**e**" or "**i**," the letter "**g**" sounds:

SP	like "**h**" in "**hero**," e.g., "**gente**" /hen-te/ *(people)*
PT	like "**s**" in "**measure**," e.g., "**gelo**" /je-lo/ *(ice)*
IT	like "**j**" in "**jam**," e.g., "**gelato**" /je-**la**-to/ *(ice cream)*
FR	like "**s**" in "**measure**," e.g., "**gilet**" /jee-**le**/ *(vest)*

  Before a letter other than "**e**" or "**i**," the letter "**g**" sounds like "**g**" in "**get**" in Spanish, Portuguese, Italian, and French.

  In Italian, in addition to the above rules, the letter "**g**" can precede "**n**" or "**li**" to form the following two special sounds:

  1. The letter "**g**" can precede the letter "**n**" to form "**gn**," pronounced like *"ny"* in *"canyon."* For example, "**gnocchi**" is pronounced as "**nyok**-kee."

  2. The letter "**g**" can precede "**li**" to form "**gli**," pronounced like *"lli"* in *"million."* [1] For example, "**figlia**," meaning *"daughter,"* is pronounced as "**fee**-lya."

  The letter "**i**" is used in Italian to change the pronunciation of "**g**" from hard to soft if the "**g**" precedes a letter that is not "**e**" or "**i**." For instance, "**giorno**" *(day)* is pronounced "**jor**-no," i.e., soft "**g**." From the perspective of an English speaker, this

---

[1] There are only few exceptions in which "**gli**" is pronounced with hard "**g**" as in "**glee**," and not with "**ly**" sound, e.g., "**anglicismo**" *(anglicism)*, "**geroglifico**" *(hieroglyph)*, "**glicerina**" *(glycerine)*, "**negligere**" *(to neglect)*, and "**gliconio**" *(glyconium)*.

explains how to produce the "**j**" sound before an "**e**" or "**i**" in Italian despite the absence of the letter "**j**" from the Italian alphabet. To summarize the possible sounds in Italian:

g	+	"**e**" or "**i**"	soft "**g**"	"**gelato**" pronounced "**je-la**-to"
gi	+	"**a**," "**o**," or "**u**"	soft "**g**"	"**giorno**" pronounced "**jor**-no"
g	+	any letter other than "**e**," "**i**," "**n**," or "**li**"	hard "**g**"	"**gatto**" pronounced "**gat**-to"
gh	+	"**e**" or "**i**"	hard "**g**"	"**spaghetti**" pronounced "spa-**get**-tee"
gn			"**ny**" sound	"**gnocchi**" pronounced "**nyok**-kee"
gli			"**ly**" sound	"**figlia**" pronounced "fee-**lya**"

- The combination "**gu**":

In Spanish, the letter "**u**" is silent after "**g**" if it is followed by "**e**" or "**i**," e.g., "**guitarra**" *(guitar)* is pronounced /gee-**ta**-rra/ and not /gwee-**ta**-rra/.

An exception is made when the "**u**" in "**gue**" or "**gui**" has a dieresis "**ü**," in which case the "**güe**" and "**güi**" sounds are pronounced as "**gwe**" and "**gwee**," respectively, e.g., "**argüir**" /ar-**gweer**/ *(to argue)*.

If the "**gu**" is not followed by "**e**" or "**i**," it is then pronounced as "**gw**," e.g., "**guardar**" *(to keep)* is pronounced /gwar-**dar**/.

In Portuguese, the letter "**u**" is mute when it falls between the letter "**g**" and "**e**" or "**i**" to maintain the hard "**g**" pronunciation, e.g., "**guerra**" /**ge**-ha/ *(war)*, "**guitarra**" /gee-**ta**-ha/ *(guitar)*, etc.[1]

In French, the letter "**u**" is almost always mute when it falls after the letter "**g**" to maintain the hard "**g**" pronunciation, e.g.,

---

[1] There are a few words in which "**gu**" is pronounced like the English "**gw**" sound before "**e**" or "**i**," e.g., "**aguentar**" /ag-wẽ-**ta**/ *(to withstand or put up with)*.

"**guerre**" /гея/ *(war)*, "**guarder**" /гая-**de**/ *(to keep)*, "**guitare**" /gee-**тая**/ *(guitar)*, etc.[1]

- The letter "**h**":

In Spanish, Portuguese, Italian, and French, the letter "**h**" is silent, unless it is combined with "**c**" to form the "**ch**" sound as in "**ch**eese" in Spanish, "**sh**" sound as in "**sh**eep" in Portuguese and French, and "**k**" sound as in "**k**it" in Italian.

In Portuguese, there are two exceptions:

a. When "**h**" is preceded by "**n**" to form the combination "**nh**," which is pronounced like "**ny**" in "can**y**on," e.g., "**lenho**" /**le**-nyo/ *(wood)*.

b. When "**h**" is preceded by "**l**" to form the combination "**lh**," which is pronounced like "**lli**" in "mi**lli**on," e.g., "**olho**" /o-lyo/ *(eye)*.

In French, there is also the combination "**ph**," which forms the equivalent English sound "**f**."

Although the "**h**" is always not pronounced in French, there is a distinction between a *mute* "**h**" and *aspirated* "**h**." This simply goes back to the origin of the word. Words of Latin origin tend to have a mute "**h**," whereas words of Germanic origin tend to have an aspirated "**h**." The difference is subtle and only appears in a few cases such as contraction with the definite article, which will be discussed in **Lesson 7** of this level.

- The letter "**j**":

In Spanish, the letter "**j**" sounds like "**h**" in "**h**ome."

In Portuguese and French, the letter "**j**" sounds more like "**s**" in "mea**s**ure."

---

[1] There are only few exceptions in which the "**u**" is pronounced after the "**g**," such as: "**Uruguay**" /µ-яµ-**gwai**/, "**jaguar**" /ja-**gwaя**/, "**aiguille**" /e-**gцy**/ *(needle)*, and "**linguiste**" /lĭ-**gweest**/ *(linguist)*.

In Italian, the letter "**j**" sounds like "**j**" in "**j**am."

- The letter "**l**":

In Spanish, Portuguese, Italian, and French, the letter "**l**" is equivalent to that in English but has a softer sound.

In Spanish, the doubled letter "**ll**" is pronounced like "**y**" in "**yes**," or in some countries, it sounds more like "**j**" in "judge."

In French, there are two cases in which "**l**" sounds like "**y**" in "**yogurt**."

Case #1: The combination *vowel* + "**il**"

Examples include: "**bail**" /bey/ *(lease)*, "**œil**" /euy/ *(eye)*, "**soleil**" /so-**ley**/ *(sun)*, etc. Words ending in "-**uile**" are an exception, e.g., "**huile**" /ə-**weel**/ *(oil)*, "**tuile**" /t-**weel**/ *(tile)*, etc.

Case #2: The combination *vowel/consonant* + "**ill**"

If the combination "**ill**" is preceded by a *vowel*, then it falls under Case #1, e.g., "**feuille**" /feuy/ *(leaf)*, "**paille**" /pay/ *(straw)*, etc., and the "**ll**" is always pronounced like English "**y**."

If the combination "**ill**" is preceded by a *consonant*, the "**ll**" is pronounced like English "**y**" in most words and like simple "**l**" in some words. Here are some examples:

"**ll**" pronounced like "**y**"		"**ll**" pronounced like "**l**"	
fille[f]	*girl*	**ville**[f]	*city*
famille[f]	*family*	**tranquille**[m,f]	*calm*
vanille[f]	*vanilla*	**Lille**	*Lille (a city)*
cédille[f]	*cedilla (ç)*	**distiller**	*to distill*
Bastille[f]	*Bastille*	**osciller**	*to swing or oscillate*

In addition to the above examples, the "**ll**" in numbers such as "**mille**[m]" /meel/ *(thousand)*, "**million**[m]" /meel-**yõ**/ *(million)*, "**milliard**[m]" /meel-**уaя**/ *(billion)*, and "**billion**[m]" /beel-**yõ**/ *(trillion)*, is pronounced like "**l**."

Finally, if the "**ll**" is preceded by a vowel other than "**i**," it is pronounced like "**l**," e.g., "**salle**" /sal/ *(room)*, "**belle**" /bel/ *(beautiful)*, "**folle**" /fol/ *(crazy)*, "**syllabe**" /see-**lab**/ *(syllable)*, etc.

- The letter "**q**":

In Spanish, Portuguese, and Italian, the letter "**q**" is always followed by the letter "**u**."

In Spanish, the combination "**qu**" is always pronounced like English "**k**" in "kit," e.g., "**querer**" /ke-**rer**/ *(to want)*.

In Portuguese, the combination "**qu**" sounds like "**kw**" before "**a**" and "**o**," and like "**k**" before "**e**" and "**i**," e.g., "**quatro**" /**kwa**-tro/ *(four)*, "**quilo**" /**kee**-lo/ *(kilo)*. In only a few words, the "**qu**" is pronounced like the English "**kw**" sound before "**e**" or "**i**," e.g., "**equestre**" /ek-**we**-stre/ *(equestrian)*.

In Italian, the combination "**qu**" always sounds like "**kw**," e.g., "**quando**" /**kwan**-do/ *(when)*, "**qui**" / kwee/ *(here)*, etc.

In French, the letter "**q**" is almost always followed by the letter "**u**" and sounds like "**k**," e.g., "**qui**"/kee/*(who/that)*. There are only a few exceptions in which the "**q**" is not followed by "**u**," such as "**cinq**" /sĩk/ *(five)* and "**coq**" /kok/ *(rooster)*. In only a few words, the "**qu**" is pronounced like the English "**kw**" sound, e.g., "**équateur**" /ek-wa-**teия**/ *(equator)*.

- The letter "**r**":

In Spanish, the letter "**r**" sounds like English "**r**" but rolled with a single flap against the upper palate.

The combination "**rr**" is considered a separate letter in Spanish, and is pronounced like a strongly trilled "**r**" sound with multiple flaps against the upper palate.

The letter "**r**" sounds also like a strongly trilled "**r**" (identical to "**rr**") when it is at the beginning of a word or after "**l**," "**n**," or "**s**," e.g., "**rojo**" *(red)* sounds like /**rro**-ho/ and "**deshonra**" *(dishonor)* sounds like /des-**on**-rra/, where the stressed syllable in the pronunciation script is in bold.

In Portuguese, the letter "**r**" is equivalent to the English "**r**" but rolled with a single flap against the upper palate, "**caro**" /ka-ro/ *(expensive)*, except: at the beginning of a word, after a nasal sound or "**l**," or when doubled "**rr**," the "**r**" sounds like "**h**," e.g., "**carro**" /ka-ho/ *(car)*, "**rato**" /ha-to/ *(mouse)*, "**genro**" /jẽ-ho/ *(son-in-law)*, etc.

At the end of a word, the "**r**" is sometimes not pronounced, e.g., "**comer**" /ko-me(r)/ *(to eat)*, depending on the regional variant of Brazilian Portuguese.

In Italian, the letter "**r**" sounds like English "**r**" but rolled with a single flap against the upper palate, similar to its pronunciation in Spanish and Portuguese.

In French, the letter "**r**" is equivalent to English "**r**" but rolled using the back of the tongue near the throat to form the distinctive French "**r**" sound, represented by the symbol /я/.

- The letter "**s**":

In Spanish, the letter "**s**" always sounds like English "**s**" in "sea."

In Portuguese, the letter "**s**" can sound like English "**s**" or "**z.**" If the "**s**" falls between two vowels or before a voiced consonant ("**b**," "**d**," "**g**," "**l**," "**m**," "**n**," "**r**," or "**v**"), it is pronounced like "**z**" in "zoo." Otherwise, it is pronounced like "**s**" in "sea." In some parts of Brazil, the final "**s**" is pronounced like "**sh**" in "sheep," e.g., "**anos**" /a-nosh/ *(years)*.

In Italian, the letter "**s**" can sound like English "**s**" or "**z.**" In most cases, the following rule applies:

If "**s**" is between two vowels or before a voiced consonant ("**b**," "**d**," "**g**," "**l**," "**m**," "**n**," "**r**," or "**v**"), it is often pronounced like English "**z**," e.g., "**rosa**" *(rose)* is pronounced /ro-za/. In most other cases, it is pronounced like the English "**s**" in "start."

The compound consonant "**sc**" is used in Italian to form the equivalents of the sounds "**sh**" and "**sk**" in English:

1. If "sc" is followed by "e" or "i," it is pronounced like *"sh"* in *"sheep,"* e.g., "scelta" *(choice)* is pronounced /<u>sh</u>el-ta/.

2. Otherwise, "sc" is pronounced like *"sk"* in *"sky,"* e.g., "scarpe" *(shoes)* is pronounced /<u>sk</u>ar-pe/.

The letter "h" is used in Italian to change the pronunciation of "sc" from "sh" to "sk" if the "sc" precedes an "e" or "i." For example, "<u>sch</u>ema" *(scheme)* is pronounced /<u>sk</u>e-ma/.

sc	+	"e" or "i"	"sh" sound	"<u>sc</u>elta" pronounced "<u>sh</u>el-ta"
sc	+	"a," "o," or "u"	"sk" sound	"<u>sc</u>arpe" pronounced "<u>sk</u>ar-pe"
sch	+	"e" or "i"	"sk" sound	"<u>sch</u>ema" pronounced "<u>sk</u>e-ma"

In French, the letter "s" can sound like English "s" or "z." If the "s" falls between two vowels, it is often pronounced like English "z," e.g., "ro<u>s</u>e" /яoz/ *(pink)*. In most other cases, it is pronounced like the English "s" in "start," e.g., "salut" /sa-lμ/ *(hi)*.

- The letter "t":

In Spanish, Portuguese, Italian, and French, the letter "t" is pronounced like an English "t" in "top."

The only exception is in Portuguese before "i" or an unstressed final "e," where it sounds like "ch" in "chip," e.g., "<u>t</u>ia" /<u>chee</u>-ya/ *(aunt)*, "brilhan<u>t</u>e" /bree-**lyã**-<u>chi</u>/ *(brilliant)*, etc.

- The letter "x":

In Spanish, the letter "x" is pronounced like "ks" in "socks," e.g., "ta<u>x</u>i" /ta<u>k</u>-see/ *(Mexico)*, and in a few exceptions pronounced like "h" in "home," e.g., "Mé<u>x</u>ico" /me-<u>h</u>ee-ko/ *(Mexico)*.

In Portuguese, the letter "x" has four possible pronunciations:

1. Like "sh" in "sh<u>o</u>p" at the beginning of a word or between vowels in most cases. Examples include: "<u>x</u>ale" /**sha**-li/ *(shawl)*, "<u>x</u>erife" /she-**ree**-fi/ *(sheriff)*, "pei<u>x</u>e" /**pey**-shi/ *(fish)*, "bai<u>x</u>o" /**bay**-sho/ *(low)*, etc.

2. Like "**s**" in "sea" before "**c**," "**f**," "**p**," "**t**," or "**qu**," e.g., "**extra**" /**es**-tra/ *(extra)*, in addition to few other words, such as: "**próximo**" /**pro**-see-mo/ *(next)*, "**máximo**" /**ma**-see-mo/ *(maximum)*, "**auxílio**" /aw-**see**-lyo/ *(aid)*, "**sintaxe**" /sĩ-**ta**-si/ *(syntax)*, and "**trouxe**" /**troo**-si/ *(he brought)*.

3. Like "**z**" in many words, especially the ones beginning with "**ex**" followed by a consonant or a voiced consonant ("**b**," "**d**," "**g**," "**l**," "**m**," "**n**," "**r**," or "**v**"), e.g., "**exame**" /e-**za**-mi/ *(exam)*, "**ex-marido**" /ez ma-**ree**-do/ *(ex-husband)*, etc.

4. Like "**ks**" in some words, e.g., "**taxi**" /**ta**-ksee/ *(taxi)*, "**axila**" /a-**ksee**-la/ *(armpit)*, "**complexo**" /kõ-**ple**-kso/ *(complex)*, "**fixo**" /**fee**-kso/ *(fixed)*, "**ortodoxo**" /or-to-**do**-kso/ *(orthodox)*, "**óxido**" /**o**-ksee-do/ *(oxide)*, "**reflexo**" /ref-**le**-kso/ *(reflex)*, "**sexo**" /**se**-kso/ *(sex)*, "**tóxico**" /**to**-ksee-ko/ *(toxic)*, etc.

In Italian, the letter "**x**" is not in the official alphabet but can still be encountered in some loanwords and acronyms, e.g., "**xeno**" /**kse**-no/ *(xenon)*.

In French, the letter "**x**" often has a "**ks**" sound like "**x**" in "**fix**" or a "**gz**" sound like "**x**" in "exam." The basic rules are:

1. If the letter "**x**" falls between two vowel sounds or at the beginning of a word, it often has a "**gz**" sound, e.g., "**examen**" /e-**gza**-mã/ *(exam)*, "**xylophone**" /**gzee**-lo-**fon**/ *(xylophone)*, etc.

2. Only at the end of the numbers "**six**" /sees/ *(six)* and "**dix**" /dees/ *(ten)* the final "**x**" is pronounced like "**s**."

3. In most other cases, the "**x**" has a "**ks**" sound, e.g., "**taxe**" /taks/ *(tax)*.

- The letter "**y**":

In Spanish, the letter "**y**" is pronounced like "**y**" in "yes," or in some countries, it sounds more like "**j**" in "judge," with two exceptions:

1. At the end of a word, it is considered a vowel, e.g., "**rey**" *(king)* and pronounced as English "**y**" in "say."

2. If used as a vowel meaning *"and,"* it is then pronounced like "**ee**" in "see."

In Portuguese, the letter "**y**" can only be encountered in loanwords and is often equivalent to English "**y**."

In Italian, the letter "**y**" is not in the official alphabet but can still be encountered in some loanwords and acronyms, e.g., "**yogurt**" /**yo**-goort/ *(yogurt)*.

In French, the letter "**y**" is considered a semi-vowel in one case, that is, when it precedes another vowel. In this case, it is pronounced like English "**y**," e.g., "**yeux**" /yeu/ *(eyes)*, "**yaourt**" /ya-**оояt**/ *(yogurt)*, etc. In all other cases, when it precedes a consonant or on its own, it is considered a vowel and is treated exactly like the vowel "**i**," e.g., "**y**" /ee/ *(there)*, "**cyclisme**" /seek-**leezm**/ *(cycling)*, "**Yves**" /eev/ *(Yves)*, etc.

- The letter "**z**":

In Latin American Spanish, the letter "**z**" is pronounced exactly like the letter "**s**." In the Spanish of Spain, it sounds like "**th**" in "**th**ree."

In Portuguese, it is equivalent to English "**z**," except at the end of a word, where it can sound like "**z**" or "**s**."

In Italian, the letter "**z**" is pronounced as "**ts**" (unvoiced) or "**dz**" (voiced). In general, the "**ts**" sound is used when the "**z**" is doubled or in the middle of a word, e.g., "**pizza**" is pronounced "**pee**-<u>ts</u>a," and "**azione**" *(action)* is pronounced "a-<u>tsyo</u>-ne." On the other hand, the "**dz**" sound is often used at the beginning of a word, e.g., "**zio**" *(uncle)* is pronounced "<u>**dzee**</u>-yo."

In French, the letter "**z**" is always equivalent to English "**z**."

- The letter "**ñ**" in Spanish:

The letter "**ñ**" exists only in Spanish and is pronounced like "**ni**" in "on**i**on" or "**ny**" in "can**y**on."

- Double letters:

In Spanish, the only case of a double consonant that one must be aware of is "**cc**," as in words like "**accidente**" *(accident)*. In such cases, one "**c**" is hard *(k-sound)* and the other is soft *(s-sound)*, in a similar fashion to the English pronunciation. Note that "**rr**" and "**ll**" are treated as single letters, not double consonants.

A much less common double-consonant is "**nn**," usually found in words having the prefix "**in-**," as in "**innavegable**" *(unnavigable)*, "**perenne**" *(perennial)*, and very few other words.

In Portuguese, only double consonants that occur in Portuguese are "**rr**" and "**ss**,", which are pronounced like "**h**" in "**h**ot" and "**s**" in "**s**et," respectively.

In Italian, of the 16 consonants in the original Italian alphabet, 14 consonants can be doubled, that is, all consonants except "**q**" and "**h**," e.g., "**caffè**" *(coffee)*, "**mamma**" *(mom)*, "**nonna**" *(grandma)*, etc. They sound stressed with a short pause. Think of the *"n"* sound in *"unnavigable,"* or *"one note"* versus *"one oat."*

In French, in most cases, other than "**ll**," double consonants generally do not change the pronunciation, e.g., "**annuler**" /a-nµ-le/ *(to cancel)*, "**essai**" /e-se/ *(essay)*, etc.

Silent Final Consonants in French

In French, the final "**e**" in most multi-syllable words tends to be silent unless it is accented, e.g., "**sucre**" /sµкя/ *(sugar)*, "**père**" /пея/ *(father)*, etc.

In addition, the final consonant(s) is(are) often silent in many French words, e.g., "**trop**" /тяо/ *(too much)*, "**temp**" /tã/ *(time)*, etc. The general rule is to assume that the final consonant is silent. However, there are many exceptions to this rule. The following notes can help you determine when to treat the final consonant of a French word as silent or pronounce it:

1. The letters "**j**," "**v**," and "**w**" are seldom found in French except in some foreign names, in which case they are likely pronounced.

2. The letters "**b**," "**k**," and "**q**" are found at the end of very few words in French. In most of these words, they are pronounced, e.g., "**club**" /klμb/ *(club)*, "**biftek**" /beef-tek/ *(steak)*, "**cinq**" /sĩk/ *(five)*, "**coq**" /kok/ *(rooster)*. One notable exception is "**plomb**" /plõ/ *(lead)*.

3. The letter "**g**" is generally pronounced when it is a final consonant of an English loanword, e.g., "**blog**" /blog/, "**iceberg**" /ayz-**beяg**/, "**parking**" /paя-**keeng**/, "**meeting**" /mee-**teeng**/, etc. The main exception of this rule is when it forms the nasal sound "**ng**" in non-"**-ing**" suffixes, e.g., "**long**" /lõ/ *(long)*, "**sang**" /sã/ *(blood)*, etc.

4. The letters "**n**" and "**m**" often result in a nasal sound when they come at the end of a word, e.g., "**un**" /ĩ/ *(a/ an)*, "**balcon**" /bal-**kõ**/ *(balcony)*, "**nom**" /nõ/ *(name)*, "**parfum**" /paя-**fĩ**/ *(perfume)*, etc. There are some notable exceptions such as: "**abdomen**" /ab-do-**men**/ *(abdomen)*, "**Amen**" /a-**men**/ *(Amen)*, "**forum**" /fo-**яμm**/ *(forum)*, and "**cadmium**" /cad-**myμm**/ *(cadmium)*.

5. The final consonants "**c**," "**r**," "**f**," and "**l**" tend to be *pronounced* especially in short words of one or two syllables. The four letters are often remembered using the word "**CaReFuL**." Here are some examples and exceptions for each case:

	Pronounced (Often)	**Silent (Exceptions)**
c	"**avec**" *(with)*, "**bloc**" *(block)*, "**sac**" *(bag)*, "**truc**" *(trick)*	"**estomac**" *(stomach)*, "**porc**" *(pork)*, "**blanc**" *(white)*, "**tronc**" *(trunk)*
r	"**cher**" *(expensive)*, "**clair**" *(clear)*, "**fier**" *(proud)*, "**mer**" *(sea)*	Infinitive of "**-er**" verbs, e.g., "**parler**" *(to speak)*
f	"**actif**" *(active)*, "**chef**" *(chef)*, "**neuf**" *(nine)*, "**œuf**" *(egg)*, "**soif**" *(thirst)*	"**clef**" *(key)*, "**nerf**" *(nerve)*
l	"**avril**" *(April)*, "**bol**" *(bowl)*, "**hôtel**" *(hotel)*, "**il**" *(he)*, "**nul**" *(nul)*	"**gentil**" *(kind)*, "**outil**" *(tool)*, vowel + "**il**": "**accueil**" *(welcome)*, "**œil**" *(eye)*

6. The final consonants "**d**," "**p**," "**s**," "**t**," "**x**," and "**z**" are often *silent* with a few exceptions. Here are some examples and exceptions for each case:

	Silent (Often)	Pronounced (Exceptions)
d	"**canard**" *(duck)*, "**chaud**" *(hot)*, "**froid**" *(cold)*, "**grand**" *(big)*,	"**sud**" *(south)*, proper names: "**David**", "**Alfred**", etc.
p	"**beaucoup**" *(a lot)*, "**champ**" *(field)*, "**drap**" *(sheet)*, "**loup**" *(wolf)*	"**cap**" *(cape)*, "**slip**" *(underpants)*
s	"**bas**" *(down)*, "**les**" *(the)*, "**nous**" *(we)*, "**temps**" *(time)*, "**trois**" *(three)*	"**autobus**" *(bus)*, "**fils**" *(son)*, "**ours**" *(bear)*, "**tennis**" *(tennis)*
t	"**abricot**" *(apricot)*, "**et**" *(and)*, "**minuit**" *(midnight)*, "**petit**" *(small)*, "**poulet**" *(chicken)*, "**salut**" *(hi)*	"**brut**" *(raw)*, "**est**" *(east)*, "**ouest**" *(west)*, -**ct** ending: e.g., "**direct**" *(direct)*, -**pt** ending: e.g., "**sept**" *(seven)*
x	"**choix**" *(choice)*, "**deux**" *(two)*, "**époux**" *(spouse)*, "**prix**" *(price)*	"**six**" *(six)*, "**dix**" *(ten)*, "**index**" *(index)*
z	"**chez**" *(at the place of)*, "**riz**" *(rice)*, "**parlez**" *(you speak)*	"**gaz**" *(gas)*

7. As we will learn in **Lesson 6** of this level, the third-person plural verb conjugation suffix "-**ent**" in the present indicative tense is always *silent*, e.g., "**ils parlent**" /eel paʁl/ *(they speak)*.

Vowels

Let us now look at vowels in Spanish, Portuguese, Italian, and French. The letters "**a**," "**e**," "**i**," "**o**," and "**u**" are treated as vowels in all four languages.

In Spanish, the letter "**y**" is considered a vowel when it is at the end of a word or when used as a conjunction meaning *"and."*

In French, the letter "**y**" is considered a vowel, except when it precedes another vowel, where it is considered a semi-vowel.

Portuguese and French have nasal vowels, whereas Spanish and Italian do not have nasal vowels.

#1: Vowels in Spanish

The vowels in Spanish are "**a**," "**e**," "**i**," "**o**," and "**u**." The letter "**y**" is considered a vowel when used as a conjunction meaning *"and,"* e.g., **"Adán y Eva"** (*Adam and Eve*) where **"y"** is pronounced **"ee"** as in "b**ee**f." The letter **"y"** is also considered a vowel at the end of a word, e.g., **"rey"** (*king*), where it is pronounced as English **"y"** in "ra**y**" or "sa**y**."

Spanish vowels are classified as strong (**a**, **e**, and **o**) and weak (**i** and **u**).

Every vowel is pronounced separately, and each with its alphabetical sound. Thus, there are no diphthongs in the English sense.

#2: Vowels in Portuguese

The letters **"a," "u," "o," "e,"** and **"i"** are the vowel letters in Portuguese. There are two types of vowels in Portuguese: oral vowels and nasal vowels. Both oral and nasal vowels can have a combination of vowel letters.

1. Oral Vowels

The five vowel letters in Portuguese have a slightly different pronunciation in Portuguese than in English. Notice that we use different symbols from the standard International Phonetic Alphabet (IPA) for simplicity.

Let us start with the main five vowels in Portuguese:

a /a/	**"falar"** /fa-**lar**/ (*to speak*)	always sounds like **"a"** in "f**a**ther"
u /oo/	**"muro"** /m**oo**-ro/ (*wall*)	always sounds like **"oo"** in "f**oo**d"
i /ee/	**"girafa"** /j**ee**-**ra**-fa/ (*giraffe*)	like **"ee"** in "s**ee**" or **"i"** in "mar**i**ne"
e /e/, /i/	**"cego"** /s**e**-go/ (*blind*) - open **"seda"** /s**e**-da" (*silk*) - closed **"noite"** /**noy**-ch**i**/ (*night*) - at word-end	1. open: like **"e"** in "b**e**d" 2. closed (*stressed or unstressed*): like **"ay"** in "s**ay**" but without the final **"y"** sound 3. Like **"i"** in "k**i**d" when it is unstressed at word-end

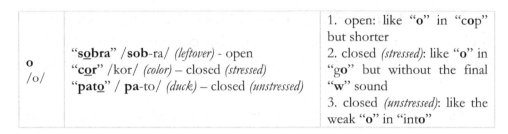

o /o/	"s<u>o</u>bra" /sob-ra/ *(leftover)* - open "c<u>o</u>r" /kor/ *(color)* – closed *(stressed)* "pat<u>o</u>" / pa-to/ *(duck)* – closed *(unstressed)*	1. open: like "o" in "cop" but shorter 2. closed *(stressed)*: like "o" in "go" but without the final "w" sound 3. closed *(unstressed)*: like the weak "o" in "into"

- The Vowel Letter "e"

The letter "e" can have one of three sounds:

1. An open "e" sounds similar to the "e" in "bed" or "set." Examples include:

c<u>e</u>go	/s<u>e</u>-go/	*blind*
f<u>é</u>	/f<u>e</u>/	*faith*

2. A closed "e" sounds similar to the "ay" sound in *"say"* but without the final "y" sound. Examples include:

s<u>e</u>da	/s<u>e</u>-da/	*silk*
voc<u>ê</u>	/vo-s<u>e</u>/	*you (singular)*

3. Like "i" in *"kid"* when it is unstressed at the end of a word. Examples include:

mol<u>e</u>	/mo-li/	*soft*
noit<u>e</u>	/noy-ch<u>i</u>/	*night*

If the "e" has a circumflex, that is "ê," it is pronounced like a closed "e." If the "e" has an acute accent, that is "é," it is pronounced like an open "e."

If the "e" has no circumflex or acute accent, which is often the case, knowing whether to use a closed or open sound is not always clear and it requires some practice and a good dictionary.

- The Vowel Letter "o"

The letter "o" can have one of three sounds:

1. An open "**o**" sounds like the "**o**" in "c**o**p" but shorter. Examples include:

r<u>o</u>cha	/h<u>o</u>-sha/	*rock*
p<u>ó</u>	/p<u>o</u>/	*dust or powder*

2. A closed stressed "**o**" sounds like the "**o**" sound in "g**o**" but without the final "**w**" sound. Examples include:

b<u>o</u>ca	/b<u>o</u>-ka/	*mouth*
av<u>ô</u>	/a-v<u>o</u>/	*grandfather*

3. A closed unstressed "**o**" sounds like the weak "**o**" in "int**o**." Examples include:

ceg<u>o</u>	/se-g<u>o</u>/	*blind*
sapat<u>o</u>	/sa-**pa**-t<u>o</u>/	*shoe*

If the "**o**" has a circumflex, that is "**ô**," it is pronounced like a closed "**o**." If the "**o**" has an acute accent, that is "**ó**," it is pronounced like an open "**o**."

If the "**o**" has no circumflex or acute accent, which is often the case, knowing whether to use a closed or open sound is not always clear and requires some practice and a good dictionary.

In addition to the main six vowels, there are 13 diphthong vowels. These are summarized as follows:

ai /ay/	"**pai**" /pay/ *(father)* "**mais**" /mays / *(more)*	Pronounced like the English word *"eye"*
au, al /aw/	"**saudar**" /saw-**dar**/ *(to salute)* "**mal**" /maw/ *(badly)*	Pronounced like *"ow"* in the English word *"now"*
ei /ey/	"**lei**" /ley/ *(law)* "**rei**" /hey / *(king)*	Pronounced like *"ay"* in the English word *"day"*
éi /ey/	"**anéis**" /a-**neys**/ *(rings)* "**hotéis**" /o-**teys**/ *(hotels)*	Pronounced like *"e"* in *"set"* followed by *"y"* sound
eu /ew/	"**teu**" /tew/ *(your)* "**pneu**" /pnew/ *(tire)*	Pronounced like *"ay"* in *"day"* followed by *"w"* sound instead of the *"y"* sound
éu /ew/	"**véu**" /vew/ *(veil)* "**chapéu**" /sha-**pew**/ *(hat)*	Pronounced like *"e"* in *"set"* followed by *"w"* sound
iu, il /eew/	"**partiu**" /par-**cheew**/ *(he left)* "**útil**" /oo-**teew**/ *(useful)*	Pronounced like *"ee"* in *"feed"* followed by *"w"* sound

oi /oy/	"noite" /**noy**-chi/ (night) "foi" /foy/ (he was/went)	Pronounced like "o" in "old" followed by "y" sound
ói /oy/	"sóis" /soys/ (suns) "herói" /e-**roy**/ (hero)	Pronounced like "o" in "cop" followed by "y" sound
ou /ow/	"sou" /sow/ (I am) "vou" /vow/ (I go)	Pronounced like "o" in "old" followed by "w" sound
ol /ow/	"sol" /soy/ (sun) "farol" /fa-**roy**/ (lighthouse)	Pronounced like "o" in "cop" followed by "w" sound
ui /ooy/	"fluido" /**flooy**-do/ (fluid) "fui" /fooy/ (I was/went)	Pronounced like "oo" in "food" followed by "y" sound
ul /oow/	"sul" /soow/ (south) "azul" /a-**zoow**/ (blue)	Pronounced like "oo" in "food" followed by "w" sound

There are also four triphthongs:

uai /way/	"quais" /kways/ (which ones)	This triphthong sounds like the English interrogative "Why?"
ual /waw/	"qual" /kwaw/ (which one)	This triphthong sounds like the English exclamation "Wow!"
uei /wey/	"continuei" /cõ-teen-**wey**/ (I continued)	Sounds like the English word "way." Exceptionally, the "u" (and the "w" sound) is mute if preceded by "q" or "g," e.g., "joguei" /jo-**gey**/ (I played)
uou /wow/	"atuou" /at-**wow**/ (he acted)	This triphthong sounds like the English exclamation "Whoa!"

2. Nasal Vowels

One main challenge in Portuguese is mastering the nasal vowel sounds.

A nasal pronunciation occurs in Portuguese in one of two cases:

1. When an "n" or "m" preceded by a vowel is at the end of a word or anywhere else in the word but followed by a consonant. To summarize:

at word end	vowel + "n" or "m"	nasal
anywhere else in a word	vowel + "n" or "m" + consonant	nasal
	vowel + "n" or "m" + vowel	not nasal

Notice that the "**m**" or "**n**" is not actually pronounced but is instead assimilated in the nasal vowel. If a vowel follows the "**m**" or "**n**," the nasalization often does not occur and the "**m**" or "**n**" is pronounced, e.g., "**ano**" /a-no/ *(year)*, "**como**" /ko-mo/ *(how)*, "**cama**" /ka-ma/ *(bed)*, "**amar**" /a-**mar**/ *(to love)*, etc.

2. When the vowel "**a**" or "**o**" is marked by a *tilde*, that is, "**ã**" or "**õ**," e.g., "**alemã**" /a-le-**mã**/ *(German)*.

Nasal Sounds

The five nasal vowel sounds in Portuguese are: nasal "**a**," nasal "**e**," nasal "**i**," nasal "**o**," and nasal "**u**." We refer to these five sounds throughout the book using the symbols: "**ã**," "**ẽ**," "**ĩ**," "**õ**," and "**ũ**."

The five nasal sounds occur in the following cases:

ã, am, an /ã/	"**ímã**" /ee-mã/ *(magnet)* "**ambos**" /ã-bos/ *(both)* "**antes**" /ã-chis/ *(before)*	Similar to "**an**" in the English word "**an**t" but with a stronger nasal sound
em, en /ẽ/	"**tempo**" /tẽ-po/ *(time)* "**vento**" /vẽ-to/ *(wind)*	Similar to "**ai**" in the English word "p**ai**nt" but with a stronger nasal sound
im, in /ĩ/	"**sim**" /sĩ/ *(without)* "**lindo**" /lĩ-do/ *(beautiful)*	Similar to "**ea**" in the English word "m**ea**ns" but with a stronger nasal sound
om, on /õ/	"**bom**" /bõ/ *(good)* "**onde**" /õ-ji/ *(where)*	Similar to "**o**" in the English word "d**o**n't" but with a stronger nasal sound
um, un /ũ/	"**um**" /ũ/ *(a/an)* "**uns**" /ũs/ *(some)*	Similar to "**oo**" in the English word "m**oo**ns" but with a stronger nasal sound

In addition to the main five nasal vowels, there are five diphthong vowels. These are summarized as follows:

ãe, ãi /ãy/	"**mãe**" /mãy/ *(mother)*	Similar to "**an**" in the English word "**an**t," but with a stronger nasal sound, followed by a *"y"* sound
ão /ãw/	"**mão**" /mãw/ *(hand)*	Similar to "**an**" in the English word "**an**t," but with a stronger nasal sound, followed by a *"w"* sound
em /ẽy/	"**trem**" /trẽy/ *(train)*	Similar to "**ai**" in the English word "p**ai**nt," but with a stronger nasal sound, followed by a *"y"* sound
õe /õy/	"**põe**" /põy/ *(he/she puts)*	Similar to "**o**" in the English word "d**o**n't," but with a stronger nasal sound, followed by a *"y"* sound

ui /ũy/	"muito" /mũy-to/ (very)	Similar to "oo" in the English word "moons," but with a stronger nasal sound, followed by a "y" sound

It is important to notice the following:

1. The "em" combination results in the diphthong nasal sound /ẽy/ only when "em" is at the end of a word, e.g., "bem" /bẽy/ (well). If "em" is not at a word end, it is pronounced like a simple nasal sound /ẽ/, e.g., "tempo" /tẽ-po/ (time).

2. The "ui" combination results in the diphthong nasal sound /ũy/ only in the word "muito" /mũy-to/ (very, much). In all other cases, "ui" is pronounced as an oral diphthong vowel /ooy/, e.g., "fui" /fooy/ (he was/went).

Finally, there are also two less-common triphthong nasal vowels that only occur before "g" or "q":

uão /wãw/	"saguão" /sag-wãw/ (lobby)	"w" sound + diphthong "ão" /ãw/
uõe /wõy/	"saguões" /sag-wõys/ (lobbies)	"w" sound + diphthong "õe" /õy/

#3: Vowels in Italian

The letters "a," "e," "i," "o," and "u" are treated as vowels, except when the letters "e" and "i" are used to indicate different pronunciation of a preceding "c" or "g," as discussed earlier.

The vowels "a," "e," and "o," are considered *strong* vowels, whereas "i" and "u" are considered *weak* vowels.

The week vowels "i" and "u" form the sounds "y" and "w" when unstressed and preceded or followed by another vowel. Below are some examples:

ai	"ay" sound	"zaino" (backpack) pronounced "dzay-no"
ie	"ye" sound	"ieri" (yesterday) pronounced "ee-ye-ree"
io	"yo" sound	"fiore" (flower) pronounced "fyo-re"
ua	"wa" sound	"guardare" (to look) pronounced "gwar-da-re"
uo	"wo" sound	"uomo" (man) pronounced "wo-mo"
au	"aw" sound	"audio" (audio) pronounced "aw-dyo"
iu	"yoo" sound	"più" (more) pronounced "pyoo"

Italian is considered to have five vowel letters and seven vowel sounds. Each of the vowels "**e**" and "**o**" has an *open* and *closed* sound. The differences are summarized in the following table:

o	open sound	like "**o**" in "**cop**"
	closed sound	like "**o**" in "**go**" but without the final "**w**" sound
e	open sound	like "**e**" in "**bed**" but a little more open
	closed sound	like "**e**" in "**they**" but without the final "**y**" sound

In general, the open sound is used when the syllable is stressed; otherwise, the closed sound is often used. Knowing when to use the open or closed sound can sometimes be tricky. The best way to master the difference is oral practice and referring to a good dictionary.

Every vowel is pronounced separately, and each with its alphabetical sound. Thus, there are no diphthongs in the English sense, except for the "**i**" and "**u**" when used as weak vowels to form the sounds "**y**" and "**w**," respectively, as discussed earlier.

#4: Vowels in French

The letters "**a**," "**u**," "**o**," "**e**," "**i**," and "**y**" are the vowel letters in French. There are two types of vowels in French: oral vowels and nasal vowels. Both oral and nasal vowels can have a combination of vowel letters.

1. Oral Vowels

The vowels "**a**," "**u**," and "**o**" are considered *hard* vowels, whereas "**e**," "**i**," and "**y**" are considered *soft* vowels. When soft vowels come after letters like "**c**" and "**g**," they dictate the pronunciation of that letter to be hard or soft.

The six vowel letters in French have a slightly different pronunciation in French than in English. Notice that we use different symbols from the standard International Phonetic Alphabet (IPA) for simplicity.

Let us start with the main six vowels in French:

a /a/	"**pa**rler" /рая-le/ *(to speak)*	always sounds like "**a**" in "father"
u /μ/	"m**u**r" /мµя/ *(wall)*	This sound does not exist in English. Make your lips round as if you want to say "**o**" and say "**ee**" instead
o /o/	"tr**o**p" /тяо/ *(very)* - closed "c**o**rps" /коя/ *(body)* - open	1. closed: like "**o**" in "**go**" but without the final "**w**" sound 2. open: like "**o**" in "**cop**" but shorter
e /ə/, /e/	"l**e**" /lə/ *(the)* - schwa "all**e**r" /a-le/ *(to go)* - closed "**e**lle" /el/ *(she)* - open	1. like a *schwa* sound in English but more rounded, and sometimes ignored 2. closed: like "**ay**" in "**say**" but without the final "**y**" sound, sometimes spelled "**é**" 3. open: like "**e**" in "**bed**," sometimes spelled "**è**" or "**ê**"
i /ee/	"**gi**rafe" /jee-яaf/ *(giraffe)*	like "**ee**" in "**see**" or "**i**" in "**marine**"
y /ee/	"c**y**cle" /seekl/ *(cycle)*	like "**ee**" in "**see**" or "**i**" in "**marine**"

The letter "**o**" has a closed sound and open sound. The closed "**o**" sound is often used when the "**o**" is the final sound of a word, e.g., "**trop**" /тяо/ *(too much)*; is followed by a "**z**" sound, e.g., "**rose**" /яoz/ *(pink)*; or has a circumflex, e.g., "**hôpital**" /o-pee-**tal**/ *(hospital)*. Otherwise, the open short sound is used. The open sound is similar to the "**o**" in "**cop**" but shorter, e.g., "**corps**" /коя/ *(body)*.

The letter "**e**" can have one of three sounds:

- Schwa sound

This sound is similar to the English schwa[1] but more rounded. This sound is often encountered at the end of single-syllable words, such as "**le**" /lə/ *(the)*, "**te**" /tə/ *(you)*, etc. In multi-syllable words, the schwa pronunciation is *sometimes* optional and can be omitted, e.g., "**devoirs**" /d(ə)v-**waя**/ *(homework)*, "**samedi**" /sam(ə)-**dee**/ *(Saturday)*, "**acheter**" /a-sh(ə)-**te**/ *(to buy)*, etc.

---

[1] A schwa sound in English is the relaxed unstressed vowel sound that we encounter in some pronunciations such as "**a**" in "**about**" or "**e**" in "**taken**."

- Closed sound

The closed "**e**" sound is similar to the "**ay**" sound in *"say"* but without the final "**y**" sound. This sound is often encountered when the syllable sound ends in a *vowel*. For example, the last syllable in the verb "**aller**" /a-**le**/ *(to go)* has the *sound* "**le**," which ends in a vowel sound even though the spelling of the syllable ends in the consonant "**r**." If the "**e**" has an acute accent, it is also pronounced with a closed "**e**" sound, e.g., "**clé**" /kle/ *(key)*, "**désolé**" /de-zo-**le**/ *(sorry)*, etc.

- Open sound

The open "**e**" sound is similar to the "**e**" in *"bed"* or *"set."* This sound is often encountered when the syllable ends in a *consonant* sound, e.g., "**sept**" /s<u>e</u>t/ *(seven)*, "**elle**" /<u>e</u>l/ *(she)*, etc. If the "**e**" has a grave accent or a circumflex, it is pronounced with an open "**e**" sound, e.g., "**mère**" /m<u>e</u>я/ *(mother)*, "**prêt**" /пя<u>e</u>/ *(ready)*, etc. The circumflex often indicates that the original word had an "**s**" in the source language that was later dropped as the language developed.

In addition to the main six vowels, there are some compound vowel sounds that result from different combinations of the six vowels. Some are familiar and easy to grasp, such as:

ai /e/	"**faire**" /feя/ *(to do)* "**jamais**" /ja-**me**/ *(never)*	Similar to closed "e" sound (especially at verb ends), or open "e" sound (in most other cases)
au /o/	"**aussi**" /o-**see**/ *(also)* "**paume**" /pom/ *(palm)*	Similar to closed "o" sound
ei /e/	"**neige**" /nej/ *(snow)* "**peiner**" /pe-**ne**/ *(to struggle)*	Similar to closed "e" sound or open "e" sound
ua /ooa/	"**nuage**" /noo-**aj**/ *(cloud)* "**gluante**" /gloo-**ant**/ *(sticky)*	This combination is pronounced as two different vowels, that is, "oo-a"
ue /we/	"**manuel**" /man-**wel**/ *(manual)* "**usuel**" /μz-**wel**/ *(usual)*	Exceptionally, the "u" is mute if preceded by "q" or "g," e.g., "**que**" /kə/ *(that/who)*
ui /wee/	"**pluie**" /plwee/ *(rain)* "**buisson**" /bwee-**sõ**/ *(bush)*	Exceptionally, the "u" is mute if preceded by "q" or "g," e.g., "**qui**" /kee/ *(that/who)*

ie /ye/	"**tiers**" /tyeя/ *(third)* "**fier**" /fyeя/ *(proud)*	Assuming it is not followed by a third vowel, e.g., "**ieu**" /yeu/
ia /ya/	"**fiable**" /fyabl/ *(reliable)* "**social**" /so-**syal**/ *(social)*	Assuming it is not followed by a third vowel, e.g., "**iau**" /yo/
ou /oo/	"**pour**" /pooя/ *(for)* "**rouge**" /яooj/ *(red)*	Pronounced like "**oo**" in "**food**," unless followed by a vowel, e.g., "**oue**" /we/

On the other hand, the following compound vowels are tricky and are often confusing to English learners:

eu /eu/	"**deux**" /deu/ *(two)* "**heure**" /euя/ *(hour)*	This sound does not exist in English. Make your lips round as if you want to say "**o**" and say "**e**" instead. Depending on whether the "**e**" sound is open or closed, the "**eu**" sound can have an open or closed sound as well.
œu /eu/	"**cœur**" /keuя/ *(heart)* "**œuf**" /euf/ *(egg)*	This vowel is treated like the "**eu**" vowel.
eau /o/	"**eau**" /o/ *(water)* "**beau**" /bo/ *(beautiful)*	This sounds like a closed "**o**."
ieu /yeu/	"**lieu**" /lyeu/ *(place)* "**mieux**" /myeu/ *(better)*	Combining the "**y**" sound with the "**eu**" sound.
iau /yo/	"**sociaux**" /so-**syo**/ *(social)* "**piauler**" /pyo-**le**/ *(peep)*	Found only in a few words.
oi /wa/	"**armoire**" /aя-**mwaя**/ *(cabinet)* "**chinois**" /sheen-**wa**/ *(Chinese)*	Pronounced "**wa**" and not like the English "**oy**" sound.
oue /we/	"**ouest**" /west/ *(west)* "**jouer**" /jwe/ *(to play)*	An exception is at the end of a word when "**e**" is silent, e.g., "**boue**" /boo/ *(mud)*.
oui /wee/	"**oui**" /wee/ *(yes)* "**jouir**" /jweeя/ *(to enjoy)*	An exception is the letter combination "**ouil**" and "**ouille**," both pronounced "**ooy**," e.g., "**bouillir**" /boo-**yeeя**/ *(to boil)*.

Notice that when the "**o**" and "**e**" are combined into one symbol, called a ligature, "**œ**," they form a single sound. As we have seen, when followed by "**u**," the combination "**œu**" has a sound identical to "**eu**." This is the most common sound of the ligature "**œ**" in French. Here are four cases that produce the three possible sounds of the ligature "**œ**" in French:

œ + u /eu/	"**cœur**" /keuя/ *(heart)* "**œuf**" /euf/ *(egg)*	Preceding "**u**," the "**œu**" combination sounds like "**eu**."

œ + il /eu/	"œil" /euy/ *(eye)* "œillet" /eu-**ye**/ *(eyelet)*	Preceding "il," the "œil" combination also sounds like "eu."
œ + st /e/ (open)	"œstrogène" /est-яo-**jen**/ *(estrogen)*	Preceding "st," the "œ" sounds like an open "e."
œ + consonant /e/ (closed)	"œsophage" /e-zo-**faj**/ *(esophagus)*	Preceding any other consonant, the "œ" sounds like a closed "e."

Finally, there is the *dieresis*, which can be found on "e," "i," or "u." It is used on the second vowel of a two-vowel combination to denote that the two vowels must be pronounced separately. For example, "**naïve**" is pronounced /na-**eev**/, not /**nev**/, despite the "**ai**" combination.

2. Nasal Vowels

A nasal pronunciation occurs in French often when a vowel precedes an "n" or "m," but not always. The nasal sound occurs when the "n" or "m" preceded by a vowel is at the end of a word or anywhere else in the word but followed by a consonant.

To summarize:

at word end	*vowel* + "n" or "m"	nasal
anywhere else in a word	*vowel* + "n" or "m" + *consonant*	nasal
	vowel + "n" or "m" + *vowel*	not nasal

For example, the "n" in "**un**" *(a/an – masculine)* and "**anglais**" *(English)* is nasal, but the "n" in "**une**" *(a/an – feminine)* and "**reine**" *(queen)* is not nasal.

The three nasal vowel sounds in French are: nasal "a," nasal "i," and nasal "o." We refer to these three sounds throughout the book here using the symbols: "ã," "ĩ," and "õ." The three sounds occur in the following cases:

- The nasal sound "õ" occurs when "o" is followed by "n" or "m," i.e., "on" or "om."

- The nasal sound "ã" occurs when "a," "e," or "ao" is followed by "n" or "m," i.e., "an," "am," "en," "em," "aon," or "aom."

- The nasal sound "ĩ" occurs when "i," "u," "y," "ai," "ei," or "ie" is followed by "n" or "m," e.g., "in," "im," "un," "um," "yn," "ym," "ain," "aim," "ein," "eim," "ien," or "iem."

Here are some examples of words that contain each of the three nasal sounds:

	an/am		en/em		aon/aom	
ã	"blanc"	"ambre"	"encore"	"temps"	"faon"	"paon"
	/blã/	/ãbя/	/ã-koя/	/tã/	/fã/	/pã/
	(white)	(amber)	(again)	(time)	(fawn)	(peacock)
	in/im	un/um	yn/ym	ain/aim	ien/iem	ein/eim
ĩ	"vin"	"un"	"lynx"	"faim"	"chien"	"rein"
	/vĩ/	/ĩ/	/lĩks/	/fĩ/	/shyĩ/	/яĩ/
	(wine)	(a/ an)	(lynx)	(hunger)	(dog)	(kidney)
	on/om					
õ	"bon"		"sombre"		"ombre"	
	/bõ/		/sõbя/		/õbя/	
	(good)		(dark)		(shadow)	

In the past, there used to be a distinction between the nasal sound from the combination "un" or "um" and the rest of nasal "ĩ" sounds. This is characterized by a fourth distinct nasal sound "œ̃." However, this sound is no longer in use in much of France and has been assimilated into the nasal "ĩ" sound.

Syllable Stress

Knowing which syllable to stress in Spanish, Portuguese, Italian, or French is critical to speaking comprehensibly and achieving fluency. The good news is that, unlike in English, where syllable stress seems more arbitrary, there are well-established rules in these four languages that eliminate the need for guessing. It is important to ensure that you master these rules early on as you build your vocabulary.

- In Spanish:

Spanish is a phonetic language. If you practice enough, you should eventually be able to pronounce any Spanish word without listening to an audio transcription or referring to a dictionary. At the start, some beginner Spanish learners complain that most Spanish learning books do not have a phonetic transcription. They, hopefully then, realize that once you learn some basic rules, you will be able to figure it out more easily with sufficient practice.

The three main rules are:

1. If the last syllable is a vowel (**a, o, u, i**), "**s,**" or "**n,**" the stress falls on the second-to-last syllable, also called the penultimate syllable. For example, "**factura**" /fak-**too**-ra/ *(invoice)*, "**joven**" /**ho**-ben/ *(young)*, and "**lunes**" /**loo**-nes/ *(Monday)*, where the stressed syllable in the pronunciation script is in bold.

2. If the last syllable is *not* a vowel (**a, o, u, i**), "**s,**" or "**n,**" the stress falls on the last syllable. For example, "**azul**" /a-**sool**/ *(blue)*, "**abril**" /ab-**reel**/ *(April)*, "**hablar**" /hab-**lar**/ *(to speak)*.

3. If the word has a written accent (´), this overrides the two previous rules, and we simply stress the syllable that contains the accent. For example, the word "**inglés**" *(English)*, if not marked by an accent, following the first rule, would be pronounced as /**een**-gles/. However, the accent on the second syllable overrides that rule and necessitates that we pronounce it correctly as /een-**gles**/. Other examples include "**útil**" /**oo**-teel/ *(useful)*, "**habló**" /ab-**lo**/ *(spoke)*, and "**jóvenes**" /**ho**-be-nes/ *(youth)*.

The above three rules constitute the basic guidelines that should be practiced frequently as you read Spanish text. In addition to these rules, here are two less important rules to remove any confusion:

1. Spanish vowels are classified as strong (**a, e,** and **o**) and weak (**i** and **u**).

    o   If the stressed syllable contains two vowels, one is strong and the other is weak, the stress falls on the strong vowel, e.g., "**reina**" /rre̲y̲-na/ (*queen*), "**igual**" /ee-g̲wa̲l/ (*equal*), "**cielo**" /cy̲e̲-lo/ (*sky*).

o If the stressed syllable contains two weak vowels, the stress falls on the last of the two vowels, e.g., "**viuda**" /by̲oo̲-da/ (*widow*), "**ruido**" /rrw̲ee̲-do/ (*noise*).

o If the stressed syllable contains two strong vowels, the two vowels are pronounced as two distinct syllables, also known as *hiatus*, and normal stress rules apply, e.g., "**europeo**" /eyoo-ro-**pe**-o/ (*European*), "**maestro**" /ma-**es**-tro/ (*teacher*), "**empleado**" /em-ple-**a**-do/ (*employee*).

A word in its plural form stresses the same syllable as in its singular form. A written accent may be added or removed to enforce this rule. For example, the plural of "**joven**" /**ho**-ben/ (*young*) is "**jóvenes**" /**ho**-be-nes/, and the plural of "**inglés**" /een-**gles**/ (*Englishman*) is "**ingleses**" /een-**gles**-es/.

- In Portuguese:

Portuguese is a phonetic language, and like Spanish, there are well-established rules to determine the stressed syllable. The three main rules are:

1. If the last letter is "**a**," "**o**," or "**e**" (after removing any final "**s**," "**ns**," or "**m**"), the stress falls on the second-to-last syllable, also called the penultimate syllable. For example, "**fatura**" (*invoice*) /fa-**too**-ra/, "**bracelete**" (*bracelet*) /bra-se-**le**-chi/, "**falam**" (*they speak*) /**fa**-lã /, etc. The stressed syllable in the pronunciation script is in bold.

2. If the last letter is not "**a**," "**o**," or "**e**" (after removing any final "**s**," "**ns**," or "**m**"), the stress falls on the last syllable. For example, "**azul**" (*blue*) /a-**zoow**/, "**abril**" (*April*) /ab-**reew**/, "**falar**" (*to speak*) /fa-**lar**/.

3. If the word has an acute accent (´), a circumflex (^), or a tilde (~), this overrides the two previous rules, and we simply stress the syllable that contains the accent or the tilde. For example, the word "**inglês**" (*English*), if not marked by an accent, following the first rule, would be pronounced as "ĩ-gles." However, the accent on the second syllable overrides that rule and necessitates that we pronounce it correctly as "ĩ-**gles**." Other examples include "**útil**" (*useful*) /**oo**-cheew/, "**fácil**" (*easy*) /**fa**-seew/, and "**médico**" (*doctor*) /**me**-dee-ko/.

There are two exceptions to the last rule:

1. If a word has both a tilde and an acute or circumflex accent, the stress falls on the syllable with the acute or circumflex accent, e.g., "**bênção**" /**bẽ**-sãw/ (*blessing*), "**órgão**" /**or**-gãw/ (*organ*), etc.
2. In words that have suffixes, e.g., "**-mente**," "**-zinho**," etc., the tilde does not indicate stress when it falls before the second-to-last syllable, e.g., "**irmãmente**" /eer-mã-**mẽ**-chi/ (*sisterly*), "**Joãozinho**" /jwãw-**zĩ**-nyo/ (*diminutive of* "**João**"), etc.

- In Italian:

In general, Italian is a phonetic language. Knowing which syllable to stress in a polysyllabic[1] word in Italian is critical to speaking comprehensibly and achieving fluency. The main syllable stress rules are:

1. If the last letter is a vowel with an accent, the stress falls on the last syllable. For example, "**città**" (*city*) /cheet-**ta**/, "**caffè**" (*coffee*) /kaf-**fe**/, and "**perché**" (*why*) /per-**ke**/, where the stressed syllable in the pronunciation script is in bold.

2. Most other words in Italian stress the *second-to-last* syllable, also called the *penultimate* syllable.

---

[1] Having more than one syllable

3. Some words stress the *third-to-last* syllable. Most of these words end with the following suffixes:

-agine	-aggine	-igine	-iggine	-uggine
-edine	-udine	-abile	-ibile	-atico
-ico	-aceo	-ognolo	-oide	-tesi
-dromo	-fago	-filo	-fobo	-fono
-metro	-nomo	-gono	-grafo	-logo
-crate	-cefalo	-gamo	-geno	-mane
-stato	-ttero	-fero	-fugo	-evole

For example, **"microfono"** *(microphone)*: mee-**kro**-fo-no, **"fotografo"** *(photograph)*: fo-**to**-gra-fo, **"sinonimo"** *(synonym)*: see-**no**-nee-mo, etc.

4. In rare cases, and often in some conjugated verbs, the stress falls on the *fourth-to-last* syllable, e.g., **"telefonano"** *(they call)*: te-**le**-fo-na-no.

- In French:

In French, the stress always falls on the last syllable of the word. Here are some examples of French words:

"police"	"politque"	"aliment"	"téléphone"
/po-**lees**/	/po-lee-**teek**/	/a-lee-**mã**/	/te-le-**fon**/
(police)	*(policy)*	*(food)*	*(phone)*

If the words are strung together to form a phrase, the stress often falls on the last syllable of the phrase, for example:

une mai**son** /μn me-**zõ**/	*a house*
une petite mai**son** /μn p(ə)-teet me-**zõ**/	*a small house*
une petite maison **blanche** /μn p(ə)-teet me-zõ **blãsh**/	*a small white house*
une belle petite maison **blanche** /μn bel p(ə)-teet me-zõ **blãsh**/	*a small beautiful white house*

Liaison in French

A liaison occurs in French when a word that normally ends with a silent consonant is followed by a vowel or a mute "**h**" (but not an aspirated "**h**"). In this case, the final consonant is pronounced. For example, the word "**trois**" *(three)* on its own is pronounced /tʀwa/, where the final "**s**" is silent. However, in the phrase "**trois amis**" /tʀwaz̲ a-**mee**/ *(three friends)*, the final "**s**" in "**trois**" is pronounced as a "**z**" sound. Here are some more liaison examples:

les /le/ *(the - plural)*	**le̲s amis** /lez̲ a-**mee**/ *(the friends)*
un /ĩ/ *(a/ an)*	**u̲n homme** /ĩn̲ om/ *(a man)*
vous /voo/ *(you)*	**vou̲s avez** /vooz̲ a-**ve**/ *(you have)*
très /tʀe/ *(very)*	**trè̲s utile** /tʀez̲ μ-**teel**/ *(very useful)*
Je suis /j(ə) swee/ *(I am/ have)*	**Je sui̲s allé** /j(ə) sweez̲ a-**le**/ *(I have gone)*
Il est /eel e/ *(He is)*	**Il es̲t ici** /eel et̲ ee-**see**/ *(He is here)*

There are a few cases in which a liaison is prohibited. A liaison is prohibited *before* the following:

1. An aspirated "**h**," e.g., "**les héros**" /le e-ʀo/ *(the heroes)*, "**en haut**" /ã o/ *(up or on top)*, etc.
2. The words "**oui**" *(yes)* and "**onze**" *(eleven)*, e.g., "**les onze ans**" /le õz ã/ *(the eleven years)*.

A liaison is generally avoided or prohibited *after* the following:

1. The conjunction "**et**" *(and)*, e.g., "**adultes et enfants**" /a-dμlt e ã-**fã**/ *(adults and children)*, "**fort et utile**" /foʀ e μ-**teel**/ *(strong and useful)*, etc.
2. The word "**toujours**" *(always)*, e.g., "**toujours ici**" /too-jooʀ ee-**see**/ *(always here)*.
3. Singular nouns, e.g., "**éléphant énorme**" /e-le-fã e-**noʀm**/ *(huge elephant)*, "**chat amical**" /sha a-mee-**kal**/ *(friendly cat)*, etc.
4. Proper nouns, e.g., "**Robert est là**" /ʀo-beʀ e la/ *(Robert is there)*.

Understanding all liaison cases can be complicated and may require some deep linguistic knowledge. Nevertheless, you simply need to recognize it when applied in normal speech. The above cases provide a good starting point and summary on the uses of liaisons.

2. SIMILARITIES TO ENGLISH

English is considered a Germanic language, whereas Spanish, Portuguese, Italian, and French are Romance languages. Yet, English shares a substantial amount of vocabulary with Romance languages. The main reason is attributed to the Norman Conquest of England in the eleventh century, as a result of which, the English language borrowed a lot of French words. French Prime Minister Georges Clemenceau (1841-1929) famously claimed that "English is just badly pronounced French." French is a Romance language and shares Latin roots, and thus a lot of vocabulary, with Spanish, Portuguese, and Italian. You can see the connection here between these languages and English via the French language. This is why the US Foreign Service Institute (FSI), which provides language training to diplomats and government employees, ranks Spanish, Portuguese, Italian, and French in the easiest language learning category for English speakers.

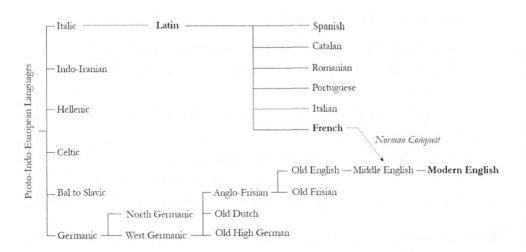

English Cognates

History aside, we can capitalize on this connection. There are a lot of English cognates in the Romance languages. English cognates are words that are directly descended from a common ancestor language, in this case, mostly French. Moreover, since English has become a universal language, some English words have obviously found their way directly into many languages, including Romance languages.

As we delve into the English cognates, do not feel overwhelmed with the vocabulary. You are not expected to memorize all of the cognates at this basic level. It is only meant to give you an idea about the similarities with English and help provide a sense of the Romance languages based on prior knowledge of English.

Take, for example, the Latin verb "claudere," meaning *"to close."* In the development of the Italian language, the "l" preceded by a consonant, e.g., "cl," "pl," "fl," etc., has often changed to "i." Knowing that, you would be more likely to recognize the similarity between the adjectives "**chiuso**" (pronounced "**kyoo**-zo") in Italian and *"closed"* in English, both derived from the Latin "claudere." Similar is the case with words such as "**fiamma**" *(flame)*, "**fiore**" *(flower)*, and "**piazza**" *(square or place)*.

Many words that begin with "h" in Spanish correspond to words that begin with "f" in Portuguese, Italian, and French, which is the original spelling in the Latin source. Here are some examples:

EN	SP	PT	IT	FR	Latin
to do	hacer	fazer	fare	faire	facĕre
falcon	halcón	falcão	falcone	faucon	falco
hunger	hambre	fome	fame	faim	fames
liver	hígado	fígado	fegato	foie	ficātum
fig	higo	figo	fico	figue	ficus
flour	harina	farinha	farina	farine	farīna
thread	hilo	fio	filo	fil	filum
aunt	hormiga	formiga	formica	fourmi	formīca
oven	horno	forno	forno	four	furnus

| *smoke* | humo | fumaça | fumo | fumée | fumus |
| *to flee* | huir | fugir | fuggire | fuir | fugĕre |

Here, we list some parallels between English and words in the four Romance languages covered in this book. We hope that will make you realize how many words you already know or perhaps are able to guess correctly.

It is also important to note that these are not considered strict rules, but rather useful guidelines to make learning Romance languages easier for English speakers.

EN	SP	PT	IT	FR	Examples	
-ile	-il	-il	-ile	-ile	SP	ágil, frágil, hostil
					PT	ágil, frágil, hostil
					IT	agile, fragile, ostile
					FR	agile, fragile, hostile
-or	-or	-or	-ore	-eur -eure	SP	interior, favor
					PT	interior, favor
					IT	interiore, favore
					FR	intérieur, faveur
-ble	-ble	-vel	-bile	-ble	SP	notable, posible
					PT	notável, possível
					IT	notabile, possibile
					FR	notable, possible
-al	-al	-al	-ale	-al -ale	SP	animal, canal, local
					PT	animal, canal, local
					IT	animale, canale, locale
					FR	animal, canal, local
-ical	-ico -ica	-ico -ica	-ico -ica	-ique	SP	crítico, lógico
					PT	crítico, lógico
					IT	critico, logico
					FR	critique, logique
-ic	-ico -ica	-ico -ica	-ico -ica	-ique	SP	público, romántico
					PT	público, romântico
					IT	pubblico, romantico
					FR	publique, romantique
-ant	-ante	-ante	-ante	-ant -ante	SP	elegante, importante
					PT	elegante, importante
					IT	elegante, importante
					FR	élégant, important

-ent	-ente	-ente	-ente	-ent -ente	SP	inteligente, diferente
					PT	inteligente, diferente
					IT	intelligente, differente
					FR	intelligent, différent
-ment	-mento	-mento	-mento	-ment	SP	documento, elemento
					PT	documento, elemento
					IT	documento, elemento
					FR	document, élément
-ist	-ista	-ista	-ista	-iste	SP	artista, dentista, turista
					PT	artista, dentista, turista
					IT	artista, dentista, turista
					FR	artiste, dentiste, touriste
-am	-ama	-ama	-amma	-amme	SP	diagrama, programa
					PT	diagrama, programa
					IT	diagramma, programma
					FR	diagramme, programme
-em	-ema	-ema	-ema	-ème	SP	problema, sistema
					PT	problema, sistema
					IT	problema, sistema
					FR	problème, système
-ous	-oso -osa	-oso -osa	-oso -osa	-eux -euse	SP	curioso, famoso
					PT	curioso, famoso
					IT	curioso, famoso
					FR	curieux, fameux
-ry	-rio -ria	-rio -ria	-rio -ria	-aire	SP	contrario, imaginario
					PT	contrário, imaginario
					IT	contrario, immaginario
					FR	contraire, imaginaire
-tion	-ción	-ção	-zione	-tion	SP	condición, nación
					PT	condição, nação
					IT	condizione, nazione
					FR	condition, nation
-tional	-cional	-cional	-zionale	-tionnel -tionnelle	SP	condicional, racional
					PT	condicional, racional
					IT	condizionale, razionale
					FR	conditionnel, rationnel
-tial	-cial	-cial	-ziale	-tiel -tielle	SP	esencial, parcial
					PT	essencial, parcial
					IT	essenziale, parziale
					FR	essentiel, partiel

-ce	-cia	-ça	-za -zia	-ce	SP	diferencia, justicia
					PT	diferença, justiça
					IT	differenza, giustizia
					FR	différence, justice
-cy	-cia	-cia	-za -zia	-ce -tie	SP	agencia, democracia
					PT	agência, democracia
					IT	agenza, democrazia
					FR	agence, démocratie
-ty	-dad	-dade	-tà	-té	SP	autoridad, unidad
					PT	autoridade, unidade
					IT	autorità, unità
					FR	autorité, unité
-ly	-mente	-mente	-mente	-ment	SP	totalmente, normalmente
					PT	totalmente, normalmente
					IT	totalmente, normalmente
					FR	totalement, normalement
-phy	-fía	-fia	-fia	-phie	SP	filosofía, fotografía
					PT	filosofia, fotografia
					IT	filosofia, fotografia
					FR	philosophie, photographie
-sion	-sión	-são	-sione	-sion	SP	decisión, conversión
					PT	decisão, conversão
					IT	decisione, conversione
					FR	décision, conversion
-ism	-ismo	-ismo	-ismo	-isme	SP	comunismo, organismo
					PT	comunismo, organismo
					IT	comunismo, organismo
					FR	communisme, organisme
-id	-ido -ida	-ido -ida	-ido -ida	-ide	SP	ávido, fluido, sólido
					PT	ávido, fluido, sólido
					IT	avido, fluido, solido
					FR	avide, fluide, solide
-ive	-ivo -iva	-ivo -iva	-ivo -iva	-if -ive	SP	activo, nativo, negativo
					PT	ativo, nativo, negativo
					IT	attivo, nativo, negativo
					FR	actif, natif, négatif

Although cognates will often have the same meaning as in English, it is important to note that this is not always the case, as languages have evolved separately. For example, the Italian word "**camera**" means *room*, not the device you use to take photos. That would be **"macchina fotografica."** Similarly, the word **"fabbrica"** in Italian means *"factory"* and not *"fabric,"* as you may have guessed.

It can be useful to be familiar with these false friends to avoid some embarrassing errors. Here are some examples where the English cognate can give a false indication of the real meaning:

SP	PT	IT	FR	EN real meaning	EN cognate (false meaning)
actual	atual	attuale	actuel	*current*	actual
recordar	recordar	ricordare	rappeler	*to remind*	to record
enviar	enviar	inviare	envoyer	*to send*	to envy
librería	livraria	libreria	librairie	*bookstore*	library

Negation

In general, forming the negation in Spanish, Portuguese, Italian, and French is a simple procedure, without many exceptions:

1. To form the negation in *Spanish*, we add **"no"** in front of the verb (and before any object pronoun before the verb).
2. To form the negation in *Portuguese*, we add **"não"** /nãw/ in front of the verb (and before any object pronoun before the verb).
3. To form the negation in *Italian*, we add **"non"** in front of the verb (and before any object pronoun before the verb).
4. To form the negation in *French*, we add **"ne"** in front of the verb (and before any object pronoun before the verb) and **"pas"** after the verb.

Here are some examples:

SP	**No** juego al fútbol.	
PT	**Não** jogo futebol.	*I **don't** play soccer.*
IT	**Non** gioco a calcio.	
FR	Je **ne** joue **pas** au football.	
SP	**No** lo quiero.	
PT	**Não** o quero.	*I **don't** want it.*
IT	**Non** lo voglio.	
FR	Je **ne** le veux **pas**.	

In many cases, we can have a double negative in Spanish, Portuguese, Italian, and French, without changing the meaning to affirmative. For example:

SP	**No** quiero <u>nada</u>.	
PT	**Não** quero <u>nada</u>.	*I don't want <u>anything</u>.*
IT	**Non** voglio <u>niente</u>.	
FR	Je **ne** veux <u>rien</u>.	

Notice that when another negation word is used in French, e.g., **"jamais"** *(never)*, **"rien"** *(nothing/anything)*, **"personne"** *(nobody/anybody)*, **"plus"** *(anymore)*, etc., it often replaces **"pas"** following the verb to form the negative. Here are some examples:

Je **n'**ai **rien** fait de mal.	*I didn't do **anything** wrong.*
Je **ne** vois **personne** ici.	*I don't see **anybody** here.*
Il **ne** répond **plus**.	*He doesn't respond **anymore**.*

Notice that **"ne"** is contracted to **"n'"** before a vowel or a mute **"h."** If a compound tense (a tense that uses an auxiliary verb) is used in French, the **"ne … pas,"** or a similar negative construction like the aforementioned examples, is placed around the first verb, that is, the auxiliary verb, e.g., **"Je n'ai pas <u>mangé</u>"** *(I <u>have</u> not <u>eaten</u>)*.

Uses of the Written Accents

Spanish, Portuguese, Italian, and French use written accents.

- In Spanish:

The most important written accent in the Spanish language is the acute accent (´). In addition to marking the exceptions to the syllable stress rules, the acute accent has the following two uses:

❖ To distinguish between the meaning of words that would otherwise be written in the same manner. For example, **"el"** is the masculine definite article *"the,"* whereas **"él"** is the personal pronoun *"he,"* **"mas"** (formal use only) is a conjunction meaning *"but,"* whereas **"más"** means *"more."*

❖ To distinguish between interrogative and relative pronouns, e.g., "**¿Dónde vives?**" *(Where do you live?)* vs. "**No hay transporte donde vivo**" *(There is no transportation where I live)*. Notice that the interrogative pronoun "**dónde**" *(where)* has an accent on the vowel of the first syllable in the first example. The same concept applies to some other interrogative pronouns, such as "**¿Quién?**" *(who?)*, "**¿Qué?**" *(what?)*, "**¿Cuál?**" *(which?)*, "**¿Dónde?**" *(where?)*.

- In Portuguese:

In Portuguese, there are five written accents: acute (´), grave (`), circumflex (ˆ), tilde (˜), and cedilla (¸). Let us discuss each in more detail:

1. Acute (´): This written accent can be found on any of the five vowels: "**a**," "**u**," "**i**," "**o**," or "**e**." It indicates that the syllable should be stressed, and when used with "**a**," "**e**," or "**o**," it also indicates an open sound.

2. Circumflex (ˆ): The pointy hat-like accent can be used with any of the three vowels: "**a**," "**e**," or "**o**." The circumflex indicates a closed sound and that the syllable should be stressed.

3. Tilde (˜): The tilde can only appear on the letter "**a**" or "**o**" to denote nasal pronunciation. e.g., "**nação**" /na-**sãw**/ *(nation)*, "**põe**" /põy / *(he/she puts)*, etc.

4. Grave (`): The grave accent is often used to mark the contraction of two consecutive vowels, with the first vowel often being a preposition, e.g., "**a**" + "**as**" = "**às**" *(at the)*. More details on this in **Level II, Lesson 1**.

5. Cedilla (¸): This accent is used uniquely with the letter "**c**" to denote a soft "**s**" sound even though the letter is followed by "**a**," "**o**," or "**u**," e.g., "**maçã**" *(apple)*, "**ação**" *(action)*, etc.

- In Italian:

In Italian, there are two written accents: acute (´) and grave (`). The only letters that can be accented in Italian are: "a," "i," "o," "u," and "e." The letter "e" can take an acute "é" or grave "è" accent to indicate a closed or open vowel sound, respectively. The other four letters can only take a grave accent, i.e., "à," "ì," "ò," and "ù."

We have encountered one common use of the written accent in Italian, that is, to indicate stress on the last syllable of a word, e.g., "**città**" *(city),* "**caffè**" *(coffee),* "**perché**" *(why),* "**ventitré**" *(twenty-three),* etc. In general, the acute accent is used with causal conjunctions ending in "-**ché**," e.g., "**perché**" *(why)* or compound words ending in "-**tré**," e.g., "**ventitré**" *(twenty-three),* whereas in most other cases, the grave accent is used.

Another important use of written accents in Italian is to distinguish between the meaning of monosyllabic words that would otherwise be written in the same manner. For example, "**e**" is used as a conjunction meaning *"and,"* whereas "**è**" is the verb *"to be"* in the third-person singular form of the present tense, meaning *"is."* Below are more examples:

Word without accent	Meaning in English	Word without accent	Meaning in English
da	*from*	dà	*gives*
ne	*of it*	nè	*neither*
si	*oneself*	sì	*yes*
se	*if*	sè	*himself/herself*
la	*the*	là	*there*

Another optional use of the written accent, that is optional, is to distinguish between different meanings of the same word depending on the syllable the stress falls on. For example, "**principi**" means *"princes,"* whereas "**princìpi**" means *"principles."* Similarly, "**ancora**" is an adverb meaning *"still,"* whereas "**àncora**" means *"anchor."* Remember that the use of the accent in these examples is optional, and the context can often determine the meaning without the need for an accent.

- In French:

In French, there are five written accents: acute (´), grave (`), circumflex (ˆ), dieresis (¨), and cedilla (¸). Let us discuss each in more detail:

1. Acute (´): This can be found only on the letter "**e**." It indicates a closed "**e**" sound. In some cases, especially at the beginning of some words, it may indicate that the word starts with "**s**" in the original Latin spelling, e.g., "**école**" *(school)*, "**état**" *(state)*, "**étudier**" *(to study)*, etc.
2. Grave (`): The grave accent is often found on the letters "**a**" and "**e**," and in only one case on the letter "**u**," that is "**où**" *(where)*. If it appears on the letter "**e**," it indicates an open "**e**" sound.
    Another use of the grave accent in French is to distinguish between the meaning of monosyllabic words that would otherwise be written in the same manner. For example, "**a**" is used as a third-person singular form of the verb *"to have,"* whereas "**à**" is a preposition that often means *"at"* or *"in."* Similarly, "**la**" is used as a feminine singular definite article meaning *"the,"* whereas "**là**" means *"there."*
3. Circumflex (ˆ): The pointy hat-like accent can be used with any of the five vowels: "**a**," "**e**," "**i**," "**o**," or "**u**." When used with "**o**," it denotes a closed "**o**" sound, whereas it denotes an open sound when used with "**a**" or "**e**." In many cases, the circumflex can point to an "**s**" that was dropped after the circumflex letter from the original source language, e.g., "**forêt**" *(forest)*, "**hôpital**" *(hospital)*, "**côte**" *(coast)*, "**pâté**" *(paste)*, "**rôtir**" *(to roast)*, etc.
    Similar to the grave accent, the circumflex is sometimes used to distinguish between the meaning of monosyllabic words that would otherwise be written in the same manner. For example,

"**sur**" is a preposition meaning *"above,"* whereas "**sûr**" is an adjective meaning *"sure"* or *"certain."* Similarly, "**mur**" means *"wall,"* whereas "**mûr**" means *"ripe"* or *"mature."*

4. Dieresis (¨): The dieresis is a special accent that is often used on the second vowel of a two-vowel combination to denote that the two vowels must be pronounced separately. The dieresis is often found on the letter "**e**" or "**i**," and in rare cases on the letter "**u**." For example, "**naïve**" *(naïve)* is pronounced /na-**eev**/, not /**nev**/, despite the "**ai**" combination. Similarly, "**Noël**" *(Christmas)* is pronounced /no-**el**/, not /**neul**/, despite the "**oe**" combination.

5. Cedilla (¸): This accent is used uniquely with the letter "**c**" to denote a soft "**s**" sound even though the letter is followed by "**a**," "**o**," or "**u**," e.g., "**français**" *(French)*, "**garçon**" *(boy)*, "**ça**" *(this)*, "**leçon**" *(lesson)*, "**reçu**" *(receipt)*, "**façon**" *(way or method)*, and "**façade**" *(façade)*.

Punctuation

In general, punctuation marks in Spanish, Portuguese, Italian, and French are used the same way as in English. One notable exception is the following:

❖ Interrogation and exclamation marks are used in Spanish both at the beginning and at the end of the question or exclamation with the inverted sign at the beginning, such as "**¿Cómo estás?**" *(How are you?)* and "**¡Qué lástima!**" *(What a pity!).*

Notice that this rule is not always enforced in many countries except in formal and legal documents.

Punctuation is also important to distinguish a question from a statement in Spanish, Portuguese, Italian, and French. For instance, the following sentence is a statement:

SP	Tú hablas inglés.	
PT	Você fala inglês.	*You speak English.*
IT	Tu parli inglese.	
FR	Tu parles anglais.	

Adding a question mark to the end of the sentence (and adding an inverted question mark to its beginning in Spanish only) makes it a question:

SP	¿Tú hablas inglés?	
PT	Você fala inglês?	*Do you speak English?*
IT	Tu parli inglese?	
FR	Tu parles anglais?	

This is one way to form a *"yes"* or *"no"* question in Spanish, Portuguese, Italian, and French. Obviously, the intonation needs to change in the spoken language.

Another way to form a **"sì"** *(yes)* or **"no"** *(no)* question from a statement in Italian is to place the subject to the end, e.g., "**È caldo il caffè?**" *(Is the coffee hot?)*.

Another more formal way to form a **"oui"** *(yes)* or **"non"** *(no)* question from a statement in French is to place the phrase "**Est-ce que**" before the statement, e.g., "**Est-ce que tu parles français?**" *(Do you speak French?)*. The introductory phrase "**Est-ce que...**" translates literally as *"Is it that ..."*

Another way to form a **"oui"** *(yes)* or **"non"** *(no)* question from a statement in French is called *inversion*. The subject pronoun and the verb are inverted and a hyphen is placed in between, e.g., "**Parles-tu français?**" *(Do you speak French?)*. This method is more common in written language. Notice that inversion requires a subject pronoun such as "**je**" *(I)*, "**tu**" *(you)*, or "**il/elle**" *(he/she/it)*. If the subject is a noun instead of a subject pronoun, the subject is maintained and repeated using the proper subject pronoun, e.g., "**Le café, est-il chaud**" *(Is the coffee hot?)*. If a verb that ends in a vowel precedes "**il/elle**" *(he/she/it)* or "**on**" *(we/one)*, the letter "**t**" must be added before the subject pronoun that begins with a vowel, e.g., "**Parle-t-il français?**" *(Does he speak French?)*.

We do not use any auxiliary to reorder the sentence using the English approach to form a question.

Finally, there are only two contractions in Spanish that involve the singular masculine definite article "**el**," and, unlike in English, these contractions are not optional and must be applied:

a + el = **al**	e.g., "Yo voy **al** restaurante" *(I go to the restaurant)*.
de + el = **del**	e.g., "Yo vengo **del** café" *(I come from the café)*.

In Portuguese and French, all contractions are also mandatory.

In Italian, some contractions are mandatory, such as "**l'acqua**" *(the water)*, while others are optional, e.g., "**dove è**" *(where is)* is optionally contracted as "**dov'è**." Unfortunately, there is no universal rule. You will know which contractions are optional as you practice and go through the lessons.

Abbreviations

The concepts behind the formation of acronyms and abbreviations in Romance languages are very similar to those in English. One notable exception is the doubling of the letters in the abbreviation of some plural nouns in Spanish and Italian. For example, in Spanish, "**Estados Unidos**" *(United States)* is abbreviated as "**EE. UU.**" Similarly, in Italian "**Poste e Telegrafi**" *(Posts and Telegraphs)* is abbreviated as "**PP. TT.**"

Capitalization

The words are capitalized in cases almost identical to those in English, with a few notable exceptions that are not capitalized in Spanish, Portuguese, Italian, and French, mainly:

❖ Adjectives of nationalities and languages, for example:

SP	italiano	
PT	italiano	*Italian*
IT	italiano	
FR	italien	
SP	canadiense	
PT	canadense	*Canadian*
IT	canadese	
FR	canadien	

SP	español	
PT	espanhol	*Spanish*
IT	spagnolo	
FR	espagnol	

❖ Days and months, for example:

SP	martes	
PT	terça-feira	*Tuesday*
IT	martedì	
FR	mardi	
SP	enero	
PT	janeiro	*January*
IT	gennaio	
FR	janvier	
SP	julio	
PT	julho	*July*
IT	luglio	
FR	juillet	

3. GENDER AND PLURAL

Each noun and adjective in Spanish, Portuguese, Italian, and French has a gender. Nouns and adjectives have only two genders: *masculine* and *feminine*. There is no neuter gender. Throughout the book, we use the superscripts [m] and [f] to refer to masculine and feminine genders, respectively.

The adjective follows the noun it describes in gender and number. The only certain way to determine the gender of a noun is by looking it up in a dictionary. Nevertheless, there are some general rules that can help you be right most of the time. Remember, however, that these are general rules, and there are many exceptions.

For the purpose of brevity throughout the book, we often refer only to the masculine singular form of an adjective. We trust that by learning the following basic rules, you will be able to guess the feminine and plural forms most of the time.

Gender & Plural in Spanish

Let us discuss some general rules to determine the gender of a noun or adjective in Spanish. We will also cover forming the plural in Spanish.

1. Gender of a Nouns & Adjectives in Spanish

There are general rules that help determine the gender of a noun or adjective in Spanish. However, there remain many exceptions that can only be learned by practice.

As a very loose and general rule, words ending in "**o**" are likely to be masculine, and most words ending in "**a**" are likely to be feminine. However, this rule—if it is even reasonable to consider it a rule—has many exceptions. Thus, we will have sub-rules that are more specific.

- Most words ending in "**-a**" are feminine. The following are some exceptions:
    1. Words that end in "**-ma**," "**-pa**," or "**-ta**" and originate from *Greek*. These are masculine. Examples are: "**el idioma**" *(language)*, "**el problema**" *(problem)*, "**el sistema**" *(system)*, "**el clima**" *(climate)*, "**el tema**" *(topic)*, "**el diploma**" *(diploma)*, "**el drama**" *(drama)*, "**el dilema**" *(dilemma)*, "**el diagrama**" *(diagram)*, "**el mapa**" *(map)*, "**el planeta**" *(planet)*, "**el cometa**" *(comet)*, etc. This exception does not apply to words that did *not* originate from *Greek*, such as "**la forma**" *(form)* and "**la plataforma**" *(platform)*.
    2. Words that end in "**-ista**" and refer to masculine or feminine people performing a profession, such as: "**el taxista**" *(taxi driver)*, "**el artista**" *(artist)*, "**el analista**" *(analyst)*, "**el pianista**" *(pianist)*, etc.
    3. Words that end in "**-a**" and refer to professions with the same masculine and feminine forms. For example, "**atleta**" can refer to a male or female *"athlete,"* and "**espía**" can refer to a male or female *"spy."*

4. A few other words that are learned by practice, such as "**el día**" (*day*), "**el Buda**" (*Buddha*), and "**el panda**" (*panda*).

- Most words ending in "-**d**," "-**z**," and "-**ión**" are feminine, e.g., "**la ciudad**" (*city*), "**la escasez**" (*shortage*), "**la religión**" (*religion*), etc. The following are some exceptions:

  1. Some masculine words with a "-**d**" ending are: "**el huésped**" (*guest*), "**el césped**" (*grass*), "**el récord**" (*record*), "**el ataúd**" (*coffin*), "**el abad**" (*abbot*), "**el milord**" (*milord*), and "**el lord**" (*lord*).

  2. Some masculine words with a "-**z**" ending are: "**el aprendiz**" (*apprentice*), "**el pez**" (*fish*), "**el arroz**" (*rice*), "**el lápiz**" (*pencil*), "**el ajedrez**" (*chess*), "**el antifaz**" (*mask*), "**el maíz**" (*corn*), "**el disfraz**" (*costume*), "**el haz**" (*beam*), "**el albornoz**" (*bathrobe*), and "**el altavoz**" (*speaker*).

  3. Some masculine words with "-**ión**" ending are: "**el avión**" (*plane*), "**el camión**" (*truck*), and "**el embrión**" (*embryo*).

- Most words ending in "-**o**" are masculine, with a few exceptions that are feminine, such as: "**la mano**" (*hand*), "**la radio**[1]" (*radio*), "**la foto**" (*photo*), "**la moto**" (*motorcycle*), and "**la libido**" (*libido*), in addition to words that end with "-**o**" used to refer to professions that have the same masculine and feminine forms, e.g., "**piloto**" can refer to a male or female *pilot*, where "**el piloto**" is masculine and "**la piloto**" is feminine.

- Words ending with an accented vowel (**á, é, í, ó, ú**) are generally masculine, e.g., "**el maní**" (*peanut*), "**el ají**" (*chili pepper*), "**el ñandú**" (*rhea*), "**el colibrí**" (*hummingbird*), "**el bambú**" (*bamboo*), etc.

- Most words ending with a consonant other than "**d**" or "**z**" are masculine, with some exceptions, such as: "**la miel**" (*honey*), "**la**

---

[1] According to the Real Academia Española (RAE), the word "**radio**" is *feminine* when referring to the broadcast or programming of the radio, e.g., "**Lo escuché en la radio**" (*I heard it on the radio*). When referring to the radio set or device, the word "**radio**" is *feminine* in Spain and the southern cone of South America, but *masculine* in most of the rest of Latin America.

piel" *(skin),* "la sal" *(salt),* "la hiel" *(gall),* "la flor" *(flower),* "la coliflor" *(cauliflower),* and "la labor" *(labor).*

- Words ending with "-e" tend to be masculine, especially those ending in "-aje" or "-ambre," but with a lot of exceptions that are feminine, such as: "la calle" *(street),* "la carne" *(meat),* "la gente" *(people),* "la llave" *(key),* "la fiebre" *(fever),* "la noche" *(night),* "la nube" *(cloud),* "la sangre" *(blood),* "la suerte" *(luck),* "la tarde" *(afternoon* or *evening),* "la fuente" *(source* or *fountain),* "la torre" *(tower),* "la sede" *(headquarters),* "la serpiente" *(snake),* "la corriente" *(current),* "la clave" *(key code),* "la clase" *(class),* "la base" *(base),* "la madre" *(mother),* "la muerte" *(death),* "la nieve" *(snow),* and "la frase" *(phrase).*

Although not a universal rule, many feminine words can be formed from masculine words that end with a consonant by adding an "a" at the end, e.g., "jugador" *(player)* (feminine "jugadora"), "juez" *(judge)* (feminine "jueza"), and from masculine words that end with an "o" by replacing the last "o" with an "a," e.g., "ingeniero" *(engineer)* (feminine "ingeniera"), "alto" *(tall)* (feminine "alta"). As we shall see, there are exceptions, as some words deviate from this simple rule to form the feminine. In addition, there are many words that do not change form based on gender. For example, "artista" *(artist),* "piloto" *(pilot),* and "estudiante" *(student)* all have the same form in both masculine and feminine.

2. Forming the Plural in Spanish

Forming the plural in Spanish is similar to forming a regular plural in English. To form the plural, the letter "s" is added if the noun or adjective ends with a vowel[1], e.g., "casa" *(house),* "casas" *(houses),* and "es" is added if the noun or adjective ends with a consonant, e.g., "mujer" *(woman),* "mujeres" *(women).* Notice that Spanish

---

[1] Although the letter "y" at the end of a word is considered a vowel, the "es" ending is used to form the plural in such words, e.g., "rey" *(king)* (plural "reyes").

adjectives can also be plural, e.g., **"mujeres jóvenes"** *(young women)*. We will encounter some minor orthographic changes in the plural form of some words, but the vast majority are regular.

Gender & Plural in Portuguese

Here, we discuss the general rules to determine the gender of a noun or adjective in Portuguese. We will also cover forming the plural in Portuguese.

1. Gender of a Noun in Portuguese

As a general rule, most nouns ending in "**-o**" are masculine, whereas most nouns ending in "**-a**" are feminine. However, there are some exceptions that we must be aware of. For example, the nouns **"mão"** *(hand)* and **"tribo"** *(tribe)* are feminine despite their "**-o**" ending. Likewise, the nouns **"dia"** *(day)* and **"sofá"** *(sofa)* are masculine even though they end with "**-a**."

In addition, nouns with "**-l**," "**-r**," or "**-z**" ending are generally masculine. Many nouns with "**-ma**" and "**-pa**" ending are masculine despite their "**-a**" ending. On the other hand, nouns with "**-gem**" or "**-dade**" ending are often feminine.

To summarize:

Gender	Ending	Examples
masculine	-o	livro *(book)*, número *(number)*, tio *(uncle)*
	-ma, -pa	clima *(climate)*, poema *(poem)*, mapa *(map)*
	-l, -r, -z	papel *(paper)*, lugar *(place)*, arroz *(rice)*
feminine	-a	mesa *(table)*, bola *(ball)*, tia *(aunt)*
	-gem	imagem *(image)*, origem *(origin)*, viagem *(travel)*
	-dade	cidade *(city)*, qualidade *(quality)*, verdade *(truth)*

Notice that many words that end in "**-ma**" or "**-pa**" and originate from *Greek* are masculine, for example:

problema^m	*problem*	**drama**^m	*drama*
sistema^m	*system*	**dilema**^m	*dilemma*
tema^m	*topic or theme*	**diagrama**^m	*diagram*
diploma^m	*diploma*	**poema**^m	*poem*
clima^m	*climate*	**mapa**^m	*map*

However, this does not apply to words that do *not* originate from *Greek*, such as "**forma**" *(form)* and "**plataforma**" *(platform)*, which are feminine.

Nouns with "**-e**" (except "**-dade**") or "**-ão**" ending can be either masculine or feminine. As a general rule, nouns in this category tend to be masculine if they refer to concrete things, and feminine if they refer to abstract concepts. Here are some examples:

Ending	Gender	Examples
-e	masculine	leite *(milk)*, sanduíche *(sandwich)*, recipiente *(container)*
	feminine	crise *(crisis)*, noite *(night)*, sorte *(luck)*, corrente *(current)*
-ão	masculine	pão *(bread)*, coração *(heart)*, limão *(lemon)*
	feminine	paixão *(passion)*, exceção *(exception)*, missão *(mission)*

Some words have a different meaning when used in the masculine form versus when used in the feminine form. For example:

cara^m	*guy*	**cara**^f	*face*
capital^m	*capital (money)*	**capital**^f	*capital (city)*
grama^m	*gram (unit)*	**grama**^f	*grass*
rádio^m	*radio set or radium*	**rádio**^f	*radio station*

Some nouns that refer to people can be masculine or feminine. The most common pattern to form the feminine noun from a masculine noun is to replace the final "**-o**" with "**-a**." For example:

médico^m	*doctor*	**médica**^f	*doctor*
engenheiro^m	*engineer*	**engenheira**^f	*engineer*

Nevertheless, this is not the only gender pattern in Portuguese. Other patterns include:

Masculine	Feminine	Example
-or	-ora	pint**or** > pint**ora** *(painter)* profess**or** > profess**ora** *(teacher)*
	-triz	at**or** > a**triz** *(actor/ actress)* emperad**or** > empera**triz** *(emperor/ empress)*
	-eira	lavrad**or** > lavrad**eira** *(farmer)*
-ês	-esa	ingl**ês** > ingl**esa** *(English man/ woman)*
-ão	-ã	irm**ão** > irm**ã** *(brother/ sister)*
	-oa	le**ão** > le**oa** *(lion/ lioness)*
	-ona	sabich**ão** > sabich**ona** *(know-all person)*

Most nouns that end in "**-ista**" can refer to masculine or feminine people performing a role or profession. For example:

dentista^{m,f}	*dentist*	**analista**^{m,f}	*analyst*
artista^{m,f}	*artist*	**pianista**^{m,f}	*pianist*

Similarly, some nouns ending in "**-e**" can also refer to both male and female in some occupations. For example:

gerente^{m,f}	*manager*	**estudante**^{m,f}	*student*

Others have only one form (masculine or feminine) regardless of the gender of the person that the noun refers to, for example:

peessoa^{f}	*person*	**vítima**^{f}	*victim*
cônjuge^{m}	*spouse*	**criança**^{f}	*child*

In general, most countries ending with "**-a**" (but not "**á**" or "**ã**") are *feminine*, e.g., "**Italia**^{f}" *(Italy)*. For example:

Turquia^{f}	*Turkey*	**Rússia**^{f}	*Russia*
Colômbia^{f}	*Colombia*	**França**^{f}	*France*
Italia^{f}	*Italy*	**Alemanha**^{f}	*Germany*

Most other countries are masculine. Here are some examples:

Japão^{m}	*Japan*	**Irã**^{m}	*Iran*
Canadá^{m}	*Canada*	**Portugal**^{m}	*Portugal*

Notice that most countries are often preceded by a definite article, while only a few cannot be used by a definite article, such as:

Portugal^m	*Portugal*	**Marrocos**^m	*Morocco*
Cuba^m	*Cuba*	**Moçambique**^m	*Mozambique*

Some countries are always in plural form, such as:

Estados Unidos^m	*United States*	**Países Baixos**^m	*Netherlands*
Filipinas^f	*Philippines*	**Bahamas**^f	*Bahamas*

2. Gender of an Adjective in Portuguese

Adjectives in Portuguese, unlike in English, come after the noun they describe, for example, "**prédio histórico**" *(historic building)*. There are some exceptions to this rule, for example, "**grande cidade**" *(big or great city)*. Many adjectives that come before the noun are *indefinite adjectives*, which will be covered in **Level III, Lesson 4**.

Many masculine adjectives in Portuguese end in "**-o**." The feminine form of most masculine adjectives ending in "**-o**" is often obtained by changing the final "**-o**" to "**-a**," e.g., "**lindo/linda**" *(beautiful)*, "**alto/alta**" *(high or tall)*, "**velho/velha**" *(old)*, etc.

Generally, most masculine adjectives ending in "**-or**," "**-ês**," or "**-u**" form the feminine form by simply adding an "**-a**" to the end of the word. For example:

interior	**trabalhador**^m	**trabalhadora**^f
Chinese	**chinês**^m	**chinesa**^f
naked	**nu**^m	**nua**^f

However, there are some exceptions that follow different patterns. The following are the most common irregular patterns:

1. Adjectives ending in "**-ão**"

The feminine form of masculine adjectives ending in "**-ão**" is often obtained by changing the final "**-ão**" to "**-ã**," or in some few words to "**-ona**":

German	alemão[m]	alemã[f]
sane/healthy	são[m]	sã[f]
playful	brincalhão[m]	brincalhona[f]

2. Some adjectives ending in "-or"

The feminine form of some masculine adjectives ending in "-or" remains unchanged:

interior	interior[m]	interior[f]
exterior	exterior[m]	exterior[f]
better	melhor[m]	melhor[f]
worse	pior[m]	pior[f]
superior	superior[m]	superior[f]
bigger	maior[m]	maior[f]
smaller	menor[m]	menor[f]

3. Some adjectives ending in "-eu"

The feminine form of masculine adjectives ending in "-eu" is often obtained by changing the final "-eu" to "-eia":

European	europeu[m]	europeia[f]
Hebrew	hebreu[m]	hebreia[f]

One exception is:

Jewish	judeu[m]	judia[f]

4. Adjectives ending in "-a," "-e," "-l," "-m," "-s," "-z," or "-ar"

The feminine form of most masculine adjectives that end with "-a," "-e," "-l," "-m," "-s," "-z," or "-ar" remains unchanged:

optimist	otimista[m]	otimista[f]
idiot	idiota[m]	idiota[f]
strong	forte[m]	forte[f]
sad	triste[m]	triste[f]
cruel	cruel[m]	cruel[f]
possible	possível[m]	possível[f]
common	comum[m]	comum[f]
young	jovem[m]	jovem[f]
simple	simples[m]	simples[f]
vulgar	reles[m]	reles[f]

happy	**feliz**^m	**feliz**^f
fast	**veloz**^m	**veloz**^f
regular	**regular**^m	**regular**^f
similar	**similar**^m	**similar**^f

5. Finally, there are some irregular adjectives that do not follow any pattern and must simply be memorized, such as:

good	**bom**^m	**boa**^f
bad	**mau**^m	**má**^f

3. Forming the Plural of a Noun or Adjective in Portuguese

More often than not, forming the plural of a noun in Portuguese resembles the English common way of adding an "-s" or "-es" at the end of a word. However, some nouns do not follow this simple pattern. Here, we will examine the different rules and patterns of forming the plural in Portuguese.

Adjectives in Portuguese must also agree in gender and number with the noun they describe.

To form the plural in Portuguese, there are six main patterns:

1. Nouns and adjectives ending in a vowel

Most nouns and adjectives ending in a vowel add a final "-s" to form the plural. For example:

braço^m	*arm*	**braços**^m	*arms*
mesa^f	*table*	**mesas**^f	*tables*
caros^m	*expensive*	**caros**^m	*expensive*

2. Nouns and adjectives ending in "-s"

Most nouns and adjectives ending in "-s" that are stressed on the last syllable or has a single syllable form the plural by adding a final "-es." For example:

país^m	*country*	**países**^m	*countries*
inglês^m	*English*	**ingleses**^m	*English*
mês^m	*month*	**meses**^m	*months*

Most other nouns and adjectives ending in "-s," i.e., multi-syllable words stressed on any syllable but the last, do not change form in the plural. Here are some examples:

ônibusᵐ	*bus*	**ônibus**ᵐ	*buses*
lápisᵐ	*pencil*	**lápis**ᵐ	*pencils*
simplesᵐ,ᶠ	*simple*	**simples**ᵐ,ᶠ	*simple*

3. Nouns and adjectives ending in "-r" "-z," or "-n"

Most nouns and adjectives ending in "-r" "-z," or "-n" add a final "-es" to form the plural. For example:

professorᵐ	*teacher*	**professores**ᵐ	*teachers*
vozᶠ	*voice*	**vozes**ᶠ	*voices*
capazᵐ,ᶠ	*capable*	**capazes**ᵐ,ᶠ	*capable*
líquenᵐ	*lichen*	**líquenes**ᵐ	*lichens*

4. Nouns and adjectives ending in "-m"

Most nouns and adjectives ending in "-m" change the final "-m" to "-n" and add a final "-s" to form the plural. For example:

somᵐ	*sound*	**sons**ᵐ	*sounds*
nuvemᶠ	*cloud*	**nuvens**ᶠ	*clouds*
ruimᵐ,ᶠ	*bad*	**ruins**ᵐ,ᶠ	*bad*

5. Nouns and adjectives ending in "-ão"

Most nouns and adjectives ending in "-ão" change the final ending to "-ões" to form the plural. For example:

coraçãoᵐ	*heart*	**corações**ᵐ	*hearts*
razãoᶠ	*reason*	**razões**ᶠ	*reasons*
decisãoᶠ	*decision*	**decisões**ᶠ	*decisions*

However, there are some exceptions:

a) Some words, especially ones that are stressed on the second-last syllable, simply add an "-s" to the final "-ão" to form the plural. For example:

órfãoᵐ	*orphan*	**órfãos**ᵐ	*orphans*

órgão^m	organ	órgãos^m	organs
mão^f	hand	mãos^f	hands
irmão^m	brother	irmãos^m	brothers

b) Some words change the final "-ão" to "-ães" to form the plural. For example:

alemão^m	German	alemães^m	Germans
cão^m	dog	cães^m	dogs
pão^m	bread	pães^m	bread (loaves)
capitão^m	captain	capitães^m	captains

6. Nouns and adjectives ending in "-l"

a) Nouns and adjectives ending in "-al," "-el," "-ol," and "-ul" form the plural by changing their ending into "-ais," "-eis," "-ois," and "-uis," respectively. For example:

animal^m	animal	animais^m	animal
papel^m	paper	papéis^m	papers
sol^m	sun	sóis^m	suns
azul^{m,f}	blue	azuis^{m,f}	blues

Notice that if last syllable is stressed, an acute accent is needed on the letter before the final "-is" in the plural.

b) Nouns and adjectives ending in "-il" form the plural by changing the final ending into "-is" if the last syllable is stressed, or "-eis" if the stress falls on a different syllable. For example:

funil^m	funnel	funis^m	funnels
sutil^{m,f}	subtle	sutis^{m,f}	subtle
fóssil^m	fossil	fósseis^m	fossils
réptil^m	reptile	répteis^m	reptiles

c) Few words deviate from the above two rules and form the plural differently:

cônsul^m	consul	cônsules^m	consuls
gol^m	goal	gols^m	goals
mal^m	evil	males^m	evils

To summarize:

Singular Ending	Plural Ending	Example
vowel	-s	mesa *(table)* > mesas *(tables)*
-s	-	lápis *(pencil)* > lápis *(pencils)*
	-es	país *(country)* > países *(tables)*
-r, -z, -n	-es	voz *(voice)* > vozes *(voices)*
-m	-ns	som *(sound)* > sons *(sounds)*
-ão	-ões	razão *(reason)* > razões *(reasons)*
	-ãos	mão *(hand)* > mãos *(hands)*
	-ães	cão *(dog)* > cães *(dogs)*
-l	-al > -ais	animal *(animal)* > animais *(animals)*
	-el > -eis	hotel *(hotel)* > hotéis *(hotels)*
	-ol > -ois	sol *(sun)* > sóis *(suns)*
	-ul > -uis	azul *(blue)* > azuis *(blue)*
	-il > -is *(stressed)* -il > -eis *(unstressed)*	funil *(funnel)* > funis *(funnels)* réptil *(reptile)* > répteis *(reptiles)*

Gender & Plural in Italian

The vast majority of Italian words end in a vowel. This is part of the reason spoken Italian has a melodic recognizable tone.

This rule, however, is not universal. Not all Italian words end with a vowel, e.g., "**il**" *(the)*, "**con**" *(with)*, "**in**" *(in)*. In addition, there are many foreign words that have made inroads into the Italian life and dictionary such as "**sport**" and "**Internet.**"

The vowel at the end of the word often identifies the gender and number of a noun or adjective. Many masculine nouns and adjectives in Italian end with "-o" in singular and "-i" in plural. On the other hand, many feminine nouns and adjectives end with "-a" in singular and "-e" in plural.

Furthermore, some Italian words end in "**-e**" in their singular form, and it can be hard to tell if they are masculine or feminine. To form the plural, the final "**e**" is changed to "**i**," regardless of the gender of the word.

	Singular	Plural
Masculine	-o	-i
Masculine or Feminine	-e	
Feminine	-a	-e

Notably, the word "**gente**" *(people)* in Italian, unlike in English, is singular, e.g., "**La gente va e viene**" *(people come and go)*. There are words that are only used in plural form such as "**baffi**ᵐ" *(mustache)*, "**forbici**ᶠ" *(scissors)*, "**occhiali**ᵐ" *(glasses)*, and "**pantaloni**ᵐ" *(pants)*.

Adjectives in Italian, unlike in English, come after the noun they describe, for example, "**edificio alto**" *(tall building)*. There are some exceptions to this rule, for example, "**grande**[1] **città**" *(big or great city)*. Many adjectives that come before the noun are *indefinite adjectives*, which will be covered in **Level III, Lesson 4**.

Let us summarize some important rules in the context of examples:

1. Words ending in "**-o**" are generally masculine, and the plural is formed by changing the final "**o**" to "**i**." For example:

libroᵐ	*book*	**libri**ᵐ	*books*
gattoᵐ	*cat*	**gatti**ᵐ	*cats*
telefonoᵐ	*phone*	**telefoni**ᵐ	*phones*
zioᵐ	*uncle*	**zii**ᵐ	*uncles*

There are only a few exceptions of words ending in "**-o**" that are feminine, such as: "**mano**" *(hand)*, "**radio**" *(radio)*, "**libido**" *(libido)*, "**foto**" *(photo)*, "**auto**" *(car)*, and "**moto**" *(motorcycle)*.

---

[1] If the adjective "**grande**" is placed after the noun, it means *"big"* or *"large,"* e.g., "**una città grande**" *(a big city)*. On the other hand, if it is placed before the noun, it can also mean *"great,"* e.g., "**una grande città**" *(a great city)*, "**una grande amica**" *(a great friend)*, etc.

2. Words ending in "**-a**" are generally feminine, and the plural is formed by changing the final "**a**" to "**e**." For example:

casa[f]	*house*	**case**[f]	*houses*
camicia[f]	*shirt*	**camicie**[f]	*shirts*
sedia[f]	*chair*	**sedie**[f]	*chairs*
zia[f]	*aunt*	**zie**[f]	*aunts*

There are some exceptions such as:

a. Words that end in "**-ma**" or "**-ta**" and originate from *Greek*. These are masculine, and the plural is formed by changing the final "**a**" to "**i**." For example:

problema[m]	*problem*	**problemi**[m]	*problems*
sistema[m]	*system*	**sistemi**[m]	*systems*
clima[m]	*climate*	**climi**[m]	*climates*
tema[m]	*topic*	**temi**[m]	*topics*
diploma[m]	*diploma*	**diplomi**[m]	*diplomas*
dramma[m]	*drama*	**drammi**[m]	*dramas*
dilemma[m]	*dilemma*	**dilemmi**[m]	*dilemmas*
diagramma[m]	*diagram*	**diagrammi**[m]	*diagrams*
pianeta[m]	*planet*	**pianeti**[m]	*planets*
poeta[m]	*poet*	**poeti**[m]	*poets*

This exception does not apply to words that did *not* originate from *Greek*, such as "**forma**[f]" *(form)* and "**piattaforma**[f]" *(platform)*, whose plurals are "**forme**[f]" and "**piattaforme**[f]," respectively.

b. Words that end in "**-ista**" and refer to masculine or feminine people performing a profession, such as:

tassista[m,f]	*taxi driver*	**tassisti**[m] **tassiste**[f]	*taxi drivers*
artista[m,f]	*artist*	**artisti**[m] **artiste**[f]	*artists*
analista[m,f]	*analyst*	**analisti**[m] **analiste**[f]	*analysts*
pianista[m,f]	*pianist*	**pianisti**[m] **pianiste**[f]	*pianists*

The feminine form is used for groups that consist exclusively of feminine-gender members. Even if one masculine-gender member of that group exists, we must use the masculine form.

3. Words ending in "-e" can be masculine or feminine, and the plural is formed by changing the final "e" to "i." For example:

colore[m]	color	colori[m]	colors
madre[f]	mother	madri[f]	mothers
padre[m]	father	padri[m]	fathers
chiave[f]	key	chiavi[f]	keys

It can be difficult to determine if a noun ending with "-e" is masculine or feminine and a dictionary is often needed. Most nouns ending in "-ice" are feminine. They are often the feminine forms of masculine nouns ending in "-ore."

attore[m] attrice[f]	actor actress	attori[m] attrici[f]	actors actresses
autore[m] autrice[f]	author	autori[m] autrici[f]	authors
direttore[m] direttrice[f]	director	direttori[m] direttrici[f]	directors
imperatore[m] imperatrice[f]	emperor empress	imperatori[m] imperatrici[f]	emperors empresses
pittore[m] pittrice[f]	painter	pittori[m] pittrici[f]	painters
scrittore[m] scrittrice[m]	writer	scrittori[m] scrittrici[m]	writers

In general, most nouns ending with "-ione" are feminine, and most nouns ending in "-one," but not "-ione," are masculine. For example:

nazione[f]	nation	nazioni[f]	nations
televisione[f]	television	televisioni[f]	televisions
opinione[f]	opinion	opinioni[f]	opinions
cordone[m]	rope	cordoni[m]	ropes
mattone[m]	brick	mattoni[m]	bricks
pallone[m]	ball	palloni[m]	balls

However, there are few exceptions, such as "**copione**" *(script)* which is masculine.

4. Although the most common gender pattern is a feminine noun with an "**-a**" ending that corresponds to a masculine noun with an "**-o**" ending, this is not the only gender pattern in Italian.

   We have encountered masculine nouns ending in "**-ore**" whose feminine forms end in "**-ice**," e.g., "**autore^m**" and "**autrice^f**," meaning *"author."* Another irregular but common feminine form is using the ending "**-essa.**" This is common with some masculine nouns ending in "**-ore**," "**-ante**," "**-ente**," "**-eta**," and "**-one.**" For example:

professore^m **professoressa^f**	*professor*	**professori^m** **professoresse^f**	*professors*
presidente^m **presidentessa^f**	*president*	**presidenti^m** **presidentesse^f**	*presidents*
poeta^m **poetessa^f**	*poet*	**poeti^m** **poetesse^f**	*poets*
leone^m **leonessa^f**	*lion* *lioness*	**leoni^m** **leonesse^f**	*lions* *lionesses*

Some nouns ending in "**-e**" in masculine have an "**-a**" ending in their feminine forms. For example:

cameriere^m **cameriera^f**	*waiter* *waitress*	**camerieri^m** **cameriere^f**	*waiters* *waitresses*
infermiere^m **infermiera^f**	*nurse*	**infermieri^m** **infermiere^f**	*nurses*

Some nouns do not change form in masculine or feminine. For example:

cantante^{m,f}	*singer*	**cantanti^{m,f}**	*singers*
francese^{m,f}	*French*	**francesi^{m,f}**	*French (plural)*
inglese^{m,f}	*English*	**inglesi^{m,f}**	*English (plural)*

Finally, there are other nouns that do not follow any pattern. For example, the feminine form of "**dio**" *(god)* is "**dea**" *(goddess).*

5. Words under the following categories have the same singular and plural forms:

   a. Foreign words used in Italian. Most such words are masculine. For example:

film^m	*film*	**film**^{m}	*films*
bar^m	*bar*	**bar**^{m}	*bars*
sport^m	*sport*	**sport**^{m}	*sports*
taxi^m	*taxi*	**taxi**^{m}	*taxis*
autobus^m	*bus*	**autobus**^{m}	*buses*
re^m	*king*	**re**^{m}	*kings*
gru^m	*crane*	**gru**^{m}	*cranes*
hotel^m	*hotel*	**hotel**^{m}	*hotels*

   b. Most words ending in an accented vowel. For example:

città^f	*city*	**città**^{f}	*cities*
caffè^m	*coffee*	**caffè**^{m}	*coffees*
università^f	*university*	**università**^{f}	*universities*
tribù^f	*tribe*	**tribù**^{f}	*tribes*
virtù^f	*virtue*	**virtù**^{f}	*virtues*

   c. Words that end in "**-si.**" Most such words are feminine. For example:

crisi^f	*crisis*	**crisi**^{f}	*crises*
analisi^f	*analysis*	**analisi**^{f}	*analyses*

   d. Feminine words that end in "**-o,**" except "**mano**^{f}" *(hand)*, whose plural is "**mani**^{f}." For example:

radio^f	*radio*	**radio**^{f}	*radios*
auto^f	*car*	**auto**^{f}	*cars*
foto^f	*photo*	**foto**^{f}	*photos*
moto^f	*motorcycle*	**moto**^{f}	*motorbikes*

Notice that the nouns "**auto,**" "**foto,**" and "**moto**" are short forms of the feminine nouns "**automobile**^{f}," "**fotografia**^{f}," and "**motocicletta**^{f}," respectively.

6. There are a few words that are masculine in singular form and feminine in plural form. For example:

braccio[m]	arm	braccia[f]	arms
dito[m]	finger	dita[f]	fingers
ginocchio[m]	knee	ginocchia[f]	knees
labbro[m]	lip	labbra[f]	lips
uovo[m]	egg	uova[f]	eggs

7. Some words undergo spelling changes to form the plural. These often fall under one of these categories:

   a. Words with "-co/-ca" and "-go/-ga" endings often add "h" to form plurals with "-chi/-che" or "-ghi/-ghe" endings, especially if the "-co/-ca" or "-go/-ga" is not preceded by "e" or "i." For example:

gioco[m]	game	giochi[m]	games
parco[m]	park	parchi[m]	parks
albergo[m]	hotel	alberghi[m]	hotels
lago[m]	lake	laghi[m]	lakes

Notice that the purpose of these changes is to maintain the desired soft or hard pronunciation of the "c" or "g."

If an "e" or "i" precedes the "-co/-ca" or "-go/-ga," the masculine plural form often ends in "-ci" or "-gi," leading to change in the "c" or "g" pronunciation from hard to soft sound. For example:

amico[m] amica[f]	friend	amici[m] amiche[f]	friends
greco[m] greca[f]	Greek	greci[m] greche[f]	Greeks
biologo[m] biologa[f]	biologist	biologi[m] biologhe[f]	biologists
psicologo[m] psicologa[f]	psychologist	psicologi[m] psicologhe[f]	psychologists

Notice that this exception applies only to the masculine form, whereas the feminine form still adds an "h" in the plural.

In general, the suffixes "**-logo**" and "**-loga**," referring to a profession in singular, change to "**-logi**" and "**-loghe**," respectively, in plural.

Finally, there are a few words, mostly masculine, that do not follow the aforementioned rules. For example:

porco^m	*pig*	**porci**^m	*pigs*
fico^m	*fig*	**fichi**^m	*figs*
sindaco^m	*mayor*	**sindaci**^m	*mayors*
monaco^m	*monk*	**monaci**^m	*monks*

b. Words with "**-cia**" and "**-gia**" endings often remove the "**i**" to form plurals with "**-ce**" and "**-ge**" endings, if the "**-cia**" or "**-gia**" ending is preceded by a consonant. For example:

arancia^f	*orange*	**arance**^f	*oranges*
faccia^f	*face*	**facce**^f	*faces*
spiaggia^f	*beach*	**spiagge**^f	*beaches*

If the "**-cia**" or "**-gia**" ending is preceded by a vowel, the regular plural is formed with "**-cie**" or "**-gie**" ending. For example:

camicia^f	*shirt*	**camicie**^f	*shirts*
ciliegia^f	*cherry*	**ciliegie**^f	*cherries*
valigia^f	*suitcase*	**valigie**^f	*suitcases*

c. Words with the the "**-io**" ending remove the final "**o**" to form plurals with the "**-i**" ending. For example:

figlio^m	*son*	**figli**^m	*sons*
occhio^m	*eye*	**occhi**^m	*eyes*
orologio^m	*clock/watch*	**orologi**^m	*clocks/watches*

If the "**i**" in the final "**-io**" is in the stressed syllable of the word, the plural is formed with the "**-ii**" ending. For example:

invio^m	*dispatch*	**invii**^m	*dispatches*
zio^m	*uncle*	**zii**^m	*uncles*

8. Some words have completely irregular plurals. For example:

uomo[m]	*man*	uomini[m]	*men*
dio[m]	*god*	dèi[m]	*gods*
bue[m]	*ox*	buoi[m]	*oxen*
ala[f]	*wing*	ali[f]	*wings*
arma[f]	*weapon*	armi[f]	*weapons*
tempio[m]	*temple*	templi[m]	*temples*

9. Some words have a different meaning when used as masculine versus when used as feminine. For example:

posto[m]	*place*	posta[f]	*mail*
modo[m]	*way*	moda[f]	*fashion*
capitale[m]	*capital (money)*	capitale[f]	*capital (city)*

Gender & Plural in French

Finally, we cover how to determine the gender of a noun or adjective in French. We will also cover forming the plural.

1. Gender of a Noun in French

On general rule is that a noun that ends with "-e" or "-ion" is likely feminine, except for nouns ending in "-ge" or "-isme," which are likely masculine even though they end with "-e." Any other noun in French that does not end with "-e" is likely, but not certainly, masculine.

Of course, there will be some obvious masculine and feminine nouns. For instance, we know that "homme" *(man)* and "prince" *(prince)* are masculine regardless of the above rule.

Let us look at some examples of nouns that follow the general rule as well as some exceptions:

Gender	Ending	Nouns that follow the rule	Exceptions
feminine	-e	couverture *(blanket)*, fenêtre *(window)*, plante *(plant)*	spectacle *(spectacle)*, stade *(stadium)*, silence *(silence)*, incendie *(fire)*
	-ion	destination *(destination)*, nation *(nation)*, production *(production)*	avion *(plane)*, camion *(truck)*

masculine	-ge	âge *(age)*, garage *(garage)*, nuage *(cloud)*, stage *(internship)*, orage *(thunderstorm)*, village *(village)*, siège *(seat)*, piège *(trap)*, liège *(cork)*, collège *(college)*	cage *(cage)*, page *(page)*, plage *(beach)*, image *(image)*, rage *(rage)*
	-isme	cyclisme *(cycling)*, prisme, schisme, tourisme *(tourism)*	-
masculine	Other	bureau *(office)*, papier *(paper)*, journal *(newspaper)*, bras *(arm)*, changement *(change)*, lit *(bed)*	eau *(water)*, peau *(skin)*, souris *(mouse)*

Some words have a different meaning when used in the masculine form versus when used in the feminine form. For example:

livre^m	*book*	livre^f	*pound*
mode^m	*mode, way or method*	mode^f	*fashion*
capitale^m	*capital (money)*	capitale^f	*capital (city)*
tour^m	*tour*	tour^f	*tower*
mémoire^m	*report*	mémoire^f	*memory*
poste^m	*job*	poste^f	*post office*
vase^m	*vase*	vase^f	*mud*

Notice that many words that end in "-me" and originate from *Greek* are masculine, for example:

problème^m	*problem*	drame^m	*drama*
système^m	*system*	dilemme^m	*dilemma*
thème^m	*topic or theme*	diagramme^m	*diagram*
diplôme^m	*diploma*	poème^m	*poem*

This exception does not apply to words that do *not* originate from *Greek*, such as "**forme**" *(form)* and "**plateforme**" *(platform)*, which are feminine.

In addition, there are many foreign nouns that have made inroads into the French life and dictionary such as "**sport**" and "**Internet**." In general, most of these nouns are masculine.

Some nouns that refer to people can be masculine or feminine. The most common pattern to form the feminine noun from a masculine noun is to add an "**e**" at the end, for example:

| étudiant[m] | student | étudiante[f] | student |
| ingénieur[m] | engineer | ingénieure[f] | engineer |

Nouns that end with a vowel followed by "**n**" or "**t**" often double the last consonant and add an "**e**" at the end, for example:

| lion[m] | lion | lionne[f] | lioness |
| chat[m] | cat | chatte[f] | cat |

Nevertheless, this is not the only gender pattern in French. Other patterns include:

-teur/-trice	actor/actress	acteur[m]	actrice[f]
	director	directeur[m]	directrice[f]
-eur/-euse	hair dresser	coiffeur[m]	coiffeuse[f]
	waiter/waitress	serveur[m]	serveuse[f]
-e/-esse	poet	poète[m]	poétesse[f]
	host/hostess	hôte[m]	hôtesse[f]

Most nouns that end in "**-iste**," "**-yste**," or "**-naire**" can refer to masculine or feminine people performing a role or profession, for example:

dentiste[m,f]	dentist	analyste[m,f]	analyst
artiste[m,f]	artist	pianiste[m,f]	pianist
vétérinaire[m,f]	veterinary	partenaire[m,f]	partner
millionaire[m,f]	millionaire	révolutionnaire[m,f]	revolutionary

Others may only have one form (masculine or feminine) regardless of the gender of the person that the noun refers to, for example:

personne[f]	person	victime[f]	victim
professeur[m]	teacher	médecin[m]	doctor
écrivain[m]	writer	juge[m]	judge

It is also commonly acceptable to add the word "**femme**" *(woman)* to describe a female with a non-form changing masculine noun, e.g., "**une femme médecin**" *(a female doctor)*.

In general, most countries ending with "**-e**" are *feminine*, e.g., "**la France**" *(France)*. Exceptionally, the following six countries end with "**-e**" but are *masculine*:

Mexique^m	Mexico	Belize^m	Belize
Cambodge^m	Cambodia	Mozambique^m	Mozambique
Zimbabwe^m	Zimbabwe	Suriname^m	Surinam

Most other countries that do not end in "-e" are masculine. Here are some examples:

| Maroc^m | Morocco | Iran^m | Iran |
| Canada^m | Canada | Portugal^m | Portugal |

Notice that most countries are often preceded by a definite article, while only a few cannot be used by a definite article, such as:

Bahreïn^m	Bahrain	Chypre^f	Cyprus
Singapour^m	Singapore	Haïti^m	Haiti
Cuba^m	Cuba	Sri Lanka^m	Sri Lanka
Malte^f	Malta	Monaco^m	Monaco

Some countries are always in plural form, such as:

| États-Unis^m | United States | Pays-Bas^m | Netherlands |
| Philippines^f | Philippines | Bahamas^m | Bahamas |

2. Gender of an Adjective in French

Adjectives in French, unlike in English, come after the noun they describe, for example, "**bâtiment historique**" *(historic building)*. There are some exceptions to this rule, for example, "**grande ville**" *(big or great city)*. Many adjectives that come before the noun are *indefinite adjectives*, which will be covered in **Level III, Lesson 4**.

Most adjectives form the feminine singular by adding a final "-e" to the masculine singular form. However, there are many exceptions that follow different patterns. The following are the most common patterns:

1. Adjectives ending in "-eux"

The feminine form of masculine adjectives ending in "-eux" is often obtained by changing the final "-eux" to "-euse":

happy	**heureux**[m]	**heureuse**[f]
joyful	**joyeux**[m]	**joyeuse**[f]
serious	**sérieux**[m]	**sérieuse**[f]
curious	**curieux**[m]	**curieuse**[f]
nervous	**nerveux**[m]	**nerveuse**[f]
religious	**religieux**[m]	**religieuse**[f]

2. Adjectives ending in "-é"

The feminine form of masculine adjectives ending in "-é" is often obtained by adding an extra "-e":

tired	**fatigué**[m]	**fatiguée**[f]
busy	**occupé**[m]	**occupée**[f]
complicated	**compliqué**[m]	**compliquée**[f]
salty	**salé**[m]	**salée**[f]

3. Adjectives ending in a silent "-e"

The feminine form of masculine adjectives ending in a silent "-e" is the same, for example:

clean	**propre**[m]	**propre**[f]
comfortable	**confortable**[m]	**confortable**[f]
dirty	**sale**[m]	**sale**[f]
easy	**facile**[m]	**facile**[f]
empty	**vide**[m]	**vide**[f]
funny	**drôle**[m]	**drôle**[f]
honest	**honnête**[m]	**honnête**[f]
poor	**pauvre**[m]	**pauvre**[f]
pleasant	**aimable**[m]	**aimable**[f]
sad	**triste**[m]	**triste**[f]
weak	**faible**[m]	**faible**[f]

4. Adjectives ending in "-f"

The feminine form of masculine adjectives ending in "-f" is often obtained by changing the final "-f" to "-ve":

active	**actif**[m]	**active**[f]
attractive	**attractif**[m]	**attractive**[f]
decisive	**décisif**[m]	**décisive**[f]
positive	**positif**[m]	**positive**[f]
negative	**négatif**[m]	**négative**[f]

| widower/widow | veuf^m | veuve^f |

5. Adjectives ending in a consonant "**l**," "**n**," or "**s**"

The feminine form of many masculine adjectives ending in the consonant "**l**," "**n**," or "**s**" is obtained by adding an "**-e**" to the end of the word and doubling the consonant before the final "**-e**":

cruel	cruel^m	cruelle^f
European	européen^m	européenne^f
fat	gros^m	grosse^f
former, old, or ancient	ancien^m	ancienne^f
good	bon^m	bonne^f
kind or nice	gentil^m	gentille^f
low	bas^m	basse^f

Finally, there are some irregular adjectives that do not follow any pattern and must simply be memorized. Here are some examples:

beautiful	beau^m	belle^f
dry	sec^m	seche^f
false	faux^m	fausse^f
favorite	favori^m	favorite^f
frank	franc^m	franche^f
fresh	frais^m	fraîche^f
long	long^m	longue^f
new	nouveau^m	nouvelle^f
old	vieux^m	vieille^f
public	public^m	publique^f
soft/sweet	doux^m	douce^f
white	blanc^m	blanche^f

Among the above irregular adjectives, there are three adjectives that change form only if they come before a *masculine* noun that starts with a vowel or mute "**h**." The three adjectives are: "**beau**" *(beautiful)*, "**nouveau**" *(new)*, and "**vieux**" *(old)*. Here are some examples:

beau^m *(beautiful)*	**beau pays** *(beautiful country)*	**bel animal** *(beautiful animal)*
nouveau^m *(new)*	**nouveau livre** *(new book)*	**nouvel ami** *(new friend)*
vieux^m *(old)*	**vieux port** *(old port)*	**vieil homme** *(old man)*

If the noun is feminine or the adjective is placed after the noun, the change of form is not applied even if the noun starts with a vowel or a mute "**h**," e.g., "**Cet animal est beau**" *(This animal is beautiful)*, "**nouvelle année**" *(new year)*, etc.

3. Forming the Plural of a Noun or Adjective in French

Forming the plural of a singular noun or adjective is often straightforward and resembles the English common way of adding an "-**s**" at the end of a word. Here are some examples:

livreᵐ	*book*	**livres**ᵐ	*books*
chatᵐ	*cat*	**chats**ᵐ	*cats*
téléphoneᵐ	*phone*	**téléphones**ᵐ	*phones*
balleᶠ	*ball*	**balles**ᶠ	*balls*
maisonᶠ	*house*	**maisons**ᶠ	*houses*

However, there are four main categories of nouns that do not follow the above simple rule to form the plural:

1. Nouns ending in "-**s**," "-**x**," or "-**z**"

The majority of nouns under this category do not change form in the plural, for example:

brasᵐ	*arm*	**bras**ᵐ	*arms*
choixᶠ	*choice*	**choix**ᶠ	*choices*
gazᵐ	*gas*	**gaz**ᵐ	*gasses*

2. Nouns ending in "-**au**" or "-**eu**"

Nouns ending in "-**au**" or "-**eu**" add an "-**x**" to the ending to form the plural, for example:

chapeauᵐ	*hat*	**chapeaux**ᵐ	*hats*
rideauᵐ	*curtain*	**rideaux**ᵐ	*curtains*
feuᵐ	*fire*	**feux**ᵐ	*fires*
lieuᵐ	*place*	**lieux**ᵐ	*places*

A notable exception is "**pneu**ᵐ" *(tire)*, whose plural is "**pneus**."

3. Nouns ending in "-**ail**" or "-**al**"

Nouns ending in "**-ail**" or "**-al**" change the ending to "**-aux**" to form the plural, for example:

animal^m	*animal*	**animaux**^m	*animals*
cheval^m	*horse*	**chevaux**^m	*horses*
travail^m	*work*	**travaux**^m	*works*
corail^m	*coral*	**coraux**^m	*corals*

4. Some nouns ending in "**-ou**"

The following nouns ending in "**-ou**" add "**-x**" to the ending to form the plural. These words need to be memorized.

bijou^m	*jewel*	**bijoux**^m	*jewels*
caillou^m	*pebble*	**cailloux**^m	*pebbles*
chou^m	*cabbage*	**choux**^m	*cabbages*
genou^m	*knee*	**genoux**^m	*knees*
hibou^m	*owl*	**hiboux**^m	*owls*
pou^m	*louse*	**poux**^m	*louses*
joujou^m	*toy*	**joujoux**^m	*toys*

Although the categories above cover most irregular plurals. There are a few words that do not fall under any of these categories. For instance, the plural of "**l'œil**^m" *(the eye)* is "**les yeux**" *(the eyes)*. Moreover, some words are only used in plural form such as "**ciseaux**^m" *(scissors)* and "**lunettes**^f" *(glasses)*.

To form the plural of an adjective, the general rule is to add an "**-s**" to the end of the adjective, e.g., "**petits**" is the plural of "**petit**" *(small)*, with the following exceptions:

1. If the adjective ends with "**-s**" or "**-x**," the plural form is the same as the singular, e.g., "**français**" is the plural of "**français**" *(French)*, and "**heureux**" is the plural of "**heureux**" *(happy)*.

2. If the adjective ends with "**-al**" or "**-eau**," the plural form ends in "**-aux**," e.g., "**principaux**" is the plural of "**principal**" *(main or principal)*, and "**nouveaux**" is the plural of "**nouveau**" *(new)*.

4. CARDINAL NUMBERS

SP		cero		veintiuno		doscientos
PT	0	zero	21	vinte e um	200	duzentos
IT		zero		ventuno		duecento
FR		zéro		vingt et un		deux cents
SP		uno, una		veintidós		trescientos
PT	1	um, uma	22	vinte e dois	300	trezentos
IT		uno, una		ventidue		trecento
FR		un, une		vingt-deux		trois cents
SP		dos		veintitrés		cuatrocientos
PT	2	dois, duas	23	vinte e três	400	quatrocentos
IT		due		ventitré		quattrocento
FR		deux		vingt-trois		quatre cents
SP		tres		treinta		quinientos
PT	3	três	30	trinta	500	quinhentos
IT		tre		trenta		cinquecento
FR		trois		trente		cinq cents
SP		cuatro		treinta y uno		seiscientos
PT	4	quatro	31	trinta e um	600	seiscentos
IT		quattro		trentuno		seicento
FR		quatre		trente et un		six cents
SP		cinco		treinta y dos		setecientos
PT	5	cinco	32	trinta e dois	700	setecentos
IT		cinque		trentadue		settecento
FR		cinq		trente-deux		sept cents
SP		seis		treinta y tres		ochocientos
PT	6	seis	33	trinta e três	800	oitocentos
IT		sei		trentatré		ottocento
FR		six		trente trois		huit cents
SP		siete		cuarenta		novecientos
PT	7	sete	40	quarenta	900	novecentos
IT		sette		quaranta		novecento
FR		sept		quarante		neuf cents
SP		ocho		cuarenta y uno		mil
PT	8	oito	41	quarenta e um	1.000	mil
IT		otto		quarantuno		mille
FR		huit		quarante et un		mille
SP		nueve		cuarenta y dos		dos mil
PT	9	nove	42	quarenta e dois	2.000	dois mil
IT		nove		quarantadue		duemila
FR		neuf		quarante-deux		deux mille

SP		diez		cincuenta		tres mil
PT	10	dez	50	cinquenta	3.000	três mil
IT		dieci		cinquanta		tremila
FR		dix		cinquante		trois mille
SP		once		cincuenta y uno		diez mil
PT	11	onze	51	cinquenta e um	10.000	dez mil
IT		undici		cinquantuno		diecimila
FR		onze		cinquante et un		dix mille
SP		doce		sesenta		cien mil
PT	12	doze	60	sessenta	100.000	cem mil
IT		dodici		sessanta		centomila
FR		douze		soixante		cent mille
SP		trece		setenta		cien mil uno
PT	13	treze	70	setenta	100.001	cem mil e um
IT		tredici		settanta		centomilauno
FR		treize		soixante-dix		cent mille un
SP		catorce		setenta y uno		cien mil diez
PT	14	quatorze	71	setenta e um	100.010	cem mil e dez
IT		quattordici		settantuno		centomiladieci
FR		quatorze		soixante et onze		cent mille dix
SP		quince		setenta y dos		doscientos mil
PT	15	quinze	72	setenta e dois	200.000	duzentos mil
IT		quindici		settantadue		duecentomila
FR		quinze		soixante-douze		deux cent mille
SP		dieciséis		ochenta		un millón
PT	16	dezesseis	80	oitenta	1.000.000	um milhão
IT		sedici		ottanta		un milione
FR		seize		quatre-vingts		un million
SP		diecisiete		noventa		dos millones
PT	17	dezessete	90	noventa	2.000.000	dois milhões
IT		diciassette		novanta		due milioni
FR		dix-sept		quatre-vingt-dix		deux millions
SP		dieciocho		cien		diez millones
PT	18	dezoito	100	cem	10.000.000	dez milhões
IT		diciotto		cento		dieci milioni
FR		dix-huit		cent		dix millions
SP		diecinueve		ciento uno		mil millones
PT	19	dezenove	101	cento e um	1.000.000.000	um bilhão
IT		diciannove		centouno		un miliardo
FR		dix-neuf		cent un		un milliard

SP		veinte		ciento dos		dos mil millones
PT	20	vinte	102	cento e dois	2.000.000.000	dois bilhões
IT		venti		centodue		due miliardi
FR		vingt		cent deux		deux milliard

❖ In Spanish and Italian, before a masculine noun, "**uno**" becomes "**un**," for example:

SP	"**un perro**" *(a dog)*, "**un gato**" *(a cat)*
IT	"**un cane**" *(a dog)*, "**un gatto**" *(a cat)*

You will encounter a similar dropping of the final "**o**" with a few other words in Spanish and Italian, such as:

	Adjective	Example
SP	"**bueno**" *(good)* "**malo**" *(bad)* "**alguno**" *(some)*	e.g., "Este restaurante es **bueno**" *(This restaurant is good)*, "Este es un **buen** restaurante" *(This is a good restaurant)*
IT	"**buono**" *(good)* "**bello**" *(beautiful)*	e.g., "Questo ristorante è **buono**" *(This restaurant is good)*, "Questo è un **buon** ristorante" *(This is a good restaurant)*

❖ The numbers 21-99 are formed by contracting the combination of tens and units.

In Italian, the following two changes apply, if necessary:

1. The vowel at the end of the tens is dropped if the unit starts with a vowel ("**uno**" and "**otto**"), e.g., "**ventuno**" (21), "**trentotto**" (38), "**quarantuno**" (41), "**novantotto**" (98), etc.

2. Numbers with *"three"* in their units are written with an acute accent on their endings, e.g., "**ventitré**" (23), "**trentatré**" (33), "**ottantatré**" (83), etc.

❖ In French, the number "**soixante-dix**" (70) is formed by combining "**soixante**" (60) and "**dix**" (10), and the number "**quatre-vingts**" (80) literally means *"four-twenties,"* i.e., 4 X 20.

❖ We use a *comma* to separate *decimals* and a *period* to separate *thousands* in Spanish, Portuguese, Italian, and French. For instance, the number **2.155,25** in any of the four languages is equivalent to *2,155.25* in English.

❖ In Spanish and Portuguese, to refer to the number 100 or thousand multiples of the number 100, we use **"cien"** and **"cem,"** respectively.

100	*a hundred*	**SP**	**cien**
		PT	**cem**
		IT	cento
		FR	cent
100.000	*a hundred thousand*	**SP**	**cien** mil
		PT	**cem** mil
		IT	centomila
		FR	cent mille
100.000.000	*a hundred million*	**SP**	**cien** millones
		PT	**cem** milhões
		IT	cento milioni
		FR	cent millions

Otherwise, if preceded or followed by a number, **"ciento(s)"** in Spanish and **"cento(s)"** in Portuguese must be used instead:

101	*a hundred and one*	**SP**	ciento uno
		PT	cento e um
		IT	centouno
		FR	cent un
300	*three hundred*	**SP**	trescientos
		PT	trezentos
		IT	trecento
		FR	trois cents

❖ In Spanish and Portuguese, the multiples of hundred (200-900) can have a masculine **"-os"** or a feminine **"-as"** ending depending on the nouns they describe, for example:

SP	doscient**os** libros	*200 books*
PT	duzent**os** livros	
IT	duecento libri	
FR	deux cents livres	
SP	doscient**as** manzanas	*200 apples*
PT	duzent**as** maçãs	
IT	duecento mele	
FR	deux cents pommes	

❖ The word for *a thousand* in Italian is "**mille**." To refer to multiples of a thousand, we use "**mila**" instead, e.g., "**tremila**" (3.000), "**cinquemila**" (5.000), etc. The words "**mil**" in Spanish and Portuguese, and "**mille**" in French, remain the same in plural.

❖ The words *"million"* and *"billion"* have plural forms in Spanish, Portuguese, Italian, and French. Notice that *a billion* and *a trillion* are different in the four languages.

1.000.000	*a million*	**SP**	un millón
		PT	um milhão
		IT	un milione
		FR	um milhão
1.000.000.000	*a billion*	**SP**	mil millones
		PT	um bilhão (or) mil milhões
		IT	un miliardo
		FR	un milliard
1.000.000.000.000	*a trillion*	**SP**	un billón
		PT	um trilhão
		IT	un trilione
		FR	un billion

❖ When describing items in millions or billions, one must add "**de**" in Spanish, Portuguese, and French, and "**di**" in Italian after *"million"* or *"billion,"* for example:

SP	un **millón** <u>de</u> estudiantes	
PT	um **milhão** <u>de</u> estudantes	*a **million** students*
IT	un **milione** <u>di</u> studenti	
FR	un **million** <u>d</u>'étudiants	
SP	dos **mil millones** <u>de</u> habitantes	
PT	dois **milhões** <u>de</u> habitantes	*two **billion** inhabitants*
IT	due **miliardi** <u>di</u> abitanti	
FR	deux **milliards** <u>d</u>'habitants	

❖ The basic arithmetic operations are as follows:

+	*plus*	**SP**	más
		PT	mais
		IT	più
		FR	plus

-	*minus*	**SP**	menos
		PT	menos
		IT	meno
		FR	moins
×	*times*	**SP**	por/veces
		PT	vezes
		IT	per/volte
		FR	fois
÷	*divided by*	**SP**	dividido por
		PT	dividido por
		IT	diviso per
		FR	divisé par
=	*equals*	**SP**	igual a
		PT	igual a
		IT	fa, uguale (a)
		FR	égalent/font

5. SUBJECT PERSONAL PRONOUNS

Subject personal pronouns in Spanish, Portuguese, Italian, and French serve the same function as their English counterparts by pointing out who carries out the action described by the verb.

SP	yo		
PT	eu	*I*	1st person singular
IT	io		
FR	je		
SP	tú		
PT	você/tu	*you (informal)*	2nd person singular
IT	tu		
FR	tu		
SP	usted		
PT	o senhor/a senhora	*you (formal)*	2nd person singular
IT	Lei		
FR	vous		
SP	él/ella		
PT	ele/ela	*he/she*	3rd person singular
IT	lui/lei		
FR	il/elle		

SP	nosotros/-as		
PT	nós	*we*	11ˢᵗ person plural
IT	noi		
FR	nous		
SP	vosotros/-as		
PT	vocês	*you (informal)*	2ⁿᵈ person plural
IT	voi		
FR	vous		
SP	ustedes		
PT	vocês	*you (formal)*	2ⁿᵈ person plural
IT	Loro		
FR	vous		
SP	ellos/ellas		
PT	eles/elas	*they*	3ʳᵈ person plural
IT	loro		
FR	ils/elles		

❖ More often than not, the subject personal pronoun is dropped in Spanish, Portuguese, and Italian because the verb endings can be sufficient to refer to the subject, as you will learn in **Lesson 6** of this level.

❖ There are two forms of the singular *"you"* in Spanish, Portuguese, Italian, and French: the first is *informal* and is used with familiar people (e.g., child, relative, friend, peer, etc.), and the second is *formal*, which is used with older people and with people we are not familiar with or to show respect.

	Informal Singular "you"	*Formal Singular "you"*
SP	tú	usted
PT	você/tu	o senhor/a senhora
IT	tu	Lei
FR	tu	vous

❖ Similarly, there are two forms of the plural *"you"* in Spanish and Italian:

	Informal Plural "you"	*Formal Plural "you"*
SP	vosotros/ustedes	ustedes
PT	vocês	
IT	voi	Loro
FR	vous	

In Latin America, "**vosotros**" is not used; instead, "**ustedes**" is used for both the formal and informal plural versions of *"you."* Throughout the book, we keep the "**vosotros**" conjugation for reference only. However, feel free to ignore it if you want to focus exclusively on Latin American Spanish.

❖ In some Spanish-speaking countries like Argentina, Uruguay, Paraguay, El Salvador, and Nicaragua, the informal "**tú**" is replaced with "**vos**."

❖ The second-person singular form "**tu**" is used in Portugal and in some parts of Brazil:

1. In Portugal, the form "**tu**" is informal and "**você**" is formal. The form "**tu**" is conjugated differently but will not be discussed in the lessons to come.

2. In Brazil, the form "**você**" is the widely used form for the informal second-person singular pronoun. However, some parts of Brazil use "**tu**" instead but keep the verb conjugation the same as "**você**." In general, "**o senhor**" *(literally, "the gentleman")* and "**a senhora**" *(literally, "the lady")* are used in Brazil as a formal way to address older people, with people we are not familiar with, or to show respect.

Throughout the book, we use the standard Brazilian Portuguese "**você**" with informal second-person singular and "**o senhor/a senhora**" with formal second-person singular.

❖ In everyday life in Brazil, there is an informal alternative to the first-person plural "**nós**" *(we)*, that is "**a gente**" *(literally "the people")*. We use the third-person singular verb conjugation with "**a gente**."

❖ Notice that, in Italian, the formal (or polite) forms "**Lei**" *(you - singular)* and "**Loro**" *(you - plural)* are capitalized to distinguish them from the non-capitalized "**lei**" *(she)* and "**loro**" *(they)*, respectively.

❖ There are two more pronouns in Italian that can replace "**lui**" *(he)* and "**lei**" *(she)*. The two pronouns are: "**egli**" *(he)* and "**ella**" *(she)*, and are rarely used in ordinary conversation.

❖ Notice that we did not include an equivalent to the English subject pronoun *"it."* Since the subject pronoun is often dropped in Spanish, Portuguese, and Italian, as we will see in **Lesson 6** of this level, the pronoun *"it"* is often not used. In formal speech, these are the alternatives:

- **Spanish**: The neuter personal pronoun "**ello**," often translated as *"it,"* can be used to refers to a statement or a situation, e.g., "**Ello no significa mucho**" *(It does not mean much)*. In spoken Spanish, we can also use the masculine demonstrative article "**esto**," meaning *"this,"* e.g., "**Esto no significa mucho**" *(It does not mean much)*.

- **Portuguese**: We can use a neuter demonstrative pronoun like "**isso**," meaning *"this/that,"* e.g., "**Isso não significa muito**" *(It does not mean much)*.

- **Italian**: The pronouns "**esso**," *(masculine)* and "**essa**," *(feminine)*, meaning *"it,"* can be used. The plural equivalents are: "**essi**," *(masculine)* and "**esse**," *(feminine)*, respectively.

- **French**: The third-person singular pronouns "**il**" and "**elle**" are also used as the equivalent to the English subject pronoun *"it,"* when referring to a masculine or feminine object. When referring to a statement or a fact, the masculine pronoun "**il**" is often used, e.g., "**il est important**" *(it is important)*.

In Summary:

	"it"
SP	ello, esto, esta
PT	isso, este, esse
IT	esso, essa, questo
FR	il, elle

❖ In French, the special pronoun "**on**" can mean *"we," "one,"* or *"they,"* especially in passive constructions, e.g., "**On va à la plage aujourd'hui**" *(We go to the beach today)*, "**On parle français ici**" *(We/They speak French here)*, etc. Note that the pronoun "**on**" uses the third-person singular conjugation.

6. PRESENT INDICATIVE TENSE I

Verbs in their infinitive form in Spanish, Portuguese, Italian, and French have one of three endings:

SP	-ar	-er	-ir
PT	-ar	-er	-ir
IT	-are	-ere	-ire
FR	-er	-ir	-re

When conjugated, these endings are replaced with different conjugation suffixes based on the subject.

In English, verb conjugation in the present tense is quite simple. For example, the verb *"to break"* is conjugated as follows: *I/you/we/they break, he/she/it breaks*. Thus, there are only two conjugation forms of the verb *"to break"* in the simple present tense, which are *"break"* and *"breaks."*

In Spanish, Portuguese, Italian, and French, it is a little more complicated.

Regular Verbs

Regular verbs in the present indicative tense follow the conjugation rules discussed here with an example from each verb group:

- In Spanish:

The stem is formed by removing the final "**-ar**," "**-er**," or "**-ir**." Then, the conjugation ending is added depending on the personal pronoun, as follows:

	-ar ending habl<u>ar</u> *(to speak)*	-er ending com<u>er</u> *(to eat)*	-ir ending viv<u>ir</u> *(to live)*
yo	habl**o**	com**o**	viv**o**
tú	habl**as**	com**es**	viv**es**
él/ella/usted	habl**a**	com**e**	viv**e**
nosotros/-as	habl**amos**	com**emos**	viv**imos**
vosotros/-as	habl**áis**	com**éis**	viv**ís**
ellos/ellas/ustedes	habl**an**	com**en**	viv**en**

- In Portuguese:

The stem is formed by removing the final "**-ar**," "**-er**," or "**-ir**." Then, the conjugation ending is added depending on the personal pronoun, as follows:

	-ar ending fal<u>ar</u> *(to speak)*	-er ending com<u>er</u> *(to eat)*	-ir ending part<u>ir</u> *(to leave)*
eu	fal**o**	com**o**	part**o**
ele/ela/você	fal**a**	com**e**	part**e**
nós	fal**amos**	com**emos**	part**imos**
eles/elas/vocês	fal**am**	com**em**	part**em**

- In Italian:

The stem is formed by removing the final "**-are**," "**-ere**," or "**-ire**." Then, the conjugation ending is added depending on the personal pronoun, as follows:

	-are ending parl<u>are</u> *(to speak)*	-ere ending vend<u>ere</u> *(to sell)*	-ire ending (Type I) part<u>ire</u> *(to leave)*	-ire ending (Type II) fin<u>ire</u> *(to finish)*
io	parl**o**	vend**o**	part**o**	fin**isco**
tu	parl**i**	vend**i**	part**i**	fin**isci**
lui/lei	parl**a**	vend**e**	part**e**	fin**isce**
noi	parl**iamo**	vend**iamo**	part**iamo**	fin**iamo**
voi	parl**ate**	vend**ete**	part**ite**	fin**ite**
loro	parl**ano**	vend**ono**	part**ono**	fin**iscono**

Notice that there are two types of "**-ire**" verbs in Italian. Type II requires the addition of "**-isc-**" between the stem and the conjugation suffix normally used with Type I for all forms except "**noi**" and "**voi**." Unfortunately, only practice and a good dictionary can help you determine the type of an "**-ire**" verb.

- In French:

The stem is formed by removing the final "**-er**," "**-ir**," or "**-re**." Then, the conjugation ending is added depending on the personal pronoun, as follows:

	-er ending parler *(to speak)*	-ir ending finir *(to finish)*	-re ending vendre *(to sell)*
je	parle /paяl/	finis /fee-**nee**/	vends /vã/
tu	parles /paяl/	finis /fee-**nee**/	vends /vã/
il/elle/on	parle /paяl/	finit /fee-**nee**/	vend /vã/
nous	parlons /paя-lõ/	finissons /fee-nee-**sõ**/	vendons /vã-**dõ**/
vous	parlez /paя-le/	finissez /fee-nee-**se**/	vendez /vã-**de**/
ils/elles	parlent /paяl/	finissent /fee-**nees**/	vendent /vãd/

Notice that the conjugation suffixes of the singular forms in the table above are not pronounced. In other words, "**parle**" and "**parles**" are both pronounced the same i.e., /paяl/. Similarly, "**finis**" and "**finit**" are both pronounced the same, i.e., /fee-**nee**/. In addition, the third-person plural suffix "**-ent**" is never pronounced, e.g., "**parlent**" /paяl/, "**vendent**" / vãd /, etc.

Dropping the Subject Pronoun

In Spanish, Portuguese, and Italian, unlike in English, we generally drop the subject pronoun because the conjugation is usually sufficient to indicate the subject.

Notice that the subject pronoun cannot be dropped in French because, as we have seen, the pronunciation is not sufficient to distinguish between the different forms.

Here is an example:

SP	**Yo** hablo inglés.	Hablo inglés.	*I speak English.*
PT	**Eu** falo inglês.	Falo inglês.	
IT	**Io** parlo inglese.	Parlo inglese.	
FR	**Je** parle anglais.	-	

Both options are considered perfect speech and grammatically correct. It even sounds more native to drop the subject pronoun in informal speech. Opting to use the subject pronoun can sound less natural in some contexts, because it can indicate an emphasis on the subject rather than the verb.

Irregular Verbs

Not all verbs are regular in the present indicative tense. For example, the verbs *"to be"* and *"to have"* are two important verbs in Spanish, Portuguese, Italian, and French, used to form sentences and as auxiliary verbs. Both are completely irregular and are conjugated as follows:

- In Spanish:

	ser *(to be)*	**tener** *(to have)*
yo	soy	tengo
tú	eres	tienes
él/ella/usted	es	tiene
nosotros/-as	somos	tenemos
vosotros/-as	sois	tenéis
ellos/ellas/ustedes	son	tienen

- In Portuguese:

	ser *(to be)*	**ter** *(to have)*
eu	sou	tenho
ele/ela/você	é	tem
nós	somos	temos
eles/elas/vocês	são	têm

- In Italian:

	essere *(to be)*	**avere** *(to have)*
io	sono	ho
tu	sei	hai
lui/lei	è	ha
noi	siamo	abbiamo
voi	siete	avete
loro	sono	hanno

- In French:

	être *(to be)*		avoir *(to have)*	
je/j'	suis	/swee/	ai	/e/
tu	es	/e/	as	/a/
il/elle/on	est	/e/	a	/a/
nous	sommes	/som/	avons	/a-**võ**/
vous	êtes	/et/	avez	/a-**ve**/
ils/elles	sont	/sõ/	ont	/õ/

We will learn more about irregular verbs in the present indicative tense in **Level II, Lesson 2**.

It is important to note that the present tense we have discussed so far is also called the present *indicative* tense to distinguish it from the present *subjunctive* tense. The indicative and the subjunctive are two different moods. You do not have to worry about the difference for now. We will cover the subjunctive mood in more advanced lessons starting in **Level IV, Lesson 5**. As we progress with more advanced tenses in the levels to come, refer to **Appendix B** to use the provided verb conjugation chart as a cheat sheet and gain perspective on the different moods and tenses.

7. THE ARTICLES

In Spanish, Portuguese, Italian, and French, both definite and indefinite articles must agree with the noun they describe in gender and number.

1. Definite Articles

The following definite articles are equivalent to *"the"* in English.

- In Spanish:

We have four definite articles in Spanish because the definite article must agree with the noun in both gender and number:

el	Before a **singular masculine** noun	e.g., el hombre (*the man*)
la	Before a **singular feminine** noun	e.g., la casa (*the house*)
los	Before a **plural masculine** noun	e.g., los hombres (*the men*)
las	Before a **plural feminine** noun	e.g., las casas (*the houses*)

There are only two contractions in Spanish that involve the singular masculine definite article "**el**," and, unlike in English, these contractions are not optional and must be applied:

a + el = **al**	e.g., "Yo voy **al** restaurante" (*I go to the restaurant*).
de + el = **del**	e.g., "Yo vengo **del** café" (*I come from the café*).

Before a singular feminine noun that starts with "**a**" or "**ha**," the definite article "**el**" is used instead of "**la**." For instance, both nouns "**agua**" (*water*) and "**águila**" (*eagle*) are feminine. When singular, we use "**el**," i.e., "**el agua**" (*the water*), "**el águila**" (*the eagle*). However, the plural is regular; thus, "**las**" is used, e.g., "**las águilas**" (*the eagles*).

- In Portuguese:

We have four definite articles in Portuguese because the definite article has to agree with the noun in both gender and number:

o	Before a **singular masculine** noun	e.g., o homem (*the man*)
a	Before a **singular feminine** noun	e.g., a casa (*the house*)
os	Before a **plural masculine** noun	e.g., os homens (*the men*)
as	Before a **plural feminine** noun	e.g., as casas (*the houses*)

- In Italian:

Below are the definite articles in Italian, equivalent to *"the"* in English. We have seven definite articles in Italian because the definite article has to agree with the noun in both gender and number. In addition, some nouns that begin with a vowel or certain consonants require different definite articles.

	Singular	Plural
Before a **masculine** noun that begins with a vowel	**l'**	
Before a **masculine** noun that begins with "**z**," "**gn**," "**ps**," or "**s**" + consonant	**lo**	**gli**
Before any other **masculine** noun	**il**	**i**
Before a **feminine** noun that begins with a vowel	**l'**	
Before any other **feminine** noun	**la**	**le**

If an adjective precedes the noun, the definite article is adjusted according to the beginning of the adjective. For example, "**l'amico**" means *"the friend,"* whereas "**il buon amico**" means *"the good friend."* Notice the change in the definite article from "**l'**" to "**il.**"

The article "**gli**" is used before any plural masculine noun (or preceding adjective) that begins with a vowel, "**z**," "**gn**," "**ps**," or "**s**" + consonant, e.g., "**gli amici**" *(the friends)*, "**gli gnocchi**" *(the dumplings)*, "**gli studenti**" *(the students)*, etc.

The feminine plural article "**le**" is used before any plural feminine plural noun (or preceding adjective), regardless of whether it begins with a vowel or consonant, e.g., "**le ore**" *(the hours)*, "**le donne**" *(the women)*, "**le zone**" *(the zones)*, etc.

Using the proper article in Italian is more complicated than in English or other Romance languages.

There are two common adjectives in Italian that undergo similar form-changing contractions to the definite articles: "**bello**" *(beautiful)* and "**quello**" *(that)*, e.g., "**quell'amico**" *(that friend)*, "**begli uccelli**" *(beautiful birds)*.[1]

	l'	lo	il	la	i	gli	le
bello	bell'	bello	bel	bella	bei	begli	belle
quello	quell'	quello	quel	quella	quei	quegli	quelle

The adjective "**bello**" can be placed before or after the noun. Notice that the contraction applies to the adjective "**bello**" only if it precedes the noun. Otherwise, the contractions are not applied, e.g., "**uccelli belli**" *(beautiful birds)*.

---

[1] Another adjective that changes form, but only in the singular before a proper noun, is "**santo**" *(saint)*, which has the form:
- "**Sant'**": before a proper masculine or feminine noun that starts with a vowel, e.g., "**Sant'Antonio**" *(St. Anthony)*, "**Sant'Anna**" *(St. Ann)*.
- "**Santo**": before a proper masculine noun that starts with "**z**," "**gn**," "**ps**," or "**s**" + consonant, e.g., "**Santo Stefano**" *(St. Stephen)*.
- "**San**": before any other proper masculine noun, e.g., "**San Marco**" *(St. Mark)*.
- "**Santa**": before any other proper feminine noun, e.g., "**Santa Maria**" *(St. Mary)*.

There will be more detail on **"quello"** and other demonstrative adjectives and pronouns in **Level II, Lesson 4**.

- In French:

Below are the definite articles in French, equivalent to *"the"* in English:

	Singular	Plural
Before a **masculine** or **feminine** noun that begins with a vowel or a mute "**h**"	l'	les
Before a **masculine** noun that does not begin with a vowel or a mute "**h**"	le	
Before a **feminine** noun that does not begin with a vowel or a mute "**h**"	la	

If an adjective precedes the noun, the definite article is adjusted according to the beginning of the adjective. For example, "**l'ami**" means *"the friend,"* whereas "**le bon ami**" means *"the good friend."* Notice the change in the definite article from "**l'**" to "**le**."

Notice that only a mute "**h**" takes the definite article "**l'**" in singular form, e.g., "**l'homme**" /lom/ *(the man)*, and a liaison is applied in plural form, i.e., "**les hommes**" /le<u>z</u>-om/ *(the men)*. On the other hand, an aspirated "**h**" takes the definite article "**le**" in singular form, e.g., "**le héros**" /lə e-яo/ *(the hero)*, and a liaison is prohibited in plural form, i.e., "**les héros**" /le e-яo/ *(the heroes)*, not /le<u>z</u> e-яo/.

2. Indefinite Articles

The following indefinite articles are equivalent to *"a"* or *"an"* in English.

- In Spanish:

The indefinite articles in Spanish are "**un**" (for singular masculine) and "**una**" (for singular feminine).

un	Before a **singular masculine** noun	e.g., un hombre *(a man)*
una	Before a **singular feminine** noun	e.g., una casa *(a house)*

The plural forms "**unos**" and "**unas**" are used to mean *"some,"* e.g., "**unos momentos**" (*some moments*), "**unas palabras**" (*some words*), etc.

Before a singular feminine noun that starts with "**a**" or "**ha**," "**un**" is used instead of "**una**," e.g., "**un águila**." The plural is regular, thus "**unas**" is used, e.g., "**unas águilas**."

- In Portuguese:

The indefinite articles in Portuguese are "**um**" (for singular masculine) and "**uma**" (for singular feminine).

um	Before a **singular masculine** noun	e.g., um homem (*a man*)
uma	Before a **singular feminine** noun	e.g., uma casa (*a house*)

The plural forms "**uns**" and "**umas**" are used to mean *"some,"* e.g., "**uns momentos**" (*some moments*), "**umas palavras**" (*some words*), etc.

- In Italian:

There are four indefinite articles in Italian; two masculine articles: "**un**" and "**uno**," and two feminine articles: "**un'**" and "**una**." The table below indicates when to use each of these four indefinite articles:

Before a **masculine** noun that begins with "**z**," "**gn**," "**ps**," or "**s**" + consonant	uno
Before any other **masculine** noun	un
Before a **feminine** noun that begins with a vowel	un'
Before any other **feminine** noun	una

Similar to the definite articles, if an adjective precedes the noun, the indefinite article is adjusted according to the beginning of the adjective. For example, "**un'amica**" means *"a (female) friend,"* whereas "**una buona amica**" means *"a good (female) friend."* Notice the change in the indefinite article from "**un'**" to "**una**."

The indefinite article "**uno**" is used before any masculine noun (or preceding adjective) that begins with "**z**," "**gn**," "**ps**," or "**s**" + *consonant*, e.g., "**uno sport**" (*a sport*), "**uno gnocco**" (*a dumpling*), "**uno zio**" *(an uncle)*, etc. All other masculine nouns use the indefinite article "**un**," e.g., "**un amico**" *(a friend)*, "**un ragazzo**" *(a boy)*, "**un gatto**" *(a cat)*, etc.

The article "**un'**" is used before any feminine noun (or preceding adjective) that begins with a vowel, e.g., "**un'amica**" *(a friend)*, "**un'ora**" *(an hour)*, "**un'isola**" *(an island)*, etc. All other feminine nouns use the indefinite article "**una**," e.g., "**una casa**" *(a house)*, "**una zia**" *(an aunt)*, "**una porta**" *(a door)*, etc.

- In French:

The singular definite articles "**un**" (masculine) and "**une**" (feminine) in French are equivalent to *"a"* or *"an"* in English, whereas "**des**" is used with plurals and often translated as *"some."* The table below summarizes the indefinite articles in French:

	Singular	Plural
Before a **masculine** noun	un	des
Before a **feminine** noun	une	

Use of the Definite Article versus English "The"

There are cases in which Spanish, Portuguese, Italian, and French use the definite article when in English, it would be omitted, such as:

1. Abstract concepts or speaking in a general sense, for example:

SP	**La** ciencia es importante.	*Science is important.*
PT	**A** ciência é importante.	
IT	**La** scienza è importante.	
FR	**La** science est importante.	
SP	**Los** animales son inteligentes.	*Animals are intelligent.*
PT	**Os** animais são inteligentes.	
IT	**Gli** animali sono intelligenti.	
FR	**Les** animaux sont intelligents.	

2. Languages and nationalities, for example:

SP	**Los** alemanes	
PT	**os** alemães	
IT	**i** tedeschi	*Germans*
FR	**les** allemands	
SP	**El** italiano	
PT	**o** italiano	
IT	**l'**italiano	*Italian*
FR	**l'**italien	

Exceptionally, we drop the definite article when the language name is an object of some verbs or after the preposition *"in,"* for example:

SP	Hablo inglés.	
PT	Falo inglês.	
IT	Parlo inglese.	*I speak English.*
FR	Je parle anglais.	
SP	escrito **en** italiano	
PT	escrito **em** italiano	
IT	scritto **in** italiano	*written **in** Italian*
FR	écrit **en** italien	

3. Days of the week when referring to a repeated action or habit on the same day of every week, for example:

SP	Voy al gimnasio **los** jueves.	
PT	Vou à academia **às** quintas-feiras.	
IT	Vado in palestra **il** giovedì.	*I go to the gym on Thursdays.*
FR	Je vais à la gym **le** jeudi.	

If we do not refer to a repeated action, we do not use the definite article in Italian and French, for example:

SP	Llego **el** lunes.	
PT	Chego **na** segunda-feira.	
IT	Arrivo lunedì.	*I arrive on Monday.*
FR	J'arrive lundi.	

4. Body parts and clothes, for example:

SP	Se lava **la** mano.	
PT	Ele lava **a** mão.	*He washes his hand.*

IT	Si lava **la** mano.	
FR	Il se lave **la** main.	
SP	Me cepillo **el** cabello.	*I brush my hair.*
PT	Escovo **o** cabelo.	
IT	Mi spazzolo **i** capelli.	
FR	Je me brosse **les** cheveux.	

5. Telling time in Spanish and Italian, for example:

SP	Son **las** dos en punto.	
PT	São duas horas.	*It's two o'clock.*
IT	Sono **le** due.	
FR	Il est deux heures.	
SP	Nos reunimos pasada **la** una de la tarde.	*We meet after one o'clock.*
PT	Nos encontramos depois de uma da tarde.	
IT	Ci incontriamo dopo **l'**una.	
FR	Nous nous retrouvons après une heure.	

6. Before a personal title, such as *"Mr.," "Mrs.," "doctor," "professor,"* etc. In French, some titles like *"Mr."* and *"Mrs."* are not preceded by a definite article. For example:

SP	**el** profesor Kennedy	
PT	**o** professor Kennedy	*Professor Kennedy*
IT	**il** professor Kennedy	
FR	**le** professeur Kennedy	
SP	**la** señora María	
PT	**a** señora Maria	*Mrs. Maria*
IT	**la** signora Maria	
FR	Madame Maria	
SP	**el** doctor Marco	
PT	**o** doutor Marco	*Dr. Marco*
IT	**il** dottor Marco	
FR	**le** docteur Marco	

An exception is made when addressing the person directly. In this case, a definite article is not used. For example:

SP	Señor Flavio, ¿cómo está?	
PT	Senhor Flávio, como está?	*Mr. Flavio, how are you?*
IT	Signor Flavio, come sta?	
FR	Monsieur Flavio, comment allez-vous?	

Notice that in Italian we drop the final "**e**" in titles like "**professore**," "**signore**," and "**dottore**" when followed by a masculine proper name. This is common in Italian with many profession titles.

7. Before each noun in the case of multiple nouns, for example:

SP	<u>el</u> padre y <u>la</u> madre	*the father and mother*
PT	<u>o</u> pai e <u>a</u> mãe	
IT	<u>il</u> padre e <u>la</u> madre	
FR	<u>le</u> père et <u>la</u> mère	
SP	<u>los</u> perros y <u>los</u> gatos	*the dogs and cats*
PT	<u>os</u> cães e <u>os</u> gatos	
IT	<u>i</u> cani e <u>i</u> gatti	
FR	<u>les</u> chiens et <u>les</u> chats	

Although you can use one definite article in English to refer to all nouns, the grammatically correct way in Spanish, Portuguese, Italian, and French is to repeat the definite article for each noun.

Like in English, it is common to omit the definite article before the seasons of the year, especially in Spanish, Italian, and French, for example:

SP	en verano	*in summer*
PT	no verão	
IT	in estate	
FR	en été	
SP	en invierno	*in winter*
PT	no inverno	
IT	in inverno	
FR	en hiver	
SP	en otoño	*in autumn*
PT	no outono	
IT	in autunno	
FR	en automne	
SP	en primavera	*in spring*
PT	na primavera	
IT	in primavera	
FR	au printemps	

Notice that we maintain the definite article in **"au printemps"** *(in spring)* in French, and in most cases in Portuguese.

8. INTERROGATIVE PRONOUNS & ADJECTIVES

Interrogative pronouns are important tools that we use to form questions. If the interrogative pronoun is followed by a noun, it becomes an interrogative adjective.

Interrogative pronoun/adjective	English meaning	Examples
SP: ¿Qué? **PT**: O que? **IT**: Che? Che cosa? Cosa? **FR**: Que? Quoi?	*What?*	**EN**: *What are you doing?* **SP**: ¿**Qué** estás haciendo? **PT**: **O que** você está fazendo? **IT**: **Cosa** stai facendo? **FR**: **Que** fais-tu?
SP: ¿Quién(es)? **PT**: Quem? **IT**: Chi? **FR**: Qui?	*Who?* *Whom?*	**EN**: *Who did this?* **SP**: ¿**Quién** hizo esto? **PT**: **Quem** fez isto? **IT**: **Chi** ha fatto questo? **FR**: **Qui** a fait cela?
SP: ¿De quién? **PT**: De quem? **IT**: Di chi? **FR**: À qui?	*Whose?*	**EN**: *Whose book is this?* **SP**: ¿**De quién** es este libro? **PT**: **De quem** é esse livro? **IT**: **Di chi** è questo libro? **FR**: **À qui** est ce livre?
SP: ¿Cómo? **PT**: Como? **IT**: Come? **FR**: Comment?	*How?*	**EN**: *How did you do it?* **SP**: ¿**Cómo** hiciste eso? **PT**: **Como** fez isso? **IT**: **Come** lo hai fatto? **FR**: **Comment** as-tu fais cela?
SP: ¿Cuál(es)? **PT**: Qual(-is)? **IT**: Quale(-i)? **FR**: Quel(s)? Quelle(s)?	*Which?*	**EN**: *Which ones are your keys?* **SP**: ¿**Cuáles** son tus llaves? **PT**: **Quais** são suas chaves? **IT**: **Quali** sono le tue chiavi? **FR**: **Quelles** sont tes clés?

SP: ¿Cuánto(-a,-os,-as)? **PT**: Quanto(-a,-os,-as)? **IT**: Quanto(-a,-i,-e)? **FR**: Combien?	*How much?* *How many?*	**EN**: *How much* does this coat cost? **SP**: ¿**Cuánto** cuesta este abrigo? **PT**: **Quanto** custa este casaco? **IT**: **Quanto** costa questo cappotto? **FR**: **Combien** coûte ce manteau?
SP: ¿Cuándo? **PT**: Quando? **IT**: Quando? **FR**: Quand?	*When?*	**EN**: *When* do you want to come? **SP**: ¿**Cuándo** quieres venir? **PT**: **Quando** você quer vir? **IT**: **Quando** vuoi venire? **FR**: **Quand** veux-tu venir?
SP: ¿Dónde? **PT**: Onde? **IT**: Dove? **FR**: Où?	*Where?*	**EN**: *Where* are you now? **SP**: ¿**Dónde** estás ahora? **PT**: **Onde** você está agora? **IT**: **Dove** sei ora? **FR**: **Où** es-tu en ce moment?
SP: ¿Por/Para qué? **PT**: Por/Para que? **IT**: Perché? **FR**: Pourquoi?	*Why?*	**EN**: *Why* don't you want to eat? **SP**: ¿**Por qué** no quieres comer? **PT**: **Por que** você não quer comer? **IT**: **Perché** non vuoi mangiare? **FR**: **Pourquoi** ne veux-tu pas manger?

In Spanish and Portuguese, the interrogative pronoun "**por que**" means *"Why?"* If written without the space, i.e., "**porque**," it means *"because."* In Italian, "**perché**," can mean *"why"* or *"because,"* depending on the context. In French, "**parce que**" means *"because"*:

	"*why*"	"*because*"
SP	¿por qué?	porque
PT	por que?	porque
IT	perché	
FR	pourquoi?	parce que

In Spanish and Portuguese, both "**por que**" and "**para qué**" are often translated as *"Why?"* However, there is a subtle difference. Whereas "¿**por qué**?" enquires about the reason, "¿**para qué**?" enquires about the purpose and can be better translated as *"What for?"*, for example:

SP	¿**Para qué** necesitas eso?	***What** do you need this **for**?*
PT	**Para que** você precisa disso?	

Although we can use "**che**" as an interrogative pronoun in Italian, e.g., "**Che hai letto?**" *(What did you read?)*, the more accepted forms are "**che cosa**" and "**cosa**," both meaning *"what,"* e.g., "**Che cosa hai letto?**" and "**Cosa hai letto?**" both mean *"What book did you read?"*

When the Italian interrogatives "**cosa**," "**come**," "**dove**," and "**quale**" are followed by "**è**" *(is)*, the following abbreviations are common but not mandatory in written Italian:

What is ...?	**Cos'è ...?**	**Cosa è ...?**
How is ...?	**Com'è ...?**	**Come è ...?**
Where is ...?	**Dov'è ...?**	**Dove è ...?**
Which is ...?	**Qual è ...?**	**Quale è ...?**

Notice that an apostrophe is needed with the interrogatives "**cosa**," "**come**," and "**dove**," but not in the case of "**quale**."

The French interrogative "**que**" has a longer form that is more formal and polite, which is "**qu'est-ce que**" /kes-kə/, e.g., "**Qu'est-ce que vous voudriez manger?**" *(What would you like to eat?)*. Notice that the subject always precedes the verb when "**qu'est-ce que**" is used.

9. BASIC VOCABULARY

We will examine and compare some basic vocabulary in Spanish, Portuguese, Italian, and French. The five categories that we will examine are: colors, times and seasons, directions, family, and anatomy.

COLORS

SP	*color*	**color**[m]	*orange*	**naranja**[m,f]
PT		**cor**[f]		**laranja**[m,f]
IT		**colore**[m]		**arancione**[m,f]
FR		**couleur**[f]		**orange**[m,f]

SP		negro/-a		rosa^{m,f} rosado/-a
PT	black	preto/-a	pink	rosa^{m,f}
IT		nero/-a		rosa^{m,f}
FR		noir(e)		rose^{m,f}
SP		azul^{m,f}		morado/-a púrpura^{m,f}
PT		azul^{m,f}		roxo/-a
IT	blue	blu^{m,f} azzurro/-a	purple	viola^{m,f} porpora^{m,f}
FR		bleu(e)		violet(te) pourpre^{m,f}
SP		marrón^{m,f}		rojo/-a
PT		marrom^{m,f}		vermelho/-a
IT	brown	marrone^{m,f} bruno/-a	red	rosso/-a
FR		matron^{m,f} brun(e)		rouge^{m,f}
SP		gris^{m,f}		blanco/-a
PT		cinza^{m,f}		branco/-a
IT	gray	grigio/-a	white	bianco/-a
FR		gris(e)		blanc^m blanche^f
SP		verde^{m,f}		amarillo/-a
PT		verde^{m,f}		amarelo/-a
IT	green	verde^{m,f}	yellow	giallo/-a
FR		vert(e)		jaune^{m,f}

TIMES & SEASONS

SP		día^m		semana^f
PT	day	dia^m	week	semana^f
IT		giorno^m		settimana^f
FR		jour^m		semaine^f
SP		mes^m		año^m
PT	month	mês^m	year	ano^m
IT		mese^m		anno^m
FR		mois^m		an^m
SP		hoy		fin^m de semana
PT	today	hoje	weekend	fim^m de semana
IT		oggi		fine^m settimana
FR		aujourd'hui		fin^f de semaine

SP	tomorrow	mañana	tomorrow morning	mañana por la mañana
PT		amanhã		amanhã de manhã
IT		domani		domattina
FR		demain		demain matin
SP	yesterday	ayer	day after tomorrow	pasado mañana
PT		ontem		depois de amanhã
IT		ieri		dopodomani
FR		hier		après-demain
SP	tonight	esta noche	day before yesterday	anteayer
PT		esta noite		anteontem
IT		stanotte		avantieri
FR		ce soir		avant-hier
SP	tomorrow night	mañana por la noche	last night	anoche
PT		manhã à noite		noite passada / ontem à noite
IT		domani notte		ieri notte
FR		demain soir		hier soir
SP	afternoon	tarde^f	morning	mañana^f
PT		tarde^f		manhã^f
IT		pomeriggio^m		mattina^f
FR		après-midi^m		matin^m
SP	decade	década^f	night	noche^f
PT		década^f		noite^f
IT		decennio^m		notte^f
FR		décennie^f		nuit^f
SP	season	estación^f	century	siglo^m
PT		estação^f		século^m
IT		stagione^f		secolo^m
FR		saison^f		siècle^m

The *days of the week* are:

SP	Monday	lunes^m	Friday	viernes^m
PT		segunda-feira^f		sexta-feira^f
IT		lunedì^m		venerdì^m
FR		lundi^m		vendredi^m
SP	Tuesday	martes^m	Saturday	sábado^m
PT		terça-feira^f		sábado^m
IT		martedì^m		sabato^m
FR		mardi^m		samedi^m

SP		miércoles^m		domingo^m
PT	Wednesday	quarta-feira^f	Sunday	domingo^m
IT		mercoledì^m		domenica^f
FR		mercredi^m		dimanche^m
SP		jueves^m		fin^m de semana
PT	Thursday	quinta-feira^f	weekend	fim^m de semana
IT		giovedì^m		fine^m settimana
FR		jeudi^m		fin^f de semaine

Notice that the days of the week are significantly different in Portuguese from other Romance languages. The reason is that most Romance languages, derived from Latin, were named by the Romans after celestial bodies – Mars for Tuesday, Mercury for Wednesday, and so on. But in Portugal, a 6th-century bishop named Martin of Braga rejected the idea of associating days with pagan deities, so he opted for a radical change.

Martin adopted the Latin word *"feria,"* meaning *"feast day"* or *"day of rest,"* and used it to create a new naming system, counting from Sunday. Thus, *Monday* became **"segunda-feira,"** meaning *"second feria,"* *Tuesday* turned into **"terça-feira"** *(third feria)*, and so on. This system made sense because, in early Christianity, *Sunday* was considered the first day of the week and the day of worship.

The existing names for *Saturday* and *Sunday* were not changed. These names already held religious significance, with Saturday derived from the Hebrew *"sabbath"* and *Sunday* which signifies *"dies Dominica" (Lord's Day)* in Latin.

The *months of the year* are:

SP		enero^m		julio^m
PT	January	janeiro^m	July	julho^m
IT		gennaio^m		luglio^m
FR		janvier^m		juillet^m
SP		febrero^m		agosto^m
PT	February	fevereiro^m	August	agosto^m
IT		febbraio^m		agosto^m
FR		février^m		août^m

SP		marzo^m		septiembre^m
PT	March	março^m	September	setembro^m
IT		marzo^m		settembre^m
FR		mars^m		septembre^m
SP		abril^m		octubre^m
PT	April	abril^m	October	outubro^m
IT		aprile^m		ottobre^m
FR		avril^m		octobre^m
SP		mayo^m		noviembre^m
PT	May	maio^m	November	novembro^m
IT		maggio^m		novembre^m
FR		mai^m		novembre^m
SP		junio^m		diciembre^m
PT	June	junho^m	December	dezembro^m
IT		giugno^m		dicembre^m
FR		juin^m		décembre^m

Notice from the two tables above that the days and months are not capitalized.

The *seasons of the year* are:

SP		otoño^m		verano^m
PT	autumn, fall	outono^m	summer	verão^m
IT		autunno^m		estate^f
FR		automne^m		été^m
SP		primavera^f		invierno^m
PT	spring	primavera^f	winter	inverno^m
IT		primavera^f		inverno^m
FR		printemps^m		hiver^m

DIRECTIONS

SP		dirección^f		mapa^m
PT	direction	direção^f	map	mapa^m
IT		indicazione^f		mappa^f
FR		direction^f		carte^f
SP		calle^f		brújula^f
PT	street	rua^f	compass	bússola^f
IT		via^f		bussola^f
FR		rue^f		boussole^f

The *four geographical directions* are:

SP	east	este^{m}	south	sur^{m} sud^{m}
PT		leste^{m} [1] este^{m}		sul^{m}
IT		est^{m}		sud^{m}
FR		est^{m}		sud^{m}
SP	north	norte^{m}	west	oeste^{m}
PT		norte^{m}		oeste^{m}
IT		nord^{m}		ovest^{m}
FR		nord^{m}		ouest^{m}

And the four main directions *right*, *left*, *up*, and *down* are:

SP	right	derecha	up	arriba
PT		direita		acima
IT		destra		su
FR		droite		haut
SP	left	izquierda	down	abajo
PT		esquerda		abaixo
IT		sinistra		giù
FR		gauche		bas

To describe the location of an object with respect to another, one can use:

SP	above on top (of)	sobre encima (de)	there	ahí allá allí
PT		em cima (de) acima (de) sobre		lá ali aí
IT		sopra		lì là
FR		au-dessus de		là

---

[1] Both "**leste**" and "**este**" are equally correct when referring to the direction of the "*east.*" However, "**este**" is rarely used to avoid confusion when the definite article is added to "**este**," in which case "**o este**" *(the east)* may sound the same as "**oeste**" *(west)*.

SP	here	acá aquí	to the left of	a la izquierda de
PT		aqui cá		à esquerda de
IT		qui qua		a sinistra di
FR		ici		à gauche de
SP	inside	dentro (de)	to the right of	a la derecha de
PT		dentro (de)		à direita de
IT		dentro		a destra di
FR		à l'intérieur (de)		à droite de
SP	near	cerca (de)	far (from)	lejos (de)
PT		perto (de)		longe (de)
IT		vicino (a)		lontano (da)
FR		près de		loin (de)
SP	outside	fuera (de)	toward	hacia
PT		fora (de)		na direção
IT		fuori (da)		verso
FR		dehors		vers
SP	straight ahead	derecho recto	under beneath	bajo debajo (de)
PT		direto em frente sempre em frente		debaixo (de) sob
IT		dritto		sotto
FR		tout droit		sous

FAMILY

SP	family	familia[f]	family members	miembros[m] de la familia
PT		família[f]		membros[m] da família
IT		famiglia[f]		membri[m] della famiglia
FR		famille[f]		membres[m] de la famille
SP	aunt	tía[f]	girlfriend	novia[f]
PT		tia[m]		namorada[f] noiva[f]
IT		zia[f]		fidanzata[f]
FR		tante[f]		petite amie[f] copine[f]

SP	boyfriend	novio^m	grandson	nieto^m
PT		namorado^m novio^m		neto^m
IT		fidanzato^m		nipote^m
FR		petit ami^m copain^m		petit-fils^m
SP	couple	pareja^f	husband	marido^m
PT		casal^m		marido^m
IT		coppia^f		marito^m
FR		couple^m		mari^m
SP	cousin	primo/-a	married	casado/-a
PT		primo/-a		casado/-a
IT		cugino/-a		sposato/-a
FR		cousin(e)		marié(e)
SP	daughter	hija^f	mother	madre^f
PT		filha^f		mãe^f
IT		figlia^f		madre^f
FR		fille^f		mère^f
SP	daughter-in-law	nuera^f	relatives	parientes^m familiares^m
PT		nora^f		parentes^{m,f}
IT		nuora^f		parenti^m famigliari^m
FR		belle-fille^f bru^f		parents^m
SP	father	padre^m	single	soltero/-a
PT		pai^m		solteiro/-a
IT		padre^m		celibe^m nubile^f
FR		père^m		célibataire^{m,f}
SP	granddaughter	nieta^f	son	hijo^m
PT		neta^f		filho^m
IT		nipote^f		figlio^m
FR		petite fille^f		fils^m
SP	grandfather	abuelo^m	son-in-law	yerno^m
PT		avô^m		genro^m
IT		nonno^m		genero^m
FR		grand-père^m		gendre^m beau-fils^m

SP	*grandmother*	abuela[f]	*spouse*	esposo/-a cónyuge[m,f]
PT		avó[f]		esposo/-a cônjuge[m,f]
IT		nonna[f]		sposo/-a coniuge[m]
FR		grand-mère[f]		époux[m]/épouse[f] conjoint(e)
SP	*uncle*	tío[m]	*wife*	mujer[f] esposa[f]
PT		tio[m]		mulher[f] esposa[f]
IT		zio[m]		moglie[f] sposa[f]
FR		oncle[m]		femme[f] épouse[f]

ANATOMY

SP	*body*	cuerpo[m]	*body parts*	partes[f] del cuerpo
PT		corpo[m]		partes[f] do corpo
IT		corpo[m]		parti[f] del corpo
FR		corps[m]		parties[f] du corps
SP	*arm*	brazo[m]	*hand*	mano[f]
PT		braço[m]		mão[f]
IT		braccio[m]		mano[f]
FR		bras[m]		main[f]
SP	*back*	espalda[f]	*head*	cabeza[f]
PT		costas[f]		cabeça[f]
IT		schiena[f]		testa[f]
FR		dos[m]		tête[f]
SP	*blood*	sangre[f]	*heart*	corazón[m]
PT		sangue[m]		coração[m]
IT		sangue[m]		cuore[m]
FR		sang[m]		cœur[m]
SP	*brain*	cerebro[m]	*leg*	pierna[f]
PT		cérebro[m]		perna[f]
IT		cervello[m]		gamba[f]
FR		cerveau[m]		jambe[f]

SP	ear	oreja^f	lip	labio^m
PT		orelha^f		lábio^m
IT		orecchio^m		labbro^m
FR		oreille^f		lèvre^f
SP	eye	ojo^m	mouth	boca^f
PT		olho^m		boca^f
IT		occhio^m		bocca^f
FR		œil^m		bouche^f
SP	face	cara^f	nose	nariz^f
PT		rosto^m face^f cara^f		nariz^m
IT		faccia^f		naso^m
FR		visage^m figure^f face^f		nez^m
SP	finger	dedo^m	shoulder	hombro^m
PT		dedo^m		ombro^m
IT		dito^m		spalla^f
FR		doigt^m		épaule^f
SP	foot	pie^m	stomach	estómago^m
PT		pé^m		estômago^m
IT		piede^f		stomaco^m
FR		pied^m		estomac^m
SP	hair	pelo^m	toe	dedo^m del pie
PT		cabelo^m		dedo^m do pé
IT		capelli^m		dito^m del piede
FR		cheveux^m		doigt^m de pied orteil^m

LEVEL II: BEGINNER

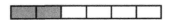

At this level, you will continue to familiarize yourself with some of the fundamental grammar rules and basic topics that will enhance your language knowledge.

1. PREPOSITIONS

Here are some of the most used prepositions in Spanish, Portuguese, Italian, and French with the most common meanings in different contexts.

Prep.	Meaning	Examples
a (SP)(PT)(IT) à (FR)	*to*	**EN**: *I go to school in the morning.* **SP**: Voy **a** la escuela por la mañana. **PT**: Eu vou **à** escola pela manhã. **IT**: Vado **a** scuola la mattina. **FR**: Je vais **à** l'école le matin.
	at	**EN**: *I will finish at noon.* **SP**: Terminaré **al** mediodía. **PT**: Terminarei **ao** meio-dia. **IT**: Finirò **a** mezzogiorno. **FR**: Je finirai **à** midi.
	by	**EN**: *Made by hand (handmade).* **SP**: Hecho **a** mano. **PT**: Feito **à** mão. **IT**: Fatto **a** mano. **FR**: Fait **à** la main.
	in	**EN**: *I live in London.* **SP**: - **PT**: - **IT**: Io vivo **a** Londra. **FR**: J'habite **à** Londres.
	on	**EN**: *I will come back home on foot.* **SP**: Volveré a casa **a** pie. **PT**: Vou voltar para casa **a** pé. **IT**: Tornerò a casa **a** piedi. **FR**: Je reviendrai **à** pied.

	per	**EN**: *It costs 20 dollars **per** night.* **SP**: - **PT**: - **IT**: Costa 20 dollari **a** notte. **FR**: -
al lado de (SP) ao lado de (PT) accanto a (IT) à côté de (FR)	*beside* *next to*	**EN**: *There is a cat **beside** the chair.* **SP**: Hay un gato **al lado de** la silla. **PT**: Há um gato **ao lado d**a cadeira. **IT**: C'è un gatto **accanto a**lla sedia. **FR**: Il y a un chat **à côté de** la chaise.
a través de (SP) através de (PT) attraverso (IT) à travers (FR)	*across* *through*	**EN**: *We walk **through** the fields.* **SP**: Caminamos **a través de** los campos. **PT**: Caminhamos **através d**os campos. **IT**: Camminiamo **attraverso** i campi. **FR**: Nous marchons **à travers** les champs.
con (SP)(IT) com (PT) avec (FR)	*with*	**EN**: *He speaks **with** his friend.* **SP**: Él habla **con** su amigo. **PT**: Ele fala **com** o amigo. **IT**: Parla **con** il suo amico. **FR**: Il parle **avec** son ami.
contra (SP)(PT) contro (IT) contre (FR)	*against*	**EN**: *I am **against** injustice.* **SP**: Estoy **contra** la injusticia **PT**: Eu sou **contra** a injustiça. **IT**: Sono **contro** l'ingiustizia. **FR**: Je suis **contre** l'injustice.
da (IT)	*from*	**EN**: *I traveled **from** London to Korea.* **IT**: Ho viaggiato **da** Londra alla Corea.
	since	**EN**: *I haven't smoked **since** April.* **IT**: Non fumo **da** aprile.
	for	**EN**: *I haven't smoked **for** two years.* **IT**: Non fumo **da** due anni.
	as (a)	**EN**: ***As a** kid, I was shy.* **IT**: **Da** bambino, ero timido.
	by	**EN**: *It was painted **by** Bosch.* **IT**: È stato dipinto **da** Bosch.
delante de (SP) diante de (PT) davanti a (IT) devant (FR)	*in front of*	**EN**: *I am **in front of** the school.* **SP**: Estoy **delante de** la escuela. **PT**: Estou **diante d**a escola. **IT**: Sono **davanti a**lla scuola. **FR**: Je suis **devant** l'école.
dentro de (SP)(PT) dentro (IT) dans (FR)	*inside*	**EN**: *The ball is **inside** the box.* **SP**: La bola está **dentro de** la caja. **PT**: A bola está **dentro d**a caixa. **IT**: La palla è **dentro** la scatola. **FR**: Le ballon est **dans** la surface.

de (SP)(PT)(FR) di (IT)	*of*	**EN**: *The color **of** that car is blue.* **SP**: El color **de** ese auto es azul. **PT**: A cor **d**esse carro é azul. **IT**: Il colore **di** quella macchina è blu. **FR**: La couleur **de** cette voiture est bleue.
	from	**EN**: *She is **from** Madrid.* **SP**: Ella es **de** Madrid. **PT**: Ela é **de** Madri. **IT**: Lei è **di** Madrid. **FR**: Elle est **de** Madrid.
	about	**EN**: *They talk **about** him.* **SP**: Hablan **de** él. **PT**: Eles falam **d**ele. **IT**: Parlano **di** lui. **FR**: Ils parlent **de** lui.
detrás de (SP) atrás de (PT) dietro (IT) derrière (FR)	*behind*	**EN**: *The tree is **behind** the house.* **SP**: El árbol está **detrás de** la casa. **PT**: A árvore está **atrás d**a casa. **IT**: L'albero è **dietro** la casa. **FR**: L'arbre est **derrière** la maison.
después de (SP) depois de (PT) dopo (IT) après (FR)	*after*	**EN**: *I slept **after** lunch today.* **SP**: Hoy dormí **después d**el almuerzo. **PT**: Hoje eu dormi **depois d**o almoço. **IT**: Ho dormito **dopo** pranzo oggi. **FR**: J'ai dormi **après** le déjeuner aujourd'hui.
durante (SP)(PT)(IT) pendant, durant (FR)	*during*	**EN**: *We can go out **during** the day.* **SP**: Podemos salir **durante** el día. **PT**: Podemos sair **durante** o dia. **IT**: Possiamo uscire **durante** il giorno. **FR**: Nous pouvons sortir **pendant** la journée.
hasta (SP) até (PT) fino a (IT) jusqu'à (FR)	*until*	**EN**: *I worked **until** midnight.* **SP**: Trabajé **hasta** medianoche. **PT**: Trabalhei **até** meia-noite. **IT**: Ho lavorato **fino a** mezzanotte. **FR**: J'ai travaillé **jusqu'à** minuit.
	as far as	**EN**: *The light reaches **as far as** the park.* **SP**: La luz alcanza **hasta** el parque. **PT**: A luz alcança **até** o parque. **IT**: La luce arriva **fino a**l parco. **FR**: La lumière s'étend **jusqu'a**u parc.
fuera de (SP) fora de (PT) fuori di (IT) à l'extérieur de (FR)	*outside*	**EN**: *The garage is **outside** the house.* **SP**: El garaje está **fuera de** la casa. **PT**: A garagem fica **fora d**a casa. **IT**: Il garage è **fuori d**alla casa. **FR**: Le garage est **à l'extérieur de** la maison.

en (SP) em (PT) in (IT) dans (FR)	*in*	**EN**: *I live in a small house.* **SP**: Vivo **en** una casa pequeña. **PT**: Eu moro **em** uma pequena casa. **IT**: Vivo **in** una piccola casa. **FR**: Je vis **dans** une petite maison.
a lo largo de (SP) ao longo de (PT) lungo (IT) le long de (FR)	*along*	**EN**: *There are houses along the lake.* **SP**: Hay casas **a lo largo d**el lago. **PT**: Há casas **ao longo d**o lago. **IT**: Ci sono case **lungo** il lago. **FR**: Il y a des maisons **le long d**u lac.
por/para (SP)(PT) per (IT) pour/par (FR)	*for* *(destination)*	**EN**: *I will leave for Barcelona tomorrow.* **SP**: Salgo **para** Barcelona mañana. **PT**: Parto **para** Barcelona amanhã. **IT**: Domani partirò **per** Barcellona. **FR**: Je pars **pour** Barcelone demain.
	by	**EN**: *I contacted you by phone.* **SP**: Te contacté **por** teléfono. **PT**: Entrei em contato com você **por** telefone. **IT**: Ti ho contattato **per** telefono. **FR**: Je t'ai contacté **par** téléphone.
	because of	**EN**: *They suffered because of the lack of water.* **SP**: Sufrieron **por** falta de agua. **PT**: Sofriam **por** falta de água. **IT**: Soffrivano **per** la mancanza d'acqua. **FR**: -
	in order to	**EN**: *We study in order to learn.* **SP**: Estudiamos **para** aprender. **PT**: Estudamos **para** aprender. **IT**: Studiamo **per** imparare. **FR**: On étudie **pour** apprendre.
antes de (SP)(PT) prima di (IT) avant de (FR)	*before*	**EN**: *I will call you before leaving.* **SP**: Te voy a llamar **antes de** irme. **PT**: Eu te ligo **antes de** ir. **IT**: Ti chiamo **prima di** partire. **FR**: Je t'appellerai **avant de** partir.
según (SP) de acordo com (PT) secondo (IT) selon (FR)	*according to*	**EN**: *According to the law, it is prohibited.* **SP**: **Según** la ley, está prohibido. **PT**: **De acordo com** a lei, é proibido. **IT**: **Secondo** la legge, è vietato. **FR**: **Selon** la loi, c'est interdit.
sin (SP) sem (PT) senza (IT) sans (FR)	*without*	**EN**: *A fish can't live without water.* **SP**: Un pez no puede vivir **sin** agua. **PT**: Um peixe não pode viver **sem** água. **IT**: Un pesce non può vivere **senza** acqua. **FR**: Un poisson ne peut pas vivre **sans** eau.

bajo, debajo de (SP) baixo, debaixo de (PT) sotto (IT) sous (FR)	*under*	**EN**: *The cat is* **under** *the chair.* **SP**: El gato está **bajo** la silla. **PT**: O gato está **debaixo d**a cadeira. **IT**: Il gatto è **sotto** la sedia. **FR**: Le chat est **sous** la chaise.
sobre (SP)(PT) su, sopra (IT) sur (FR)	*on*	**EN**: *The fly is* **on** *the table.* **SP**: La mosca está **sobre** la mesa. **PT**: A mosca está **sobre** a mesa. **IT**: La mosca è **sul** tavolo. **FR**: La mouche est **sur** la table.
	about	**EN**: *The debate* **about** *that incident is over.* **SP**: El debate **sobre** ese incidente ha terminado. **PT**: O debate **sobre** esse incidente acabou. **IT**: Il dibattito **su** quell'incidente è finito. **FR**: Le débat **sur** cet incident est clos.
entre (SP)(PT)(FR) tra, fra (IT)	*between*	**EN**: *The bird is stuck* **between** *the branches.* **SP**: El pájaro está atrapado **entre** las ramas. **PT**: O pássaro está preso **entre** os galhos. **IT**: L'uccello è bloccato **tra** i rami. **FR**: L'oiseau est coincé **entre** les branches.
	among	**EN**: *I am the tallest* **among** *my friends.* **SP**: Soy el más alto **entre** mis amigos. **PT**: Eu sou o mais alto **entre** meus amigos. **IT**: Sono il più alto **tra** i miei amici. **FR**: -
	in	**EN**: *We will leave* **in** *a week.* **SP**: - **PT**: - **IT**: Partiremo **tra** una settimana. **FR**: -
parmi (FR)	*among*	**EN**: *I am the tallest* **among** *my friends.* **FR**: Je suis le plus grand **parmi** mes amis.
hacia (SP) em direção a (PT) verso (IT) vers (FR)	*toward*	**EN**: *She ran* **toward** *the exit.* **SP**: Ella corrió **hacia** la salida. **PT**: Ela correu **em direção à** saída. **IT**: Corse **verso** l'uscita. **FR**: Elle courut **vers** la sortie.
cerca de (SP) perto de (PT) vicino a (IT) près de (FR)	*near*	**EN**: *I live* **near** *the city.* **SP**: Vivo **cerca de** la ciudad. **PT**: Eu moro **perto d**a cidade. **IT**: Vivo **vicino a**lla città. **FR**: J'habite **près de** la ville.

Contractions

❖ In Spanish, there are only two contractions that involve the singular masculine definite article "**el**," and, unlike in English, these contractions are not optional and must be applied:

a + el = al	Yo voy **al** restaurante. *I go to the restaurant.*
de + el = del	Yo vengo **del** café. *I come from the café.*

❖ In Portuguese, the propositions "**a**," "**de**," "**em**," and "**por**" contract when followed by the definite article as shown below:

Preposition	Reduced Form	o	os	a	as
a	-	ao	aos	à	às
de	d-	do	dos	da	das
em	n-	no	nos	na	nas
por	pel-	pelo	pelos	pela	pelas

Notice that the above contractions are not optional. They are mandatory in all cases.

Notice also the use of the grave accent to mark the contraction of two consecutive vowels, where the first vowel is the preposition "**a**," i.e., "**a**" + "**a**" = "**à**" and "**a**" + "**as**" = "**às**."

❖ In Italian, the prepositions "**a**," "**da**," "**di**," "**in**," and "**su**" contract when followed by a definite article. Remember that there are seven definite articles in Italian: "**l'**," "**lo**," "**il**," "**la**," "**i**," "**gli**," and "**le**." This results in the following possible combinations:

	l'	lo	il	la	i	gli	le
a	all'	allo	al	alla	ai	agli	alle
da	dall'	dallo	dal	dalla	dai	dagli	dalle
di	dell'	dello	del	della	dei	degli	delle
in	nell'	nello	nel	nella	nei	negli	nelle
su	sull'	sullo	sul	sulla	sui	sugli	sulle

Although optional, you may also use or encounter the following three contractions of the preposition "**con**" *(with)*, especially in spoken Italian:

	il	la	l'
con	col	colla	coll'

Other prepositions do not contract.

Contractions add to the complexity of the prepositions in Italian. Practice is your best approach to learn them. Here are some examples:

a + lo = allo	Verrò con te **allo** stadio. *I'll go with you **to the** stadium.*
da + il = dal	Voglio imparare **dal** libro. *I want to learn **from the** book.*
di + la = della	Il colore **della** macchina è blu. *The color **of the** car is blue.*
in + l' = nell'	La valigia è **nell'**armadio. *The suitcase is **in the** wardrobe.*
su + gli = sugli	C'è molta polvere **sugli** occhiali. *There is a lot of dust **on the** glasses.*

The definite article is dropped from some expressions that are commonly used in daily life such as: "**a casa**" *(at home)*, "**in macchina**" *(by car)*, "**in centro**" *(in downtown)*, etc.

❖ In French, the prepositions "**à**" and "**de**" contract when followed by the definite article "**le**" (in its non-contracted form) or "**les**." Other prepositions do not contract with the definite article.

	le	la	l'	les
à	au	à la	à l'	aux
de	du	de la	de l'	des

Here are some examples:

à + le = au	J'irai avec toi **au** stade. *I'll go with you **to the** stadium.*

à + les = aux	Le professeur parle **aux** élèves. *The teacher speaks **to the** students.*
de + le = du	Toutes les photos sont supprimées **du** livre. *All photos are removed **from the** book.*
de + les = des	C'est l'un **des** meilleurs quartiers ici. *It is one **of the** best areas here.*
de + la = de la	La couleur **de la** voiture est bleue. *The color **of the** car is blue.*

Prepositions meaning *"in"* in Italian & French

The prepositions **"a"** in Italian and **"à"** in French are used to mean *"in"* when referring to the proper name of a city (or a smaller area), for example:

IT	Vivo **a** Roma.	*I live **in** Rome.*
FR	Je vis **à** Rome.	

For larger areas, we use the prepositions **"in"** in Italian and **"en"** in French, for example:

IT	Vivo **in** California.	*I live **in** California.*
FR	Je vis **en** Californie.	
IT	L'ho visto **in** Spagna.	*I saw it **in** Spain.*
FR	Je l'ai vu **en** Espagne.	

In most contexts, the prepositions **"in"** in Italian and **"en"** in French generally mean *"in"* in English. However, when referring to a destination that is larger than a city, these prepositions can also be translated as *"to,"* for example:

IT	Andrò **in** California.	*I will go **to** California.*
FR	J'irai **en** Californie.	
IT	Ho viaggiato **in** Spagna.	*I traveled **to** Spain.*
FR	J'ai voyagé **en** Espagne.	

When referring to a means of transportation, the preposition **"en"** in French is often translated as *"by,"* e.g., **"On voyage en train"** *(We travel by train).*

The Preposition "da" in Italian

The preposition "**da**" in Italian can have several meanings:

1. The basic meaning of *"from"* in English with its versatile use to indicate the starting point of a movement, source or origin, separation, etc. For example:

Ho viaggiato **da** Londra alla Corea.	*I traveled **from** London to Korea.*
Vengo **da** Firenze.	*I come (am) **from** Florence.*
Separa l'acqua **da** questa miscela.	*Separate the water **from** this mixture.*

2. The equivalent of *"since"* or *"for"* in time expressions that typically use the present perfect or present perfect continuous tense in English. For example:

Non fumo **da** aprile.	*I haven't smoked **since** April.*
Non fumo **da** due anni.	*I haven't smoked **for** two years.*

Notice that, in Italian, the present tense is used before "**da**" to convey the equivalent meaning in English.

Keep in mind that to describe a defined duration in the future, the preposition "**per**" must be used instead. For example:

Lavoro lì **da** due anni.	*I have worked there **for** two years.*
Lavorerò lì **per** due anni.	*I will work there **for** two years.*

3. The equivalent of *"to"* or *"for"* when used to indicate purpose or reason. For example:

Qualcosa **da** bere	*Something **to** drink*
Una casa **da** vendere	*A house **for** sale*

4. The meaning of being at someone's house or workplace. In this context, "**da**" is often translated as *"at,"* but can also mean *"to"* if preceded by the verb *"go."* For example:

Siamo **da** Marco.	*We are **at** Marco's place.*
Domani vado **dal** dentista.	*I will go **to** the dentist tomorrow.*

5. The meaning of the preposition *"by"* in English, referring to an agent in the passive voice. For example:

| Un software sviluppato **da** Microsoft. | *A software developed **by** Microsoft.* |
| Dipinto **da** un artista anonimo. | *Painted **by** an anonymous artist.* |

6. The expression *"as (a) …"* in English. For example:

| Te lo dico **da amico**. | *I tell you **as a** friend.* |
| **Da bambini**, ci divertivamo molto. | ***As** kids, we had a lot of fun.* |

The Preposition "depuis" in French

The preposition **"depuis"** in French is used as the equivalent of *"since"* and *"for"* in time expressions that typically use the present perfect or present perfect continuous tense in English. For example:

| Je n'ai pas fumé **depuis** avril. | *I haven't smoked **since** April.* |
| Je n'ai pas fumé **depuis** deux ans. | *I haven't smoked **for** two years.* |

The Preposition "chez" in French

In French, we use **"chez"** to refer to being at someone's house or workplace. In this context, **"chez"** is often translated as *"at"* or *"to."* For example:

Nous sommes **chez** Marco.	*We are **at** Marco's place.*
Es-tu **chez** Anne?	*Are you **at** Anne's place?*
Nous sommes **chez** Burger King.	*We are **at** Burger King.*
Je viendrai **chez** toi.	*I will come **to** your house.*
J'irai **chez** le dentiste demain.	*I will go **to** the dentist tomorrow.*

Prepositions meaning "about"

To express the meaning of *"about"* (e.g., to talk *about* someone or watch a documentary *about* something), we often use one of the following prepositions:

SP	Vi un documental **sobre** la guerra.	
PT	Eu vi um documentário **sobre** a guerra.	*I watched a documentary **about** that war.*
IT	Ho visto un documentario **su** quella guerra.	
FR	J'ai regardé un documentaire **sur** cette guerre.	

SP	Leí un libro **acerca de** la vida en Japón.	*I read a book **about** life in Japan.*
PT	Eu li um livro **acerca d**a vida no Japão.	
IT	Ho letto un libro **circa** la vita in Giappone.	
FR	J'ai lu un livre **sur** la vie au Japon.	
SP	Ellos hablan **de** él.	*They talk **about** him.*
PT	Eles falam **de**le.	
IT	Parlano **di** lui.	
FR	Ils parlent **de** lui.	

Further Notes on Prepositions

❖ In Spanish and Portuguese, both "**para**" and "**por**" can be used to mean *"for."* Differences between the two with examples will be explained in **Level II, Lesson 8**.

❖ In Italian, the preposition "**tra**" or "**fra**" often means *"between."* If used to indicate the future, it can mean *"in,"* as in: "**Ci vediamo tra un mese**" *(See you in a month)*.

2. PRESENT INDICATIVE TENSE II

Some verbs deviate from the general conjugation rules in the present indicative tense outlined in **Level I, Lesson 6**. Some of these deviations are simple and easy to apply, while others may require some practice. Use your Anki cards to practice more examples until you master this lesson. In addition, you can use the summary in the cheat sheets in **Appendix B** as a quick reference.

Irregular Verbs in Spanish

To examine the irregular verbs in the present indicative tense in Spanish, we will categorize these verbs in five main groups.

#1: Irregular Verbs in "Yo" Form

Let us start with the easier irregularities. In the *first* group, the following four sets of irregular verbs are only irregular in the first-person singular form, that is, with the subject "**yo**."

1. The verbs "**estar**" *(to be)* and "**dar**" *(to give)* are conjugated with "-**oy**" ending in the first-person "**yo**" form as "**estoy**" and "**doy**," respectively, e.g., "**Yo estoy aquí**" (*I am here*), "**Yo le doy dinero a mi hermano**" (*I give money to my brother*).

2. The verbs "**hacer**" *(to do)*, "**poner**" *(to put)*, "**valer**" *(to be worth)*, "**salir**" *(to go out or to exit)*, "**traer**" *(to bring)*, and "**caer**" *(to drop)* are conjugated with "-**go**" ending in the first-person "**yo**" as "**hago**," "**pongo**," "**valgo**," "**salgo**," "**traigo**," and "**caigo**," respectively, e.g., "**Yo salgo con mis amigos**" (*I go out with my friends*).

3. The verbs ending in a vowel followed by "-**cer**" or "-**cir**" are conjugated with "-**zco**" in the first-person "**yo**." Examples are "**conocer**" *(to know)*, "**ofrecer**" *(to offer)*, "**conducir**" *(to drive)*, and "**traducir**" *(to translate)*.

4. The verbs "**saber**" *(to know)*, "**caber**" *(to fit)*, and "**ver**" *(to see)* do not follow any rules and are conjugated in first-person "**yo**" form as "**sé**," "**quepo**," and "**veo**," respectively.

Remember that these three sets of irregular verbs are only irregular in their first-person "**yo**" form. In other forms, they are conjugated as regular verbs.

	estar	dar	hacer	salir	conocer	saber
yo	est**oy**	d**oy**	ha**go**	sal**go**	cono**zco**	s**é**
tú	est**ás**	das	haces	sales	conoces	sabes
él/ella/usted	est**á**	da	hace	sale	conoce	sabe
nosotros/-as	est**amos**	d**amos**	hac**emos**	sal**imos**	conoc**emos**	sab**emos**
vosotros/-as	est**áis**	dais	hac**éis**	sal**ís**	conoc**éis**	sab**éis**
ellos/-as/ustedes	est**án**	dan	hacen	salen	conocen	saben

Added to these four sets are three more sets of verbs that are regular in essence but change spelling when conjugated in first-person "**yo**" form. These are the verbs ending in "-**guir**," "-**ger**," "-**gir**," and "-**quir**."

1. Verbs ending in "-**guir**" in first-person "**yo**" form end in "-**go**," e.g., "**extinguir**" *(to extinguish)* becomes "**yo extingo**."

2. Verbs ending in "-**ger**" and "-**gir**" in first-person "**yo**" form end in "-**jo**," e.g., "**escoger**" *(to choose)* becomes "**yo escojo**," and "**exigir**" *(to demand)* becomes "**yo exijo**."

3. Verbs ending in "-**quir**" in first-person "**yo**" form end in "-**co**," e.g., "**delinquir**" *(to commit an offense or a crime)* becomes "**yo delinco**."

	-guir ending extinguir	-ger ending proteger	-gir ending exigir
yo	extin**go**	prote**jo**	exi**jo**
tú	extin**gues**	prote**ges**	exi**ges**
él/ella/usted	extin**gue**	prote**ge**	exi**ge**
nosotros/-as	extin**guimos**	prote**gemos**	exi**gimos**
vosotros/-as	extin**guís**	prote**géis**	exi**gís**
ellos/ellas/ustedes	extin**guen**	prote**gen**	exi**gen**

The justification for such a spelling change is to maintain the pronunciation rules. For instance, the letter "**g**" sounds like the "*g*" in "*get*," except when it is followed by "**e**" or "**i**," in which case it is pronounced like the "*h*" in "*hero*." Similarly, the letter "**c**" sounds like "*c*" in "*car*," except when it is followed by "**e**" or "**i**," in which case it is pronounced like the "*c*" in "*city*."

#2: Irregular Verbs with Stem Change

The *second* group of irregular verbs includes verbs with stem changes. In these verbs, the irregular conjugation is applied to all forms except with the subject pronouns "**nosotros/-as**" and "**vosotros/-as**." The verbs in this group are divided into five categories:

1. Verbs that change stem from "**e**" to "**i**," e.g., "**corregir**" *(to correct)*, "**elegir**" *(to choose or to elect)*, "**medir**" *(to measure)*, "**pedir**" *(to ask for or to request)*, "**reír**" *(to laugh)*, "**repetir**" *(to repeat)*, "**seguir**" *(to follow)*, "**servir**" *(to serve)*.

2. Verbs that change stem from "**e**" to "**ie**," e.g., "**advertir**" (*to warn*), "**atender**" (*to attend to*), "**atravesar**" (*to cross*), "**calentar**" (*to heat*), "**cerrar**" (*to close*), "**comenzar**" (*to commence* or *to start*), "**confesar**" (*to confess*), "**convertir**" (*to convert*), "**defender**" (*to defend*), "**divertir**" (*to amuse*), "**empezar**" (*to begin*), "**encender**" (*to light*), "**entender**" (*to understand*), "**enterrar**" (*to bury*), "**fregar**" (*to scrub*), "**herir**" (*to injure*), "**hervir**" (*to boil*), "**mentir**" (*to lie*), "**negar**" (*to deny*), "**pensar**" (*to think*), "**perder**" (*to lose*), "**preferir**" (*to prefer*), "**querer**" (*to want*), "**regar**" (*to water*), "**sugerir**" (*to suggest*), "**temblar**" (*to tremble*), "**tropezar**" (*to trip* or *to stumble*), "**verter**" (*to pour*).

3. Verbs that change stem from "**o**" to "**ue**," e.g., "**acordar**" (*to agree*), "**almorzar**" (*to have lunch*), "**aprobar**" (*to approve*), "**contar**" (*to count*), "**costar**" (*to cost*), "**dormir**" (*to sleep*), "**encontrar**" (*to find*), "**forzar**" (*to force*), "**morder**" (*to bite*), "**mostrar**" (*to show*), "**poder**" (*to be able to*), "**probar**" (*to test* or *to taste*), "**volar**" (*to fly*), "**volver**" (*to return*).

4. Verbs that change stem from "**u**" to "**ue**" include only one verb, which happens to be commonly used, that is, "**jugar**" (*to play*).

5. Verbs that change stem from "**i**" to "**ie**" include only two verbs "**adquirir**" (*to acquire*) and "**inquirir**" (*to inquire*).

The table below summarizes the stem change rules with examples.

	pedir e➔i	pensar e➔ie	dormir o➔ue	jugar u➔ue	adquirir i➔ie
yo	pido	pienso	duermo	juego	adquiero
tú	pides	piensas	duermes	juegas	adquieres
él/ella/usted	pide	piensa	duerme	juega	adquiere
nosotros/-as	pedimos	pensamos	dormimos	jugamos	adquirimos
vosotros/-as	pedís	pensáis	dormís	jugáis	adquirís
ellos/ellas/ustedes	piden	piensan	duermen	juegan	adquieren

Notice again how the conjugation remains regular with the subject pronouns "**nosotros/-as**" and "**vosotros/-as**."

The rules about verbs ending in "-**guir**," "-**ger**," and "-**gir**" should be respected in the first-person "**yo**" form if a verb happens to belong to one of the abovementioned categories. For example, the verb "**seguir**" changes stem from "**e**" to "**i**." In the first-person "**yo**" form, in addition to the stem change, the "**gu**" is replaced with "**g**," while the other forms only change the stem. Similarly, the verb "**elegir**" changes stem from "**e**" to "**i**." In the first-person "**yo**" form, in addition to stem change, the "**g**" is replaced with "**j**," while the other forms only change the stem.

	"**-guir**" ending e.g., **seguir**	"**-gir**" ending e.g., **elegir**
yo	si**go**	eli**jo**
tú	sigu**es**	elig**es**
él/ella/usted	sigu**e**	elig**e**
nosotros/-as	segu**imos**	eleg**imos**
vosotros/-as	segu**ís**	eleg**ís**
ellos/ellas/ustedes	sigu**en**	elig**en**

#3: Irregular Verbs in "Yo" Form + Stem Change

The *third* group of verbs includes the verbs that are irregular in the first-person "**yo**" form with a "-**go**" ending and have a stem change in all other forms except the "**nosotros/-as**" and "**vosotros/-as**" forms. This group includes the commonly used verbs "**decir**" (*to say*), "**venir**" (*to come*), and "**tener**" (*to have*).

	decir	venir	tener
yo	di**go**	ven**go**	ten**go**
tú	dic**es**	vien**es**	tien**es**
él/ella/usted	dic**e**	vien**e**	tien**e**
nosotros/-as	dec**imos**	ven**imos**	ten**emos**
vosotros/-as	dec**ís**	ven**ís**	ten**éis**
ellos/ellas/ustedes	dic**en**	vien**en**	tien**en**

#4: Completely Irregular Verbs

The *fourth* group of verbs includes completely irregular verbs. These must be practiced until memorized. Verbs in this group include "**ser**" *(to be)*, "**ir**" *(to go)*, "**oler**" *(to smell)*, and **oír** *(to hear)*. Note that "**ser**" and "**estar**" both mean *"to be."* Differences between the two will be explained in **Lesson 9** of this level.

	ser	ir	oler	oír
yo	soy	voy	huelo	oigo
tú	eres	vas	hueles	oyes
él/ella/usted	es	va	huele	oye
nosotros/-as	somos	vamos	olemos	oímos
vosotros/-as	sois	vais	oléis	oís
ellos/ellas/ustedes	son	van	huelen	oyen

#5: Irregular Verbs with Orthographic Changes

The *fifth* group includes verbs that undergo some other orthographic changes when conjugated. We have already encountered the verbs with "**-guir**," "**-ger**," and "**-gir**" endings, which undergo some orthographic change when conjugated in the first-person "**yo**" form. We have also encountered verbs that end in a vowel followed by "**-cer**" or "**-cir**," whose conjugation in the first-person "**yo**" form ends in "**-zco**." Here we discuss two more orthographic changes:

1. Verbs ending in "**-uir**" (excluding "**-guir**") add "**y**" between the stem and the conjugation suffix in all forms except with "**nosotros/-as**" and "**vosotros/-as**," e.g., "**atribuir**" *(to attribute)*, "**construir**" *(to construct)*, "**contribuir**" *(to contribute)*, "**disminuir**" *(to diminish* or *to decrease)*, "**distribuir**" *(to distribute)*, "**huir**" *(to escape* or *to run away)*, "**incluir**" *(to include)*, "**sustituir**" *(to substitute)*.

	construir	incluir	huir
yo	constru**yo**	inclu**yo**	hu**yo**
tú	constru**yes**	inclu**yes**	hu**yes**
él/ella/usted	constru**ye**	inclu**ye**	hu**ye**
nosotros/-as	constru**imos**	inclu**imos**	hu**imos**
vosotros/-as	constru**ís**	inclu**ís**	hu**ís**
ellos/ellas/ustedes	constru**yen**	inclu**yen**	hu**yen**

2. Some verbs ending in "**-iar**" or "**-uar**" add an accent to the "**i**" or "**u**" before the conjugation suffix in all forms except with "**nosotros/-as**" and "**vosotros/-as**," e.g., "**enviar**" *(to send),* "**fiar**" *(to trust or to believe in),* "**liar**" *(to bundle or to bind),* "**variar**" *(to vary),* "**actuar**" *(to act),* "**continuar**" *(to continue),* "**habituar**" *(to get used to),* "**situar**" *(to position or to situate).*

	enviar	actuar	continuar
yo	envío	actúo	continúo
tú	envías	actúas	continúas
él/ella/usted	envía	actúa	continúa
nosotros/-as	enviamos	actuamos	continuamos
vosotros/-as	enviáis	actuáis	continuáis
ellos/ellas/ustedes	envían	actúan	continúan

Irregular Verbs in Portuguese

Let us examine the irregular verbs in the present indicative tense in the three verb groups: "**-ar**," "**-er**," and "**-ir**."

#1: "-ar" Verbs

The verbs "**estar**" *(to be)* and "**dar**" *(to give)* are the most common irregular "**-ar**" verbs that do not follow a particular pattern of conjugation. They are important verbs that should be practiced and memorized.

	estar *(to be)*	dar *(to give)*
eu	estou	dou
ele/ela/você	está	dá
nós	estamos	damos
eles/elas/vocês	estão	dão

In addition to the above two verbs, the following "**-ar**" verbs ending in "**-iar**" change the "**i**" to "**ei**" in all forms except "**nós**":

	eu	ele/ela/você	nós	eles/elas/vocês
odiar *to hate*	od**ei**o	od**ei**a	odiamos	od**ei**am

ansiar *to long for*	ans**eio**	ans**eia**	ansi**amos**	ans**eiam**
incendiar *to set alight*	incend**eio**	incend**eia**	incendi**amos**	incend**eiam**
mediar *to mediate*	med**eio**	med**eia**	medi**amos**	med**eiam**
remediar *to remedy*	remed**eio**	remed**eia**	remedi**amos**	remed**eiam**

#2: "-er" Verbs

The most common irregular "-**er**" verbs are:

	eu	ele/ela/você	nós	eles/elas/vocês
ser *to be*	sou	é	somos	são
ter *to have*	tenho	tem	temos	têm
ver *to see*	vejo	vê	vemos	vêem
poder *can*	posso	pode	podemos	podem
dizer *to say*	digo	diz	dizemos	dizem
trazer *to bring*	trago	traz	trazemos	trazem
fazer *to do or make*	faço	faz	fazemos	fazem
caber *to fit*	caibo	cabe	cabemos	cabem
saber *to know*	sei	sabe	sabemos	sabem
querer *to want*	quero	quer	queremos	querem
haver *to have*	hei	há	hemos	hão
ler *to read*	leio	lê	lemos	leem
crer *to believe*	creio	crê	cremos	creem
perder *to lose*	perco	perde	perdemos	perdem
valer *to be worth*	valho	vale	valemos	valem

In addition to the above verbs, there are some "-**er**" verbs that undergo minor spelling changes, such as:

a) Verbs that change "**c**" to "**ç**"

If the stem ends in "**c**," the final stem "**c**" is changed into "**ç**" in the first-person singular to maintain the soft sound of the letter "**c**." For example:

	eu	ele/ela/você	nós	eles/elas/vocês
vencer *to win*	venço	vence	vencemos	vencem
parecer *to seem*	pareço	parece	parecemos	parecem

b) Verbs that change "**g**" to "**j**"

If the stem ends in "**g**," the final stem "**g**" is changed into "**j**" in the first-person singular to maintain the proper pronunciation sound. For example:

	eu	ele/ela/você	nós	eles/elas/vocês
eleger *to elect*	elejo	elege	elegemos	elegem
proteger *to protect*	protejo	protege	protegemos	protegem

c) Verbs that change "**gu**" to "**g**"

If the stem ends in "**gu**," the final stem "**gu**" is changed into "**g**" in the first-person singular to maintain the hard sound of the letter "**g**." For example:

	eu	ele/ela/você	nós	eles/elas/vocês
erguer *to raise*	ergo	ergue	erguemos	erguem

#3: "-ir" Verbs

The most common irregular "-**ir**" verbs are:

	eu	ele/ela/você	nós	eles/elas/vocês
ir *to go*	vou	vai	vamos	vão
vir *to come*	venho	vem	vimos	vêm
rir *to laugh*	rio	ri	rimos	riem
sorrir *to smile*	sorrio	sorri	sorrimos	sorriem
sair *to leave*	saio	sai	saímos	saem
cair *to fall*	caio	cai	caímos	caem
ouvir *to hear*	ouço	ouve	ouvimos	ouvem

In addition to the above verbs, there are a few verbs that undergo minor spelling and stem changes. Most of these verbs follow some pattern and fall under one of these five categories:

1. Verbs that undergo stem changes

a) Verbs that change "**e**" to "**i**"

Many "**-ir**" verbs change the stem vowel from "**e**" to "**i**" in the first-person singular. For example:

	eu	ele/ela/você	nós	eles/elas/vocês
mentir *to lie*	minto	mente	mentimos	mentem
repetir *to repeat*	repito	repete	repetimos	repetem
servir *to serve*	sirvo	serve	servimos	servem

Other examples include: "**aderir**" *(to adhere)*, "**advertir**" *(to warn)*, "**convergir**" *(to converge)*, "**diferir**" *(to differ)*, "**digerir**" *(to digest)*, "**divergir**" *(to diverge)*, "**divertir**" *(to amuse)*, "**ferir**" *(to injure)*, "**preferir**" *(to prefer)*, "**refletir**" *(to reflect)*, "**referir**" *(to refer)*, "**repelir**" *(to repel)*, "**seguir**" *(to follow)*, "**sentir**" *(to feel)*, "**sugerir**" *(to suggest)*, and "**vestir**" *(to dress)*.

In addition to the above verbs, there are a few verbs that change the stem vowel from "**e**" to "**i**" in all conjugation forms except the "**nós**" form. For example:

	eu	ele/ela/você	nós	eles/elas/vocês
prevenir *to prevent*	previno	previne	prevenimos	previnem
agredir *to attack*	agrido	agride	agredimos	agridem
progredir *to progress*	progrido	progride	progredimos	progridem
regredir *to regress*	regrido	regride	regredimos	regridem

b) Verbs that change "**o**" to "**u**"

Many "**-ir**" verbs change the stem vowel from "**o**" to "**u**" in the first-person singular. For example:

	eu	ele/ela/você	nós	eles/elas/vocês
dormir *to sleep*	durmo	dorme	dormimos	dormem
cobrir *to cover*	cubro	cobre	cobrimos	cobrem
descobrir *to discover*	descubro	descobre	descobrimos	descobrem
encobrir *to cover up*	encubro	encobre	encobrimos	encobrem
tossir *to cough*	tusso	tosse	tossimos	tossem

Exceptionally, the verb "**polir**" *(to polish)* changes the stem vowel from "**o**" to "**u**" in all conjugation forms except the "**nós**" form:

	eu	ele/ela/você	nós	eles/elas/vocês
polir *to polish*	pulo	pule	polimos	pulem

c) Verbs that change "**u**" to "**o**"

Some "**-ir**" verbs change the stem vowel from "**u**" to "**o**" in the third-person singular and plural forms. For example:

	eu	ele/ela/você	nós	eles/elas/vocês
subir *to go up*	subo	<u>sobe</u>	sub**imos**	<u>sobem</u>
fugir *to escape*	fujo	<u>foge</u>	fug**imos**	<u>fogem</u>
cuspir *to spit*	cuspo	<u>cospe</u>	cusp**imos**	<u>cospem</u>
sacudir *to shake*	sacudo	<u>sacode</u>	sacud**imos**	<u>sacodem</u>

2. Verbs that undergo minor spelling changes

Similar to the orthographic changes we encountered in some "**-er**" verbs, if the stem of an "**-ir**" verb ends in "**c**," "**g**," or "**gu**," the final stem letter is changed into "**ç**," "**j**," or "**g**," respectively, in the first-person singular to maintain the proper sound. For example:

	eu	ele/ela/você	nós	eles/elas/vocês
ressarcir *to compensate*	<u>ressarço</u>	ressarce	ressarc**imos**	ressarcem
dirigir *to drive*	<u>dirijo</u>	dirige	dirig**imos**	dirigem
seguir *to follow*	<u>sigo</u>	segue	segu**imos**	seguem

3. Verbs ending in "**-dir**"

There are a few verbs ending in "**-dir**" that change the "**d**" into "**ç**" in the first-person singular only. For example:

	eu	ele/ela/você	nós	eles/elas/vocês
pedir *to ask for*	<u>peço</u>	pede	ped**imos**	pedem
medir *to measure*	<u>meço</u>	mede	med**imos**	medem
despedir *to dismiss*	<u>despeço</u>	despede	despedi**mos**	despedem

4. Verbs ending in "-zir"

Verbs that end in "-zir" normally have no ending in the third-person singular form. For example:

	eu	ele/ela/você	nós	eles/elas/vocês
conduzir *to drive*	conduzo	conduz	conduzimos	conduzem
deduzir *to deduce*	deduzo	deduz	deduzimos	denduzem
introduzir *to introduce*	introduzo	introduz	introduzimos	introduzem
produzir *to produce*	produzo	produz	produzimos	produzem
traduzir *to translate*	traduzo	traduz	traduzimos	traduzem

5. Verbs ending in "-uir"

a) Verbs like "seguir"

Many verbs like "**seguir**" change the "**egu**" to "**ig**" in the first-person singular only. For example:

	eu	ele/ela/você	nós	eles/elas/vocês
seguir *to follow*	sigo	segue	seguimos	seguem
conseguir *to get*	consigo	consegue	conseguimos	conseguem
perseguir *to chase*	persigo	persegue	perseguimos	perseguem

b) Verbs that end in "-buir"

Verbs that end in "-**buir**" are normally irregular in the third-person singular and the first-person plural, and have the following pattern:

	eu	ele/ela/você	nós	eles/elas/vocês
distribuir *to distribute*	distribuo	distribui	distribuímos	distribuem

contribuir *to contribute*	contribuo	contribui	contribuímos	contribuem
atribuir *to attribute*	atribuo	atribui	atribuímos	atribuem

c) Verbs that end in "**-truir**"

Some verbs that end in "**-truir**" are irregular in all forms except the first-person singular, and have the following pattern:

	eu	ele/ela/você	nós	eles/elas/vocês
construir *to construct*	construo	constrói	construímos	constroem
destruir *to destroy*	destruo	destrói	destruímos	destroem

Irregular Verbs in Italian

We examine five groups of irregular verbs in the present indicative tense.

#1: Completely Irregular Verbs

The *first* group contains 14 verbs that are common, yet completely irregular, that is, they do not follow a particular pattern of conjugation. These verbs should be practiced and memorized.

	io	tu	lui/lei	noi	voi	loro
andare *(to go)*	vado	vai	va	andiamo	andate	vanno
avere *(to have)*	ho	hai	ha	abbiamo	avete	hanno
bere *(to drink)*	bevo	bevi	beve	beviamo	bevete	bevono
essere *(to be)*	sono	sei	è	siamo	siete	sono
dare *(to give)*	do	dai	dà	diamo	date	danno
dire *(to say/tell)*	dico	dici	dice	diciamo	dite	dicono
dovere *(must)*	devo/debbo	devi	deve	dobbiamo	dovete	devono/debbono
fare *(to do/make)*	faccio	fai	fa	facciamo	fate	fanno
potere *(can)*	posso	puoi	può	possiamo	potete	possono
sapere *(to know)*	so	sai	sa	sappiamo	sapete	sanno

stare *(to stay)*	sto	stai	sta	stiamo	state	stanno
scegliere *(to choose)*	scelgo	scegli	sceglie	scegliamo	scegliete	scelgono
uscire *(to go out)*	esco	esci	esce	usciamo	uscite	escono
volere *(to want)*	voglio	vuoi	vuole	vogliamo	volete	vogliono

Notice that the verb "**stare**" can also mean *"to be"* in some contexts, e.g., "**Come stai?**" *(How are you?)*, "**Sto bene**" *(I am well)*, etc.

In addition to these 14 verbs, any verb that is derived from or written similar to these verbs uses the same conjugation patterns. For example, the verb "**rifare**" *(to redo or remake)* is conjugated like the verb "**fare**," and the verb "**riuscire**" *(to succeed)* is conjugated like the verb "**uscire**."

#2: Add "g" to the stem in "io" and "loro" forms

The *second* group adds a "**g**" to the stem of the verb in the "**io**" and "**loro**" forms. There are four common verbs in this group:

	salire *(to go up)*	rimanere *(to remain)*	venire *(to come)*	tenere *(to hold)*
io	sal**g**o	riman**g**o	ven**g**o	ten**g**o
tu	sali	rimani	vieni	tieni
lui/lei	sale	rimane	viene	tiene
noi	saliamo	rimaniamo	veniamo	teniamo
voi	salite	rimanete	venite	tenete
loro	sal**g**ono	riman**g**ono	ven**g**ono	ten**g**ono

Notice that the verbs "**venire**" and "**tenere**" also change the stem in the "**tu**" and "**lui/lei**" forms from "**ven-**" and "**ten-**" to "**vien-**" and "**tien-**," respectively.

Verbs that derive from the four verbs in this group are conjugated similarly. For example, the verbs "**contenere**" *(to contain)* and "**intervenire**" *(to intervene)* follow the same conjugation patterns of the verbs "**tenere**" and "**venire**," respectively.

#3: Other Minor Stem Changes

The *third* group includes verbs with relatively minor stem changes. For example, the verb "**apparire**" *(to appear)* changes the stem from "**appar-**" to "**appai-**" when conjugated in the "**io**" and "**loro**" forms, whereas the verb "**udire**" *(to hear)* changes the stem from "**ud-**" to "**od-**" in all forms except "**noi**" and "**voi**." In general, the "**noi**" and "**voi**" forms remain unchanged in this group of verbs. Here are four common verbs in this group:

	apparire *(to appear)*	morire *(to die)*	sedere *(to sit)*	udire *(to hear)*
io	appaio	muoio	siedo[1]	odo
tu	appari	muori	siedi	odi
lui/lei	appare	muore	siede	ode
noi	appariamo	moriamo	sediamo	udiamo
voi	apparite	morite	sedete	udite
loro	appaiono	muoiono	siedono[2]	odono

In addition to these four verbs, similar verbs follow the same conjugation patterns. For example, the verbs "**comparire**" *(to appear or become visible)*, "**riapparire**" *(to reappear)*, "**scomparire**" *(to disappear)*, "**sparire**" *(to disappear or vanish)*, and "**trasparire**" *(to transpire)* follow the same conjugation patterns of the verb "**apparirie**," and the verb "**possedere**" *(to possess)* follows the same conjugation patterns of the verb "**sedere**."

#4: Orthographic Changes

The *fourth* group includes verbs that are regular in essence but change spelling to maintain proper pronunciation. These are the verbs ending in "**-care**," "**-gare**," "**-ciare**," "**-giare**," and "**-gliare**."

1. Verbs ending in "**-care**" and "**-gare**" add an "**h**" to the stem in the "**tu**" and "**noi**" forms before the "**-i**" and "**-iamo**" endings, respectively, e.g., "**cercare**" *(to search)*, "**pagare**" *(to pay)*, "**giocare**" *(to play)*, "**praticare**" *(to practice)*, "**negare**" *(to deny or refuse)*, "**caricare**" *(to load)*, "**pregare**" *(to pray or beg)*, "**sporcare**" *(to make dirty)*, and "**litigare**" *(to argue)*.

---

[1] Another accepted irregular conjugation of the "**io**" form is "**seggo**."
[2] Another accepted irregular conjugation of the "**loro**" form is "**seggono**."

2. Verbs in "-**ciare**," "-**giare**," and "-**gliare**" drop the "i" from the stem in the "**tu**" and "**noi**" forms before the "-**i**" and "-**iamo**" endings, respectively, to avoid the double "i," e.g., "**cominciare**" *(to start or begin)*, "**mangiare**" *(to eat)*, "**baciare**" *(to kiss)*, "**lasciare**" *(to leave)*, "**strisciare**" *(to crawl)*, "**arrangiare**" *(to arrange)*, "**viaggiare**" *(to travel)*, "**tagliare**" *(to cut)*, and "**sbagliare**" *(to make a mistake)*.

3. Most other verbs that end in "-**iare**," that is, excluding "-**ciare**," "-**giare**," and "-**gliare**," follow the same pattern and drop the "i" from the stem in the "**tu**" and "**noi**" forms before the "-**i**" and "-**iamo**" endings, respectively, to avoid the double "i," e.g., "**abbreviare**" *(to abbreviate)*, "**cambiare**" *(to change)*, "**copiare**" *(to copy)*, "**iniziare**" *(to begin)*, "**studiare**" *(to study)*, and "**variare**" *(to vary)*.

However, the exception to the rule is that some verbs drop the "i" from the stem only in the "**noi**" form and maintain the double "i" in the "**tu**" form, e.g., "**avviare**" *(to start)*, "**fuorviare**" *(to mislead)*, "**inviare**" *(to send)*, "**obliare**" *(to forget)*, "**rinviare**" *(to postpone)*, "**sciare**" *(to ski)*, and "**spiare**" *(to spy)*.

Finally, keep in mind that verbs ending in "-**cere**" and "-**gere**" do not undergo any spelling change, but instead change the pronunciation to the hard sounds "**k**" (as in *"kit"*) and "**g**" (as in *"get"*) in the "**io**" and "**loro**" forms before the "-**o**" and "-**ono**" endings, respectively, e.g., "**conoscere**" *(to know)*, "**piangere**" *(to cry)*, and "**vincere**" *(to win)*.

Here is a summary in the context of some examples:

	io	tu	lui/lei	noi	voi	loro
cer<u>c</u>are	cerco	cerchi	cerca	cerchiamo	cercate	cercano
pa<u>g</u>are	pago	paghi	paga	paghiamo	pagate	pagano
ba<u>ci</u>are	bacio	baci	bacia	baciamo	baciate	baciano
man<u>gi</u>are	mangio	mangi	mangia	mangiamo	mangiate	mangiano
ta<u>gli</u>are	taglio	tagli	taglia	tagliamo	tagliate	tagliano

studiare	studio	studi	studia	studiamo	studiate	studiano
inviare	invio	invii	invia	inviamo	inviate	inviano
vincere	vinco	vinci	vince	vinciamo	vincete	vincono
piangere	piango	piangi	piange	piangiamo	piangete	piangono

#5: Contracted Infinitive Verbs with "-rre" Endings

Finally, the *fifth* group includes some special, but not so common, verbs that end in "-**arre**," "-**orre**," and "-**urre**." These verbs did not initially appear under the three main verb types in Italian with "-**are**," "-**ere**," and "-**ire**" endings. These verbs belong to a group of verbs called *contracted infinitive* verbs. In these verbs, the stem of the infinitive is shorter than that of the conjugated verb. For instance, the verb "**tradurre**" *(to translate)* is conjugated in the "**io**" form as "**traduco**." Notice that the stem of the infinitive is "**trad-**," whereas the stem of the conjugated verb is "**traduc-**." The reason for that often goes back to the Latin origin of the verb, which is "traducere." This explains the irregular conjugation of many Italian verbs, some of which even belong to the three main verb types, for example, "**dire**" *(to say*, Latin: "dicere"), "**fare**" *(to do or make*, Latin: "facere"), and "**porre**" *(to put*, Latin: "ponere"). In general, verbs in this group are considered "-**ere**" verbs because they lost an internal "-**e-**" when derived from their Latin origin.

Let us examine some conjugation examples of contracted infinitive verbs that end with "-**arre**," "-**orre**," and "-**urre**."

	-arre ending trarre *(to pull)*	-orre ending porre *(to put)*	-urre ending tradurre *(to translate)*
io	traggo	pongo	traduco
tu	trai	poni	traduci
lui/lei	trae	pone	traduce
noi	traiamo	poniamo	traduciamo
voi	traete	ponete	traducete
loro	traggono	pongono	traducono

Other examples include:

-arre ending	-orre ending	-urre ending

"contrarre" *(to contract)*	"comporre" *(to compose)*	"condurre" *(to lead or conduct)*
"distrarre" *(to distract)*	"esporre" *(to exhibit)*	"dedurre" *(to deduce)*
"sottrarre" *(to subtract)*	"imporre" *(to impose)*	"produrre" *(to produce)*

Irregular Verbs in French

Let us examine the irregular verbs in the three verb groups "**-er**," "**-ir**," and "**-re**" in the present indicative tense.

#1: "-er" Verbs

The verb "**aller**" *(to go)* is essentially the *only* irregular "**-er**" verb that does not follow a particular pattern of conjugation. This is an important verb that should be practiced and memorized.

	je	**tu**	**il/elle**	**nous**	**vous**	**ils/elles**
aller *to go*	vais	vas	va	allons	allez	vont

Notice that the verb "**aller**" is used instead of the verb "**être**" *(to be)* in some contexts, e.g., "**Comment <u>allez</u>-vous?**" *(How <u>are</u> you?)*, "**Je <u>vais</u> bien**" *(I <u>am</u> well)*, etc.

Some "**-er**" verbs undergo minor spelling changes of the stem when conjugated in some forms. These are classified in the following five categories:

1. Verbs ending in "-cer"

Verbs ending in "**-cer**" add a *cedilla* to the "**c**" only when conjugated in the first-person plural form "**nous**." This is required to maintain the soft "**c**" sound when the "**-ons**" suffix is added. Other conjugations are unchanged. Here are some examples:

nous commençons	*we start*	**nous effaçons**	*we erase*
nous finançons	*we finance*	**nous influençons**	*we influence*
nous menaçons	*we threaten*	**nous plaçons**	*we place*
nous remplaçons	*we replace*	**nous renonçons**	*we renounce*

2. Verbs ending in "-ger"

Verbs ending in "-**ger**" add an "**e**" after the "**g**" only when conjugated in the first-person plural form "**nous**." This is required to maintain the soft "**g**" sound when the "-**ons**" suffix is added. Other conjugations are unchanged. Here are some examples:

nous boug<u>e</u>ons	*we move*	nous chang<u>e</u>ons	*we change*
nous corrig<u>e</u>ons	*we correct*	nous dégag<u>e</u>ons	*we release*
nous exig<u>e</u>ons	*we demand*	nous mang<u>e</u>ons	*we eat*
nous nag<u>e</u>ons	*we swim*	nous voyag<u>e</u>ons	*we travel*

3. Verbs ending in "-**yer**"

Verbs ending in "-**yer**" change the "**y**" to "**i**" in all forms except "**nous**" and "**vous**." For instance, the verb "**envoyer**" *(to send)* in the first-person singular is conjugated as "**j'envoie**" /jã-**vwa**/. Notice that the letter "**y**" is replaced with "**i**" and the "**y**" sound at the end no longer exists in pronunciation. Let us look at some examples:

	"appuyer" (to lean on)	"dévoyer" (to mislead)	"ennuyer" (to bore or annoy)	"envoyer" (to send)
je/j'	appuie	dévoie	ennuie	envoie
tu	appuies	dévoies	ennuies	envoies
il/elle/on	appuie	dévoie	ennuie	envoie
nous	appuyons	dévoyons	ennuyons	envoyons
vous	appuyez	dévoyez	ennuyez	envoyez
ils/elles	appuient	dévoient	ennuient	envoient

One exception is the verb "**payer**" *(to pay)* which can be conjugated both ways. For instance, the verb "**payer**" in the first-person singular can be conjugated as "**je paye**" /j(ə) pey/ or "**je paie**" /j(ə) pe/.

4. Verbs ending in "-**eler**"

Some verbs ending in "-**eler**" double the "**l**" at the end of their stem in all forms except "**nous**" and "**vous**." For instance, the verb "**appeler**" *(to call)* in the first-person singular is conjugated as "**j'appe<u>ll</u>e**" /ja-**pel**/. Here are some more examples:

	"épeler" (to spell)	"étinceler" (to sparkle)	"rappeler" (to remind)	"renouveler" (to renew)
je/j'	épelle	étincelle	rappelle	renouvelle
tu	épelles	étincelles	rappelles	renouvelles
il/elle/on	épelle	étincelle	rappelle	renouvelle
nous	épelons	étincelons	rappelons	renouvelons
vous	épelez	étincelez	rappelez	renouvelez
ils/elles	épellent	étincellent	rappellent	renouvellent

5. Verbs ending in "-e-" + *consonant* + "-er"

Some verbs ending in "-e-" followed by a *consonant* followed by "-er" add a *grave accent* to the "e" in the stem before the consonant in all forms except "**nous**" and "**vous**." This changes the "e" sound to an open "e" sound instead of a schwa sound. For instance, the verb "**lever**" /lə-ve/ *(to raise)* in the first-person singular is conjugated as "**je lève**" /j(ə) lev/. Here are some more examples:

	"acheter" (to buy)	"enlever" (to remove)	"mener" (to lead)	"peser" (to weigh)
je/j'	achète	enlève	mène	pèse
tu	achètes	enlèves	mènes	pèses
il/elle/on	achète	enlève	mène	pèse
nous	achetons	enlevons	menons	pesons
vous	achetez	enlevez	menez	pesez
ils/elles	achètent	enlèvent	mènent	pèsent

If the "e" in the stem before the consonant already has an acute accent in the infinitive, the acute accent is replaced with a grave accent in all forms except "**nous**" and "**vous**." Here are some examples:

	"célébrer" (to celebrate)	"espérer" (to hope)	"gérer" (to manage)	"préférer" (to prefer)
je/j'	célèbre	espère	gère	préfère
tu	célèbres	espères	gères	préfères
il/elle/on	célèbre	espère	gère	préfère
nous	célébrons	espérons	gérons	préférons
vous	célébrez	espérez	gérez	préférez
ils/elles	célèbrent	espèrent	gèrent	préfèrent

#2: "-ir" Verbs

We covered the conjugation of regular "-**ir**" verbs in **Level I, Lesson 6**. Here is an example of a regular "-**ir**" verb conjugated in the present indicative tense:

	je	tu	il/elle	nous	vous	ils/elles
finir *to finish*	finis	finis	finit	finissons	finissez	finissent

Unfortunately, not all "-**ir**" verbs are regular. There are many irregular verbs in this verb group. We will classify them into five main categories:

1. Verbs ending in "-**tir**," "-**mir**," and "-**vir**"

Many verbs in this category are conjugated with the same pattern. Notice the dropping of the last letter of the stem in the three singular forms.

	partir *(to leave)*	**dormir** *(to sleep)*	**servir** *(to serve)*
je	pars	dors	sers
tu	pars	dors	sers
il/elle/on	part	dort	sert
nous	partons	dormons	servons
vous	partez	dormez	servez
ils/elles	partent	dorment	servent

2. Verbs ending in "-**vrir**," "-**frir**," and "-**llir**"

Many verbs in this category are conjugated like regular "-**er**" verbs, for example:

	ouvrir *(to open)*	**offrir** *(to offer)*	**cueillir** *(to pick)*
je/j'	ouvre	offre	cueille
tu	ouvres	offres	cueilles
il/elle/on	ouvre	offre	cueille
nous	ouvrons	offrons	cueillons
vous	ouvrez	offrez	cueillez
ils/elles	ouvrent	offrent	cueillent

Other examples include: "**couvrir**" *(to cover)*, "**souffrir**" *(to suffer)*, "**découvrir**" *(to discover)*, "**assaillir**" *(to assault)*, and "**accueillir**" *(to welcome)*.

3. The verbs "**venir**," "**tenir**," and their derivations

Verbs in this category are conjugated as follows:

	venir *(to come)*	tenir *(to hold)*	devenir *(to become)*	obtenir *(to obtain)*
je/j'	viens	tiens	deviens	obtiens
tu	viens	tiens	deviens	obtiens
il/elle/on	vient	tient	devient	obtient
nous	venons	tenons	devenons	obtenons
vous	venez	tenez	devenez	obtenez
ils/elles	viennent	tiennent	deviennent	obtiennent

Other examples include: "**advenir**" *(to happen)*, "**revenir**" *(to come back)*, "**convenir**" *(to suit)*, "**provenir**" *(to arise from)*, "**prévenir**" *(to prevent)*, "**survenir**" *(to occur)*, "**intervenir**" *(to intervene)*, "**détenir**" *(to hold or detain)*, "**retenir**" *(to retain or hold)*, "**abstenir**" *(to abstain)*, "**contenir**" *(to contain)*, "**soutenir**" *(to sustain or support)*, "**maintenir**" *(to maintain)*, "**appartenir**" *(to belong)*, and "**entretenir**" *(to entertain)*.

4. Verbs ending with "-oir"

Verbs ending in "-oir" do not follow a single conjugation pattern. Thus, one must practice and memorize as many verbs as possible in this category. Here are some common examples:

	je	tu	il/elle	nous	vous	ils/elles
avoir *to have*	ai	as	a	avons	avez	ont
savoir *to know*	sais	sais	sait	savons	savez	savent
devoir *must*	dois	dois	doit	devons	devez	doivent
pouvoir *can*	peux	peux	peut	pouvons	pouvez	peuvent
vouloir *to want*	veux	veux	veut	voulons	voulez	veulent

voir *to see*	vois	vois	voit	voyons	voyez	voient
falloir *to be necessary*	-	-	faut	-	-	-
pleuvoir *to rain*	-	-	pleut	-	-	-
asseoir *to sit*	assieds	assieds	assied	asseyons	asseyez	asseyent
décevoir *to disappoint*	déçois	déçois	déçoit	décevons	décevez	déçoivent
prévoir *to predict*	prévois	prévois	prévoit	prévoyons	prévoyez	prévoient
recevoir *to receive*	reçois	reçois	reçoit	recevons	recevez	reçoivent
valoir *to be worth*	-	-	vaut	-	-	-

5. Other irregular "-ir" verbs

There remain a few irregular "-ir" verbs that do not fall under any of the four previous categories, such as:

	je	**tu**	**il/elle**	**nous**	**vous**	**ils/elles**
acquérir *to acquire*	acquiers	acquiers	acquiert	acquérons	acquérez	acquièrent
conquérir *to conquer*	conquiers	conquiers	conquiert	conquérons	conquérez	conquièrent
bouillir *to boil*	bous	bous	bout	bouillons	bouillez	bouillent
courir *to run*	cours	cours	court	courons	courez	courent
parcourir *to run through*	parcours	parcours	parcourt	parcourons	parcourez	parcourent
secourir *to rescue*	secours	secours	secourt	secourons	secourez	secourent
mourir *to die*	meurs	meurs	meurt	mourons	mourez	meurent

#3: "-re" Verbs

The irregular "-re" verbs group includes some important verbs in French such as: "**être**" *(to be)*, "**faire**" *(to do or make)*, and "**boire**" *(to drink)*.

	être	faire	boire
	(to be)	*(to do or make)*	*(to drink)*
je	suis	fais	bois
tu	es	fais	bois
il/elle/on	est	fait	boit
nous	sommes	faisons	buvons
vous	êtes	faites	buvez
ils/elles	sont	font	boivent

Most verbs in this group fall under one of these eight categories that can help you recognize them:

1. The verb "**prendre**" and its derivations

The verb "**prendre**" and its derivations are conjugated with the same pattern. Notice the removal of the "**d**" in all three plural forms and the extra "**n**" in the third-person plural forms "**ils**" and "**elles**."

	prendre	apprendre	comprendre
	(to take)	*(to learn)*	*(to understand)*
je/j'	prends	apprends	comprends
tu	prends	apprends	comprends
il/elle/on	prend	apprend	comprend
nous	pren**ons**	appren**ons**	compren**ons**
vous	pren**ez**	appren**ez**	compren**ez**
ils/elles	pren**n**ent	appren**n**ent	compren**n**ent

Other examples include: "**entreprendre**" *(to undertake)*, "**surprendre**" *(to surprise)*, "**reprendre**" *(to retake)*, and "**méprendre**" *(to mistake)*.

2. The verbs "**mettre**," "**battre**," and their derivations

The verbs "**mettre**," "**battre**," and their derivations are conjugated with the same pattern. Notice the dropping of the second "**t**" in all three singular forms.

	mettre	battre	promettre	débattre
	(to put)	*(to beat)*	*(to promise)*	*(to debate)*

je	mets	bats	promets	débats
tu	mets	bats	promets	débats
il/elle/on	met	bat	promet	débat
nous	mettons	battons	promettons	débattons
vous	mettez	battez	promettez	débattez
ils/elles	mettent	battent	promettent	débattent

Other examples include: "**admettre**" *(to admit)*, "**commettre**" *(to commit)*, "**compromettre**" *(to compromise)*, "**permettre**" *(to permit)*, "**soumettre**" *(to submit)*, "**transmettre**" *(to transmit)*, "**abattre**" *(to knock down)*, and "**combattre**" *(to combat)*.

3. The verb "**rompre**" and its derivations

The verb "**rompre**" and its derivations are conjugated with the same pattern. Notice that these verbs are conjugated just like regular "**-re**" verbs, except in the third-person singular form which takes the suffix "**t**."

	rompre *(to break)*	corrompre *(to corrupt)*	interrompre *(to interrupt)*
je/j'	romps	corromps	interromps
tu	romps	corromps	interromps
il/elle/on	rompt	corrompt	interrompt
nous	rompons	corrompons	interrompons
vous	rompez	corrompez	interrompez
ils/elles	rompent	corrompent	interrompent

4. Verbs ending in "-**aindre**," "-**eindre**," and "-**oindre**"

Verbs in this category drop the "**d**" in their root in all forms, and add a "**g**" before the "**n**" in the three plural forms.

	craindre *(to fear)*	peindre *(to paint)*	joindre *(to join)*
je	crains	peins	joins
tu	crains	peins	joins
il/elle/on	craint	peint	joint
nous	craignons	peignons	joignons
vous	craignez	peignez	joignez
ils/elles	craignent	peignent	joignent

Other examples include: "**adjoindre**" *(to appoint)*, "**astreindre**" *(to compel or force)*, "**atteindre**" *(to attain or reach)*, "**ceindre**" *(to put on)*, "**contraindre**" *(to force)*, "**dépeindre**" *(to depict)*, "**disjoindre**" *(to disconnect)*, "**empreindre**" *(to imprint)*, "**éteindre**" *(to extinguish)*, "**feindre**" *(to feign)*, "**geindre**" *(to groan or whine)*, "**plaindre**" *(to pity)*, "**rejoindre**" *(to rejoin)*, "**restreindre**" *(to restrict)*, and "**teindre**" *(to dye)*.

5. Verbs ending in "-uire," "-dire," "-fire," and "-lire"

Verbs in this category are conjugated with the same pattern. Notice that these verbs add an "**s**" to the end of the stem in the three plural forms. One exception is the second-person plural of the verb "**dire**" (and its derivations), which is conjugated as "**vous dites**."

	cuire	dire	confire	lire
	(to cook)	*(to beat)*	*(to preserve)*	*(to debate)*
je	cuis	dis	confis	lis
tu	cuis	dis	confis	lis
il/elle/on	cuit	dit	confit	lit
nous	cuisons	disons	confisons	lisons
vous	cuisez	dites	confisez	lisez
ils/elles	cuisent	disent	confisent	lisent

Other examples include: "**conduire**" *(to drive)*, "**construire**" *(to build)*, "**contredire**" *(to contradict)*, "**déduire**" *(to deduce or deduct)*, "**détruire**" *(to destroy)*, "**élire**" *(to elect)*, "**induire**" *(to mislead)*, "**instruire**" *(to instruct)*, "**interdire**" *(to forbid)*, "**induire**" *(to mislead)*, "**introduire**" *(to insert or introduce)*, "**luire**" *(to shine)*, "**médire**" *(to malign)*, "**nuire**" *(to harm)*, "**prédire**" *(to predict)*, "**produire**" *(to produce)*, "**reconduire**" *(to renew)*, "**reconstuire**" *(to rebuild)*, "**réduire**" *(to reduce)*, "**séduire**" *(to seduce)*, "**suffire**" *(to suffer)*, and "**traduire**" *(to translate)*.

6. Verbs ending in "-crire"

Verbs in this category are conjugated with the same pattern. Notice that these verbs add a "**v**" to the end of the stem in the three plural forms.

	écrire *(to write)*	décrire *(to describe)*	souscrire *(to subscribe)*
je/j'	écris	décris	souscris
tu	écris	décris	souscris
il/elle/on	écrit	décrit	souscrit
nous	écrivons	décrivons	souscrivons
vous	écrivez	décrivez	souscrivez
ils/elles	écrivent	décrivent	souscrivent

Other examples include: "**inscrire**" *(to inscribe or write down)*, "**prescrire**" *(to prescribe)*, "**proscrire**" *(to prohibit or ban)*, "**récrire**" *(to rewrite)*, "**transcrire**" *(to transcribe)*, and "**circonscrire**" *(to contain or confine)*.

7. Verbs ending in "-**aître**"

Verbs in this category, except "**naître**," follow the same conjugation pattern. Notice the circumflex in the third-person singular form.

	apparaître *(to appear)*	connaître *(to know)*	paraître *(to seem)*
je/j'	apparais	connais	parais
tu	apparais	connais	parais
il/elle/on	apparaît	connaît	paraît
nous	apparaissons	connaissons	paraissons
vous	apparaissez	connaissez	paraissez
ils/elles	apparaissent	connaissent	paraissent

Other examples include: "**comparaître**" *(to appear in court)*, "**disparaître**" *(to disappear)*, "**méconnaître**" *(to be unaware of)*, "**reconnaître**" *(to recognize)*, "**reapparaître**" *(to reappear)*, and "**transparaître**" *(to show through)*.

8. Other irregular "-**re**" verbs

Finally, there remain a few verbs that do not belong to any of the previous categories like the verbs "**être**" *(to be)*, "**faire**" *(to do or make)*, and "**boire**" *(to drink)*, which we discussed at the beginning of this section. Here are a few other examples:

	je/j'	tu	il/elle	nous	vous	ils/elles
clore *to close*	clos	clos	clôt	-	-	closent
conclure *to conclude*	conclus	conclus	conclut	concluons	concluez	concluent
coudre *to sew*	couds	couds	coud	cousons	cousez	cousent
croire *to believe*	crois	crois	croit	croyons	croyez	croient
dissoudre *to dissolve*	dissous	dissous	dissout	dissolvons	dissolvez	dissolvent
distraire *to distract*	distrais	distrais	distrait	distrayons	distrayez	distraient
exclure *to exclude*	exclus	exclus	exclut	excluons	excluez	excluent
inclure *to include*	inclus	inclus	inclut	incluons	incluez	incluent
moudre *to grind*	mouds	mouds	moud	moulons	moulez	moulent
plaire *to please*	plais	plais	plait	plaisons	plaisez	plaisent
résoudre *to resolve*	résous	résous	résout	résolvons	résolvez	résolvent
rire *to laugh*	ris	ris	rit	rions	riez	rient
sourire *to smile*	souris	souris	sourit	sourions	souriez	sourient
suivre *to follow*	suis	suis	suit	suivons	suivez	suivent
vivre *to live*	vis	vis	vit	vivons	vivez	vivent

3. POSSESSIVE ADJECTIVES & PRONOUNS

Possessive adjectives *(my, your, his/her, our, their)* come before a noun, e.g., "*This is my house*," while possessive pronouns *(mine, yours, his/hers, ours, theirs*) are used to replace a noun and its possessive adjective, e.g., *"This house is mine."*

Possessive Adjectives & Pronouns in Spanish

In Spanish, possessive adjectives and pronouns must agree in gender and number with the noun they describe. Fortunately, only **"nosotros/-as"** and **"vosotros/-as"** have distinct masculine and feminine possessive adjective forms.

	Singular	Plural
my	mi	mis
your (informal singular)	tu	tus
his/her/your (formal singular)	su	sus
our	nuestro/-a	nuestros/-as
your (informal plural)	vuestro/-a	vuestros/-as
their/your (formal plural)	su	sus

❖ Note that, unlike in English, the possessive adjective agrees in number and gender with the noun it describes and not the possessor, e.g., **"mis hermanos"** (*my brothers*). Note that we use **"mis"** because the *noun* we describe is *plural*, although the possessor is singular. Similarly, in the example **"nuestras madres"** (*our mothers*), the possessive adjective **"nuestras"** agrees in gender and number with the noun it describes, i.e., **"madres."**

❖ Notice the lack of accent on the vowel in the possessive adjectives **"mi"** and **"tu"** to distinguish them from the prepositional object pronoun **"mí"** meaning *"me,"* and the subject pronoun for second-person singular informal **"tú"** meaning *"you,"* respectively. This is inconsequential in spoken Spanish and does not affect pronunciation.

❖ The possessive adjective can come after the noun if the emphasis is placed on the possessor, e.g., **"un amigo mío"** (*a friend of mine*), **"la casa tuya"** (*your house*), etc.

Let us now examine the *possessive pronouns* in Spanish. Unlike possessive adjectives, all possessive pronouns have masculine and feminine forms as well as singular and plural forms. One must use the correct form that agrees in gender and number with the noun being described.

	Masc. Sing.	Masc. Plural	Fem. Sing.	Fem. Plural
mine	mío	míos	mía	mías
yours (informal singular)	tuyo	tuyos	tuya	tuyas
his/hers/yours (formal singular)	suyo	suyos	suya	suyas
ours	nuestro	nuestros	nuestra	nuestras
yours (informal plural)	vuestro	vuestros	vuestra	vuestras
theirs/yours (formal plural)	suyo	suyos	suya	suyas

❖ Possessive pronouns are normally preceded with a definite article "**el**," "**la**," "**los**," or "**las**" that agrees in gender and number with the possessive pronoun, e.g., "**Tu celular es mejor que el <u>mío</u>**" (*Your cell phone is better than <u>mine</u>*), "**Esa casa es la <u>nuestra</u>**" (*That house is <u>ours</u>*). The only exception is after the verb "**ser**," where it is *optional* and can be dropped, e.g., "**No es tuyo, es <u>mío</u>**" (*It is not <u>yours</u>, it's <u>mine</u>*), "**Esa casa es <u>nuestra</u>**" (*That house is <u>ours</u>*).

❖ In another special case, the possessive pronoun can be preceded by the neuter article "**lo**" to denote property, e.g., "**lo <u>mío</u>**" (*that which is <u>mine</u>*), "**lo <u>nuestro</u>**" (*that which is <u>ours</u>*), "**lo <u>suyo</u>/lo propio**" (*one's own property*), "**lo <u>ajeno</u>**" (*that which belongs to <u>others</u>*).

Possessive Adjectives & Pronouns in Portuguese

In Portuguese, possessive adjectives and pronouns must agree in gender and number with the noun they describe.

	Sing. Masc.	Sing. Fem.	Plural Masc.	Plural Fem.
my (mine)	meu	minha	meus	minhas
his/her(s)/their(s)/your(s)	seu	sua	seus	suas
our(s)	nosso	nossa	nossos	nossas

❖ Note that, unlike in English, the possessive adjective agrees in number and gender with the noun it describes and not the possessor, e.g., "**meus irmãos**" (*my brothers*). Note that we use "**meus**" because the *noun* we describe is *plural*, although the possessor is singular. Similarly, in the example "**nossas mães**" (*our mothers*), the possessive adjective "**nossas**" agrees in gender and number with the noun it describes, i.e., "**mães**."

❖ Notice that possessive adjectives "**seu(s)**" and "**sua(s)**" can mean *"his," "her," "their,"* or *"your."* This could create ambiguity. For example, "**o seu livro**" can be translated as *"his/her/their/your book."* Similarly, "**os seus livros**" can mean *"his/her/their/your books."* To avoid such confusion, especially in the daily spoken language, the following expressions can be used instead:

his	o(s)/a(s) … dele	*the … of him*
her	o(s)/a(s) … dela	*the … of her*
their (masculine)	o(s)/a(s) … deles	*the … of them*
their (feminine)	o(s)/a(s) … delas	*the … of them*
your (informal singular)	seu(s)/sua(s) …	
your (formal singular)	o(s)/a(s) … do senhor o(s)/a(s) … da senhora	*the … of the sir/lady*
your (plural)	seu(s)/sua(s) …	

For example, "**o livro dele**" means *"his book,"* "**o livro dela**" means *"her book,"* "**os livro dela**" means *"her books,"* etc.

If "**seu(s)**" or "**sua(s)**" is used in spoken language, it is often assumed to mean *"your"* in the singular informal form, e.g., "**o seu livro**" (*your book*) unless the meaning indicates otherwise. Another equivalent to "**o seu livro**" (*your book*) is "**o teu livro**," where the possessive adjective "**teu**" comes from the less-common "**tu**" form, the subject personal pronoun discussed in **Level I, Lesson 5**. The feminine form of "**teu**" is "**tua**."

Some people may avoid using "**seu(s)**" and "**sua(s)**" to mean *"his,"* *"her,"* or *"their,"* and reserve its use to mean *"your"* in singular or plural forms.

Notice that, in many cases, the correct interpretation of "**seu(s)**" or "**sua(s)**" is easily understood from the context. Here are some examples:

Ele emprestou **seu** livro para ela.	*He lent her **his** book.*
A mãe comprou um presente para **sua** filha.	*The mother bought a present for **her** daughter.*
Eles cuidam do **seu** jardim com muito carinho.	*They look after **their** garden with great care.*
Os funcionários adoraram **seu** novo emprego.	*The employees loved **their** new job.*
Ela encontrou **sua** amiga no shopping.	*She met **her** friend at the mall.*
Eles visitam **seus** amigos todo fim de semana.	*They visit **their** friends every weekend.*

The informal first-person plural "**a gente**" can be used in a similar way instead of the formal "**nosso(s)**" and "**nossa(s)**" forms:

our (informal)	o(s)/a(s) ... da gente	*the ... of us (the people)*

❖ The possessive adjective can come after the noun if the emphasis is placed on the possessor, e.g., "**um amigo <u>meu</u>**" (*a friend of <u>mine</u>*), "**aquela casa <u>sua</u>**" (*that house of <u>yours</u>*), etc.

❖ Possessive *adjectives* can be preceded with a definite article that agrees in gender and number with the possessive adjective. This may sound a little unfamiliar and less natural to English speakers. For example, both "**meus livros**" and "**os meus livros**" mean *"my books."* In general, adding the definite article before the possessive adjective is optional.

❖ Possessive *pronouns* are normally preceded with a definite article that agrees in gender and number with the possessive pronoun, e.g., "**Seu celular é melhor que <u>o meu</u>**" (*Your cell phone is better than <u>mine</u>*), "**A casa dela é maior que <u>a nossa</u>**" (*Her house is bigger than <u>ours</u>*). The only exception is after the verb "**ser**," where it is often dropped, e.g., "**Não é <u>seu</u>, é <u>meu</u>**" (*It is not <u>yours</u>, it's <u>mine</u>*), "**Essa casa é <u>nossa</u>**" (*That house is <u>ours</u>*).

❖ One can also insert the adjective "**proprio/-a**" *(own)* between the possessive pronoun and the noun for emphasis, e.g., "**o <u>próprio</u> telefone dele**" (*his <u>own</u> phone*), "**sua <u>própria</u> casa**" (*your <u>own</u> house*), etc. The plural forms of "**proprio**" and "**propria**" are "**proprios**" and "**proprias**," respectively, e.g., "**com as <u>próprias</u> mãos**" *(with one's <u>own</u> hands)*.

It is common in Portuguese to use the definite article instead of the possessive adjective when referring to members of one's family, "**Eles vão ficar com <u>o</u> pai**" *(They will stay with their father)*, "**Ele gosta de sair com <u>a</u> tia**" *(He likes to go out with his aunt)*, etc.

Possessive Adjectives & Pronouns in Italian

In Italian, possessive adjectives and pronouns must agree in gender and number with the noun they describe, except for the possessive "**loro**" *(their)*, which is invariable.

Moreover, the definite article must precede the possessive as an essential part that agrees with it in gender and number. This may sound a little unfamiliar and less natural to English speakers.

	Sing. Masc.	Sing. Fem.	Plural Masc.	Plural Fem.
my (mine)	il mio	la mia	i miei	le mie
your(s) (informal singular)	il tuo	la tua	i tuoi	le tue
his/her(s)/your(s) (form. sing.)	il suo	la sua	i suoi	le sue
our(s)	il nostro	la nostra	i nostri	le nostre
your(s) (informal plural)	il vostro	la vostra	i vostri	le vostre
their(s)/your(s) (formal plural)	il loro	la loro	i loro	le loro

❖ The *formal* possessive *"your(s)"* should be capitalized in plural "**il/la/i/le Loro**," and singular: "**il Suo**," "**la Sua**," "**i Suoi**," and "**le Sue**."

❖ Note that, unlike in English, the possessive adjective agrees in number and gender with the noun it describes and not the possessor, e.g., "**i miei fratelli**" (*my brothers*). Note that we use "**i miei**" because the *noun* we describe is *masculine* and *plural*, although the possessor is singular. Similarly, in the example "**le nostre madri**" (*our mothers*), the possessive adjective "**le nostre**" agrees in gender and number with the noun it describes.

❖ The possessive adjective can come after the noun if the emphasis is placed on the possessor and the noun is preceded by an indefinite article or a verb, e.g., "**un amico <u>mio</u>**" (*a friend of <u>mine</u>*), "**un problema <u>tuo</u>**" (<u>your</u> *problem*), "**Sono affari <u>tuoi</u>**" (*That's <u>your</u> business*), etc.

❖ One can also insert the adjective "**proprio/-a**" (*own*) between the possessive pronoun and the noun for emphasis, e.g., "**il suo proprio telefono**" (*his <u>own</u> phone*), "**la tua <u>propria</u> casa**" (*your <u>own</u> house*), etc. The plural forms of "**proprio**" and "**propria**" are "**propri**" and "**proprie**," respectively, e.g., "**con le <u>proprie</u> mani**" (*with one's <u>own</u> hands*).

❖ The definite article is *optional* and can be dropped after the verb "**essere**," e.g., "**Non è <u>tuo</u>, è <u>mio</u>**," (*It is not <u>yours</u>, it's <u>mine</u>*), "**Quella casa, è <u>nostra</u>**" (*That house is <u>ours</u>*).

❖ The definite article is not used to precede the possessive adjective with the following singular unmodified kinship nouns, except for "**loro**":

padre *(father)*	**marito** *(husband)*	**suocero** *(father-in-law)*
madre *(mother)*	**moglie** *(wife)*	**suocera** *(mother-in-law)*
figlio *(son)*	**zio** *(uncle)*	**cognato** *(brother-in-law)*
figlia *(daughter)*	**zia** *(aunt)*	**cognata** *(sister-in-law)*
fratello *(brother)*	**genero** *(son-in-law)*	**cugino** *(male cousin)*
sorella *(sister)*	**nuora** *(daughter-in-law)*	**cugina** *(female cousin)*

For example:

mio padre	*my father*
tua madre	*your mother*
sua zia	*his/her aunt*
le sue zie	*his/her aunts*
la sua zia vecchia	*his/her old aunt*
il loro figlio	*their brother*

Notice that, in the last three examples, the kinship name is either not singular, modified, or preceded by "**loro**." Thus, the definite article is needed before the possessive adjective.

The definite article is still needed, if a possessive pronoun is used, e.g., "**Mio padre sta bene, e il tuo,?**" *(My father is well, and yours?).*

The definite article with the following kinship nouns is optional, when singular and unmodified, except for "**loro**":

papà *(dad)*	e.g., mio papà	(or)	il mio papà
mamma *(mom)*	e.g., tua mamma	(or)	la tua mamma
nonno *(grandfather)*	e.g., suo nonno	(or)	il suo nonno
nonna *(grandmother)*	e.g., sua nonna	(or)	la sua nonna

Possessive Adjectives & Pronouns in French

In French, possessive adjectives and pronouns must agree in gender and number with the noun they describe.

The possessive adjectives are:

	Sing. Masc.	Sing. Fem.	Plural Masc.	Plural Fem.
my	mon	ma	mes	
your (informal singular)	ton	ta	tes	
his/her	son	sa	ses	
our	notre		nos	
your (plural or formal singular)	votre		vos	
their	leur		leurs	

On the other hand, the possessive pronouns in French are:

	Sing. Masc.	Sing. Fem.	Plural Masc.	Plural Fem.
mine	le mien	la mienne	les miens	les miennes
yours (informal singular)	le tien	la tienne	les tiens	les tiennes
his/hers	le sien	la sienne	les siens	les siennes
ours	le nôtre	la nôtre	les nôtres	
yours (plural or formal singular)	le vôtre	la vôtre	les vôtres	
theirs	le leur	la leur	les leurs	

❖ Note that the *masculine* form "**mon**," "**ton**," or "**son**" is used before a singular *feminine* noun that starts with a vowel or a mute "**h**," e.g., "**mon armoire**" *(my cabinet)*, "**son horloge**" *(his clock)*, etc.

❖ Note that, unlike in English, the possessive adjective agrees in number and gender with the noun it describes and not the possessor, e.g., "**mes frères**" *(my brothers)*. Note that we use "**mes**" because the *noun* we describe is *plural*, although the possessor is singular. Similarly, in the example "**sa mère**" *(his/her mother)*, the possessive adjective "**sa**" agrees in gender and number with the noun it describes, "**mère**," and can mean *"his"* or *"her"* depending on the gender of the possessor. The context often clears up this ambiguity.

❖ Another way to express possession is using the proposition "**à**" followed by a noun or object pronoun, e.g., "**C'est à toi**" *(This is yours)*, "**Je ne sais pas c'est à qui**" *(I don't know whose it is)*, "**Ce n'est pas à Robert**" *(It's not Robert's)*, etc.

❖ One can also insert the adjective "**propre(s)**" *(own)* between the possessive pronoun and the noun for emphasis, e.g., "**son propre téléphone**" *(his/her own phone)*, "**ta propre maison**" *(your own house)*, "**ses propres mains**" *(his/her own hands)*, etc.

4. DEMONSTRATIVE PRONOUNS & ADJECTIVES

Demonstrative adjectives (*this, that, these, those*) come before a noun, e.g., "*I want this book*," while possessive pronouns (same as demonstrative adjectives: *this, that, these, those*) are used to replace a noun and its possessive adjective, e.g., "*I want this*."

Demonstrative pronouns and adjectives must agree in gender and number with the noun being described.

Demonstrative Pronouns & Adjectives in Spanish

The following are the demonstrative adjectives in Spanish:

	Masc. Singular	Masc. Plural	Feminine Singular	Feminine Plural
this/these	este	estos	esta	estas
that/those	ese	esos	esa	esas
that/those (over there)	aquel	aquellos	aquella	aquellas

In general, **"este," "esta," "estos,"** and **"estas"** are used to refer to nouns close to the speaker and listener. On the other hand, **"ese," "esa," "esos,"** and **"esas"** are used to refer to nouns close to the listener but far away from the speaker, whereas **"aquel," "aquella," "aquellos,"** and **"aquellas"** are used to refer to nouns far away from both the speaker and the listener.

Demonstrative pronouns are the same as demonstrative adjectives in addition to the set of neuter demonstrative pronouns **"esto," "eso,"** and **"aquello,"** which mean *"this," "that,"* and *"that over there,"* respectively. These are used to refer to a whole sentence or concept, e.g., **"Esto no es aceptable"** (*This is not acceptable*), or to point at something without mentioning it, e.g., **"¿Qué es eso?"** (*What is that?*). The following are the demonstrative pronouns in Spanish:

	Masc. Sing.	Masc. Plural	Fem. Sing.	Fem. Plural	Neuter
this/these	este	estos	esta	estas	esto
that/those	ese	esos	esa	esas	eso
that/those (over there)	aquel	aquellos	aquella	aquellas	aquello

Demonstrative Pronouns & Adjectives in Portuguese

Demonstrative adjectives and pronouns in Portuguese are similar to those in Spanish.

The following are the demonstrative adjectives in Portuguese:

	Masc. Singular	Masc. Plural	Feminine Singular	Feminine Plural
this/these	este	estes	esta	estas
that/those	esse	esses	essa	essas
that/those (over there)	aquele	aqueles	aquela	aquelas

In general, "**este**," "**esta**," "**estes**," and "**estas**" are used to refer to nouns close to the speaker and listener. On the other hand, "**esse**," "**essa**," "**esses**," and "**essas**" are used to refer to nouns close to the listener but far away from the speaker, whereas "**aquele**," "**aquela**," "**aqueles**," and "**aquelas**" are used to refer to nouns far away from both the speaker and the listener.

Demonstrative pronouns are the same as demonstrative adjectives in addition to the set of invariable neuter demonstrative pronouns "**isto**," "**isso**," and "**aquilo**," which mean *"this," "that,"* and *"that over there,"* respectively. The neuter demonstrative pronouns have no gender or plural forms. These are used to refer to a whole sentence or concept, e.g., "**Isto não é aceitável**" (*This is not acceptable*), or to point at something without mentioning it, e.g., "**O que é isso?**" (*What is that?*). The following are the demonstrative pronouns in Portuguese:

	Masc. Sing.	Masc. Plural	Fem. Sing.	Fem. Plural	Neuter
this/these	este	estes	esta	estas	isto
that/those	esse	esses	essa	essas	isso
that/those (over there)	aquele	aqueles	aquela	aquelas	aquilo

Demonstrative Pronouns & Adjectives in Italian

Demonstrative pronouns and adjectives in Italian are more challenging.

Let us start with the demonstrative pronouns:

	Masc. Singular	Feminine Singular	Masc. Plural	Feminine Plural
this (one)/these (ones)	questo	questa	questi	queste
that (one)/those (ones)	quello	quella	quelli	quelle

In general, "**questo**," "**questa**," "**questi**," and "**queste**" are used to refer to nouns close to the speaker. On the other hand, "**quello**," "**quella**," "**quelli**," and "**quelle**" are used to refer to nouns far away from the speaker.

Let us take some examples:

A: Which chair do you want? B: *That one.*	A: Quale sedia[f] vuoi? B: **Quella**.
A: Which language do you prefer? B: *This one.*	A: Quale lingua[f] preferisci? B: **Questa**.
A: Which books did you read? B: *These ones.*	A: Quali libri[m] hai letto? B: **Questi**.
A: Which cell phone do you use? B: *This one.*	A: Quale cellulare[m] utilizzi? B: **Questo**.
A: Which schools are the best? B: *Those ones.*	A: Quali scuole[f] sono le migliori? B: **Quelle**.

The demonstrative pronouns "**questo**" and "**quello**" can also be used to refer to a whole sentence or concept, e.g., "**Questo non è accettabile**" (*This is not acceptable*), or to point at something without mentioning it, e.g., "**Deve essere quello**" (*It has to be that*).

Let us now examine the demonstrative adjectives.

In the case of the demonstrative adjectives of nearness, i.e., *"this"* and *"these,"* the demonstrative adjectives are identical to the demonstrative pronouns, that is, "**questo**," "**questa**," "**questi**," and "**queste**." For example, "**questo ragazzo**" *(this boy)*, "**questa macchina**" *(this car)*.

Notice that it is optional to use the form "**quest'**" instead of "**questo**" or "**questa**" before a noun that begins with a vowel, e.g., "**quest'amica**" *(this friend)* is short for "**questa amica**."

In the case of the demonstrative adjectives of farness, i.e., *"that"* and *"those,"* recall from **Level I, Lesson 7** that "**quello**" is one of two common adjectives that change form like the definite articles, depending on the number and gender of the following noun and whether the noun begins with a vowel or certain consonants.

	l'	lo	il	la	i	gli	le
quello	quell'	quello	quel	quella	quei	quegli	quelle

To summarize, the following are the demonstrative adjectives in Italian:

	Masc. Singular	Feminine Singular	Masc. Plural	Feminine Plural
this/these	questo	questa	questi	queste
that/those	quell'$^{(V)}$ quello$^{(Z)}$ quel	quell'$^{(V)}$ quella	quegli$^{(V)(Z)}$ quei	quelle

$^{(V)}$ before a noun (or preceding adjective) that begins with a **vowel**
$^{(Z)}$ before a noun (or preceding adjective) that begins with "**z**," "**gn**," "**ps**," or "**s**" + consonant

Let us take some examples:

A: Which chair do you want? B: *That chair.*	A: Quale sedia^f vuoi? B: **Quella** sedia.
A: Which language do you prefer? B: *This language.*	A: Quale lingua^f preferisci? B: **Questa** lingua.
A: Which books did you read? B: *These books.*	A: Quali libri^m hai letto? B: **Questi** libri.
A: Which cell phone do you use? B: *This cell phone.*	A: Quale cellulare^m utilizzi? B: **Questo** cellulare.
A: Which schools are the best? B: *Those schools.*	A: Quali scuole^f sono le migliori? B: **Quelle** scuole.
A: Which of your uncles lives here? B: *That uncle.*	A: Quale dei tuoi zii^m abita qui? B: **Quello** zio.
A: Which lawyers have you contacted? B: *Those lawyers.*	A: Quali avvocati^m hai contattato? B: **Quegli** avvocati.

| A: Which pants should I wear?
B: _Those_ pants. | A: Quali pantaloni[m] dovrei indossare?
B: **Quei** pantaloni. |
| A: Which of your friends works here?
B: _That_ friend. | A: Quale dei tuoi amici[m] lavora qui?
B: **Quell'** amico. |

Demonstrative Pronouns & Adjectives in French

In French, the demonstratives pronouns and adjectives are slightly different.

Let us start with the demonstrative adjectives.

	Masc. Singular	Feminine Singular	Masc. Plural	Feminine Plural
this/that/these/those	ce/cet	cette	ces	

In French, the demonstrative adjectives "**ce**," "**cet**," and "**cette**" can mean both _"this"_ and _"that."_ The demonstrative adjective "**cet**" is used before a singular masculine noun that starts with a vowel or mute "**h**," e.g., "**cet arbre**" _(this/that tree)_, "**cet homme**" _(this/that man)_, etc., whereas "**ce**" is used before any other singular masculine noun, e.g., "**ce garcon**" _(this/that boy)_. The demonstrative adjective "**cette**" is used before a singular feminine noun.

Similarly, "**ces**" can mean both _"these"_ and _"those."_ There is no real distinction of nearness and farness in the simple forms of the demonstrative adjectives.

To make such a distinction, we can add "**-ci**" or "**-là**" after the noun, for example:

ce livre-ci	_this book_	ce livre-là	_that book_
cet homme-ci	_this man_	cet homme-là	_that man_
cette femme-ci	_this woman_	cette femme-là	_that woman_
ces chemises-ci	_these shirts_	ces chemises-là	_those shirts_

Let us now examine the demonstrative pronouns:

	Masc. Singular	Feminine Singular	Masc. Plural	Feminine Plural
this/that (one) **these/those (ones)**	celui	celle	ceux	celles

In general, "**celui**," "**celle**," "**ceux**," and "**celles**" do not appear on their own. They can appear with "**-ci**" or "**-là**" attached to the end of the demonstrative pronoun, or followed by "**que**," "**qui**," "**de**," or a prepositional phrase. In the latter case, the demonstrative pronoun is often translated as *"the one(s)."* Let us look at some examples:

*Do you want this book or **that one**?*	Voulez-vous ce livre ou **celui-là**?
*I have two cars; **this one** is my favorite.*	J'ai deux voitures; **celle-ci** est ma préférée.
*For **those** who are overweight, exercise is very important.*	Pour **ceux** qui sont en surpoids, l'exercice est très important.
*I'm looking for the car; not mine but Pierre's (**that** of Pierre).*	Je cherche la voiture; pas la mienne mais **celle** de Pierre.
*Which shirts? **The ones** that are there are not mine.*	Quelles chemises? **Celles** qui sont là ne sont pas les miennes.

When referring to a statement, an indefinite thing, or a previously mentioned idea, we use one of the following pronouns:

ce/c'	*this/that*	Used with the verb "**être**"	*informal*
ça	*this/that*	Used with verbs other than "**être**"	
ceci	*this*	Both "**ceci**" and "**cela**" can be used with any verb including "**être**"	*formal*
cela	*that*		

The pronouns "**ce**" and "**ça**" are often used in familiar situations in daily spoken language. The pronoun "**ce**" (or "**c'**" before a vowel or a mute "**h**") is used before the verb "**être**" *(to be)*, whereas "**ça**" is used with other verbs.

On the other hand, the pronouns "**ceci**" *(this)* and "**cela**" *(that)* are more formal and are often encountered in written French.

Here are some examples:

***That** is interesting.*	**C'est** intéressant.
***This** is a good idea.*	**C'est** une bonne idée.
***That** is good news.*	**Ce** sont de bonnes nouvelles.
*Look at **that**.*	Regarde **ça**.
*I didn't say **that**.*	Je n'ai pas dit **ça**.
***This** is not acceptable.*	**Ceci** n'est pas acceptable.
***That** has already been discussed.*	**Cela** a déjà été discuté.

5. OBJECT PERSONAL PRONOUNS

Object pronouns can be divided into three classes: *prepositional*, *direct*, and *indirect* object pronouns.

Prepositional Object Pronouns

Prepositional object pronouns come after a preposition, such as *"about," "from," "in," "on," "of," "with," "without,"* etc. Prepositional object pronouns are the same as subject pronouns in most cases except in the underlined cases in the following table.

	Subj. Pron.	Prep. Obj. Pronoun	Examples	
SP	yo	mí	Ellos hablan de **mí**.	
PT	eu	mim	Eles falam de **mim**.	
IT	io	me	Parlano di **me**.	*They talk about* **me**.
FR	je	moi	Ils parlent de **moi**.	
SP	tú	ti	Este regalo es para **ti**.	
PT	você	você	Este presente é para **você**.	
IT	tu	te	Questo regalo è per **te**.	*This gift is for* **you**.
FR	tu	toi	Ce cadeau est pour **toi**.	
SP	él	él	Salgo con **él**.	
PT	ele	ele	Eu saio com **ele**.	
IT	lui	lui	Esco con **lui**.	*I go out with* **him**.
FR	il	lui	Je sors avec **lui**.	
SP	ella	ella	Salgo con **ella**.	
PT	ela	ela	Eu saio com **ela**.	
IT	lei	lei	Esco con **lei**.	*I go out with* **her**.
FR	elle	elle	Je sors avec **elle**.	
SP	nosotros	nosotros	No está contra **nosotros**.	
PT	nós	nós	Ele não está contra **nós**.	
IT	noi	noi	Non è contro di **noi**.	*He is not against* **us**.
FR	nous	nous	Il n'est pas contre **nous**.	
SP	ustedes	ustedes	Confío en **ustedes**.	
PT	vocês	vocês	Eu confio em **vocês**.	
IT	voi	voi	Mi fido di **voi**.	*I trust in* **you**.
FR	vous	vous	Ce cadeau est pour **vous**.	
SP	ellos/-as	ellos/-as	No voy sin **ellos**.	
PT	eles/elas	eles/elas	Eu não vou sem **eles**.	
IT	loro	loro	Non vado senza di **loro**.	*I won't go without* **them**.
FR	ils/elles	eux	Je ne pars pas sans **eux**.	

The reflexive prepositional pronouns are a special case of the prepositional object pronouns, such as *"myself," "yourself," "himself,"* etc. This is used when the subject and the object pronoun refer to the same person.

	Subj. Pron.	Ref. Prep. Obj. Pron.	Examples	
SP	yo	mí	Yo no hablo de **mí**.	*I don't talk about **myself**.*
PT	eu	mim	Eu não falo de **mim**.	
IT	io	me	Non parlo di **me**.	
FR	je	moi	Je ne parle pas de **moi**.	
SP	tú	ti	Compraste un regalo para **ti**.	*You bought a gift for **yourself**.*
PT	você	você	Comprou um presente para **você**.	
IT	tu	te	Hai comprato un regalo per **te**.	
FR	tu	toi	Tu as acheté un cadeau pour **toi**-même.	
SP	él	sí	Él se alaba a **sí** mismo.	*He praises **himself**.*
PT	ele	si	Ele elogia a **si** mesmo.	
IT	lui	se	Lui loda **se** stesso.	
FR	il	lui	Elle se loue **lui**-même	
SP	ella	sí	Ella se alaba a **sí** misma.	*She praises **herself**.*
PT	ela	si	Ela elogia a **si** mesma.	
IT	lei	se	Lei loda **se** stessa.	
FR	elle	elle	Elle se loue **elle**-même.	
SP	nosotros	nosotros	Lo hacemos para **nosotros**.	*We do it for **ourselves**.*
PT	nós	nós	Nós fazemos isso por **nós**.	
IT	noi	noi	Lo facciamo per **noi**.	
FR	nous	nous	Nous le faisons pour **nous**-mêmes.	
SP	ustedes	ustedes	Piensan solo en **ustedes**.	*You only think of **yourselves**.*
PT	vocês	vocês	Vocês só pensa em **vocês** mesmos.	
IT	voi	voi	Pensate solo a **voi**.	
FR	vous	vous	Vous ne pensez qu'à **vous**.	
SP	ellos/-as	sí	Ellos hablan de **sí** mismos.	*They talk about **themselves**.*
PT	eles/elas	si	Eles querem tudo para **si**.	
IT	loro	se	Parlano di **se** stessi.	
FR	ils/elles	eux	Ils parlent d'**eux**-mêmes	

More often than not, the reflexive prepositional object pronoun is followed by the following adjective meaning *"same"* for emphasis:

	Masculine Singular	Feminine Singular	Masculine Plural	Feminine Plural
SP	mismo	misma	mismos	mismas
PT	mesmo	mesma	mesmos	mesmas
IT	stesso	stessa	stessi	stesse
FR	même		mêmes	

Direct and Indirect Object Pronouns

The second and third classes of object pronouns are direct and indirect object pronouns. This tends to be one of the most challenging grammar lessons for English-speaking students. Nevertheless, the use of direct and indirect objects is so ubiquitous that we feel obliged to cover it at this beginner level. Feel free to return to this lesson at times of confusion if you do not fully grasp all the details.

Before we delve into the details, let us first define the difference between the two classes, since the distinction in English is not always clear. The direct object is the noun directly acted upon, whereas the indirect object is usually the noun (or person) receiving the direct object. For example, in the expressions *"He gives it to us"* and *"I give it to you,"* the *"it"* is the direct object acted upon in both examples, whereas *"us"* is the indirect object in the first example and *"you"* in the second. In English, we use *"me," "you," "him," "her," "us,"* and *"them,"* regardless of whether we are referring to a direct or indirect object. In Spanish, Portuguese, Italian, and French, there are some differences:

❖ The direct and indirect object pronouns generally come before the verb, e.g., in Spanish: **"Nos lo da"** (He gives *it* to *us*). Attachment to the end of the verb will be discussed as an exception.

❖ The indirect object always comes before the direct object when they are both in the same sentence. One exception is in French when the indirect object is in the third person, in which case the indirect object comes *after* the direct object.

❖ Unlike in English, we do not add the equivalent of *"to"* before the indirect object, e.g., *"I give it to you"* becomes **"Te lo doy"** in Spanish, where **"te"** means *"to you"* in this context.

Now, let us learn the direct and indirect object pronouns and their equivalents in English.

	Direct Object Pronoun	Indirect Object Pronoun	English Equivalent
SP	me	me	me
PT	me	me	
IT	mi	mi	
FR	me (m')	me (m')	
SP	te	te	you (informal singular)
PT	o/a	lhe	
IT	ti	ti	
FR	te (t')	te (t')	
SP	lo/la	le	him/her/it/you (formal singular)
PT	o/a	lhe	
IT	lo/la	gli/le	
FR	le (l')/ la (l')	lui	
SP	nos	nos	us
PT	nos	nos	
IT	ci	ci	
FR	nous	nous	
SP	los/las	les	you (informal plural)
PT	os/as	lhes	
IT	vi	vi	
FR	vous	vous	
SP	los/las	les	them/you (formal plural)
PT	os/as	lhes	
IT	li/le	gli/gli	
FR	les	leur	

Note that, in Italian, the direct and indirect objects for the formal *"you,"* in singular and plural forms, should be capitalized.

Let us take some examples:

He knows me.	**SP**	Él **me** conoce.	"**me**" is a direct object
	PT	Ele **me** conhece.	"**me**" is a direct object
	IT	Lui **mi** conosce.	"**mi**" is a direct object
	FR	Il **me** connaît.	"**me**" is a direct object
He knows us.	**SP**	Él **nos** conoce.	"**nos**" is a direct obj.
	PT	Ele **nos** conhece.	"**nos**" is a direct obj.
	IT	Lui **ci** conosce.	"**ci**" is a direct object
	FR	Il **nous** connaît.	"**nous**" is a direct obj.
That book! I want it. *That pen! I want it.*	**SP**	¡Este libro! **Lo** quiero. ¡Esa pluma! **La** quiero.	Depending on gender, "**lo**" or "**la**" is used
	PT	Aquele livro! Eu **o** quero. Essa caneta! Eu **a** quero.	Depending on gender, "**o**" or "**a**" is used
	IT	Quel libro! **Lo** voglio. Quella penna! **La** voglio.	Depending on gender, "**lo**" or "**la**" is used
	FR	Ce livre! Je **le** veux. Ce stylo! Je **le** veux.	Depending on gender, "**le**" or "**la**" is used
I know him. *I will give him something.*	**SP**	**Lo** conozco. **Le** daré algo.	"**lo**" is a direct object "**le**" is an indirect obj.
	PT	Eu **o** conheço. Vou dar-**lhe** algo.	"**o**" is a direct object "**lhe**" is an indirect obj.
	IT	**Lo** conosco. **Gli** darò qualcosa.	"**lo**" is a direct object "**gli**" is an indirect obj.
	FR	Je **le** connais. Je **lui** donnerai quelque chose.	"**le**" is a direct object "**lui**" is an indirect obj.
I know her. *I will give her something.*	**SP**	**La** conozco. **Le** daré algo.	"**la**" is a direct object "**le**" is an indirect obj.
	PT	Eu **a** conheço. Vou dar-**lhe** algo.	"**a**" is a direct object "**lhe**" is an indirect obj.
	IT	**La** conosco. **Le** darò qualcosa.	"**la**" is a direct object "**le**" is an indirect obj.
	FR	Je **la** connais. Je **lui** donnerai quelque chose.	"**la**" is a direct object "**lui**" is an indirect obj.
Those guys! I know them. *I will give them something.*	**SP**	¡Esos tipos! **Los** conozco **Les** daré algo.	"**los**" is a direct object "**les**" is an indirect obj.
	PT	Aqueles rapazes! Eu **os** conheço. Eu **lhes** darei algo.	"**os**" is a direct object "**lhes**" is an indirect obj.
	IT	Quei ragazzi! **Li** conosco. **Gli** darò qualcosa.	"**li**" is a direct object "**gli**" is an indirect obj.
	FR	Ces gars! Je **les** connais. Je **leur** donnerai quelque chose.	"**les**" is a direct object "**leur**" is an indirect obj.

Those girls! I know them. *I will give them something.*	**SP**	¡Esas chicas! **Las** conozco. **Les** daré algo.	"las" is a direct object "les" is an indirect obj.
	PT	Essas garotas! Eu **as** conheço. Eu **lhes** darei algo.	"as" is a direct object "lhes" is an indirect obj.
	IT	Quelle ragazze! **Le** conosco. **Gli** darò qualcosa.	"le" is a direct object "gli" is an indirect obj.
	FR	Ces gars! Je **les** connais. Je **leur** donnerai quelque chose.	"les" is a direct object "leur" is an indirect obj.

In daily spoken Portuguese, we use the following informal sets of the direct and indirect object pronouns:

Direct Object Pronoun	Indirect Object Pronoun	English Equivalent
me	me para mim	me
você/te	para você/ti	you (singular)
ele/ela	para ele/ela	him/her
nos	nos para nós	us
eles/elas	para eles/elas	them/you (plural)

The first-person singular and plural indirect object pronouns have unstressed forms, i.e., "**me**" and "**nos**," and stressed forms, i.e., "**para mim**" and "**para nós**." For example, the sentence *"He sent me a letter"* can be translated using one of two forms:

Ele **me** enviou uma carta.	*formal or unstressed informal*
Ele enviou uma carta **para mim**.	*stressed informal*

There are two ways to express the second-person informal singular direct object pronoun *"you"* in spoken Portuguese: using "**você**" after the verb, or more colloquially using "**te**" before the verb. Remember that the formal written direct object pronoun meaning *"you"* is "**o**" or "**a**," depending on the gender of the addressee. Thus, the following three sentences can have the same meaning:

Eu **o/a** amo (a você).	
Eu amo **você**.	*I love you.*
Eu **te** amo.	

The formal second-person *"you"* can also be expressed using the indirect object pronouns **"para o senhor"** and **"para a senhora"** for masculine and feminine, respectively. For example:

Vou vender a casa **para o senhor**.	*I will sell **you** the house, sir.*
Vou vender a casa **para a senhora**.	*I will sell **you** the house, madam.*

Attaching Object Pronouns to Verb Ends

Now, let us look at the three cases in which the direct or indirect object pronoun attaches to the end of the verb. Object pronouns attach to the infinitive, gerund, or affirmative imperative. Keep in mind that attachment is optional in some of the cases above. Notice that, in French, only in the case of the affirmative imperative, the object pronoun is attached to the end of the verb.

SP	Quiero hacer<u>lo</u>. (or) <u>Lo</u> quiero hacer.	*I want to do <u>it</u>.*	obj. pron. + infinitive
PT	Eu quero fazê-<u>lo</u>. (or) Eu <u>o</u> quero fazer.		
IT	Voglio far<u>lo</u>.		
FR	Je veux <u>le</u> faire.		
SP	<u>Lo</u> estoy viendo. (or) Estoy viendo<u>lo</u>.	*I am watching <u>it</u>.*	direct obj. pron. + gerund
PT	Eu <u>o</u> estou vendo. (or) Eu estou vendo-<u>o</u>.		
IT	Sto guardando<u>lo</u>.		
FR	Je <u>le</u> regarde.		
SP	Ábre<u>lo</u>.	*Open <u>it</u>.*	dir. obj. pron. + imperative
PT	Abra-<u>o</u>.		
IT	Apri<u>lo</u>.		
FR	Ouvrez-<u>le</u>.		
SP	Píde<u>le</u> dinero.	*Ask <u>him</u> for money.*	ind. obj. pron. + imperative
PT	Peça-<u>lhe</u> dinheiro.		
IT	Chiedi<u>gli</u> dei soldi.		
FR	Demandez-<u>lui</u> de l'argent.		

Notice that in Portuguese, the object pronouns **"me,"** **"te,"** **"o(s),"** **"a(s),"** **"se,"** **"nos,"** and **"lhe(s)"** can be placed before the verb or attached, with a hyphen, to the end the verb. Let us consider these cases:

1. In formal writing, one must not start a sentence or phrase with an object pronoun. If the explicit subject is removed, the object pronoun is attached to the end the verb.

Eu **o** vejo. Vejo-**o**.	*I see **him**.*
Eu **lhe** mando cartas. Mando-**lhe** cartas.	*I send **him** letters.*

In informal spoken language, there is no such restriction. Avoiding object pronoun attachment to the verb-end can sound more natural in an informal dialogue.

2. If the subject is a noun, rather than a subject pronoun, attachment to the verb-end is optional and tends to be more formal. For example:

O homem **o** visitou. O homem visitou-**o**.	*The man visited **him**.*
Os fãs **lhe** mandam cartas. Os fãs mandam-**lhe** cartas.	*The fans send **him** letters.*

3. Object pronouns often attach to the infinitive in formal writing, but are placed before the infinitive in informal speech.

Ele quer **me** ver. Ele quer ver-**me**.	*He wants to see **me**.*
Ela quer **nos** ligar. Ela quer ligar-**nos**.	*She wants to call **us**.*

If the object pronoun is "**o(s)**" or "**a(s)**," the pronoun is changed to "**lo(s)**" or "**la(s)**," respectively, and the final "**r**" of the infinitive is dropped. For example:

Eu **o** quero ver. Quero vê-**lo**.	*I want to see **him**.*
Eu **os** quero enviar. Quero enviá-**los**.	*I want to send **them**.*

4. If the verb is in the first-person plural ending in "-**mos**" and the object pronouns is "**o(s)**" or "**a(s)**," the pronoun is changed to "**lo(s)**" or "**la(s)**," respectively, and the final "**s**" of the verb ending is dropped. For example:

Nós **a** visitamos. Visitamo-**la**.	*We visit **her**.*
Nós **os** vemos. Vemo-**los**.	*We see **them**.*

5. If the verb ends in a nasal sound "-**am**," "-**em**," "-**ão**," or "-**õe**," and the object pronouns is "**o(s)**" or "**a(s)**," the pronoun is changed to "**no(s)**" or "**na(s)**," respectively. For example:

Eles **o** visitam. Visitam-**no**.	*They visit **him**.*
Ela **os** põe em risco. Ela põe-**nos** em risco.	*She puts **them** at risk.*

Combining Direct and Indirect Object Pronouns

We will examine how to combine direct and indirect objects in the same sentence in Spanish, Italian, and French through the following two examples:

❖ Let us take the example: *"She sells me the house."* This translates to:

SP	Ella **me** vende la casa.
IT	Lei **mi** vende la casa.
FR	Elle **me** vend la maison.

In the above example, we recognize that *"the house"* is the direct object being acted upon, i.e., being sold, whereas *"me"* is the indirect object that receives the direct object, i.e., the house is being sold *to me.*

Let us first focus on the direct object in *"She sells the house."* If we remove the direct object, *"the house,"* to say *"She sells it,"* we must use the proper direct object pronoun meaning *"it."* Since *"the house"* is feminine is Spanish, Italian, and French, we must use **"la"**:

SP	Ella la vende.
IT	Lei la vende.
FR	Elle la vend.

Next, we add the indirect object meaning *"to me" before* the direct object **"la"** to say *"She sells it to me"*:

SP	Ella me la vende.
IT	Lei me la vende.
FR	Elle me la vend.

Notice that in Italian, when the indirect object **"mi"** is followed by the direct object **"la,"** the indirect object is changed to **"me."**

As a general rule, in Italian, when the indirect object **"mi,"** **"ti,"** **"ci,"** or **"vi"** is followed by the direct object **"lo,"** **"la,"** **"li,"** or **"le,"** the indirect object is changed to **"me,"** **"te,"** **"ce,"** or **"ve,"** respectively.

mi/ti/ci/vi +	lo	=	me/te/ce/ve lo
	la	=	me/te/ce/ve la
	li	=	me/te/ce/ve li
	le	=	me/te/ce/ve le

❖ Let us take another example: *"I send him a gift."* This translates to:

SP	Yo le mando un regalo.
IT	Io gli mando un regalo.
FR	Je lui envoie un cadeau.

Here, *"a gift"* is the direct object, whereas *"him"* is the indirect object.

Let us first focus on the direct object *"I send a gift ...."* If we remove the direct object *"a gift"* to say *"I send it ...,"* we must use the proper direct object pronoun meaning *"it."* Since *"a gift"* is masculine in Spanish, Italian, and French, we must use **"lo"** in Spanish and Italian, and **"le"** in French:

SP	Yo lo mando.
IT	Io lo mando.
FR	Je l'envoie

Next, we add the indirect object meaning *"to him"* to say *"I send it to him"*:

SP	Yo se lo mando.
IT	Io glielo mando.
FR	Je le lui envoie

Note the following:

1. In Spanish, to avoid alliteration when saying **"le lo"** in this case, one must replace the indirect object with **"se."** Thus, we instead say: **"Yo se lo mando."**

   As a general rule to avoid *alliteration*:

   (le/les)   +   (lo/la/los/las)   =   **se** (lo/la/los/las)

*I send **them to her**.*	Yo **se los** mando.	*le + los = se los*
*I send **it to them**.*	Yo **se lo** mando.	*les + lo = se lo*

2. In Italian, when the indirect object **"gli"** is followed by the direct object **"lo,"** they form one word **"glielo."**
   As a general rule, the indirect object **"gli"** or **"le"** is followed by the direct object **"lo," "la," "li,"** or **"le,"** they form one word:

gli/le +	lo	=	glielo
	la	=	gliela
	li	=	glieli
	le	=	gliele

Here are a few more examples:

I send *them to her*.	Io **glieli** mando.	*le + li = glieli*
I send *it to them*.	Io **glielo** mando.	*gli + lo = glielo*
I send *her to them*.	Io **gliela** mando.	*gli + la = gliela*

3. In French, when the indirect object is in the third person, i.e., "**lui**" *(to him/her)* or "**leur**" *(to them)*, the indirect object is placed *after* the direct object. Here are a few more examples:

I send *them to her*.	Je **les** **lui** envoie.
I send *it to them*.	Je **le** **leur** envoie.
I send *her to them*.	Je **la** **leur** envoie.

In Portuguese, we can also combine direct and indirect object pronouns in the same sentence. In this case, we often place the direct object pronoun before the verb and the indirect object pronoun after the verb, as shown in the following two examples:

Ela **me** vende **a casa**.	*She sells **me the house**.*
Ela **a** vende.	*She sells **it**.*
Ela **a** vende **para mim**.	*She sells **it to me**.*
Eu **lhe** dou **um presente**.	*I give **him a gift**.*
Eu **o** dou.	*I give **it**.*
Eu **o** dou **para ele**.	*I give **it to him**.*

6. RELATIVE PRONOUNS

Most interrogative pronouns can be used as relative pronouns, e.g., *"Here is where I want to be," "I will tell you when I remember,"* etc. Here is a summary of some relative pronouns in Spanish, Portuguese, and Italian:

Relative pronoun	English meaning	Examples
que (SP)(PT) che (IT)	*that* *who*	**EN**: *The tea **that** you like is here.* **SP**: El té **que** te gusta está acá. **PT**: O chá **que** você gosta está aqui. **IT**: Il tè **che** ti piace è qui.
quien(es) (SP) quem (PT) cui (IT)	*who* *which* *whom*	**EN**: *This is the person with **whom** I talked.* **SP**: Es la persona con **quien** hablé. **PT**: É a pessoa com **quem** falei. **IT**: Questa è la persona con **cui** ho parlato.
cuyo, cuya, cuyos, cuyas (SP) cujo, cuja, cujos, cujas (PT) il cui, la cui, i cui, le cui (IT)	*whose*	**EN**: *This is the man **whose** two sons are doctors.* **SP**: Es el hombre **cuyos** dos hijos son médicos. **PT**: Ele é o homem **cujos** dois filhos são médicos. **IT**: È l'uomo **i cui** due figli sono dottori.
el cual, la cual, los cuales, las cuales (SP) o qual, a qual, os quais, as quais (PT) il quale, la quale, i quali, le quali (IT)	*which*	**EN**: *They are discussing an important topic, one **which** affects you.* **SP**: Ellos discuten sobre un tema importante, **el cual** te afecta. **PT**: Eles discutem um tópico importante, **o qual** afeta você. **IT**: Discutono di un argomento importante, **il quale** ti riguarda.

In Italian, the relative pronoun "**chi**" can be used to refer only to a person or persons, and cannot refer to a thing or a place. It is always singular even if it refers to multiple persons, and is often used in proverbs and general statements meaning *"those who"* or *"whoever,"* e.g., "**Chi vince, detta le regole**" (*Whoever wins sets the rules*), "**Non mi piace chi giura**" (*I don't like those who swear*), etc.

As a general rule, if you refer to a person and follow that by a simple relative pronoun such as *"who"* or *"that,"* "**che**" is often used instead, e.g., "**Il mio amico, che è ingegnere, me lo ha detto**" (*My friend, who is an engineer, told me this*).

The following is a summary in the context of some examples:

EN: *This is the restaurant **that** opened last week.* **SP**: Este es el restaurante **que** abrió la semana pasada. **PT**: Este é o restaurante **que** abriu na semana passada. **IT**: Questo è il ristorante **che** ha aperto la scorsa settimana.	Referring to a place using the simple relative pronoun *"that"* right after the noun. Thus, use "**que**" in Spanish and Portuguese, and "**che**" in Italian.
EN: *This is the teacher **who** taught me.* **SP**: Es el profesor **que** me enseñó. **PT**: É o professor **que** me ensinou. **IT**: Questo è l'insegnante **che** mi ha insegnato.	Referring to a person using the simple relative pronoun *"who"* right after the noun. Thus, use "**que**" in Spanish and Portuguese, and "**che**" in Italian.
EN: *They are the players **with** **whom** I used to play.* **SP**: Ellos son los jugadores **con quienes** yo jugaba. **PT**: São os jogadores **com quem** joguei. **IT**: Sono i giocatori **con cui** giocavo.	Referring to a person using the relative pronoun *"whom"* preceded by a preposition. Thus, use "**quien(es)**" in Spanish, "**quem**" in Portuguese, and "**cui**" in Italian.

Relative Pronouns in French

In French, relative pronouns function differently from their English counterparts. Thus, it is difficult to have a direct translation. Consider the following examples of the relative pronouns "**qui**," "**que**," and "**dont**," which can refer to persons or things:

C'est le livre **qui** a remporté le prix.	*This is the book **that** won the award.*
C'est le livre **que** j'ai acheté.	*This is the book **that** I bought.*
C'est le livre **dont** je parlais.	*This is the book **that** I was talking about.*

In the above example, the relative pronouns "**qui**," "**que**," and "**dont**" are all translated as *"that."* The relative pronoun "**qui**" is used when referring to a *subject*, i.e., *"the book that won the award."* The relative pronoun "**que**" is used when referring to an *object*, i.e., *"the book that I bought."* Finally, the relative pronoun "**dont**" is used when referring to an *object* of a verb or verbal expression that includes the preposition "**de**," such as: "**parler de**" *(talk about)*, "**avoir besoin de**" *(to need)*, etc.

Similarly, the relative pronouns "**qui**," "**que**," and "**dont**" can refer to people and have different meanings:

C'est le garçon **qui** jouait ici.	*This is the boy **who** used to play here.*
C'est le médecin **que** j'ai consulté.	*This is the doctor **whom** I consulted.*
C'est le genre de joueur **dont** notre équipe a besoin.	*This is the kind of player **that** our team needs.*
C'est l'homme **dont** les deux fils sont médecins.	*This is the man **whose** two sons are doctors.*

Notice that "**qui**" is used when referring to a *subject*, i.e., *"the boy who used to play here;"* "**que**" is used when referring to an *object*, i.e., *"the doctor I consulted;"* and "**dont**" is used when referring to an *object* of a verb or verbal expression that includes the preposition "**de**," in this case: "**avoir besoin de**" *(to need)*, i.e., *"the player that our team needs."* The relative pronoun "**dont**" is also used to express possession if the verb is preceded by the subject and followed by the object. In this case, it is often translated as *"whose," "of which,"* or *"of whom."*

Another relative pronoun that can also mean *"that," "which,"* or *"whom"* is "**lequel**" and its gender and number variants: "**laquelle**," "**lequels**," and "**lesquelles**." When preceded by a preposition, these pronouns are often used to refer to things more specifically. When referring to people, "**qui**" preceded with a preposition is often used instead, for example:

Ce sont les joueurs <u>avec</u> **lesquels** je jouais.	*They are the players <u>with</u> **whom** I used to play.*
Je nettoierai la chaise <u>derrière</u> **laquelle** le chat joue.	*I will clean the chair <u>behind</u> **which** the cat plays.*
C'est le bâtiment <u>dans</u> **lequel** je vis.	*This is the building <u>in</u> **which** I live.*
C'est la personne <u>à</u> **qui** ils ont demandé.	*This is the person **whom** they asked.*

Notice that "**lequel**" (and its gender and number variants) is treated the same way as the definite article when contracted with the preceding preposition, e.g., "**C'est le projet <u>auquel</u> je pense**" *(This is the project I am thinking of).*

We have previously encountered the interrogative pronoun "**où**," meaning *"where."* As a relative pronoun, it is used meaning *"where"* or *"when,"* referring to a certain moment of time. Here are some examples:

C'est **où** je veux être maintenant.	*This is **where** I want to be now.*
Nous ne savons pas **où** aller.	*We don't know **where** to go.*
C'est le moment **où** j'ai pris la décision.	*This is the time **when** I made the decision.*
Il a probablement appelé au moment **où** j'étais occupé.	*He probably called at the time **when** I was busy.*

Another common pronoun that means *"when"* is "**lorsque**," e.g., "**Dis-moi lorsqe tu es de retour**" *(Tell me when you are back).* Remember that "**quand**" can be used as an interrogative or relative pronoun, whereas "**lorsque**" cannot be used as an interrogative pronoun to ask questions about time.

Here is a summary of some relative pronouns in French:

Relative pronoun	English meaning
que	*that, which, who*
qui	*that, which, who, whom*
dont	*that, whose, of which, of whom*
lequel (sing. m.) laquelle (sing. f.) lesquels (pl. m.) lesquelles (pl. f.)	*that, which, whom*
où	*where, when*
quand	*when*
lorsque	*when*

7. ORDINAL NUMBERS I

Ordinal numbers describe the order of a noun. Thus, it is considered an adjective and must agree in gender and number with the noun. Here are the ordinal numbers in Spanish, Portuguese, Italian, and French from 1 to 10.

1	**SP**	uno, una	primer(o), primera	1.º / 1.ª
	PT	um, uma	primeiro/-a	1.º / 1.ª
	IT	uno, una, un'	primo/-a	1.º / 1.ª
	FR	un, une	premier/première	1er/1ère
2	**SP**	dos	segundo/-a	2.º / 2.ª
	PT	dois, duas	segundo/-a	2.º / 2.ª
	IT	due	secondo/-a	2.º / 2.ª
	FR	deux	deuxième	2e
3	**SP**	tres	tercer(o), tercera	3.º / 3.ª
	PT	três	terceiro/-a	3.º / 3.ª
	IT	tre	terzo/-a	3.º / 3.ª
	FR	trois	troisième	3e
4	**SP**	cuatro	cuarto/-a	4.º / 4.ª
	PT	quatro	quarto/-a	4.º / 4.ª
	IT	quattro	quarto/-a	4.º / 4.ª
	FR	quatre	quatrième	4e
5	**SP**	cinco	quinto/-a	5.º / 5.ª
	PT	cinco	quinto/-a	5.º / 5.ª
	IT	cinque	quinto/-a	5.º / 5.ª
	FR	cinq	cinquième	5e
6	**SP**	seis	sexto/-a	6.º / 6.ª
	PT	seis	sexto/-a	6.º / 6.ª
	IT	sei	sesto/-a	6.º / 6.ª
	FR	six	sixième	6e
7	**SP**	siete	séptimo/-a	7.º / 7.ª
	PT	sete	sétimo/-a	7.º / 7.ª
	IT	sette	settimo/-a	7.º / 7.ª
	FR	sept	septième	7e
8	**SP**	ocho	octavo/-a	8.º / 8.ª
	PT	oito	oitavo/-a	8.º / 8.ª
	IT	otto	ottavo/-a	8.º / 8.ª
	FR	huit	huitième	8e
9	**SP**	nueve	noveno/-a	9.º / 9.ª
	PT	nove	nono/-a	9.º / 9.ª
	IT	nove	nono/-a	9.º / 9.ª
	FR	neuf	neuvième	9e
10	**SP**	diez	décimo/-a	10.º / 10.ª
	PT	dez	décimo/-a	10.º / 10.ª
	IT	dieci	decimo/-a	10.º / 10.ª
	FR	dix	dixième	10e

In Spanish, when the masculine form **"primero"** or **"tercero"** is placed before a noun, the **"o"** is dropped, e.g., **"Es el primero"** (*He is the first*) versus **"Es el primer atleta"** (*He is the first athlete*).

Unlike in English, where dates are described using ordinal numbers, e.g., *"the 24th of October,"* in Spanish, Portuguese, Italian, and French, dates are expressed using cardinal numbers:

SP	el 24 de octubre	
PT	24 de outubro	*the 24th of October*
IT	il 24 (di) ottobre	
FR	le 24 octobre	

A notable exception is the first day of the month, in which case the ordinal number is used. In Spanish, the ordinal or the cardinal number can be used. The use of the ordinal number **"primero"** is more common in Latin America, whereas the use of the cardinal number **"uno"** is more common in Spain. For example:

SP	el primero de noviembre el uno de noviembre	
PT	primeiro de novembro	*the 1st of November*
IT	il primo (di) novembre	
FR	le premier novembre	

Fractional Numbers

❖ Fractional numbers from *fourth* to *tenth* are the same as the ordinal numbers in Spanish and Portuguese. Fractional numbers from *third* to *tenth* are the same as the ordinal numbers in Italian. Fractional numbers from *fifth* to *tenth* are the same as the ordinal numbers in French. To summarize:

	1/2	1/3	1/4	1/5 … 1/10
SP	medio	tercio		*Same as ordinal number*
PT	meio	terço		*Same as ordinal number*
IT	mezzo			*Same as ordinal number*
FR	demi	tiers	quart	*Same as ordinal number*

Here are some examples:

SP	un **tercio** de la población	
PT	um **terço** da população	*a **third** of the population*
IT	un **terzo** della popolazione	
FR	un **tiers** de la population	
SP	un **cuarto** de los jugadores	
PT	um **quarto** dos jogadores	*a **fourth** of the players*
IT	un **quarto** dei giocatori	
FR	un **quart** des joueurs	
SP	un **quinto** de los recursos	
PT	um **quinto** dos recursos	*a **fifth** of the resources*
IT	un **quinto** delle risorse	
FR	un **cinquième** des ressources	

❖ To describe the fractional number 1/2 *(half)*, we use the following adjective:

SP	**medio** kilo	
PT	**meio** quilo	*half a kilo*
IT	**mezzo** chilo	
FR	**demi**-kilo	
SP	**media** hora	
PT	**meia** hora	*half an hour*
IT	**mezz'**ora	
FR	**demi**-heure	
SP	**media** docena	
PT	**meia** dúzia	*half a dozen*
IT	**mezza** dozzina	
FR	**demi**-douzaine	

❖ We can also use the following feminine *noun* to describe half the quantity of something, and it is often followed by a preposition meaning *"of,"* for example:

SP	**mitad** <u>de</u> la tierra	
PT	**metade** <u>do</u> terreno	*half of the land*
IT	**metà** <u>del</u> terreno	
FR	**moitié** <u>du</u> terrain	

❖ In numbers formed by an integer and a fraction, the indefinite article can be dropped before 1/2, if preceded by an integer in Spanish, Portuguese, Italian, and French, and before 1/4, if preceded by an integer in French. For example:

SP	uno y medio	
PT	um e meio	1 ½
IT	uno e mezzo	
FR	un et demi	
SP	tres y <u>un</u> cuarto	
PT	três e <u>um</u> quarto	3 ¼
IT	tre e <u>un</u> quarto	
FR	trois et quart	
SP	cinco y <u>un</u> octavo	
PT	cinco e <u>um</u> oitavo	5 ⅛
IT	cinque e <u>un</u> ottavo	
FR	cinq et <u>un</u> huitième	

We will cover higher ordinal numbers and fractions in **Level VI, Lesson 1**.

8. "POR" VS. "PARA" IN SPANISH & PORTUGUESE

The difference between the prepositions "**por**" and "**para**" is challenging for most Spanish and Portuguese learners. There are a few rules that you need to follow and some expressions that you need to memorize. However, with practice, you can get this right. In general, both "**por**" and "**para**" can mean *"for."* Nevertheless, in many contexts, they can also mean *"by," "per," "in order to," "because of,"* and some other meanings. Let us take a look at some of these contexts.

Uses of "Por"

1. To denote *reason* or *motive*, for example:

SP	Llegaremos tarde **por** el tráfico.	
PT	Estaremos atrasados **por** causa do trânsito.	*We'll be late **because of** the traffic.*
SP	Él murió **por** falta de agua.	
PT	Ele morreu **por** falta de água.	*He died **due to** a lack of water.*

2. To denote *duration*, for example:

SP	Te Espero **por** dos horas.	
PT	Te espero **por** duas horas.	*I'll wait for you for two hours.*

SP	Estaré en España **por** tres días.	*I will be in Spain **for** three days.*
PT	Estarei na Espanha **por** três dias.	

3. To denote *agency*, usually meaning *"by,"* for example:

SP	El libro fue escrito **por** un autor anónimo.	*The book was written **by** an anonymous author.*
PT	O livro foi escrito **por** um autor anônimo.	
SP	Ellos son amados **por** sus padres.	*They are loved **by** their parents.*
PT	Eles são amados **por** seus pais.	

4. To denote *equivalency* or *exchange*, for example:

SP	Cambié mi auto **por** otro nuevo.	*I changed my car **for** a new one.*
PT	Troquei meu carro **por** um novo.	
SP	La harina cuesta dos dólares **por** kilo.	*The flour costs two dollars **per** kilo.*
PT	A farinha custa dois dólares **por** quilo.	

5. To denote *travel itinerary*, usually meaning *"through,"* for example:

SP	Quiero ir a Suiza **por** Italia.	*I want to go to Switzerland **through** Italy.*
PT	Eu quero ir para a Suíça **pela** Itália.	
SP	Podemos pasar **por** el parque.	*We can go **through** the park.*
PT	Podemos ir **pelo** parque.	

6. To denote *means of communication*, usually meaning *"by"* or *"via,"* for example:

SP	Enviaron el documento **por** fax.	*They sent the document **by** fax.*
PT	Enviaram o documento **por** fax.	
SP	Te voy a contactar **por** teléfono.	*I am going to contact you **by** phone.*
PT	Entrarei em contato **por** telefone.	

Uses of "Para"

1. To denote a *goal* or *objective*, meaning *"in order to,"* for example:

SP	Trabajo **para** ganar dinero.	*I work **in order to** earn money.*
PT	Trabalho **para** ganhar dinheiro.	

SP	Voy a la universidad **para** estudiar.	*I go to the university **to** study.*
PT	Vou para a universidade **para** estudar.	

2. To denote *destination* or *direction*, for example:

SP	El tren sale **para** Nueva York.	*The train leaves **for** New York.*
PT	O trem parte **para** Nova York.	
SP	Viajaremos **para** Colombia.	*We will travel **to** Colombia.*
PT	Viajaremos **para** a Colômbia.	

3. To denote the *recipient of an object*, for example:

SP	Es **para** ti.	*This is **for** you.*
PT	É **para** você.	
SP	Este regalo es **para** mi amigo.	*This gift is **for** my friend.*
PT	Este presente é **para** o meu amigo.	

4. To denote an *opinion*, for example:

SP	**Para** mí, es ridículo.	***For** me, it's ridiculous.*
PT	**Para** mim, é ridículo.	
SP	**Para** ella, el fútbol no es divertido.	***In her opinion**, soccer is not fun.*
PT	**Para** ela, futebol não é diversão.	

5. To denote the *contrast of an idea*, for example:

SP	**Para** un niño, él habla muy bien.	***For** a child, he speaks very well.*
PT	**Para** uma criança, ele fala muito bem.	
SP	Tiene buena salud **para** su edad.	*He's in good health **for** his age.*
PT	Ele está bem de saúde **para** sua idade.	

Common Expressions with "Por" and "Para"

There are certain expressions that use "**por**," such as:

SP	por Dios	*Oh my God!*	por las dudas por si acaso	*just in case*
PT	por Deus		pelas dúvidas se por acaso	
SP	por favor	*please*	por ejemplo	*for example*
PT	por favor		por exemplo	

SP	por suerte	*luckily*	por eso	*that's why*
PT	por sorte		por isso	
SP	por ciento	*percent*	por tu culpa	*because of you*
PT	por cento		por tua culpa	

and others that use "**para**," such as:

SP	para siempre	*forever*	para variar	*just for a change*
PT	para sempre		para variar	
SP	para colmo	*to top it all*	para empezar	*for starters*
PT	para completar		para começar	
SP	para otra ocasión para otro momento	*for another time*	para que	*so that*
PT	para outra hora para outro momento		para que	

9. THE VERB "TO BE": "SER" VS. "ESTAR" IN SPANISH & PORTUGUESE

There are two verbs in Spanish and Portuguese that are translated as the verb *"to be"* in English. The two verbs are: "**ser**" and "**estar**." It is often tricky for English speakers to wrap their heads around the difference, but we will explain the difference in a simple manner. Before we do that, you need to recognize the two verbs in their present indicative conjugated forms:

- In Spanish:

	ser	estar
yo	soy	estoy
tú	eres	estás
él/ella/usted	es	está
nosotros/-as	somos	estamos
vosotros/-as	sois	estáis
ellos/ellas/ustedes	son	están

- In Portuguese:

	ser	estar
eu	sou	estou
ele/ela/você	é	está
nós	somos	estamos
eles/elas/vocês	são	estão

Both "**ser**" and "**estar**" are irregular in Spanish and Portuguese. The two verbs are encountered frequently. Thus, it is important to memorize how they are conjugated.

Now, let us look at the difference in meaning between "**ser**" and "**estar**." The easiest way to distinguish between the two is to remember the uses of "**estar**." These tend to be more limited than the uses of "**ser**." If you remember the uses of "**estar**," you can safely assume that everything else should take the verb "**ser**."

Uses of the Verb "estar"

1. To describe location, for example:

SP	¿Dónde **está** él?	*Where is he?*
PT	Onde **está** ele?	
SP	Yo **estoy** aquí.	*I am here.*
PT	**Estou** aqui.	
SP	No sé donde **están** las llaves.	*I don't know where the keys are.*
PT	Eu não sei onde **estão** as chaves.	

There are two exceptions:

o One notable exception is when we describe where an event (and not a physical thing) is taking place. In that case, we use "**ser**," for example:

SP	El partido **es** en el estadio.	*The match is in the stadium.*
PT	O jogo **é** no estádio.	
SP	¿Dónde **es** la reunión?	*Where is the meeting?*
PT	Onde **é** o encontro?	

o The second exception applies only in Portuguese: to describe a permanent geographical location, we use the verb "**ser**" in Portuguese but "**estar**" in Spanish, for example:

SP	Sao Paulo **está** en Brasil.	*Sao Paulo is in Brazil.*
PT	São Paulo **é** no Brasil.	
SP	Manaus **está** en el norte de Brasil.	*Manaus is in the north of Brazil.*
PT	Manaus **é** no norte do Brasil.	

Alternatively, the verb "**quedar**" in Spanish or the verb "**ficar**" in Portuguese can be used instead of "**ser**" to provide the same meaning, for example:

SP	Sao Paulo **queda** en Brasil.	*Sao Paulo is in Brazil.*
PT	São Paulo **fica** no Brasil.	

2. To describe a *temporary* state, condition, or emotion, for example:

SP	**Estoy** acostado.	*I am lying down.*
PT	**Estou** deitado.	
SP	Mi amigo **está** enfermo.	*My friend is sick.*
PT	Meu amigo **está** doente.	
SP	Ellos **están** felices.	*They are happy.*
PT	Eles **estão** felizes.	

As you can observe, lying down, being sick, and being happy are temporary states. Therefore, we use the verb "**estar**." There are a few exceptions:

o Occupation, religion, nationality, and political affiliation: Although one may change any of those, we use the verb "**ser**" to describe these states, for example:

SP	**Soy** ingeniero.	*I am an engineer.*
PT	**Sou** engenheiro.	
SP	Ella **es** católica.	*She is Catholic.*
PT	Ela **é** católica.	
SP	Él **es** portugués.	*He is Portuguese.*
PT	Ele **é** português.	
SP	Ellos **son** socialistas.	*They are socialists.*
PT	Eles **são** socialistas.	

o Time: Although time changes, we use the verb "**ser**" to describe it, for example:

SP	¿Qué hora **es**?	*What time is it?*
PT	Que horas **são**?	
SP	**Son** las 9.	*It is 9 o'clock.*
PT	**São** 9 horas.	
SP	Hoy **es** viernes.	*Today is Friday.*
PT	Hoje **é** sexta-feira.	

o Physical description: Although one may grow up taller, lose, or gain weight, we still use the verb "**ser**," for example:

SP	Él **es** alto y delgado.	*He __is__ tall and thin.*
PT	Ele **é** alto e magro.	

o Relationships: whether they are changeable or unchangeable, for example:

SP	Ella **es** mi madre.	*She __is__ my mother.*
PT	Ela **é** minha mãe.	
SP	Él **es** mi jefe.	*He __is__ my boss.*
PT	Ele **é** meu chefe.	
SP	Ella **es** mi esposa.	*She __is__ my spouse.*
PT	Ela **é** minha esposa.	

Uses of the Verb "ser"

Most other cases use the verb "**ser**," especially if they describe the essence, origin, or characteristics of something or someone, for example:

SP	**Soy** Diego.	*I __am__ Diego.*
PT	**Sou** Diego.	
SP	Ella **es** de Chile.	*She __is__ from Chile.*
PT	Ela **é** do Chile.	
SP	Esta silla **es** de madera.	*This chair __is__ made of wood.*
PT	Essa cadeira **é** de madeira.	
SP	Él **es** amigable.	*He __is__ friendly.*
PT	Ele **é** amigável.	
SP	Ella **es** inteligente.	*She __is__ intelligent.*
PT	Ela **é** inteligente.	

In some cases, using "**ser**" or "**estar**" can convey a different meaning. For example, "**Él es celoso**" and "**Él está celoso**" in Spanish both are translated as *"He __is__ jealous."* However, "**Él es celoso**" conveys that someone is jealous by *nature* and that this is a *characteristic* of him, whereas "**Él está celoso**" conveys that he is *feeling* jealous in response to a certain *condition* or event.

The statement "**O sorvete é delicioso**" *(Ice cream __is__ delicious)* in Portuguese means that ice cream, in general, has the characteristic of being delicious, whereas "**O sorvete <u>está</u> delicioso**" likely refers to a specific ice cream that tastes delicious because of its ingredients, flavor, preparation, etc.

Similarly, in Spanish "**La manzana <u>es</u> verde**" and "**La manzana <u>está</u> verde**" both are translated as "*The apple <u>is</u> green.*" However, "**La manzana <u>es</u> verde**" describes the color of the apple as an *intrinsic characteristic* of the apple, whereas "**La manzana <u>está</u> verde**" refers more to the *state* of the apple being unripe.

Another more common example is when we describe the climate of a place versus the weather at a particular time, e.g., "**Canadá <u>é</u> muito frio**" *(Canada <u>is</u> very cold)* in Portuguese describes Canada as a cold place, indicating that being cold is a permanent trait of the place. On the other hand, "**<u>Está</u> frio hoje**" *(It <u>is</u> cold today)* simply means that the weather is cold at a specific time, that is, today.

We use the verb "**estar**" to describe being *alive* or *dead*. We do not use "**ser**" in this case, for example:

SP	<u>Está</u> muerta.	*She <u>is</u> dead.*
PT	<u>Está</u> morta.	

To describe one's marital status, we often use "**ser**" even though marital status is subject to change. In Spanish, we could use either "**ser**" or "**estar**." Although legal documents may use "**ser**," you may hear "**estar**" more often by Spanish speakers, for example:

SP	<u>Estoy</u>/<u>Soy</u> casado.	*I <u>am</u> married.*
PT	<u>Sou</u> casado.	
SP	<u>Está</u>/<u>Es</u> soltera.	*She <u>is</u> single.*
PT	<u>É</u> solteira.	

LEVEL III: ELEMENTARY

Start by reading the introductory topics of this level. You will notice that some concepts are unique to the Romance languages covered in the book. You could also use Anki cards to practice with reviews and exercises.

1. VERBS LIKE "GUSTAR" IN SPANISH & "PIACERE" IN ITALIAN

Some expressions use a different sentence structure in Spanish, Portuguese, Italian, and French, compared to that used in English to express the same meaning. One of the most common examples is the use of verbs like "**gustar**" in Spanish and "**piacere**" in Italian, both meaning *"to please."*

Let us examine this sentence in Spanish and Italian:

SP	Me gusta el auto.
IT	Mi piace la macchina.

Both sentences above are translated as: *"I like the car."*

A more accurate and literal translation would be:

"The car is pleasing to me."

Note that the verb conjugation is in the third-person singular form, **"gusta"** or **"piace,"** because **"el auto"** or **"la macchina"** is the subject that does the act of pleasing, and **"me"** or **"mi"** is the object. Thus, the conjugation of the verb must agree with the subject.

Let us take another example. If you want to say that someone is interested in ancient cultures, the best way to say that is:

SP	Le interesan las culturas antiguas.
IT	Gli interessano le culture antiche.

Here, we use the verb **"interesar"** in Spanish or **"interessare"** in Italian, and the sentence is translated as:

"Ancient cultures interest him."

Note that the verb is conjugated as **"interesan"** in Spanish or **"interessano"** in Italian because *"ancient cultures"* is the subject, and **"le"** in Spanish or **"gli"** in Italian is the object. Thus, the conjugation of the verb must agree with the subject.

As you can see, we use the indirect object **"le"** in Spanish or **"gli"** in Italian to express the meaning *"to him,"* that is, that the ancient cultures interest him. However, remember that **"le"** and **"gli"** can also mean *"to him"* or *"to them."* To remove ambiguity and sometimes to show emphasis, we can use the prepositional **"a"** followed by the object or the prepositional object pronoun:

SP	**"A Marco** <u>le</u> interesan las culturas antiguas," or **"A lui** <u>le</u> interesan las culturas antiguas."
IT	**"A Marco** interessano le culture antiche," or **"A lui** interessano le culture antiche."

This is translated as:

"Ancient cultures interest Marco," or *"Ancient cultures interest him."*

Notice that indirect object **"le"** is used in Spanish after the prepositional **"a"** followed by the object or the prepositional object pronoun, whereas the indirect object is omitted in Italian.

Below are more examples of expressions with the verbs **"gustar"** and **"piacere"** using the prepositional **"a"** and prepositional object pronoun:

English Example	Prep. Obj. Pronoun	Ind. Obj. Pronoun		Spanish and Italian Equivalent
I like reading.	mí	me	**SP**	A **mí** me gusta leer.
	me	mi	**IT**	A **me** piace leggere.
You like reading. (singular, informal)	ti	te	**SP**	A **ti** te gusta leer.
	te	ti	**IT**	A **te** piace leggere.

He likes reading.	él	le	**SP**	A **él le** gusta leer.
	lui	lui	**IT**	A **lui** piace leggere.
She likes reading.	ella	le	**SP**	A **ella le** gusta leer.
	lei	lei	**IT**	A **lei** piace leggere.
You like reading. (singular, formal)	usted	le	**SP**	A **usted le** gusta leer.
	Lei	Lei	**IT**	A **Lei** piace leggere.
We like reading.	nosotros/-as	nos	**SP**	A **nosotros nos** gusta leer.
	noi	noi	**IT**	A **noi** piace leggere.
You like reading. (plural, informal)	vosotros/-as	os	**SP**	A **vosotros os** gusta leer.
	voi	voi	**IT**	A **voi** piace leggere.
They like reading.	ellos/-as	les	**SP**	A **ellos les** gusta leer.
	loro	loro	**IT**	A **loro** piace leggere.
You like reading. (plural, formal)	ustedes	les	**SP**	A **ustedes les** gusta leer.
	Loro	Loro	**IT**	A **Loro** piace leggere.

Note again how the verbs **"gustar"** and **"piacere"** do not change conjugation in the examples above because the subject is singular; thus, the verb takes the *third-person singular* conjugation.

Here is a list of similar verbs in Spanish and Italian:

Verb	Meaning	Example
aburrir (SP) annoiare (IT)	*to bore*	**EN**: *Video games* **are boring** *to me.* **SP**: Me **aburren** los videojuegos. **IT**: Mi **annoiano** i videogiochi.
bastar (SP) bastare (IT)	*to be enough*	**EN**: *The food* **is enough** *for him.* **SP**: La comida le **basta**. **IT**: Il cibo gli **basta**.
disgustar (SP) disgustare (IT)	*to disgust*	**EN**: *These problems* **disgust** *me.* **SP**: Estos problemas me **disgustan**. **IT**: Questi problemi mi **disgustano**.
doler (SP) fare male (IT)	*to be painful*	**EN**: *She* **has** *back* **pain**. **SP**: A ella le **duele** la espalda. **IT**: Le **fa male** la schiena.
importar (SP) importare (IT)	*to be important*	**EN**: *I don't care.* **SP**: No me **importa**. **IT**: Non mi **importa**.
parecer (SP) parere (IT)	*to seem*	**EN**: *The idea* **seems** *reasonable to me.* **SP**: La idea me **parece** razonable. **IT**: L'idea mi **pare** ragionevole.

2. PRESENT PERFECT TENSE

In English, the present perfect tense is used to describe events that happened in the past and continue in the present.

The present perfect tense in Portuguese, Italian, and French does not always correspond to the present perfect tense in English.

In Spanish, the present perfect tense, like in English, is used to describe events that happened recently or started in the past and continue in the present, e.g., *"I have spoken."*

In Portuguese, the present perfect tense is used to describe repeated actions in the past that extend to the present. It is more like the present perfect continuous tense in English, e.g., *"I have been working hard."*

In Italian and French, the present perfect tense is used to describe events that happened and were completed in the past *or* happened in the past and continue in the present. Therefore, this tense covers both the present perfect and the simple past tenses in English, that is, *"I spoke"* and *"I have spoken"* are both translated to the same tense in Italian and French. In French, this tense is also called the *composite past*.

In Spanish and Portuguese, the preterite tense is equivalent in many cases to the simple past in English. We will cover the preterite tense in Spanish and Portuguese in **Level IV, Lesson 2**.

In Summary:

	The present perfect tense is …	Example
SP	equivalent to **"present perfect tense"** in English	e.g., *"I have spoken"*
PT	equivalent to **"present perfect continuous tense"** in English	e.g., *"I have been speaking"*
IT	equivalent to **"simple past tense"** or **"present perfect tense"** in English	e.g., *"I spoke"* or *"I have spoken"*
FR		

Present Perfect Tense in Spanish

The present perfect tense in Spanish, like in English, is used to describe events that happened recently or started in the past and continue in the present.

It is a compound tense, meaning it requires an auxiliary verb, in this case, the *irregular* verb "**haber**" in the present tense, followed by the past participle. The auxiliary "**haber**" serves a similar function to the auxiliary *"have"* in English, e.g., *"I have done my homework."*

"**-ar**" verbs	subject pronoun + "**haber**" in present tense + (verb stem+ **ado**)
"**-er**" verbs	subject pronoun + "**haber**" in present tense + (verb stem+ **ido**)
"**-ir**" verbs	subject pronoun + "**haber**" in present tense + (verb stem+ **ido**)

Let us look at some verb examples and the conjugation of "**haber**."

		-ar ending e.g., hablar	-er ending e.g., comer	-ir ending e.g., vivir
yo	he			
tú	has			
él/ella/usted	ha	habl**ado**	com**ido**	viv**ido**
nosotros/-as	hemos			
vosotros/-as	habéis			
ellos/ellas/ustedes	han			

Here are some examples:

Yo **he visitado** Egipto.	*I **have visited** Egypt.*
Tú **has bebido** el café.	*You **have drunk** the coffee.*
Ella **ha hablado** con su madre.	*She **has spoken** to her mother.*
Nosotros **hemos comido**.	*We **have eaten**.*
Ellos **han vivido** aquí.	*They **have lived** here.*

Irregular Past Participles

There are a few verbs with irregular past participles that need to be memorized.

Verb	Past Participle	Meaning	Examples

abrir	abierto	to open	He **abierto** la puerta. *I have **opened** the door.*
absolver	absuelto	to absolve	Lo han **absuelto**. *They have **absolved** him.*
cubrir	cubierto	to cover	Hemos **cubierto** el suelo. *We have **covered** the floor.*
decir	dicho	to say	Te lo he **dicho**. *I have **told** you so.*
escribir	escrito	to write	Ella ha **escrito** una carta. *She has **written** a letter.*
freír	frito	to fry	¿Has **frito** la papa? *Have you **fried** the potato?*
hacer	hecho	to do	He **hecho** la tarea. *I have **done** the task.*
imprimir	impreso	to print	He **impreso** la foto. *I have **printed** the photo.*
morir	muerto	to die	Él ha **muerto**. *He has **died**.*
poner	puesto	to put	Él nos ha **puesto** en peligro. *He has **put** us in danger.*
proveer	provisto	to provide	Hemos **provisto** el agua. *We have **provided** water.*
resolver	resuelto	to resolve	Ella ha **resuelto** el problema. *She has **resolved** the problem.*
romper	roto	to break	Ella ha **roto** la ventana. *She has **broken** the window.*
satisfacer	satisfecho	to satisfy	Mi trabajo me ha **satisfecho**. *My work has **satisfied** me.*
ver	visto	to see	No lo he **visto**. *I haven't **seen** him.*
volver	vuelto	to return	Ella no ha **vuelto**. *She hasn't **returned**.*

Among the above exceptions, it is acceptable for the verbs "**freír**," "**imprimir**," and "**proveer**" to use the past participle in the regular form as "**freído**," "**imprimido**," and "**proveído**." However, only irregular forms are acceptable if used as adjectives.

The verbs above can be used with prefixes that change the meaning, but the irregular form remains the same. For example, the past participles of "**revolver**" (*to scramble*), "**devolver**" (*to return*), and "**envolver**" *(to wrap)* are "**revuelto**," "**devuelto**," and "**envuelto**," respectively, which are all similar to the past participle of the original verb "**volver**" without the prefix, i.e., "**vuelto**."

Another minor orthographic irregularity is in the case of "-**er**" and "-**ir**" verbs if the stem ends in a vowel, e.g., the stem of "**leer**" *(to read)* is "**le-**." In this case, the "**i**" in the past participle ending is accented, i.e., "-**ído**." Thus, the past participle of "**leer**" is "**leído**." Other examples include "**caer**" *(to fall)*, "**creer**" *(to believe)*, "**oír**" *(to hear)*, "**poseer**" *(to possess)*, "**reír**" *(to laugh)*, and "**traer**" *(to bring)*. An exception to the accented "**i**" rule is verbs with a "-**uir**" ending. In this case, the "**i**" is not accented, e.g., "**destruir**" *(to destroy)* becomes "**destruido**."

Present Perfect Tense in Portuguese

The present perfect tense is used in Portuguese to describe repeated actions in the past that extend to the present. It is more similar to the present perfect continuous tense in English, e.g., "*I have been working hard.*"

The present perfect is a compound tense, meaning it requires an auxiliary verb, in this case, the *irregular* verb "**ter**" or "**haver**" in the present tense, followed by the past participle. The auxiliary "**ter**" or "**haver**" serves a similar function to the auxiliary "*have*" in English, e.g., "*I have done my homework.*"

"-**ar**" verbs	"**ter**"/"**haver**" in present tense + (verb stem+ **ado**)
"-**er**" verbs	"**ter**"/"**haver**" in present tense + (verb stem+ **ido**)
"-**ir**" verbs	"**ter**"/"**haver**" in present tense + (verb stem+ **ido**)

Both "**ter**" and "**haver**" are grammatically correct and can be used interchangeably. However, the use of "**haver**" is usually limited to writing. In everyday language, the verb "**ter**" is often used.

The table below summarizes the conjugation rules of the three verb groups in the present perfect tense:

		-ar ending e.g., falar	-er ending e.g., comer	-ir ending e.g., partir
eu	tenho/hei			
ele/ela/você	tem/há	falado	comido	partido
nós	temos/havemos			
eles/elas/vocês	têm/hão			

Here are some more examples in context:

Você **tem bebido** o café.	*You **have been drinking** coffee.*
Ela **tem falado** com a mãe.	*She **has been speaking** to her mother.*
Nós **temos comido**.	*We **have been eating**.*
Eles **têm vivido** aqui.	*They **have been living** here.*

Irregular Past Participles

1. There are a few verbs with irregular past participles:

Verb	Past Participle	Meaning	Examples
abrir	aberto	*to open*	Eu **tenho aberto** a porta. *I **have been opening** the door.*
cobrir	coberto	*to cover*	Nós **temos coberto** o chão. *We **have been covering** the floor.*
dizer	dito	*to say*	Eu te **tenho dito** isso. *I **have been telling** you so.*
escrever	escrito	*to write*	Ela **tem escrito** uma carta. *She **has been writing** a letter.*
fazer	feito	*to do*	Eu **tenho feito** a tarefa. *I **have been doing** the task.*
pôr	posto	*to put*	Ele nos **tem posto** em perigo. *He **has been putting** us in danger.*
ver	visto	*to see*	Eu **tenho visto** o último evento. *I **have been seeing** the latest event.*
vir	vindo	*to come*	O homem **tem vindo** de longe. *The man **has been coming** from far away.*

❖ Notice that the past participle and the gerund of the verb "**vir**" *(to come)* are identical, i.e., "**vindo**."

❖ The verbs above can be used with prefixes that change the meaning, but the irregular form remains the same. For example, the past participles of the verb "**descobrir**" *(to discover)* is "**descoberto**," which is similar to the past participle of the original verb "**cobrir**" without the prefix, i.e., "**coberto**."

2. There are also some verbs that have both regular and irregular past participles. Here are the most common ones:

aceitar	*to accept*	aceitado, aceito
acender	*to turn on or to light*	acendido, aceso
dispersar	*to disperse*	dispersado, disperso
eleger	*to elect*	elegido, eleito
entregar	*to deliver*	entregado, entregue
expressar	*to express*	expressado, expresso
exprimir	*to express*	exprimido, expresso
expulsar	*to expel or to throw out*	expulsado, expulso
extinguir	*to extinguish*	extinguido, extinto
fritar	*to fry*	fritado, frito
ganhar	*to win*	ganhado, ganho
gastar	*to spend*	gastado, gasto
impergir	*to immerse*	imergido, imerso
limpar	*to clean*	limpado, limpo
matar	*to kill*	matado, morto
pagar	*to pay*	pagado, pago
pegar	*to get*	pegado, pego
prender	*to arrest or hold*	prendido, preso
salvar	*to save*	salvado, salvo
soltar	*to release*	soltado, solto
submergir	*to submerge*	submergido, submerso
suprimir	*to suppress*	suprimido, supresso
suspender	*to suspend*	suspendido, suspenso

In general, it is preferrable, but not always required, to use the regular form when the past participle is used after the auxiliary "**ter**" or "**haver**," e.g., "**Ele tem aceitado**" *(He has been accepting)*. On the other hand, the irregular shorter form is often used when the past participle is used as an adjective, e.g., "**É aceito aqui**" *(It is accepted here)*.

Present Perfect Tense in Italian

In Italian, the present perfect tense is used to describe events that happened and were completed in the past or happened in the past and continue in the present. Therefore, this tense covers both the present perfect and the simple past tenses in English, that is, *"I spoke"* and *"I have spoken"* are both translated to the same tense in Italian.

The present perfect is a compound tense, meaning it requires an auxiliary verb. In English, we use the verb *"to have"* in the present tense as an auxiliary, e.g., *"I have done my homework."*

In Italian, some verbs use the auxiliary **"avere"** *(to have)*, while others use the auxiliary **"essere"** *(to be)* in the present tense, followed by the past participle.

The past participle of regular verbs using the auxiliary **"avere"** *(to have)* is formed by adding the appropriate suffix for "-**are**," "-**ere**," and "-**ire**" verbs.

"-are" verbs		"verb stem" + "-ato"
"-ere" verbs	"avere" in the present tense	"verb stem" + "-uto"
"-ire" verbs		"verb stem" + "-ito"

The past participle of regular verbs using the auxiliary **"essere"** *(to be)* is formed in a similar way. One additional requirement here is that the suffix of the past participle must agree with the subject in gender and number, that is, the past participle essentially requires the treatment of an adjective.

"-are" verbs		"verb stem" + "-ato"/ "-ata"/ "-ati"/ "-ate"
"-ere" verbs	"essere" in the present tense	"verb stem" + "-uto"/ "-uta"/ "-uti"/ "-ute"
"-ire" verbs		"verb stem" + "-ito"/ "-ita"/ "-iti"/ "-ite"

Let us look at some examples of verbs conjugated using the auxiliary **"avere"**:

		-are ending e.g., parlare	-ere ending e.g., vendere	-ire ending e.g., finire

io	ho			
tu	hai			
lui/lei	ha	parl**ato**	vend**uto**	fin**ito**
noi	abbiamo			
voi	avete			
loro	hanno			

Here are some examples in context:

Io **ho visitato** l'Egitto l'anno scorso.	I **visited** Egypt last year.
Tu **hai finito** il tuo lavoro.	You **have finished** your work.
Lui **ha parlato** con sua madre.	He **spoke** with his mother.
Noi **abbiamo mangiato** tutto il cibo.	We **have eaten** all the food.
Sono sicuro che mi **avete sentito** ieri sera.	I am sure you **heard** me last night.
Loro **hanno lavorato** qui per due anni.	They **worked** here for two years.

Now, let us look at some examples of verbs conjugated using the auxiliary "**essere**":

		-are ending e.g., andare	-ere ending e.g., cadere	-ire ending e.g., partire
io	sono	and**ato**/-**a**	cad**uto**/-**a**	part**ito**/-**a**
tu	sei	and**ato**/-**a**	cad**uto**/-**a**	part**ito**/-**a**
lui	è	and**ato**	cad**uto**	part**ito**
lei	è	and**ata**	cad**uta**	part**ita**
noi	siamo	and**ati**/-**e**	cad**uti**/-**e**	part**iti**/-**e**
voi	siete	and**ati**/-**e**	cad**uti**/-**e**	part**iti**/-**e**
loro	sono	and**ati**/-**e**	cad**uti**/-**e**	part**iti**/-**e**

Here are some more examples:

Sono andato in palestra la scorsa settimana.	I **went** to the gym last week.
Sei partito presto ieri sera.	You **left** early last night.
Lui **è caduto** dalle scale.	He **fell down** the stairs.
Siamo entrati nella stanza.	We **have entered** the room.
Voi **siete arrivati** tardi la scorsa notte.	You **arrived** late last night.
Ieri loro **sono usciti** insieme.	They **went out** together yesterday.

Notice that in some of these examples, the present perfect tense in Italian corresponds to the present perfect, whereas in others it corresponds to the simple past tense depending on the context.

Using the Conjugation Auxiliary "Avere" vs. "Essere"

You are perhaps wondering when to use the auxiliary "**avere**" and when to use the auxiliary "**essere**" to form the past participle. The vast majority of Italian verbs, including all transitive[1] verbs, are conjugated using the auxiliary "**avere**." Thus, it is easier to memorize the verbs that use "**essere**." First, all transitive non-reflexive verbs use "**avere**." If you can rule that out, the following categories, although not comprehensive, contain most verbs that use "**essere**":

1. A group of intransitive verbs related to *motion* (e.g., to go, to come, to return, to enter, to leave, to fall, to enter, etc.).

andare	*to go*	scappare	*to escape*
arrivare	*to arrive*	scendere	*to go down or descend*
cadere	*to fall*	tornare	*to return*
entrare	*to enter*	uscire	*to go out*
partire	*to leave*	venire	*to come*
salire	*to go up*		

Remember that all the verbs above that use "**essere**" are motion-related. However, not all motion-related verbs use "**essere**." This should serve as a guideline to help you memorize the verbs in this category.

2. A group of intransitive verbs related to *change or transformation* (e.g., to become, to be born, to die, to appear, to disappear, to lose weight, etc.).

apparire	*to appear*	ingrandire	*to get bigger*
cambiare	*to change*	migliorare	*to get better*
crescere	*to grow*	morire	*to die*
dimagrire	*to lose weight*	nascere	*to be born*
diminuire	*to diminish*	peggiorare	*to get worse*
dipendere da	*to depend on or cause*	sparire	*to disappear*

---

[1] A verb is transitive if it requires an object. For example, the *"to bring"* can only be transitive, because the meaning is not complete without an object, e.g., *"I bring."*

diventare	to become	svanire	to vanish
guarire	to heal	volare	to fly

Notice that the above verbs use **"essere"** only when they are in transitive form, that is when there is a direct object acted upon. If the verb is transitive, **"avere"** must be used. For example:

Verb	Example	
cambiare *to change*	**È cambiato** molto di recente.	He **has changed** a lot recently.
	Ha cambiato il mondo.	He **has changed** the world.
crescere *to raise or grow*	**È cresciuta** in città.	She **grew up** in the city.
	Ha cresciuto tre figli.	She **raised** three children.
guarire *to heal*	La mia pelle **è guarita**.	My skin **has healed**.
	La crema **ha guarito** la mia pelle.	The cream **healed** my skin.

3. Verbs that are always in the third-person, e.g., **"costare"** *(to cost)*, **"durare"** *(to last)*, **"occorrere"** *(to take or to be necessary)*, **"succedere"** *(to happen)*, etc. Here are some examples:

Verb	Meaning	Example
costare	to cost	Mi **è costato** molto. / It **has cost** me a lot.
durare	to last	Il volo **è durato** un'ora. / The flight **lasted** one hour.
occorrere	to be necessary or to take	**Sono occorsi** tre giorni per dipingere la casa. / It **took** three days to paint the house.
succedere	to happen	Per favore, dimmi cosa **è successo**. / Please, tell me what **happened**.

4. Many, but not all, verbs like **"piacere."** Refer to **Lesson 1** of this level. Here are some examples:

Verb	Meaning	Example
bastare	to be enough	Il cibo gli **è bastato**. / The food **was enough** for him.
importare	to be important	Non ci **è importato**. / We didn't care.
mancare	to miss	Mi **è mancata** mia sorella. / I **missed** my sister.
parere	to seem	L'idea mi **è parsa** ragionevole. / The idea **seemed** reasonable to me.

sembrare	*to seem*	Questo ragazzo mi **è sembrato** strano. *This guy **seemed** strange to me.*
servire	*to need or be of use*	Mi **è servito** un altro libro. *I **needed** one more book.*

5. All reflexive verbs, which will be covered in detail in **Level IV, Lesson 3**, e.g., **"chiamarsi"** *(to call oneself)*, **"lavarsi"** *(to wash oneself)*, etc.

Irregular Past Participles

There are some verbs with irregular past participles that need to be memorized.

Verb	Past Participle	Meaning	Examples
accendere	acceso	*to switch on*	All'arrivo, ha **acceso** la luce. *Upon arrival, he **turned on** the light.*
aprire	aperto	*to open*	Ho **aperto** la porta. *I have **opened** the door.*
bere	bevuto	*to drink*	Quanto hai **bevuto**? *How much did you **drink**?*
chiedere	chiesto	*to ask*	Mi ha **chiesto** di aiutarlo. *He **asked** me to help him.*
chiudere	chiuso	*to close*	Oggi il negozio ha **chiuso** tardi. *The shop **closed** late today.*
coprire	coperto	*to cover*	Ho **coperto** il pavimento. *I have **covered** the floor.*
correre	corso	*to run*	Oggi ho **corso** di mattina. *Today I **ran** in the morning.*
cuocere	cotto	*to cook*	Ha **cotto** una bella bistecca. *He **cooked** a nice steak.*
decidere	deciso	*to decide*	Abbiamo **deciso** di partire. *We **decided** to leave.*
dire	detto	*to say*	Te l'ho **detto** dall'inizio. *I **told** you from the beginning.*
discutere	discusso	*to discuss*	Hanno **discusso** l'argomento. *They **discussed** the topic.*
dividere	diviso	*to divide*	Ho **diviso** la torta a fette. *I **divided** the cake into slices.*
fare	fatto	*to do*	Ho **fatto** tutto il lavoro. *I have **done** all the work.*

friggere	fritto	*to fry*	Hai **fritto** la patata? *Have you **fried** the potato?*
leggere	letto	*to read*	Hai **letto** questo articolo? *Have you **read** this article?*
mettere	messo	*to put*	Ho **messo** la roba nel furgone. *I **put** the stuff in the van.*
morire	morto	*to die*	È **morto** l'anno scorso. *He **died** last year.*
nascere	nato	*to be born*	È **nato** e cresciuto qui. *He **was born** and raised here.*
offendere	offeso	*to offend*	Mi dispiace se ti ho **offeso**. *I'm sorry if I **offended** you.*
perdere	perso	*to lose*	Ho **perso** le chiavi. *I **lost** my keys.*
piangere	pianto	*to cry*	Ha **pianto** per la sua perdita. *He **cried** over his loss.*
porre	posto	*to put*	Abbiamo **posto** fine a questo. *We have **put** an end to this.*
ridere	riso	*to laugh*	Ho **riso** quando me l'hanno detto. *I **laughed** when they told me.*
rimanere	rimasto	*to remain*	Sono **rimasti** con noi per due notti. *They **stayed** with us for two nights.*
risolvere	risolto	*to resolve*	Lei ha **risolto** il problema. *She has **resolved** the problem.*
rompere	rotto	*to break*	Lei ha **rotto** la finestra. *She has **broken** the window.*
soddisfare	soddisfatto	*to satisfy*	Il mio lavoro mi ha **soddisfatto**. *My work has **satisfied** me.*
scegliere	scelto	*to choose*	Ho **scelto** questo prodotto. *I **chose** this product.*
scendere	sceso	*to descend or go down*	Lui è **sceso** le scale. *He **went down** the stairs.*
scrivere	scritto	*to write*	Ha **scritto** una lettera. *She has **written** a letter.*
soffrire	sofferto	*to suffer*	Ha **sofferto** molto nella vita. *He has **suffered** a lot in life.*
spegnere	spento	*to switch off*	Ha **spento** la luce ed è uscito. *He **turned off** the light and went out.*
tradurre	tradotto	*to translate*	Ho **tradotto** il documento. *I have **translated** the document.*

vedere	visto	*to see*	Non l'ho **visto.** *I haven't **seen** him.*
venire	venuto	*to come*	Non è ancora **venuta.** *She hasn't **come** yet.*
vincere	vinto	*to win*	Ha **vinto** molto facilmente. *He **won** very easily.*
vivere	vissuto	*to live*	Hanno **vissuto** qui per anni. *They have **lived** here for years.*

❖ Some verbs have both regular and irregular past participle forms:

Verb	Meaning	Regular Past Part.	Irregular Past Part.
vedere	*to see*	veduto	visto
perdere	*to lose*	perduto	perso
succedere	*to happen*	succeduto	successo
seppellire	*to bury*	seppellito	sepolto
cedere	*to search*	ceduto	cesso

Although both regular and irregular forms are considered grammatically correct, note the following:

1. Except for the verb "**cedere**," the use of irregular forms is more common in daily spoken language.

2. The use of "**veduto**," "**perduto**," and "**succeduto**" is often found in literary domain and may sound archaic.

3. The regular form "**perduto**" is often used in the context of morality or soul-searching, e.g., "**anima perduta**" *(lost soul)*. In the context of losing one's way or going astray, the irregular form is often used, e.g., "**Ho perso la mia strada**" *(I have lost my way)*.

4. The regular form "**succeduto**" is often only used when "**succedere**" means *"to succeed,"* as in: "**Il re è succeduto a suo padre**" *(The king succeeded his father).*

5. The irregular form "**cesso**" of the verb "**cedere**" is used in colloquial language as a noun meaning *"toilet."*

❖ The verbs above can be used with prefixes that change the meaning, but the irregular form remains the same. For example, the verb "**rivedere**," derived from "**vedere**," has two past participle forms: "**riveduto**" and "**rivisto**." Similarly, the past participle of the verb "**assolvere**" *(to absolve)* is "**assolto**," similar to "**risolto**," the past participle of "**risolvere**" *(to resolve)*.

Composite Past Tense in French

The compound past tense, or the **passé composé** in French, is used to describe events that happened and were completed in the past or happened in the past and continue in the present. In French, this tense covers both the present perfect and the simple past tenses in English, that is, *"I spoke"* and *"I have spoken"* are both translated to the same tense in French.

The compound past is a compound tense, meaning it requires an auxiliary verb. In English, we use the verb *"to have"* in the present tense as an auxiliary to form the present perfect tense, e.g., *"I have done my homework."*

In French, some verbs use the auxiliary "**avoir**" *(to have)*, while others use the auxiliary "**être**" *(to be)* in the present tense, followed by the past participle.

The past participle of regular verbs using the auxiliary "**avoir**" *(to have)* is formed by adding the appropriate suffix for "**-er**," "**-ir**," and "**-re**" verbs.

"**-er**" verbs		"verb stem" + "**-é**"
"**-ir**" verbs	"**avoir**" in the present tense	"verb stem" + "**-i**"
"**-re**" verbs		"verb stem" + "**-u**"

The past participle of regular verbs using the auxiliary "**être**" *(to be)* is formed in a similar way. One additional requirement here is that the suffix of the past participle must agree with the subject in gender and number, that is, the past participle essentially requires the treatment of an adjective.

"**-er**" verbs		"verb stem" + "**-é**"/ "**-ée**"/ "**-és**"/ "**-ées**"
"**-ir**" verbs	"**être**" in the present tense	"verb stem" + "**-i**"/ "**-ie**"/ "**-is**"/ "**-ies**"
"**-re**" verbs		"verb stem" + "**-u**"/ "**-ue**"/ "**-us**"/ "**-ues**"

Let us look at some examples of verbs conjugated using the auxiliary "**avoir**":

		-er ending e.g., <u>parl</u>er	-ir ending e.g., <u>fin</u>ir	-re ending e.g., <u>vend</u>re
j'	ai			
tu	as			
il/elle/on	a	parlé	fini	vendu
nous	avons			
vous	avez			
ils/elles	ont			

Here are some more examples:

J'**ai visité** l'Egypte l'année dernière.	I **visited** Egypt last year.
Tu **as terminé** ton travail.	You **have finished** your work.
Il **a parlé** avec sa mère.	He **spoke** with his mother.
Nous **avons mangé** toute la nourriture.	We **have eaten** all the food.
Je suis sûr que vous m'**avez entendu** hier soir.	I am sure you **heard** me last night.
Ils **ont travaillé** ici pendant deux ans.	They **worked** here for two years.

Notice that in some of these examples, the compound past in French corresponds to the present perfect, whereas in others it corresponds to the simple past tense depending on the context.

Now, let us look at some examples of verbs conjugated using the auxiliary "**être**":

		-er ending e.g., aller	-ir ending e.g., partir	-re ending e.g., descendre
je	suis	allé(e)	parti(e)	descendu(e)
tu	es	allé(e)	parti(e)	descendu(e)
il/on	est	allé	parti	descendu
elle	est	allée	partie	descendue
nous	sommes	allé(e)s	parti(e)s	descendu(e)s
vous	êtes	allé(e)s	parti(e)s	descendu(e)s
ils	sont	allés	partis	descendus
elles	sont	allées	parties	descendues

Here are some more examples:

Je **suis allé** à la gym la semaine dernière.	*I **went** to the gym last week.*
Tu **es parti** tôt hier soir.	*You **left** early last night.*
Elle **est tombée** dans les escaliers.	*She **fell down** the stairs.*
Nous **sommes entrés** dans la salle.	*We **have entered** the room.*
Vous **êtes arrivés** tard hier soir.	*You **arrived** late last night.*
Ils **sont sortis** ensemble hier.	*They **went out** together yesterday.*

Using the Conjugation Auxiliary "Avoir" vs. "Être"

Finally, we discuss when to use the auxiliary "**avoir**" and the auxiliary "**être**" to form the past participle. The vast majority of French verbs, including all transitive[1] non-reflexive verbs, are conjugated using the auxiliary "**avoir**." Thus, it is easier to memorize the verbs that use "**être**." There are two main categories of verbs that use the auxiliary "**être**":

1. Some intransitive verbs related to *motion* (e.g., to go, to come, to return, to enter, to leave, to fall, to enter, etc.) and a few others related to *change or transformation* (e.g., to become, to be born, to die, to lose weight, etc.).

aller	*to go*	échapper	*to escape*
arriver	*to arrive*	descendre	*to go down or descend*
tomber	*to fall*	tourner	*to turn*
entrer	*to enter*	retourner revenir rentrer	*to return*[2]

---

[1] A verb is transitive if it requires an object. For example, the *"to bring"* can only be transitive, because the meaning is not complete without an object, e.g., *"I bring."*

[2] The three verbs "**retourner**," "**revenir**," and "**rentrer**" can all be used to mean *"to return"*:

- The verb "**retourner**" means *"to go back to where the speaker is not,"* e.g., "**J'habitais à Paris quand j'étais jeune. Je vais y retourner cet été**" *(I lived in Paris when I was young. I will return this summer)*. It can also mean *"to return (something),"* e.g., "**Je vais retourner le livre demain**" *(I will return the book tomorrow)*.
- The verb "**revenir**" means *"to return to where the speaker is, that is, to come back,"* e.g., "**Il est déjà parti mais il va bientôt revenir**" *(He has already left but will return soon)*.
- The verb "**rentrer**" means *"to return (home),"* where *"home"* can refer to a house, country, place of residence, etc., e.g., "**Je vais rentrer chez moi à midi**" *(I will return home at noon)*.

partir	*to leave*	**sortir**	*to go out*
monter	*to climb or go up*	**venir**	*to come*
rester	*to stay*	**demeurer**	*to remain*
naître	*to be born*	**mourir**	*to die*
devenir	*to become*	**passer**	*to pass*
diminuer	*to diminish*	**maigrir**	*to lose weight*

Remember that all the verbs above that use "**être**" are either motion or transformation-related. However, not all motion and transformation-related verbs use "**être**." This should only serve as a guideline to help you memorize the verbs in this category.

Notice that the above verbs use "**être**" only when they are in intransitive form, that is when there is no direct object acted upon. If the verb is transitive, "**avoir**" must be used. For example:

Verb	Example	
retourner *to return*	Il **est** **retourné** au travail hier.	He **returned** to work yesterday.
	J'**ai** **retourné** l'enveloppe.	I **returned** the envelope.
passer *to pass or spend*	Je **suis** **passé** par le parc.	I **passed** by the park.
	J'y **ai** **passé** deux jours.	I **spent** two days there.
entrer *to enter*	Il **est** **entré** dans la pièce.	He **entered** the room.
	Il **a** **entré** les données dans le fichier.	He **entered** the data into the file.

2. All reflexive verbs, which will be covered in detail in **Level IV, Lesson 3**, e.g., "**s'appeler**" *(to call oneself)*, "**se laver**" *(to wash oneself)*, etc.

Irregular Past Participles

Some verbs have irregular past participles and need to be memorized.

Verb	Past Participle	Meaning	Examples
acquérir	acquis	*to acquire*	Il a **acquis** la nouvelle maison. *He **acquired** the new house.*

apprendre	appris	*to learn*	Elle a **appris** le français si vite. *She **learned** French so quickly.*
avoir	eu	*to have*	J'ai **eu** mal à la tête. *I **had** a headache.*
boire	bu	*to drink*	Combien as-tu **bu**? *How much did you **drink**?*
comprendre	compris	*to understand*	J'ai **compris** les consignes. *I **understood** the instructions.*
conduire	conduit	*to drive*	J'ai **conduit** trois heures. *I **drove** three hours.*
craindre	craint	*to fear*	Ils ont **craint** l'ennemi. *They **feared** the enemy.*
devoir	dû	*must*	J'ai **dû** me lever tôt aujourd'hui. *I **had to** wake up early today.*
dire	dit	*to say*	Ils nous ont **dit** que c'était fermé. *They **told** us it was closed.*
écrire	écrit	*to write*	Elle a **écrit** une lettre. *She has **written** a letter.*
être	été	*to be*	Nous avons **été** occupés. *We have **been** busy.*
faire	fait	*to do*	J'ai **fait** tout le travail. *I have **done** all the work.*
falloir	fallu	*to have to*	Il a **fallu** ajuster la taille. *They **had to** adjust the size.*
lire	lu	*to read*	Avez-vous **lu** cet article? *Have you **read** this article?*
mettre	mis	*to put*	J'ai **mis** les affaires dans le van. *I **put** the stuff in the van.*
mourir	mort	*to die*	Il est **mort** l'année dernière. *He **died** last year.*
naître	né	*to be born*	Il est **né** et a été élevé ici. *He **was born** and raised here.*
offrir	offert	*to offer*	Il a **offert** son aide. *He **offered** to help.*
ouvrir	ouvert	*to lose*	J'ai **ouvert** la porte. *I have **opened** the door.*
peindre	peint	*to paint*	Il a **peint** le paysage. *He **painted** the landscape.*
plaire	plu	*to please*	J'espère que l'endroit t'a **plu**. *I hope you **liked** the place.*

pleuvoir	plu	*to rain*	Il a **plu** hier soir. It **rained** last night.
pouvoir	pu	*can*	Nous n'avons pas **pu** sortir hier. We **couldn't** go out yesterday.
prendre	pris	*to take*	Il a **pris** des photos de la voiture. He **took** photos of the car.
recevoir	reçu	*to receive*	Il a **reçu** ma lettre. He **received** my letter.
rire	ri	*to laugh*	J'ai **ri** quand ils me l'ont dit. I **laughed** when they told me.
savoir	su	*to know*	Il a **su** nous orienter. He **knew** how to guide us.
suivre	suivi	*to follow*	Elle a **suivi** les règles. She has **followed** the rules.
vivre	vécu	*to live*	Ils ont **vécu** ici pendant des années. They have **lived** here for years.
voir	vu	*to see*	Je ne l'ai pas **vu**. I haven't **seen** him.
vouloir	voulu	*to want*	Elle a **voulu** juste une tranche. She **wanted** just one slice.

3. THE VERB "TO KNOW"

There are two verbs in Spanish, Portuguese, Italian, and French that mean *"to know"* in English. The two verbs are:

SP	saber	conocer
PT	saber	conhecer
IT	sapere	conoscere
FR	savoir	connaître

Knowing when to use each verb should not be difficult if you understand the subtle difference between the two concepts of *"knowing."*

In short, the verbs "**saber**," "**sapere**," and "**savoir**" are used to describe knowledge of facts, concepts, skills, abilities, etc. On the other hand, the verbs "**conocer**," "**conhecer**," "**conoscere**," and "**connaître**" are used to describe recognition or familiarity with a person, a place, or an object, including a movie, a site, a brand, etc.

In Italian and French, when referring to a language, one could use either verb. The sentence "**Conosco l'italiano**" in Italian indicates that you know some Italian or that you are familiar with the language, whereas "**So l'italiano**" or "**So parlare l'italiano**" indicates that you know Italian well enough to speak it. Similarly, the sentence "**Je connais le français**" in French indicates that you know some French or that you are familiar with the language, whereas "**Je sais le français**" or "**Je sais parler français**" indicates that you know French well enough to speak it. In Spanish and Portuguese, the verb "**saber**" is often used referring to a language.

Here are some examples that highlight the difference:

	Examples	Explanation
EN	*Do you **know** if there is someone inside?*	When referring to a fact (whether someone is inside or not), use "**saber**," "**sapere**," and "**savoir**."
SP	¿**Sabes** si hay alguien dentro?	
PT	Você **sabe** se há alguém dentro?	
IT	**Sai** se c'è qualcuno dentro?	
FR	**Sais**-tu s'il y a quelqu'un à l'intérieur?	
EN	*She doesn't **know** how to swim.*	When referring to a skill, use "**saber**," "**sapere**," and "**savoir**."
SP	Ella no **sabe** nadar.	
PT	Ela não **sabe** nadar.	
IT	Lei non **sa** nuotare.	
FR	Elle ne **sait** pas nager.	
EN	*I don't **know** where there is a school.*	When referring to a fact (whether a school exists nearby), use "**saber**," "**sapere**," and "**savoir**."
SP	No **sé** dónde hay una escuela.	
PT	Não **sei** onde há uma escola.	
IT	Non **so** dove ci sia una scuola.	
FR	Je ne **sais** pas où il y a une école.	
EN	*I don't **know** the city very well.*	When referring to recognizing a place, use "**conocer**," "**conhecer**," "**conoscere**," and "**connaître**."
SP	No **conozco** la ciudad muy bien.	
PT	Não **conheço** muito bem a cidade.	
IT	Non **conosco** molto bene la città.	
FR	Je ne **connais** pas très bien la ville.	
EN	*They don't **know** my parents.*	When referring to recognizing a person, use "**conocer**," "**conhecer**," "**conoscere**," and "**connaître**."
SP	No **conocen** a mis padres.	
PT	Não **conhecem** meus pais.	
IT	Non **conoscono** i miei genitori.	
FR	Ils ne **connaissent** pas mes parents.	

EN	*Do you **know** that movie?*	When referring to recognizing a movie, use "**conocer**," "**conhecer**," "**conoscere**," or "**connaître**."
SP	¿**Conoces** esa película?	
PT	**Conhece** aquele filme?	
IT	**Conosci** quel film?	
FR	**Connaissez**-vous ce film?	
EN	*Do you **know** English?*	When referring to a language, in Spanish and Portuguese, we use "**saber**." In Italian and French, either verb can be used.
SP	¿**Sabes** inglés?	
PT	**Sabe** inglês?	
IT	**Conosci** l'inglese? (or) **Sai** l'inglese?	
FR	**Connaissez**-vous l'anglais? (or) **Savez**-vous l'anglais?	

Expressions that use "Saber," "Sapere," or "Savoir"

The verb "**saber**," "**sapere**," or "**savoir**" is used in many expressions, for example:

SP	lo sé		¿quién sabe?	
PT	eu sei	*I know*	quem sabe?	*who knows?*
IT	lo so		chissà?	
FR	je sais		qui sait?	
SP	para que lo sepas[1]		que yo sepa[1]	
PT	para que saiba[1]	*just so you know*	que eu saiba[1]	*as far as I know*
IT	perché lo sappia[1]		per quanto ne so	
FR	pour que tu le saches[1]		que je sache[1]	

To know each other

The verb "**conocer**," "**conhecer**," "**conoscere**," or "**connaître**" is used to refer to the reciprocal act of knowing each other:

SP	**Nos conocemos**[2] muy bien.	*We **know each other** very well.*
PT	**Nos conhecemos**[2] muito bem.	
IT	**Ci conosciamo**[2] molto bene.	
FR	Nous **nous connaissons**[2] très bien.	
SP	No **se conocen**.	*They don't **know each other**.*
PT	Eles não **se conhecem**.	
IT	Non **si conoscono**.	
FR	Ils ne **se connaissent** pas.	

---

[1] The subjunctive mood is used, which we will study in **Level IV Lesson 5**.
[2] More on the use of reflexive verbs will be covered in detail in **Level IV, Lesson 3**.

Referring to the Past

The verb **"conocer,"** **"conhecer,"** **"conoscere,"** or **"connaître"** can also mean *"to meet"* when referring to the past, for example:

SP	**Conocí** a mi esposa en la universidad.	
PT	**Conheci** minha esposa na faculdade.	*I **met** my wife at university.*
IT	**Ho conosciuto** mia moglie all'università.	
FR	**J'ai connu** ma femme à l'université.	

4. INDEFINITE ADJECTIVES & PRONOUNS

Indefinite adjectives describe a noun in a vague or non-specific way, e.g., *"other people," "each person," "several things," "all schools,"* etc. On the other hand, an indefinite pronoun replaces the noun in a vague and non-specific way, e.g., *"I tell you something," "I speak to someone," "All is well,"* etc. Many indefinite pronouns are identical to their indefinite adjective counterpart, e.g., *"all," "other," "many,"* etc.

Unlike most adjectives in Spanish, Portuguese, Italian, and French, indefinite adjectives precede the noun they describe. Some also change form to agree with the noun in gender and number. Indefinite adjectives and pronouns are used abundantly in the four languages. Here is a list of the most common indefinite adjectives and pronouns:

	Meaning	Examples
bastante, suficiente[1] (SP)(PT) abbastanza (IT) assez (FR)	*enough*	**EN**: *I have **enough** money.* **SP**: Tengo **bastante** dinero. **PT**: Eu tenho **bastante** dinheiro. **IT**: Ho **abbastanza** soldi. **FR**: J'ai **assez** d'argent.
mucho (SP) muito (PT) molto, troppo (IT) beaucoup (FR)	*much many*	**EN**: *There are **many** people here.* **SP**: Hay **mucha** gente aquí. **PT**: Há **muitas** pessoas aqui. **IT**: Qui c'è **troppa** gente. **FR**: Il y a **beaucoup** de monde ici.

---

[1] Although both **"bastante"** and **"suficiente"** are often translated as *"enough,"* **"suficiente"** indicates that something is just barely enough, whereas **"bastante"** often has a more positive connotation that indicates an abundance and is not typically used in negative contexts.

demasiado (SP) demasiado (PT) troppo (IT) trop (FR)	*too*	**EN**: *This car is **too** expensive.* **SP**: Este auto es **demasiado** caro. **PT**: Este carro é **demasiado** caro. **IT**: Questa macchina è **troppo** costosa. **FR**: Cette voiture est **trop** chère.
uno a otro (SP) uns aos outros (PT) l'uno l'altro (IT) l'un l'autre (FR)	*each other*	**EN**: *They must help **each other**.* **SP**: Deben ayudarse **unos a otros**. **PT**: Eles devem ajudar uns aos outros. **IT**: Devono aiutarsi **l'un l'altro**. **FR**: Ils doivent s'aider les uns les autres.
uno u otro (SP) um ou outro (PT) l'uno o l'altro (IT) l'un(e) ou l'autre (FR)	*one or the other*	**EN**: *You must choose **one or the other** of these houses.* **SP**: Debes elegir **una u otra** de estas casas. **PT**: Deve escolher **uma ou outra** dessas casas. **IT**: Devi scegliere **l'una o l'altra** di queste case. **FR**: Il faut choisir **l'une ou l'autre** de ces maisons.
ambos, -as (SP) ambos, -as (PT) entrambi, -e (IT) les deux (FR)	*both*	**EN**: ***Both** options are available.* **SP**: **Ambas** opciones están disponibles. **PT**: **Ambas** as opções estão disponíveis. **IT**: **Entrambe** le opzioni sono disponibili. **FR**: **Les deux** options sont disponibles.
los otros, las otras (SP) os outros, as outras (PT) gli altri, le altre (IT) les autres (FR)	*the others*	**EN**: ***The others** are not available.* **SP**: Los otros no están disponibles. **PT**: Os outros não estão disponíveis. **IT**: **Gli altri** non sono disponibili. **FR**: **Les autres** ne sont pas disponibles.
el resto (SP) o resto (PT) il resto (IT) le reste (FR)	*the rest*	**EN**: ***The rest** of the world is suffering.* **SP**: **El resto** del mundo está sufriendo. **PT**: **O resto** do mundo está sofrendo. **IT**: **Il resto** del mondo sta soffrendo. **FR**: **Le reste** du monde souffre.
mismo (SP) mesmo (PT) stesso (IT) même (FR)	*same, self*	**EN**: *It is the **same** person we saw last night.* **SP**: Es la **misma** persona que vimos anoche. **PT**: É a **mesma** pessoa que vimos ontem à noite. **IT**: È la **stessa** persona che abbiamo visto ieri sera. **FR**: C'est la **même** personne que nous avons vue hier soir.

cierto (SP) certo (PT) certo (IT) certain (FR)	*certain*	**EN**: *Only **certain** people can do that.* **SP**: Solo **ciertas** personas pueden hacer eso. **PT**: Somente **certas** pessoas podem fazer isso. **IT**: Solo **certe** persone possono farlo. **FR**: Seules certaines personnes peuvent le faire.
otro (SP) outro (PT) altro (IT) autre (FR)	*other,* *another*	**EN**: *I'd like **another** glass of water, please.* **SP**: Quisiera **otra** copa de agua por favor. **PT**: Eu gostaria de **outro** copo de água, por favor. **IT**: Vorrei un **altro** bicchiere d'acqua, per favore. **FR**: Je voudrais un **autre** verre d'eau, s'il vous plaît.
todo (SP) todo (PT) tutto (IT) tout (FR)	*all, every*	**EN**: ***All** year round, it rains in the country.* **SP**: **Todo** el año llueve en el país. **PT**: Durante **todo** o ano chove no país. **IT**: **Tutto** l'anno, piove nel paese. **FR**: **Toute** l'année, il pleut dans le pays.
todos (SP) todos (PT) tutti (IT) tous (FR)	*all,* *everybody*	**EN**: ***All** of us are from Australia.* **SP**: **Todos** nosotros somos de Australia. **PT**: **Todos** nós somos da Austrália. **IT**: **Tutti** noi veniamo dall'Australia. **FR**: Nous venons **tous** d'Australie.
poco (SP) pouco (PT) poco (IT) peu (FR)	*little,* *not much*	**EN**: *We need **little** time to arrive.* **SP**: Necesitamos **poco** tiempo para llegar. **PT**: Precisamos de **pouco** tempo para chegar. **IT**: Abbiamo bisogno di **poco** tempo per arrivare. **FR**: Nous avons besoin de **peu** de temps pour arriver.
pocos (SP) poucos (PT) pochi (IT) peu de (FR)	*few*	**EN**: *He has **few** friends at school.* **SP**: Tiene **pocos** amigos en la escuela. **PT**: Ele tem **poucos** amigos na escola. **IT**: Ha **pochi** amici a scuola. **FR**: Il a **peu** d'amis à l'école.
varios (SP) vários (PT) parecchi, diversi (IT) plusieurs (FR)	*several*	**EN**: *You can read **several** books on this topic.* **SP**: Puedes leer **varios** libros sobre este tema. **PT**: Você pode ler **vários** livros sobre esse assunto. **IT**: Puoi leggere **diversi** libri su questo argomento. **FR**: Vous pouvez lire plusieurs livres sur ce sujet.

cualquier (SP) qualquer (PT) qualsiasi (IT) n'importe quel (FR)	*any,* *whichever*	**EN**: *Bring me **any** book you find.* **SP**: Tráeme cualquier libro que encuentres. **PT**: Traga-me qualquer livro que encontrar. **IT**: Portami **qualsiasi** libro trovi. **FR**: Apportez-moi **n'importe quel** livre que vous trouvez.
alguno/-as (SP) alguns/-umas (PT) alcuni, qualche (IT) quelques (FR)	*some, few*	**EN**: *I only have **some** books.* **SP**: Sólo tengo **algunos** libros. **PT**: Só tenho **alguns** livros. **IT**: Ho solo **alcuni** libri. **FR**: Je n'ai que **quelques** livres.
cada (SP)(PT) ogni, ciascuno (IT) chaque (FR)	*each, every*	**EN**: *Brush your teeth after **each** meal.* **SP**: Cepilla tus dientes después de **cada** comida. **PT**: Escove os dentes após **cada** refeição. **IT**: Lavati i denti dopo **ogni** pasto. **FR**: Brossez-vous les dents après **chaque** repas.
algo (SP) (PT) qualcosa (IT) quelque chose (FR)	*something*	**EN**: *I want to say **something** very important.* **SP**: Quiero decir **algo** muy importante. **PT**: Quero dizer **algo** muito importante. **IT**: Voglio dire **qualcosa** di molto importante. **FR**: Je veux dire **quelque chose** de très important.
alguien (SP) alguém (PT) qualcuno (IT) quelqu'un (FR)	*someone*	**EN**: *I talked with **someone** very interesting.* **SP**: Hablé con **alguien** muy interesante. **PT**: Conversei com **alguém** muito interessante. **IT**: Ho parlato con **qualcuno** di molto interessante. **FR**: J'ai parlé avec **quelqu'un** de très intéressant.
nada (SP)(PT) niente (IT) rien (FR)	*nothing*	**EN**: *I am going to do **nothing** all day today.* **SP**: Hoy no voy a hacer **nada** en todo el día. **PT**: Não vou fazer **nada** o dia todo hoje. **IT**: Oggi non farò **niente** tutto il giorno. **FR**: Je ne ferai **rien** de la journée d'aujourd'hui.
nadie (SP) ninguém (PT) nessuno (IT) personne (FR)	*nobody* *not any*	**EN**: ***Nobody** is in the office today.* **SP**: Hoy no hay **nadie** en la oficina. **PT**: **Ninguém** está no escritório hoje. **IT**: Non c'è **nessuno** in ufficio oggi. **FR**: **Personne** n'est au bureau aujourd'hui.
quienquiera (SP) quem quer (PT) chiunque (IT) qui que, quiconque (FR)	*whoever*	**EN**: ***Whoever** it is, it is not important.* **SP**: **Quienquiera** que sea, no es importante. **PT**: **Quem quer** que seja, não é importante. **IT**: **Chiunque** sia, non è importante. **FR**: **Qui que** ce soit, ce n'est pas important.

5. CONJUNCTIONS

Conjunctions are important components of any language as they allow the speaker to join sentences and convey useful meanings.

The most common conjunctions in Spanish, Portuguese, Italian, and French are:

Conjunction	Meaning	Example
y (SP) e (PT)(IT) et (FR)	*and*	**EN**: *I like spring* **and** *summer.* **SP**: Me gusta la primavera **y** el verano. **PT**: Gosto da primavera **e** do verão. **IT**: Mi piacciono la primavera **e** l'estate. **FR**: J'aime le printemps **et** l'été.
o (SP)(IT) ou (PT)(FR)	*or*	**EN**: *I will drink tea* **or** *coffee.* **SP**: Voy a tomar café **o** té. **PT**: Vou tomar café **ou** chá. **IT**: Prenderò un caffè **o** un tè. **FR**: Je boirai du thé **ou** du café.
si (SP)(FR) se (PT)(IT)	*if*	**EN**: *If I am tired, I won't go out.* **SP**: **Si** estoy cansado, no voy a salir. **PT**: **Se** estou cansado, não saio. **IT**: **Se** sono stanco, non esco. **FR**: **Si** je suis fatigué, je ne sors pas.
pero, mas (SP) mas, porém (PT) ma, però (IT) mais (FR)	*but*	**EN**: *I want to sleep,* **but** *I can't.* **SP**: Quiero dormir **pero** no puedo. **PT**: Quero dormir, **mas** não consigo. **IT**: Voglio dormire **ma** non posso. **FR**: Je veux dormir, **mais** je ne peux pas.
entonces (SP) então (PT) allora, poi (IT) alors, puis (FR)	*so* *then*	**EN**: *So, what should we do?* **SP**: ¿**Entonces**, qué debemos hacer? **PT**: **Então** o que deveríamos fazer? **IT**: **Allora**, cosa dobbiamo fare? **FR**: **Alors**, que devrions-nous faire?
según (SP) segundo (PT) secondo (IT) selon (FR)	*according to*	**EN**: *According to the doctors, coffee is not bad.* **SP**: **Según** los médicos, el café no es malo. **PT**: **Segundo** os médicos, o café não faz mal. **IT**: **Secondo** i medici, il caffè non fa male. **FR**: **Selon** les médecins, le café n'est pas mauvais.

excepto, salvo (SP) exceto (PT) tranne, eccetto (IT) sauf, excepté (FR)	*except*	**EN**: *I go to the gym every day **except** Friday.* **SP**: Voy al gimnasio todos los días **excepto** los viernes. **PT**: Vou à academia todos os dias, **exceto** às sextas. **IT**: Vado in palestra tutti i giorni **tranne** il venerdi. **FR**: Je vais à la gym tous les jours **sauf** le vendredi.
sin embargo (SP) no entanto (PT) comunque, tuttavia (IT) cependant, toutefois (FR)	*however*	**EN**: *I am tired. **However,** I can go out with you.* **SP**: Estoy cansado. **Sin embargo**, puedo salir contigo. **PT**: Estou cansado. **No entanto**, posso sair com você. **IT**: Sono stanco. **Comunque**, posso uscire con te. **FR**: Je suis fatigué. **Cependant**, je peux sortir avec toi.
para que (SP)(PT) in modo che (IT) pour que (FR)	*so that* *in order to*	**EN**: *I will summarize the book **so that** you can understand it.* **SP**: Resumiré el libro **para que** puedas entenderlo. **PT**: Vou resumir o livro **para que** você possa entendê-lo. **IT**: Riassumerò il libro **in modo che** tu possa capirlo. **FR**: Je vais résumer le livre **pour que** vous puissiez le comprendre.
porque (SP)(PT) perché (IT) parce que (FR)	*because*	**EN**: *I study Spanish **because** I want to live in Mexico.* **SP**: Estudio español **porque** quiero vivir en México. **PT**: Estudo espanhol **porque** quero morar no México. **IT**: Studio spagnolo **perché** voglio vivere in Messico. **FR**: J'étudie l'espagnol **parce que** je veux vivre au Mexique.
a causa de (SP) por causa de (PT) a causa di (IT) à cause de (FR)	*because of*	**EN**: *We can't go out **because of** the snow.* **SP**: No podemos salir **a causa de** la nieve. **PT**: Não podemos sair **por causa d**a neve. **IT**: Non possiamo uscire **a causa della** neve. **FR**: Nous ne pouvons pas sortir **à cause de** la neige.

en vez de (SP) em vez de (PT) invece di (IT) au lieu de (FR)	*instead of*	**EN**: ***Instead of*** *going out tonight, we'll watch a movie.* **SP**: **En vez de** salir hoy, vamos a ver una película. **PT**: **Em vez de** sair hoje, vamos ver um filme. **IT**: **Invece di** uscire oggi, vedremo un film. **FR**: **Au lieu de** sortir ce soir, nous allons regarder un film.
dado que (SP) dado que (PT) dato che (IT) étant donné que (FR)	*given that*	**EN**: *I'll go to the coffee shop* ***given that*** *I have enough free time.* **SP**: Iré a la cafetería **dado que** tengo suficiente tiempo libre. **PT**: Irei ao café **dado que** tenho tempo livre suficiente. **IT**: Vado al bar **dato che** ho abbastanza tempo libero. **FR**: Je vais aller au café **étant donné que** j'ai assez de temps libre.
por lo tanto (SP) portanto (PT) quindi, pertanto, dunque (IT) donc, par conséquent (FR)	*therefore*	**EN**: *It was late;* ***therefore****, we didn't go out last night.* **SP**: Era tarde; **por lo tanto**, no salimos anoche. **PT**: Era tarde; **portanto**, não saímos ontem à noite. **IT**: Era tardi; **quindi**, non siamo usciti ieri sera. **FR**: Il était tard; **donc** nous ne sommes pas sortis hier soir.
de lo contrario (SP) caso contrário, do contrário (PT) altrimenti (IT) autrement, sinon (FR)	*otherwise*	**EN**: *I hope it doesn't rain;* ***otherwise****, we don't go out.* **SP**: Espero que no llueva; **de lo contrario**, no salimos. **PT**: Espero que não chova**; caso contrário**, não saímos. **IT**: Spero che non piova; **altrimenti**, non usciamo. **FR**: J'espère qu'il ne pleut pas; **sinon**, nous ne sortons pas.
aunque, si bien (SP) embora, mesmo que, se bem que (PT) anche se, benché (IT) bien que, même si, malgré que (FR)	*although*	**EN**: *I understand the problem,* ***although*** *I can't explain it.* **SP**: Entiendo el problema, **aunque** no puedo explicarlo. **PT**: Entendo o problema, **embora** não consiga explicá-lo. **IT**: Capisco il problema, **anche se** non riesco a spiegarlo. **FR**: Je comprends le problème, **même si** je ne peux pas l'expliquer.

a pesar de (SP) apesar de (PT) nonostante (IT) malgré (FR)	*in spite of despite*	**EN:** ***Despite*** *being short, he is a very good player.* **SP: A pesar de** ser bajito, es muy buen jugador. **PT: Apesar de** ser baixo, ele é um jogador muito bom. **IT: Nonostante** sia basso, è un ottimo giocatore. **FR: Malgré** sa petite taille, c'est un très bon joueur.
es decir, o sea (SP) ou seja (PT) cioè, ovvero (IT) c'est-à-dire (FR)	*that is*	**EN:** *I speak English and Spanish,* ***that is****, I'm bilingual.* **SP:** Hablo inglés y español, **es decir**, soy bilingüe. **PT:** Falo inglês e espanhol, **ou seja**, sou bilíngue. **IT:** Parlo inglese e spagnolo, **cioè** sono bilingue. **FR:** Je parle anglais et espagnol, **c'est-à-dire** que je suis bilingue.
es decir, en otras palabras (SP) ou seja, em outras palavras (PT) in altre parole (IT) autrement dit, en d'autres termes (FR)	*in other words*	**EN:** ***In other words****, we must work harder.* **SP: En otras palabras**, debemos trabajar más duro. **PT: Em outras palavras**, devemos trabalhar mais. **IT: In altre parole**, dobbiamo lavorare di più. **FR: Autrement dit**, nous devons travailler plus dur.
mientras (SP) enquanto (PT) mentre (IT) pendant que (FR)	*while*	**EN:** *Let's buy something* **while** *we are here.* **SP:** Compremos algo **mientras** estamos aquí. **PT:** Compremos algo **enquanto** estivermos aqui. **IT:** Compriamo qualcosa **mentre** siamo qui. **FR:** Allons acheter quelque chose **pendant que** nous sommes ici.
mientras (SP) contanto que, enquanto (PT) finché (IT) tant que (FR)	*as long as*	**EN:** ***As long as*** *you are prepared, you don't need to worry.* **SP: Mientras** esté preparado, no necesita preocuparse. **PT: Contanto que** você esteja preparado, não precisa se preocupar. **IT: Finché** sei preparato, non devi preoccuparti. **FR: Tant que** vous êtes prêt, vous n'avez pas à vous inquiéter.

		EN: *We **either** leave now **or** later.*
o ... o ... (SP) ou ... ou ... (PT) o ... o ... (IT) soit ... soit ... (FR)	*either... or...*	SP: **O** nos vamos ahora **o** más tarde. PT: **Ou** vamos embora agora **ou** mais tarde. IT: **O** partiamo ora **o** più tardi. FR: **Soit** nous partons maintenant, **soit** plus tard.
ni ... ni ... (SP) não... nem... (PT) né ... né ... (IT) ni ... ni ... (FR)	*neither ... nor ...*	EN: *My Italian is **neither** good **nor** bad.* SP: Mi italiano no es **ni** bueno **ni** malo. PT: Meu italiano **não** é bom **nem** ruim. IT: Il mio italiano non è **né** buono **né** cattivo. FR: Mon italien n'est **ni** bon **ni** mauvais.
además de (SP) além de (PT) oltre a (IT) en plus de (FR)	*besides*	EN: ***Besides** food, I will order drinks too.* SP: **Además de** la comida, pediré bebidas también. PT: **Além d**a comida, pedirei bebidas tamḃém. IT: **Oltre al** cibo, ordinerò anche da bere. FR: **En plus de** la nourriture, je commanderai aussi des boissons.
aparte de (SP) à parte de (PT) a parte (IT) a part (FR)	*apart from*	EN: ***Apart from** the weather, I don't like this place.* SP: **Aparte de**l clima, no me gusta este lugar. PT: **À parte d**o tempo, não gosto deste lugar. IT: **A parte** il clima, non mi piace questo posto. FR: Apart from the weather, I don't like this place.
a diferencia de (SP) ao contrário de, diferente de você (PT) a differenzia di (IT) contrairement à (FR)	*unlike*	EN: ***Unlike** you, I don't know German.* SP: **A diferencia de** usted, no sé alemán. PT: **Ao contrário de** você, não sei alemão. IT: **A differenza di** te, io non conosco il tedesco. FR: **Contrairement à** vous, je ne connais pas l'allemand.

❖ In Spanish, if the word following "**y**" *(and)* starts with an "**i**" or has the *"ee"* sound, e.g., "**hijo**" *(son)* at the beginning of the word, the "**y**" is replaced with "**e**," e.g., "**español e inglés**" *(Spanish and English)*, "**hijos e hijas**" *(sons and daughters)*, etc. An exception to this rule is if the word starts with a diphthong, such as "**ie**" or "**io**" sounds, e.g., "**agua y hielo**" *(water and ice)*.

Similarly, if the word following "**o**" *(or)* starts with an "**o**" or has the "**o**" sound (e.g., "**hogar**") at the beginning of the word, the "**o**" is replaced with "**u**," e.g., "**siete u ocho**" *(seven or eight)*, "**ayer u hoy**" *(yesterday or today)*.

❖ In Italian, if the word following "**e**" *(and)* starts with an "**e**," the "**e**" is replaced with "**ed**" to avoid the double "**e**" sound. This is called euphonic "**d**," e.g., "**corretto ed esatto**" *(correct and exact)*, "**alberi ed erba**" *(trees and grass)*, etc.

Historically, the euphonic "**d**" was used after "**e**" or "**a**" when followed by *any* vowel. Today, it is generally more accepted to use it only when the "**e**" or "**a**" is followed by the *same* vowel, e.g., "**Manderò un messaggio ad Andrea**" *(I will send a message to Andrea)*.

6. SIMPLE FUTURE TENSE

The simple future tense is used to express events in the future.

In Spanish, Portuguese, and French, there is an informal but common way to express the future tense in the indicative mood is by using the auxiliary verb "*to go.*" It is similar in purpose to the English use of the present progressive tense to talk about the future, e.g., *"I am going to travel."*

To form the informal future tense, the verb "**ir**" *(to go)* can be used in Spanish and Portuguese, and the verb "**aller**" *(to go)* in French. Notice that the verb "**ir**" is followed by prepositional "**a**" to form the informal future tense in Spanish.

- In Spanish:

		-ar ending e.g., hablar	-er ending e.g., comer	-ir ending e.g., vivir
yo	voy a			
tú	vas a			
él/ella/usted	va a	hablar	comer	vivir
nosotros/-as	vamos a			
vosotros/-as	vais a			
ellos/ellas/ustedes	van a			

- In Portuguese:

		-ar ending e.g., falar	-er ending e.g., comer	-ir ending e.g., partir

eu	vou			
ele/ela/você	vai	falar	comer	partir
nós	vamos			
eles/elas/vocês	vão			

- In French:

		-er ending e.g., parler	-ir ending e.g., finir	-re ending e.g., vendre
je	vais			
tu	vas			
il/elle/on	va	parler	finir	vendre
nous	allons			
vous	allez			
ils/elles	vont			

Regular Verb Conjugation

The formal simple future tense is also used to express events in the future and is more common in written literature.

- In Spanish:

The regular verb conjugation uses the *infinitive* as a stem. Conjugation endings are the same for all three verb groups.

	-ar ending hablar *(to speak)*	-er ending comer *(to eat)*	-ir ending vivir *(to live)*
yo	hablar**é**	comer**é**	vivir**é**
tú	hablar**ás**	comer**ás**	vivir**ás**
él/ella/usted	hablar**á**	comer**á**	vivir**á**
nosotros/-as	hablar**emos**	comer**emos**	vivir**emos**
vosotros/-as	hablar**éis**	comer**éis**	vivir**éis**
ellos/ellas/ustedes	hablar**án**	comer**án**	vivir**án**

In addition to expressing events in the future, the simple future tense can also be used to express conjecture or possibility, e.g., "**La chica tendrá 15 años**" (*The girl might be 15 years old*), "**¿Dónde estará mi celular?**" (*Where could my cell phone be?*).

Another less common use of the simple future tense is giving commands, e.g., "**No mentirás**" (*You shall/will not lie*), "**Te sentarás acá**" (*You shall/will sit here*).

- In Portuguese:

The regular verb conjugation uses the *infinitive* as a stem. Conjugation endings are the same for all three verb groups.

	-ar ending falar *(to speak)*	-er ending comer *(to eat)*	-ir ending partir *(to live)*
eu	falar**ei**	comer**ei**	partir**ei**
ele/ela/você	falar**á**	comer**á**	partir**á**
nós	falar**emos**	comer**emos**	partir**emos**
eles/elas/vocês	falar**ão**	comer**ão**	partir**ão**

As in Spanish, the simple future tense in Portuguese can also be used to express conjecture or possibility, e.g., "**A menina terá 15 anos**" (*The girl might be 15 years old*), "**Onde estará meu celular?**" (*Where could my cell phone be?*).

Another less common use of the simple future tense is giving commands, e.g., "**Não mentirá**" (*You shall/will not lie*), "**Sentará aqui**" (*You shall/will sit here*), etc.

- In Italian:

To form the stem of the verb needed for regular verb conjugation, we drop the final "**e**" of the verb and change the final "**-ar**" to "**-er**" in the case of "**-are**" verbs. The endings are the same for the three types of verbs.

	-are ending parlare *(to speak)*	-ere ending vendere *(to sell)*	-ire ending partire *(to leave)*
io	parl<u>e</u>r**ò**	vender**ò**	partir**ò**
tu	parl<u>e</u>r**ai**	vender**ai**	partir**ai**
lui/lei	parl<u>e</u>r**à**	vender**à**	partir**à**
noi	parl<u>e</u>r**emo**	vender**emo**	partir**emo**
voi	parl<u>e</u>r**ete**	vender**ete**	partir**ete**
loro	parl<u>e</u>r**anno**	vender**anno**	partir**anno**

In addition to expressing events in the future, the simple future tense can also be used to express conjecture or possibility, e.g., "**La ragazza <u>avrà</u> 15 anni**" *(The girl might be 15 years old)*, "**Dove <u>sarà</u> il mio cellulare?**" *(Where could my cell phone be?)*, etc.

- In French:

To form the stem of the verb needed for regular verb conjugation, we use the *infinitive* as a stem and drop the final "-**e**" in the case of "-**re**" verbs. The endings are the same for the three types of verbs.

	-er ending parler *(to speak)*	-ir ending finir *(to finish)*	-re ending vendre *(to sell)*
je	parler**ai**	finir**ai**	vendr**ai**
tu	parler**as**	finir**as**	vendr**as**
il/elle/on	parler**a**	finir**a**	vendr**a**
nous	parler**ons**	finir**ons**	vendr**ons**
vous	parler**ez**	finir**ez**	vendr**ez**
ils/elles	parler**ont**	finir**ont**	vendr**ont**

Uses of the simple future tense in French are very similar to that in English. Nevertheless, there are sometimes little differences. For example, in sentences that describe two events occurring in the future linked with "**quand**" *(when)* or "**dès que**" *(once)*, both events are expressed in French using verbs in the simple future tense. While in English we say *"I'll call you <u>when</u> I arrive home,"* in French, we would say "**Je t'appellerai <u>quand</u> j'arriverai à la maison.**" Notice that both verbs "**appeler**" *(to call)* and "**arriver**" *(to arrive)* are in the future tense.

Irregular Verbs in Spanish

In Spanish, there are twelve commonly used irregular verbs in the simple future tense:

1. Five verbs ending in "-**er**" and "-**ir**" drop the "**e**" or "**i**" from the infinitive and add a "**d**." There are five common verbs in this category: "**tener**" *(to have)*, "**poner**" *(to put)*, "**valer**" *(to value or be worth)*, "**venir**" *(to come)*, and "**salir**" *(to go out or to exit)*.

	tener tendr-	poner pondr-	valer valdr-	venir vendr-	salir saldr-
yo	tendré	pondré	valdré	vendré	saldré
tú	tendrás	pondrás	valdrás	vendrás	saldrás
él/ella/usted	tendrá	pondrá	valdrá	vendrá	saldrá
nosotros/-as	tendremos	pondremos	valdremos	vendremos	saldremos
vosotros/-as	tendréis	pondréis	valdréis	vendréis	saldréis
ellos/ellas/ustedes	tendrán	pondrán	valdrán	vendrán	saldrán

2. Five verbs ending in "-er" drop the "e" from the infinitive. There are also five common verbs in this category: "**saber**" *(to know)*, "**poder**" *(can)*, "**caber**" *(to fit)*, "**querer**" *(to want)*, and "**haber**," which is an auxiliary verb equivalent to the English auxiliary verb *"have."*

	saber sabr-	poder podr-	caber cabr-	querer querr-	haber habr-
yo	sabré	podré	cabré	querré	habré
tú	sabrás	podrás	cabrás	querrás	habrás
él/ella/usted	sabrá	podrá	cabrá	querrá	habrá
nosotros/-as	sabremos	podremos	cabremos	querremos	habremos
vosotros/-as	sabréis	podréis	cabréis	querréis	habréis
ellos/ellas/ustedes	sabrán	podrán	cabrán	querrán	habrán

3. The verbs "**decir**" *(to say)* and "**hacer**" *(to do* or *to make)* change their stem to "**dir-**" and "**har-**" to form the simple future tense conjugation. These two verbs are irregular and must be memorized.

	decir dir-	hacer har-
yo	diré	haré
tú	dirás	harás
él/ella/usted	dirá	hará
nosotros/-as	diremos	haremos
vosotros/-as	diréis	haréis
ellos/ellas/ustedes	dirán	harán

Irregular Verbs in Portuguese

In Portuguese, the verbs "**dizer**" (*to say*), "**fazer**" (*to do*), and "**trazer**" (*to bring*) change their stem to "**dir**-," "**far**-," and "**trar**-," respectively, to form the simple conditional tense conjugation. These three verbs are irregular and must be memorized.

	dizer dir-	fazer far-	trazer trar-
eu	dir**ei**	far**ei**	trar**ei**
ele/ela/você	dir**á**	far**á**	trar**á**
nós	dir**emos**	far**emos**	trar**emos**
eles/elas/vocês	dir**ão**	far**ão**	trar**ão**

Irregular Verbs in Italian

In Italian, there are some verbs that are irregular in the simple future tense, which we attempt to summarize here:

1. Some verbs, in addition to dropping the final "**e**," drop the vowel before the final "**r**" from the infinitive to form the stem. For example, the stem from the verb "**andare**" (*to go*) becomes "**andr**-" instead of "**andar**-." Other examples from this group are: "**avere**" (*to have*), "**cadere**" (*to fall*), "**dovere**" (*must*), "**potere**" (*can*), "**sapere**" (*to know*), "**vedere**" (*to see*), and "**vivere**" (*to live*).

	andare andr-	avere avr-	cadere cadr-	dovere dovr-	potere potr-
io	andr**ò**	avr**ò**	cadr**ò**	dovr**ò**	potr**ò**
tu	andr**ai**	avr**ai**	cadr**ai**	dovr**ai**	potr**ai**
lui/lei	andr**à**	avr**à**	cadr**à**	dovr**à**	potr**à**
noi	andr**emo**	avr**emo**	cadr**emo**	dovr**emo**	potr**emo**
voi	andr**ete**	avr**ete**	cadr**ete**	dovr**ete**	potr**ete**
loro	andr**anno**	avr**anno**	cadr**anno**	dovr**anno**	potr**anno**

2. Some short verbs with the "**-are**" ending do not change the "**-ar**" to "**-er**" after dropping the final "**e**" to form the stem. The

most common verbs in this group are: "**dare**" *(to give)*, "**fare**" *(to do or to make)*, and "**stare**" *(to stay or to be)*.

	dare dar-	fare far-	stare star-
io	darò	farò	starò
tu	darai	farai	starai
lui/lei	darà	farà	starà
noi	daremo	faremo	staremo
voi	darete	farete	starete
loro	daranno	faranno	staranno

3. Some verbs, in addition to dropping the final "**e**," replace both the consonant and the vowel preceding the final "**r**" of the infinitive with an extra "**r**" to form the stem. For example, the stem from "**tenere**" *(to hold)* is "**terr-**" instead of "**tener-**." The most common verbs in this group are: "**tenere**" *(to hold)*, "**volere**" *(to want)*, and "**venire**" *(to come)*.

	tenere terr-	volere vorr-	venire verr-
io	terrò	vorrò	verrò
tu	terrai	vorrai	verrai
lui/lei	terrà	vorrà	verrà
noi	terremo	vorremo	verremo
voi	terrete	vorrete	verrete
loro	terranno	vorranno	verranno

4. Some verbs are completely irregular, such as "**essere**" *(to be)* and "**bere**" *(to drink)*, whose stems are "**sar-**" and "**berr-**," respectively.

	essere sar-	bere berr-
io	sarò	berrò
tu	sarai	berrai
lui/lei	sarà	berrà
noi	saremo	berremo
voi	sarete	berrete
loro	saranno	berranno

5. Finally, the same orthographic changes applied to verbs ending in "-**care**," "-**gare**," "-**ciare**," "-**giare**," and "-**gliare**" in the present indicative tense are applied here to maintain the proper pronunciation.

Irregular Verbs in French

Here is a list of the most common irregular verbs in the simple future tense in French:

	je	tu	il/elle	nous	vous	ils/elles
aller *to go*	irai	iras	ira	irons	irez	iront
avoir *to have*	aurai	auras	aura	aurons	aurez	auront
courir *to run*	courrai	courras	courra	courrons	courrez	courront
devenir *to become*	deviendrai	deviendras	deviendra	deviendrons	deviendrez	deviendront
devoir *must*	devrai	devras	devra	devrons	devrez	devront
envoyer *to send*	enverrai	enverras	enverra	enverrons	enverrez	enverront
être *to be*	serai	seras	sera	serons	serez	seront
faire *to do*	ferai	feras	fera	ferons	ferez	feront
falloir *to have to*	-	-	faudra	-	-	-
mourir *to die*	mourrai	mourras	mourra	mourrons	mourrez	mourront
pleuvoir *to rain*	-	-	pleuvra	-	-	-
recevoir *to receive*	recevrai	recevras	recevra	recevrons	recevrez	recevront
revenir *to return*	reviendrai	reviendras	reviendra	reviendrons	reviendrez	reviendront
savoir *to know*	saurai	sauras	saura	saurons	saurez	sauront
tenir *to hold*	tiendrai	tiendras	tiendra	tiendrons	tiendrez	tiendront
valoir *to be worth*	-	-	vaudra	-	-	-

venir *to come*	viendrai	viendras	viendra	viendrons	viendrez	viendront
voir *to take*	verrai	verras	verra	verrons	verrez	verront
vouloir *to want*	voudrai	voudras	voudra	voudrons	voudrez	voudront

There are some verbs that undergo minor spelling changes. Here are some common examples:

	je	tu	il/elle	nous	vous	ils/elles
employer *to hire*	emploierai	emploieras	emploiera	emploierons	emploierez	emploieront
essuyer *to wipe*	essuierai	essuieras	essuiera	essuierons	essuierez	essuieront
nettoyer *to clean*	nettoierai	nettoieras	nettoiera	nettoierons	nettoierez	nettoieront
acheter *to buy*	achèterai	achèteras	achètera	achèterons	achèterez	achèteront
appeler *to call*	appellerai	appelleras	appellera	appellerons	appellerez	appelleront
jeter *to throw*	jetterai	jetteras	jettera	jetterons	jetterez	jetteront

Examples

Here are some examples that use the simple future tense:

SP	**Iré** a Italia el año que viene.	*I **will go** to Italy next year.*
PT	**Irei** para a Itália no próximo ano.	
IT	L'anno prossimo **andrò** in Italia.	
FR	J'**irai** en Italie l'année prochaine.	
SP	**No iré** al gimnasio hoy.	*I **won't go** to the gym today.*
PT	**Não irei** à academia amanhã.	
IT	Oggi **non andrò** in palestra.	
FR	Je **n'irai pas** à la gym aujourd'hui.	
SP	Ella **comprará** una casa en Roma.	*She **will buy** a house in Rome.*
PT	Ela **comprará** uma casa em Roma.	
IT	Lei **comprerà** una casa a Roma.	
FR	Elle **achètera** une maison à Rome.	

SP	**Estudiarás** mucho sólo este fin de semana.	*You **will study** hard only this weekend.*
PT	Você **estudará** muito apenas neste fim de semana.	
IT	**Studierai** duramente solo questo fine settimana.	
FR	Tu **étudieras** dur seulement ce week-end.	
SP	Ellos **vivirán** en una pequeña ciudad.	*They **will live** in a small city.*
PT	Eles **viverão** em uma cidade pequena.	
IT	**Vivranno** in una piccola città.	
FR	Ils **vivront** dans une petite ville.	
SP	Mañana **dormiremos** todo el día.	*We **will sleep** all day tomorrow.*
PT	**Dormiremos** o dia todo amanhã.	
IT	**Dormiremo** tutto il giorno domani.	
FR	Nous **dormirons** toute la journée demain.	

7. TELLING TIME & DESCRIBING THE WEATHER

Telling time and describing the weather are fundamental language skills for any language learner.

Expressing Time in Hours

In Spanish, Portuguese, Italian, and French, the verb *"to be"* is used in the third-person forms to describe time.

In Spanish, Portuguese, and Italian, the singular form of the verb *"to be"* is used for *"one o'clock,"* while other hours (from two to twelve o'clock) use the plural form of the verb *"to be."*

In French, the singular form of the verb *"to be"* is always used, i.e., **"il est"** *(it is)*.

SP	**Es** <u>la</u> una.	*It's one o'clock.*
PT	**É** uma hora.	
IT	**È** <u>l'</u>una.	
FR	**Il est** une heure.	
SP	**Son** <u>las</u> tres.	*It's three o'clock.*
PT	**São** três horas.	
IT	**Sono** <u>le</u> tre	
FR	**Il est** trois heures.	

SP	Son <u>las</u> once.	
PT	**São** onze horas.	***It's*** *eleven o'clock.*
IT	**Sono** <u>le</u> undici.	
FR	**Il est** onze heure.	

Notice the use of the definite article in the examples above in both Spanish and Italian.

To ask what time it is, use the following expression, meaning *"What time is it?"* in English, or more literally: *"What hour is it?"* or *"What hours are they?"*

SP	¿Qué hora es?
PT	Que horas são?
IT	Che ora è? (or) Che ore sono?
FR	Quelle heure est-il?

To ask *"At what time ...?"*, we use:

SP	¿A qué hora ...?
PT	A que horas ...?
IT	A che ora ...?
FR	À quelle heure ...?

Expressing Minutes

To express time in hours and minutes, we use the conjunction *"and"* in Spanish, Portuguese, and Italian. In French, we simply add the minutes after the hour. For example:

SP	Es la una **y** cincuenta.	
PT	É uma **e** cinquenta.	*It's one-fifty.*
IT	È l'una **e** cinquanta.	
FR	Il est une heure cinquante.	
SP	Son las cinco **y** veinticuatro.	
PT	São cinco **e** vinte **e** quatro.	*It's five twenty-four.*
IT	Sono le cinque **e** ventiquattro.	
FR	Il est cinq heures vingt-quatre.	

If you want to say: it is minutes to a certain hour, e.g., *"It's five to ten,"* we use:

SP	Es la una **menos** diez.	
PT	São dez minutos **para** a uma.	*It's ten to one.*
IT	È l'una **meno** dieci.	
FR	Il est une heure **moins** dix.	
SP	Son las diez **menos** cinco.	
PT	São cinco **para** as dez.	*It's five to ten.*
IT	Sono le dieci **meno** cinque.	
FR	Il est dix heures **moins** cinq.	

The *"15 minutes"* and *"30 minutes"* can sometimes be replaced with *"quarter"* and *"half,"* respectively.

SP	Es la una menos **cuarto**.	
PT	São um **quarto** para a uma.	*It's a quarter to one.*
IT	È l'una meno **un quarto**.	
FR	Il est une heure moins **le quart**.	
SP	Son las cuatro y **media**.	
PT	São quatro e **meia**.	*It's four-thirty.*
IT	Sono le quattro e **mezza**.	
FR	Il est quatre heures et **demie**.	

Other Time Expressions

The expressions "**a.m.**" and "**p.m.**" are not commonly used in Spanish, Portuguese, Italian, and French, but you will hear people tell the time using the twelve-hour clock format and expressions like *"in the morning," "in the afternoon," "in the evening,"* or *"at night."*

Here are some expressions that are used to express time with examples:

de la mañana (SP) da manhã (PT) di mattina (IT) du matin (FR)	*in the morning*	**EN**: *It's 9 a.m.* **SP**: Son las nueve **de la mañana**. **PT**: São nove **da manhã**. **IT**: Sono le nove **di mattina**. **FR**: Il est neuf heures **du matin**.

de la tarde (SP) da tarde (PT) del pomeriggio (IT) de l'après-midi (FR)	*in the afternoon*	**EN:** *It's 1 p.m.* **SP:** Es la una **de la tarde**. **PT:** É uma **da tarde**. **IT:** È l'una **del pomeriggio**. **FR:** Il est une heure **de l'après-midi**.
de la noche (SP) da noite (PT) di sera (IT) du soir (FR)	*in the evening*	**EN:** *It's 7 p.m.* **SP:** Son las siete **de la noche**. **PT:** São sete horas **da noite**. **IT:** Sono le sette **di sera**. **FR:** Il est sept heures **du soir**.
mediodía (SP) meio-dia (PT) mezzogiorno (IT) midi (FR)	*noon*	**EN:** *It's noon.* **SP:** Es **mediodía**. **PT:** É **meio-dia**. **IT:** È **mezzogiorno**. **FR:** Il est **midi**.
medianoche (SP) meia-noite (PT) mezzanotte (IT) minuit (FR)	*midnight*	**EN:** *It's midnight.* **SP:** Es **medianoche**. **PT:** É **meia-noite**. **IT:** È **mezzanotte**. **FR:** Il est **minuit**.
al amanecer (SP) ao amanhecer (PT) all'alba (IT) à l'aube (FR)	*at dawn*	**EN:** *We'll meet at dawn.* **SP:** Nos encontraremos **al amanecer**. **PT:** Nos encontraremos **ao amanhecer**. **IT:** Ci vedremo **all'alba**. **FR:** Nous nous retrouverons **à l'aube**.
en punto (SP) em ponto (PT) in punto (IT) pile(s), précise(s) (FR)	*exactly*	**EN:** *It's five o'clock **sharp**.* **SP:** Son las cinco **en punto**. **PT:** São cinco **em ponto**. **IT:** Sono le cinque **precise**. **FR:** Il est cinq heures **piles**.
más o menos (SP) mais ou menos (PT) circa (IT) environ (FR)	*about*	**EN:** *It's about three o'clock.* **SP:** Son las tres **más o menos**. **PT:** São **mais ou menos** três horas. **IT:** Sono **circa** le tre. **FR:** Il est **environ** trois heures.

Weather Expressions

Describing the weather in Spanish, Portuguese, Italian, and French often involves the use of some idiomatic expressions that make little sense if translated into English literally.

Here, we list a few common ways of describing the weather using some of these idiomatic expressions as well as other simple expressions.

Weather Expressions using the verb *"to do"*

SP	¿Qué tiempo **hace**?	*What's the weather like?*
PT	-	
IT	Che tempo **fa**?	
FR	Quel temps **fait**-il?	
SP	**Hace** buen tiempo.	*The weather is good.*
PT	-	
IT	**Fa** bel tempo.	
FR	Il **fait** beau.	
SP	**Hace** mal tiempo.	*The weather is bad.*
PT	-	
IT	**Fa** brutto tempo.	
FR	Il **fait** mauvais.	
SP	**Hace** (mucho) frío.	*It's (too) cold.*
PT	**Faz** (muito) frio.	
IT	**Fa** (molto) freddo.	
FR	Il **fait** (trop) froid.	
SP	**Hace** calor.	*It's hot.*
PT	**Faz** calor.	
IT	**Fa** caldo.	
FR	Il **fait** chaud.	

Weather using Expressions meaning "there is/are"

Expression meaning *"there is"* or *"there are"* are used in many weather expressions, such as:

SP	**Hay** sol.	*The sun is shining.*
PT	**Há** sol.	
IT	**C'è** il sole.	
FR	**Il y a** du soleil.	
SP	**Hay** nubes.	*It's cloudy.*
PT	**Há** nuvens.	
IT	**Ci sono** nuvole.	
FR	**Il y a** des nuages.	

SP	Hay niebla.	
PT	Há nevoeiro.	*It's foggy.*
IT	C'è nebbia.	
FR	Il y a du brouillard.	
SP	Hay neblina.	
PT	Há neblina.	*It's misty.*
IT	C'è foschia.	
FR	Il y a de la brume.	
SP	Hay humedad.	
PT	Há umidade.	*It's humid.*
IT	C'è umidità.	
FR	Il y a de l'humidité.	
SP	Hay relámpagos.	
PT	Há trovões.	*There is lightning.*
IT	Ci sono tuoni.	
FR	Il y a de la foudre.	
SP	Hay un vendaval.	
PT	Há um vendaval.	*There is a windstorm.*
IT	C'è una tempesta.	
FR	Il y a un orage.	

Weather Expressions using the verb *"to be"*

We can also use the verb *"to be"* in the third-person singular form followed by an adjective to describe the weather.

SP	¿Cómo está el tiempo?	
PT	Como está o tempo?	*How's the weather?*
IT	Com'è il tempo?	
FR	Comment est la météo?	
SP	Está soleado.	
PT	Está ensolarado.	*It's sunny.*
IT	È soleggiato.	
FR	C'est ensoleillé.	
SP	Está nublado.	
PT	Está nublado.	*It's cloudy.*
IT	È nuvoloso.	
FR	C'est nuageux.	
SP	Está lluvioso.	
PT	Está chuvoso.	*It's rainy.*
IT	È piovoso.	
FR	C'est pluvieux.	

Weather Expressions using a simple verb

One can also use a simple verb expression in the third-person singular form. Here are some examples:

SP	Llueve.	
PT	Chove.	*It's raining.*
IT	Piove.	
FR	Il pleut.	
SP	Nieva.	
PT	Neva.	*It's snowing.*
IT	Nevica.	
FR	Il neige.	
SP	Llovizna.	
PT	Garoa.	*It's sprinkling.*
IT	Pioviggina.	
FR	Il bruine.	
SP	Truena.	
PT	Troveja.	*It's thundering.*
IT	Tuona.	
FR	Il tonne.	

8. ADVERBS

An adverb is a word that modifies a verb, an adjective, or another adverb. Adverbs usually answer questions such as how, how often, how long, when, where, etc.

A lot of adverbs have the ending "-**mente**" in Spanish, Portuguese, and Italian, or "-**ment**" in French. This is, more or less, similar to the ending "*-ly*" in English. Nevertheless, there are many other adverbs and adverbial phrases that do not follow this simple rule. We will attempt to classify the most common adverbs into some categories for easier memorization.

Forming an Adverb

Many adverbs can be formed by simply adding "-**mente**" in Spanish, Portuguese, and Italian, or "-**ment**" in French, to the *feminine* singular adjective.

In Italian, if the adjective ends with "**-le**" or "**-re**" preceded by a vowel, we simply drop the final "**-e**."

Here are some examples:

Adverb in English		Masculine singular adjective	Feminine singular adjective	Adverb in Spanish, Portuguese, Italian, & French
slowly	SP	lento	lenta	lentamente
	PT	lento	lenta	lentamente
	IT	lento	lenta	lentamente
	FR	lent	lente	lentement
quickly	SP	rápido	rápida	rápidamente
	PT	rápido	rápida	rapidamente
	IT	rapido	rapida	rapidamente
	FR	rapide	rapide	rapidement
quietly	SP	tranquilo	tranquila	tranquilamente
	PT	tranquilo	tranquila	tranquilamente
	IT	tranquillo	tranquilla	tranquillamente
	FR	tranquille	tranquille	tranquillement
exactly	SP	exacto	exacta	exactamente
	PT	exato	exata	exatamente
	IT	esatto	esatta	esattamente
	FR	exact	exacte	exactement
easily	SP	fácil	fácil	fácilmente
	PT	fácil	fácil	facilmente
	IT	fac<u>il</u>e	facile	facilmente
	FR	facile	facile	facilement
normally	SP	normal	normal	normalmente
	PT	normal	normal	normalmente
	IT	norm<u>al</u>e	normale	normalmente
	FR	normal	normale	normalement
generally	SP	general	general	generalmente
	PT	geral	geral	geralmente
	IT	gener<u>al</u>e	generale	generalmente
	FR	général	générale	généralement

In Italian, some adverbs ending with "**-mente**" slightly deviate from the above rules. For example:

benevolent	benevolo	*benevolently*	benevolmente

light	leggero	*lightly*	leggermente
original	originale	*originally*	originariamente
violent	violento	*violently*	violentemente

In French, some adverbs ending with "**-ment**" slightly deviate from the above rules. For example:

| *recent* | récent | *recently* | récemment |
| *violent* | violent | *violently* | violemment |

Not all adverbs are formed by adding the "**-mente**" or "**-ment**" ending, similar to the fact that not all English adverbs are formed by adding "*-ly*" to the corresponding adjective. Some adverbs do not follow any particular rule.

For example:

SP	"**bueno**" *(good)* > "**bien**" *(well)*	"**malo**" *(bad)* > "**mal**" *(badly)*
PT	"**bom**" *(good)* > "**bem**" *(well)*	"**ruim**" *(bad)* > "**mal**" *(badly)*
IT	"**buono**" *(good)* > "**bene**" *(well)*	"**cattivo**" *(bad)* > "**male**" *(badly)*
FR	"**bon**" *(good)* > "**bien**" *(well)*	"**mauvais**" *(bad)* > "**mal**" *(badly)*

The Adverbs *"So"* & *"Such"*

Another common adverb that can be translated as *"such"* or *"so"* is:

SP	¡Es un gato **tan** lindo!	
PT	Ele é um gato **tão** fofo!	*He is **such** a pretty cat.*
IT	È un gatto **così** carino!	
FR	C'est un **si** joli chat.	
SP	¡Este gato es **tan** lindo!	
PT	Esse gato é **tão** fofo!	*This cat is **so** pretty.*
IT	Questo gatto è **così** carino!	
FR	Ce chat est **si** joli.	

The Adverbs *"Too"* & *"Neither"*

Here, we discuss the common adverbs used to express *agreement* with *affirmative* and *negative* statements. For example:

SP	A: Yo hablo italiano. B: Yo **también**.	
PT	A: Eu falo italiano. B: Eu **também**.	*A: I speak Italian.*
IT	A: Io parlo italiano. B: **Anche** io.	*B: Me **too**.*
FR	A: Je parle italien. B: Moi **aussi**.	
SP	A: Yo no hablo italiano. B: Yo **tampoco**.	
PT	A: Eu não falo italiano. B: Eu **também não**. (or) Eu **tampouco**.	*A: I don't speak Italian.*
IT	A: Io non parlo italiano. B: **Neanche** io. (or) **Nemmeno** io.	*B: Me **neither**.*
FR	A: Je ne parle pas italien. B: Moi **non plus**.	

To show *disagreement* with affirmative and negative statements, we simply use *"no"* and *"yes,"* respectively, for example:

SP	A: Yo hablo italiano. B: Yo **no**.	
PT	A: Eu falo italiano. B: Eu **não**.	*A: I speak Italian.*
IT	A: Io parlo italiano. B: Io **no**.	*B: I **don't**.*
FR	A: Je parle italien. B: Moi **non**.	
SP	A: Yo no hablo italiano. B: Yo **sí**.	
PT	A: Eu não falo italiano. B: Eu **sim**.	*A: I don't speak Italian.*
IT	A: Io non parlo italiano. B: Io **sì**.	*B: I **do**.*
FR	A: Je ne parle pas italien. B: Moi **oui**.	

In Spanish and Italian, if a verb like **"gustar"** or **"piacere"** is used, the subject pronoun is replaced with a prepositional **"a"** followed by the prepositional object pronoun. For example:

SP	A: Me gusta el té. B: <u>A mí</u> **también**.	*A: I like tea.* *B: Me **too**.*
IT	A: Mi piace il tè. B: **Anche** <u>a me</u>.	
SP	A: No me gusta el té. B: <u>A mí</u> **tampoco**.	*A: I don't like tea.* *B: Me **neither**.*
IT	A: Non mi piace il tè. B: **Nemmeno** <u>a me</u>.	

The same concept is applied in case of *disagreement*, for example:

SP	A: Me gusta el té. B: <u>A mí</u> **no**.	*A: I like tea.* *B: I **don't**.*
IT	A: Mi piace il tè. B: <u>A me</u> **no**.	
SP	A: No me gusta el té. B: <u>A mí</u> **sí**.	*A: I don't like tea.* *B: I **do**.*
IT	A: Non mi piace il tè. B: <u>A me</u> **sì**.	

The Adverbs "Still," "Yet," and "Already"

When followed by a verb in the present tense, "**todavía**" or "**aún**" in Spanish, "**ainda**" in Portuguese, "**ancora**" in Italian, and "**encore**" in French generally mean *"still"* in affirmative and negative expressions. The same word can also mean *"yet"* in a negative expression if a verb in the present perfect tense is used. For example:

SP	**Todavía** vivo en Italia.	*I **still** live in Italy.*
PT	**Ainda** moro na Itália.	
IT	Vivo **ancora** in Italia.	
FR	J'habite **encore** en Italie.	
SP	**Todavía** no hablo bien inglés.	*I **still** don't speak English well.*
PT	**Ainda** não falo bem inglês.	
IT	Non parlo **ancora** bene l'inglese.	
FR	Je ne parle pas **encore** bien anglais.	
SP	**Todavía** no he vuelto a casa.	*I have **not** returned home **yet**.*
PT	**Ainda** não voltei para casa.	
IT	Non sono **ancora** tornato a casa.	
FR	Je ne suis pas **encore** rentré.	

The words "**ya**" in Spanish, "**já**" in Portuguese, "**già**" in Italian, and "**déjà**" in French generally mean *"already."*

Below are some examples of the meaning of *"already"* in both the present tense and the present perfect tense:

a) Present Tense

SP	**Todavía no** hablo bien inglés.	
PT	**Ainda não** falo bem inglês.	
IT	**Non** parlo **ancora** bene l'inglese.	*I **still** don't speak English well.*
FR	Je **ne** parle **pas encore** bien anglais.	
SP	**Ya** hablo bien inglés.	
PT	**Já** falo bem inglês.	
IT	Parlo **già** bene l'inglese.	*I **already** speak English well.*
FR	Je parle **déjà** bien l'anglais.	

b) Present Perfect Tense

SP	**Todavía no** he vuelto a casa.	
PT	**Ainda não** voltei para casa.	
IT	**Non** sono **ancora** tornato a casa.	*I haven't returned home **yet**.*
FR	Je ne suis pas **encore** rentré.	
SP	**Ya** he vuelto a casa.[1]	
PT	**Já** voltei para casa.[2]	
IT	Sono **già** tornato a casa.	*I have **already** returned home.*
FR	Je suis **déjà** rentré chez moi.	

In the present tense, the opposite of *"still"* is *"no longer."* For example:

SP	**Todavía** vivo en Italia.	
PT	**Ainda** moro na Itália.	
IT	Vivo **ancora** in Italia.	*I **still** live in Italy.*
FR	J'habite **encore** en Italie.	

---

[1] In Latin American Spanish, it is common to use the preterite with "**ya**" to describe finished actions, e.g., "**Ya volví a casa**" *(I have already returned home)*. The English equivalent, however, still uses the present perfect to express the same meaning.

[2] In Portuguese, we use the preterite with "**já**" to describe finished actions, e.g., "**Já voltei para casa**" *(I have already returned home)*. Notice that the English equivalent uses the present perfect to express the same meaning.

SP	Ya no vivo en Italia.	
PT	Já não moro na Itália. Não moro mais na Itália.	*I **no longer** live in Italy.*
IT	Non vivo più in Italia.	
FR	Je n'habite plus en Italie.	

The Adverb *"Ago"*

The adverb of time meaning *"ago"* is used to describe something that happened and ended in the past. Here are the examples:

SP	Hablé con mi hermana **hace** tres meses.	
PT	Falei com minha irmã **há** três meses.	*I spoke to my sister three months*
IT	Ho parlato con mia sorella tre mesi **fa**.	***ago.***
FR	J'ai parlé à ma sœur **il y a** trois mois.	
SP	Me desperté **hace** 15 minutos.	
PT	Acordei **há** 15 minutos.	*I woke up 15 minutes **ago**.*
IT	Mi sono svegliato 15 minuti **fa**.	
FR	Je me suis réveillé **il y a** 15 minutes.	

The Adverb "Desde" in Spanish & Portuguese

Depending on the context, **"desde"** is used to indicate a point in time and can mean *"since"* or *"from."* For example:

SP	**Desde** que era niño, he jugado al fútbol.	***Since** I was a child, I have*
PT	**Desde** criança jogo futebol.	*played football.*
SP	**Desde** entonces, no fuimos allá.	***Since** then, we didn't go there.*
PT	**Desde** então, não fomos lá.	
SP	Te dije eso **desde** el principio.	*I told you that **from** the*
PT	Eu te disse isso **desde** o princípio.	*beginning.*

Adverbial Phrases Describing Frequency of Occurrence

The following feminine nouns are used to describe the frequency of occurrence:

SP	"**vez**" *(time)*	"**veces**" *(times)*
PT	"**vez**" *(time)*	"**vezes**" *(times)*
IT	"**volta**" *(time)*	"**volte**" *(times)*
FR	"**fois**" *(time)*	"**fois**" *(times)*

The English equivalents are often *"time,"* and its plural *"times,"* e.g., *"how many times did you win?"*

Here is a list of some adverbial phrases that use these nouns:

SP	esta vez		cada vez menos		
PT	desta vez	*this time*	cada vez menos		*less and less*
IT	questa volta		ogni volta meno		
FR	cette fois		de moins en moins		
SP	la próxima vez		la última vez		
PT	a próxima vez	*next time*	a última vez		*last time*
IT	la prossima volta		l'ultima volta		
FR	la prochaine fois		la dernière fois		
SP	cada vez		una vez		
PT	cada vez	*each time*	uma vez		*one time*
IT	ogni volta	*every time*	una volta		*once*
FR	chaque fois		une fois		
SP	por primera vez		por última vez		
PT	pela primeira vez	*for the first*	pela última vez		*for the last*
IT	per la prima volta	*time*	per l'ultima volta		*time*
FR	pour la première fois		pour la dernière fois		
SP	algunas veces		de vez en cuando		
PT	algumas vezes	*at times*	de vez em quando		*from time to*
IT	qualche volta	*some time*	di volta in volta		*time*
FR	quelquefois		de temps en temps		
SP	a veces		una vez		
PT	as vezes	*sometimes*	uma vez		*one time*
IT	a volte		una volta		*once*
FR	parfois		une fois		
SP	varias veces		tres veces		
PT	várias vezes		três vezes		
IT	molte volte più volte	*many times*	tre volte		*three times*
FR	plusieurs fois		trois fois		
SP	muchas veces		¿Cuántas veces?		
PT	muitas vezes	*many times*	Quantas vezes?		*How many*
IT	tante volte		Quante volte?		*times?*
FR	beaucoup de fois		Combien de fois?		

9. Present Participle & Gerund in French

The *present participle* has some important uses in French.

The conjugation of the present participle in French is straightforward. We start with the first-person plural form, that is, the "**nous**" form, and we replace the final "-**ons**" with "-**ant**." The present participle has only one form. There is no gender or number associated with the present participle. Let us look at some examples of forming the present participle:

nous parlons	*we speak*	**parlant**	*speaking*
nous mangeons	*we eat*	**mangeant**	*eating*
nous choisissons	*we choose*	**choisissant**	*choosing*
nous buvons	*we drink*	**buvant**	*drinking*

Notice that any spelling change in the "**nous**" form is carried over to the present participle.

There are only three irregular verbs in the present participle: "**être**" *(to be)*, "**avoir**" *(to have)*, and "**savoir**" *(to know)*. The present participles of these verbs are: "**étant**," "**ayant**," and "**sachant**," respectively.

The present participle is used to describe the action of a noun or pronoun that is unrelated to the action described by the main verb. For example:

Nous avons vu l'homme **entrant** dans le bâtiment.	*We saw the man **entering** the building.*
Étant occupé, il a refusé de prendre rendez-vous.	***Being** busy, he declined to make an appointment.*
Voulant être entendu, il a décidé de se lever et de parler fort.	***Wanting** to be heard, he decided to stand up and speak loudly.*

Sometimes the past participle is used to replace a relative clause, for example:

Les personnes **portant** des sacs doivent attendre.	*People **carrying** (who carry) bags must wait.*

| Les animaux domestiques **ayant** des papiers peuvent voyager. | *Pets **having** (that have) documentation can travel.* |
| Des techniciens **sachant** réparer les téléphones sont disponibles. | *Technicians **knowing** (who know) how to fix phones are available.* |

When the present participle is preceded by the preposition "**en**," it is referred to as *gerund*. In this context, the preposition "**en**" can be translated as *"while," "upon,"* or *"by,"* for example:

Il s'est dormi **en regardant** la télé.	*He slept **while watching** TV.*
Il est devenu nerveux **en me voyant**.	*He got nervous **upon seeing** me.*
En étudiant dur, il a réussi l'examen.	***By studying** hard, he passed the exam.*
C'est **en suivant** les règles qu'il a réussi.	*It is **by following** the rules that he succeeded.*

Sometimes "**tout**" *(all)* precedes the preposition "**en**" when forming the gerund. This cannot be translated literally, but often highlights a contradiction between two actions or events. The meaning becomes closer to *"even though,"* for example:

| **Tout en étant** malade, il a réussi à être le meilleur joueur sur le terrain. | ***While being** sick, he managed to be the best player on the pitch.* |
| **Tout en prétendant** être innocent, les preuves étaient contre lui. | ***While claiming** to be innocent, the evidence was against him.* |

The French language does not have a direct equivalent of the present and past continuous tense. Thus, the present participle is not used in this case.

LEVEL IV: INTERMEDIATE

At this intermediate level, we encounter new topics, some familiar thanks to our knowledge of English and some new topics that are unique to the Romance languages. Use the Anki cards to reinforce these topics in your memory with reviews and exercises.

1. DEGREES OF COMPARISON

In this lesson, we will examine different ways of comparing nouns, indicating their equality, inequality, or the extreme degree of an adjective. We will study the comparison of equality, the comparison of inequality, and superlatives.

Comparatives of Equality

The most common expressions in this category are:

1. *as (adjective/ adverb) as …*

SP	tan + (adj./adv.) + como …	
PT	tão + (adj./adv.) + quanto …	*as (adj./adv.) as …*
IT	così + (adj./adv.) + come … tanto + (adj./adv.) + quanto …	
FR	aussi + (adj./adv.) + que …	

Here are some examples:

SP	Este auto es **tan** caro **como** una casa.	
PT	Este carro é **tão** caro **quanto** uma casa.	*This car is **as***
IT	Questa macchina è **così** costosa **come** una casa. Questa macchina è **tanto** costosa **quanto** una casa.	*expensive **as** a house.*
FR	Cette voiture est **aussi** chère **qu'**une maison.	
SP	Ella es **tan** alta **como** su hermana.	
PT	Ela é **tão** alta **quanto** a irmã.	*She is **as** tall **as***
IT	Lei è **così** alta **come** sua sorella. Lei è **tanto** alta **quanto** sua sorella.	*her sister.*
FR	Elle est **aussi** grande **que** sa sœur.	

SP	Él·habla **tan** claro **como** un profesor.	*He speaks **as** clearly **as** a teacher.*
PT	Ele fala **tão** claramente **quanto** um professor.	
IT	Parla **così** chiaro **come** un insegnante. Parla **tanto** chiaro **quanto** un insegnante.	
FR	Il parle **aussi** clairement **qu'**un professeur.	

Notice that it is more common, in Italian, to drop the first word, "**così**" or "**tanto**," in the construction in informal speech, e.g., "**Lei è alta come/quanto sua sorella**" *(She is as tall as her sister).*

2. *as much/many (noun) as …*

SP	**tanto/-a(s)** + (noun) + **como** …	*as much/many (noun) as …*
PT	**tanto/-a(s)** + (noun) + **como/quanto** …	
IT	**tanto/-a/-i/-e** + (noun) + **quanto** …	
FR	**autant de** + (noun) + **que** …	

Here are some examples:

SP	Él tiene **tanto** dinero **como** un millonario.	*He has **as much** money **as** a millionaire.*
PT	Ele tem **tanto** dinheiro **quanto** um milionário.	
IT	Ha **tanti** soldi **quanto** un milionario.	
FR	Il a **autant d'**argent **qu'**un millionnaire.	
SP	Hay **tanta** gente acá **como** en Londres.	*There are **as many** people here **as** in London.*
PT	Há **tantas** pessoas aqui **como** em Londres.	
IT	Ci sono **tante** persone qui **come** a Londra.	
FR	Il y a **autant de** monde ici **qu'**à Londres.	

Comparatives of Inequality

The following formula is used to express inequality when comparing two adjectives, adverbs, or nouns:

SP	**más/menos** … **que** …	*more/less … than …*
PT	**mais/menos** … **que** …	
IT	**più/meno** … **di** …	
FR	**plus/moins (de)**… **que** …	

Notice that, in French, "**de**" is added only when comparing nouns, but not when comparing adjectives or adverbs.

Here are some examples:

SP	Ella es **más** alta **que** su hermana.	*She is taller than her sister.*
PT	Ela é **mais** alta **que** a irmã.	
IT	È **più** alta **di** sua sorella.	
FR	Elle est **plus** grande **que** sa sœur.	
SP	Él habla **más** claro **que** un profesor.	*He speaks more clearly than a teacher.*
PT	Ele fala **mais** claro **que** um professor.	
IT	Parla **più** chiaro **di** un professore.	
FR	Il **parle** plus clairement **qu'**un professeur.	
SP	Él tiene **más** dinero **que** el presidente.	*He has more money than the president.*
PT	Ele tem **mais** dinheiro **que** o presidente.	
IT	Ha **più** soldi **d**el presidente.	
FR	Il a **plus** <u>d</u>'argent **que** le président.	
SP	Somos **menos** ricos **que** nuestros padres.	*We are less rich than our parents.*
PT	Somos **menos** ricos **que** nossos pais.	
IT	Siamo **meno** ricchi **dei** nostri genitori.	
FR	Nous sommes **moins** riches **que** nos parents.	
SP	Él habla **menos** claro **que** un profesor.	*He speaks less clearly than a teacher.*
PT	Ele fala **menos** claramente **que** um professor.	
IT	Parla **meno** chiaramente **di** un professore.	
FR	Il parle **moins** clairement **qu'**un professeur.	
SP	Él tiene **menos** paciencia **que** mi hermano.	*He has less patience than my brother.*
PT	Ele tem **menos** paciência **que** o meu irmão.	
IT	Ha **meno** pazienza **di** mio fratello.	
FR	Il a **moins** <u>de</u> patience **que** mon frère.	

Some adjectives have irregular forms:

SP	bueno	*good*	mejor	*better*
PT	bom		melhor	
IT	buono		**migliore** (or) **più buono**	
FR	bon		meilleur	
SP	mal	*bad*	peor	*worse*
PT	ruim		pior	
IT	cattivo		**peggiore** (or) **più cattivo**	
FR	mauvais		**pire** (or) **plus mauvais**	
SP	viejo	*old*	mayor	*older*
PT	velho		maior	
IT	vecchio		**maggiore** (or) **più vecchio**	
FR	vieux		**plus vieux**	

SP	joven		menor	
PT	jovem	*young*	menor	*younger*
IT	giovane		minore (or) **più giovane**	
FR	jeune		**plus jeune**	
SP	grande		mayor	
PT	grande	*large*	maior	*larger*
IT	grande		maggiore (or) **più grande**	
FR	grand		**plus grand**	
SP	pequeño		menor	
PT	pequeno	*small*	menor	*smaller*
IT	piccolo		minore (or) **più piccolo**	
FR	petit		**plus petit**	

In the special case of comparing an adjective to another adjective of the same noun in Italian, we use "**che**" instead of "**di**" before the second adjective. For example:

Il suo discorso è **più** emotivo **che** accurato.	*His speech is **more** emotional **than** it is accurate.*
Sono **più** professionali **che** esperti.	*They are **more** professional **than** they are experienced.*

Superlatives

There are two ways to express the large or extreme degrees of an adjective.

1. Relative Superlatives

SP	el/la/los/las + **más/menos** + (adj.)	
PT	o/a/os/as + **mais/menos** + (adj.)	*the + most/least + (adj.)*
IT	il/la/i/le + **più/meno** + (adj.)	
FR	le/la/les + **plus/moins** + (adj.)	

Inserting a noun between the definite article and *"most/least"* is optional.

Here are some examples:

SP	Ella es **la más** inteligente de su clase.	
PT	Ela é **a mais** inteligente de sua classe.	*She is **the most** intelligent in her class.*
IT	Lei è **la più** intelligente della sua classe.	
FR	Elle est **la plus** intelligente de sa classe.	

SP	Somos **los menos** afectados por la crisis.	*We are **the least** affected by the crisis.*
PT	Somos **os menos** afetados pela crise.	
IT	Siamo **i meno** colpiti dalla crisi.	
FR	Nous sommes **les moins** touchés par la crise.	
SP	Es el <u>tema</u> **más** importante en el país.	*This is **the most** important topic in the country.*
PT	Este é o <u>tema</u> **mais** importante do país.	
IT	È la <u>questione</u> **più** importante del paese.	
FR	C'est le <u>sujet</u> **le plus** important du pays.	
SP	Es **el** <u>político</u> **menos** corrupto del parlamento.	*He is **the least** corrupt politician in the parliament.*
PT	Ele é **o** <u>político</u> **menos** corrupto do parlamento.	
IT	È **il** <u>politico</u> **meno** corrotto in parlamento.	
FR	Il est **le** <u>politicien</u> **le moins** corrompu du parlement.	
SP	Son **las** <u>mujeres</u> **más** valientes que he visto en mi vida.	*They are **the most** courageous women I have ever seen.*
PT	São **as** <u>mulheres</u> **mais** corajosas que já vi.	
IT	Sono **le** <u>donne</u> **più** coraggiose che abbia mai visto.	
FR	Ce sont **les** <u>femmes</u> **les plus** courageuses que j'ai jamais vues.	

The following adjectives (listed here in their singular masculine form) from the comparison of inequality have irregular forms as relative superlatives:

SP	**bueno**		**el mejor**	
PT	**bom**	*good*	**o melhor**	*best*
IT	**buono**		**il migliore** (or) **il più buono**	
FR	**bon**		**le meilleur**	
SP	**mal**		**el peor**	
PT	**ruim**	*bad*	**o pior**	*worst*
IT	**cattivo**		**il peggiore** (or) **il più cattivo**	
FR	**mauvais**		**le pire** (or) **le plus mauvais**	
SP	**viejo**		**el mayor**	
PT	**velho**	*old*	**o maior**	*oldest*
IT	**vecchio**		**il maggiore** (or) **il più vecchio**	
FR	**vieux**		**le plus vieux**	

SP	joven		el menor	
PT	jovem	*young*	o menor	*youngest*
IT	giovane		il minore (or) il più giovane	
FR	jeune		le plus jeune	
SP	grande		el mayor	
PT	grande	*large*	o maior	*largest*
IT	grande		il maggiore (or) il più grande	
FR	grand		le plus grand	
SP	pequeño		el menor	
PT	pequeno	*small*	o menor	*smallest*
IT	piccolo		il minore (or) il più piccolo	
FR	petit		le plus petit	

2. Absolute Superlatives

One can express an absolute superlative by simply preceding the adjective with an adverb such as *"very"* or *"extremely."* Here are some examples:

SP	Este estadio está **muy** frío.	
PT	Este estádio está **muito** frio.	*This stadium is **very** cold.*
IT	Questo stadio è **molto** freddo.	
FR	Ce stade est **très** froid.	
SP	El café está **extremamente**[1] caliente.	
PT	O café está **extremamente** quente.	*The coffee is **extremely** hot.*
IT	Il caffè è **estremamente** caldo.	
FR	Le café est **extrêmement** chaud.	

In Spanish and Italian, there is another way to express absolute superlatives by using adjectives ending in "**-ísimo/-a (s)**" in Spanish "**-issimo/-a/-i/-e**" in Italian, translated as *"very"* or *"quite."* It is constructed by removing the vowel at the end of the adjective (if it exists) and attaching the suffix.

SP	bueno		buenísimo	
IT	buono	*good*	buonissimo	*very good*

---

[1] Another common adverb in Spanish that is equivalent to "**extremamente**" is "**sumamente**."

SP	malo	*bad*	malísimo	*very bad*
IT	cattivo		cattivissimo	
SP	grande	*large*	grandísimo	*very large*
IT	grande		grandissimo	
SP	pequeño	*small*	pequeñísimo	*very small*
IT	piccolo		piccolissimo	

2. PAST TENSE: PRETERITE VS. IMPERFECT

In Spanish and Portuguese, the tense that often corresponds to the simple past tense in English is called the *preterite tense*. In Italian and French, the present perfect tense covers both the present perfect and the simple past tenses in English, that is, *"I spoke"* and *"I have spoken"* are both translated to the same tense in Italian and French. In French, this tense is also called the *composite past*.

The *past absolute tense* in Italian and the *simple past tense* in French are equivalent to the preterite tense in Spanish and Portuguese. However, they are considered more formal and are less used in common-day language. The present perfect tense is often used instead in daily life in Italian and French. We will cover the most important aspects of the past absolute tense in Italian and the simple past tense in French in **Level V, Lesson 2**.

In addition to the *preterite tense* (in Spanish and Portuguese) and the *present perfect tense* (in Italian and French), there is another past tense that is used to talk about habits, actions, and descriptions in the past. This tense is called the *imperfect indicative tense*. This tense is often translated as in the example *"I used to speak"* or *"I would speak"*

In Portuguese, the present perfect tense is used to describe repeated actions in the past that extend to the present. It is more like the present perfect continuous tense in English, e.g., *"I have been working hard."* The present perfect tense in English is often mapped into the *preterite tense* in Portuguese.

	"I have spoken"	*"I spoke"*	*"I used to speak"* or *"I would speak"*
SP	*present perfect* **"yo hé hablado"**	*preterite* **"yo hablé"**	*imperfect* **"yo hablaba"**
PT	*preterite* **"eu falei"**		*imperfect* **"eu falava"**
IT	*present perfect* **"io ho parlato"**		*imperfect* **"io parlavo"**
FR	*present perfect* **"j'ai parlé"**		*imperfect* **"je parlais"**

Uses

The *preterite tense* is used in Spanish and Portuguese to describe:

1. Completed actions that have definite beginning and end points, usually identified by expressions such as: *"yesterday," "last night," "last week," "in 1852,"* etc.
2. Actions which lasted a defined duration of time, usually identified by expressions such as: *"for two hours," "all night," "three times," "from one to three o'clock," "the other day,"* etc.

On the other hand, we use the *imperfect tense* in Spanish, Portuguese, Italian, and French to describe:

1. Habits in the past, e.g., *"I used to play volleyball when I was young."*
2. Description of people, places, and objects in the past, e.g., *"Da Vinci was a famous painter and scientist."*
3. Time and age in the past, e.g., *"When I was 15 years old, I lived in a village."*
4. Actions that were continuously happening when another action interrupted in the past, e.g., *"While you were studying, I was watching TV."*

Conjugation

Before diving into examples, let us look at the conjugation of the preterite and the imperfect.

1. Preterite Tense

Regular verbs in the preterite are conjugated as follows:

- In Spanish:

	-ar ending hablar	-er ending comer	-ir ending vivir
yo	hablé	comí	viví
tú	hablaste	comiste	viviste
él/ella/usted	habló	comió	vivió
nosotros/-as	hablamos	comimos	vivimos
vosotros/-as	hablasteis	comisteis	vivisteis
ellos/ellas/ustedes	hablaron	comieron	vivieron

Notice that the "**nosotros/-as**" conjugation is the same as that of the present tense, e.g., "**nosotros hablamos**" can mean *"we speak"* or *"we spoke,"* depending on the context.

There are quite a few verbs that are irregular in the preterite tense. The following are among the most important irregular verbs:

	ser	ir	dar	tener	estar	hacer
yo	fui	fui	di	tuve	estuve	hice
tú	fuiste	fuiste	diste	tuviste	estuviste	hiciste
él/ella/usted	fue	fue	dio	tuvo	estuvo	hizo
nosotros/-as	fuimos	fuimos	dimos	tuvimos	estuvimos	hicimos
vosotros/-as	fuisteis	fuisteis	disteis	tuvisteis	estuvisteis	hicisteis
ellos/ellas/ustedes	fueron	fueron	dieron	tuvieron	estuvieron	hicieron

Notice that the verbs "**ser**" and "**ir**" have the same conjugation in the preterite. The verbs "**ser**," "**ir**," and "**dar**" have unique patterns of conjugation in the preterite and thus must be memorized. A few other irregular verbs are conjugated in the preterite in a manner similar to "**tener**," "**estar**," and "**hacer**."

In addition to the above irregular verbs in the preterite, there are a few more verbs and patterns that are useful to memorize. Use your Anki cards to practice more examples until you master this lesson. You can also use the summary in the cheat sheets in **Appendix B** as a quick reference.

A. Verbs ending in "-ducir" as well as "decir" and "traer"

Verbs ending in "-**ducir**" replace the "**c**" with "**j**" in their stem to form the preterite stem ending in "**duj**-." The verbs "**decir**" and "**traer**" are treated similarly, and their stems are "**dij**-" and "**traj**-," respectively. Notice also that the third-person plural form of these verbs ends in "-**eron**" instead of "-**ieron**."

Examples of verbs in this category include: "**traducir**" (*to translate*), "**producir**" (*to produce*), "**reducir**" (*to reduce*), "**conducir**" (*to drive*), "**introducir**" (*to introduce*), "**deducir**" (*to deduce*), and "**seducir**" (*to seduce*).

	traducir	producir	reducir	decir	traer
yo	traduje	produje	reduje	dije	traje
tú	tradujiste	produjiste	redujiste	dijiste	trajiste
él/ella/usted	tradujo	produjo	redujo	dijo	trajo
nosotros/-as	tradujimos	produjimos	redujimos	dijimos	trajimos
vosotros/-as	tradujisteis	produjisteis	redujisteis	dijisteis	trajisteis
ellos/ellas/ustedes	tradujeron	produjeron	redujeron	dijeron	trajeron

B. Verbs "estar," "tener," and "andar"

The verbs "**estar**," "**tener**," and "**andar**" (*to walk* or *to go*) take the stems "**estuv**-," "**tuv**-," and "**anduv**-," respectively.

	estar	tener	andar
yo	estuve	tuve	anduve
tú	estuviste	tuviste	anduviste
él/ella/usted	estuvo	tuvo	anduvo
nosotros/-as	estuvimos	tuvimos	anduvimos
vosotros/-as	estuvisteis	tuvisteis	anduvisteis
ellos/ellas/ustedes	estuvieron	tuvieron	anduvieron

C. Verbs that change the first vowel from "a" or "o" to "u"

The two verbs "**haber**" and "**poder**" take the stems "**hub**-" and "**pud**-," respectively, whereas the verbs "**poner**," "**saber**," and "**caber**" (*to fit*) undergo an extra-letter change and take the stems "**pus**-," "**sup**-," and "**cup**-," respectively.

	haber	poder	poner	saber	caber
yo	hube	pude	puse	supe	cupe
tú	hubiste	pudiste	pusiste	supiste	cupiste
él/ella/usted	hubo	pudo	puso	supo	cupo
nosotros/-as	hubimos	pudimos	pusimos	supimos	cupimos
vosotros/-as	hubisteis	pudisteis	pusisteis	supisteis	cupisteis
ellos/ellas/ustedes	hubieron	pudieron	pusieron	supieron	cupieron

D. Verbs that change stem in the third-person forms

There are three groups in this category:

1. Verbs that change "**e**" to "**i**" in the third-person singular and plural forms. Examples of these verbs: "**pedir**" *(to ask or request)*, "**mentir**" *(to lie)*, "**sentir**" *(to feel)*, "**seguir**" *(to follow)*, "**servir**" *(to serve)*, "**hervir**" *(to boil)*, "**preferir**" *(to prefer)*, "**convertir**" *(to convert)*, "**despedir**" *(to dismiss)*, "**impedir**" *(to prevent)*, "**divertirse**" *(to have fun)*, "**sugerir**" *(to suggest)*, "**vestirse**" *(to dress)*, "**repetir**" *(to repeat)*, "**reír**" *(to laugh)*, and "**sonreír**" *(to smile)*. Notice that these verbs are all "-**ir**" verbs.

	pedir	mentir	seguir	preferir	reír
yo	pedí	mentí	seguí	preferí	reí
tú	pediste	mentiste	seguiste	preferiste	reíste
él/ella/usted	pidió	mintió	siguió	prefirió	rió
nosotros/-as	pedimos	mentimos	seguimos	preferimos	reímos
vosotros/-as	pedisteis	mentisteis	seguisteis	preferisteis	reísteis
ellos/ellas/ustedes	pidieron	mintieron	siguieron	prefirieron	rieron

2. Verbs that change "**o**" to "**u**" in the third-person singular and plural forms. Examples of these verbs: "**dormir**" *(to sleep)* and "**morir**" *(to die)*, which are also "-**ir**" verbs.

	dormir	morir
yo	dormí	morí
tú	dormiste	moriste
él/ella/usted	durmió	murió
nosotros/-as	dormimos	morimos
vosotros/-as	dormisteis	moristeis
ellos/ellas/ustedes	durmieron	murieron

3. Verbs that change "**e**" or "**i**" to "**y**" in the third-person singular and plural forms. Examples of these verbs: "**caer**" *(to fall)*, "**leer**" *(to read)*, "**roer**" *(to nibble)*, "**oír**" *(to hear)*, "**influir**" *(to influence)*, and "**concluir**" *(to conclude)*. Notice that if the final vowel of the stem is silent, this rule does not apply, e.g., "**seguir**" *(to follow)*, "**perseguir**" *(to chase or pursue)*, "**conseguir**" *(to get)*.

	caer	leer	roer	oír	influir
yo	caí	leí	roí	oí	influí
tú	caíste	leíste	roíste	oíste	influiste
él/ella/usted	cayó	leyó	royó	oyó	influyó
nosotros/-as	caímos	leímos	roímos	oímos	influimos
vosotros/-as	caísteis	leísteis	roísteis	oísteis	influisteis
ellos/ellas/ustedes	cayeron	leyeron	royeron	oyeron	influyeron

The changes in the table above prevent the presence of three consecutive vowels, e.g., "**cayó**" (the "**y**" replaces "**e**," preventing the presence of the three consecutive vowels "**-aeo-**").

E. Verbs "venir," "querer," and "ver"

Finally, the verbs "**venir**" and "**querer**" take the stems "**vin-**" and "**quis-**," respectively, whereas the verb "**ver**" does not follow a specific rule.

	ver	venir	querer
yo	vi	vine	quise
tú	viste	viniste	quisiste
él/ella/usted	vio	vino	quiso
nosotros/-as	vimos	vinimos	quisimos
vosotros/-as	visteis	vinisteis	quisisteis
ellos/ellas/ustedes	vieron	vinieron	quisieron

- In Portuguese:

	-ar ending e.g., falar	-er ending e.g., comer	-ir ending e.g., partir
eu	falei	comi	parti
ele/ela/você	falou	comeu	partiu
nós	falamos	comemos	partimos
eles/elas/vocês	falaram	comeram	partiram

Notice that the "**nós**" conjugation is the same as that of the present tense, e.g., "**nós comemos**" can mean *"we eat"* or *"we ate,"* depending on the context.

The verbs "**estar**" *(to be)* and "**dar**" *(to give)* are the most common irregular "**-ar**" verbs, whereas the verbs "**ir**" *(to go)* and "**vir**" *(to come)* are the most common irregular "**-ir**" verbs. Most other common irregular verbs in the preterite belong to the "**-er**" group. Here is a list of the most common irregular verbs in the preterite:

	eu	ele/ela/você	nós	eles/elas/vocês
estar *to be*	estive	esteve	estivemos	estiveram
dar *to give*	dei	deu	demos	deram
ser *to be*	fui	foi	fomos	foram
ter *to have*	tive	teve	tivemos	tiveram
ver *to see*	vi	viu	vimos	viram
poder *can*	pude	pôde	pudemos	puderam
dizer *to say*	disse	disse	dissemos	disseram
trazer *to bring*	trouxe	trouxe	trouxemos	trouxeram
fazer *to do or make*	fiz	fez	fizemos	fizeram
caber *to fit*	coube	coube	coubemos	couberam
saber *to know*	soube	soube	soubemos	souberam
querer *to want*	quis	quis	quisemos	quiseram
haver *to have*	houve	houve	houvemos	houveram
pôr *to put*	pus	pôs	pusemos	puseram
ir *to go*	fui	foi	fomos	foram

| vir
to come | vim | veio | viemos | vieram |

Notice that "**ser**" and "**ir**" have the same irregular conjugation in the preterite. Notice also that the verb "**pôr**" *(to put)* is considered an "**-er**" verb based on its Latin origin, that is, "ponere."

2. Imperfect Tense

Regular verbs in the imperfect are conjugated as follows:

- In Spanish:

To form the stem of the verb needed for regular verb conjugation, we drop the final "**-ar**," "**-er**," or "**-ir**" of the verb and attach the conjugation suffix.

	-ar ending hablar	-er ending comer	-ir ending vivir
yo	hablaba	comía	vivía
tú	hablabas	comías	vivías
él/ella/usted	hablaba	comía	vivía
nosotros/-as	hablábamos	comíamos	vivíamos
vosotros/-as	hablabais	comíais	vivíais
ellos/ellas/ustedes	hablaban	comían	vivían

There are only three verbs that are irregular in the imperfect. These verbs are:

	ser	ir	ver
yo	era	iba	veía
tú	eras	ibas	veías
él/ella/usted	era	iba	veía
nosotros/-as	éramos	íbamos	veíamos
vosotros/-as	erais	ibais	veíais
ellos/ellas/ustedes	eran	iban	veían

- In Portuguese:

To form the stem of the verb needed for regular verb conjugation, we drop the final "**-ar**," "**-er**," or "**-ir**" of the verb and attach the conjugation suffix, as follows:

	-ar ending e.g., falar	-er ending e.g., comer	-ir ending e.g., partir
eu	falava	comia	partia
ele/ela/você	falava	comia	partia
nós	falávamos	comíamos	partíamos
eles/elas/vocês	falavam	comiam	partiam

There are only four verbs that are irregular in the imperfect. These verbs are:

	vir *(to come)*	ter *(to have)*	ser *(to be)*	pôr *(to put)*
eu	vinha	tinha	era	punha
ele/ela/você	vinha	tinha	era	punha
nós	vínhamos	tínhamos	éramos	púnhamos
eles/elas/vocês	vinham	tinham	eram	punham

- In Italian:

To form the stem of the verb needed for regular verb conjugation, we drop the final "-re" of the verb and attach the conjugation suffix. The suffixes are the same for the three types of verbs.

	-are ending parlare *(to speak)*	-ere ending vendere *(to sell)*	-ire ending partire *(to leave)*
io	parlavo	vendevo	partivo
tu	parlavi	vendevi	partivi
lui/lei	parlava	vendeva	partiva
noi	parlavamo	vendevamo	partivamo
voi	parlavate	vendevate	partivate
loro	parlavano	vendevano	partivano

There are a few verbs in the imperfect indicative tense that are irregular. These should be practiced and memorized. The most common ones are: "**essere**" *(to be)*, "**bere**" *(to drink)*, "**dire**" *(to say)*, and "**fare**" *(to do)*.

	io	tu	lui/lei	noi	voi	loro
bere *(to drink)*	bevevo	bevevi	beveva	bevevamo	bevevate	bevevano
dare *(to give)*	davo	davi	dava	davamo	davate	davano
dire *(to say/tell)*	dicevo	dicevi	diceva	dicevamo	dicevate	dicevano
essere *(to be)*	ero	eri	era	eravamo	eravate	erano

fare *(to do/make)*	facevo	facevi	faceva	facevamo	facevate	facevano
stare *(to stay/be)*	stavo	stavi	stava	stavamo	stavate	stavano

- In French:

To conjugate verbs in the imperfect for all forms, we begin from the *first-person plural in the present indicative*, that is, the "**nous**" form, e.g., "**parlons**," "**finissons**," "**buvons**," "**partons**," etc., and we extract the stem "**parl-**," "**finiss-**," "**buv-**," "**part-**," etc., by dropping the last "**-ons**."

The suffixes are the same for all three types of verbs.

	parler *(to speak)* nous <u>parl</u>ons	**finir** *(to finish)* nous <u>finiss</u>ons	**boire** *(to drink)* nous <u>buv</u>ons
je	parl**ais**	finiss**ais**	buv**ais**
tu	parl**ais**	finiss**ais**	buv**ais**
il/elle/on	parl**ait**	finiss**ait**	buv**ait**
nous	parl**ions**	finiss**ions**	buv**ions**
vous	parl**iez**	finiss**iez**	buv**iez**
ils/elles	parl**aient**	finiss**aient**	buv**aient**

In essence, the verb "**être**" *(to be)* is the only irregular verb in the imperfect.

	je	tu	il/elle/on	nous	vous	ils/elles
être *to be*	étais	étais	était	étions	étiez	étaient

Some verbs in the imperfect undergo minor spelling changes similar to those encountered in conjugation in other tenses to maintain the proper pronunciation, for example:

	je	tu	il/elle/on	nous	vous	ils/elles
manger *to eat*	mangeais	mangeais	mangeait	mangions	mangiez	mangeaient
menacer *to threaten*	menaçais	menaçais	menaçait	menacions	menaciez	menaçaient

Examples

Let us now look at some examples and determine when to use the imperfect and when to use the preterite. It takes practice, but hopefully, these examples are a good start to illustrate the difference.

EN: *I **visited** my mother last night.* **SP**: Yo **visité** a mi madre anoche. **PT**: Eu **visitei** minha mãe ontem à noite. **IT**: Io **ho visitado** mia madre ieri sera. **FR**: J'**ai visité** à ma mère hier soir.	Preterite in SP/PT (or) Pres. Perfect in IT/FR	Action with defined time in the past (last night)
EN: *I **spent** two hours at the gym.* **SP**: **Pasé** dos horas en el gimnasio. **PT**: **Passei** duas horas na academia. **IT**: **Ho passato** due ore in palestra. **FR**: J'**ai passé** deux heures au gymnase.	Preterite in SP/PT (or) Pres. Perfect in IT/FR	Action with defined time in the past (for two hours)
EN: *I **talked** to her the other day.* **SP**: **Hablé** con ella el otro día. **PT**: **Falei** com ela outro dia. **IT**: Le **ho parlato** l'altro giorno. **FR**: Je lui **ai parlé** l'autre jour.	Preterite in SP/PT (or) Pres. Perfect in IT/FR	Action with defined time in the past (the other day [1])
EN: *When I was a child, I **used to live** in a village.* **SP**: De niña, **vivía** en un pueblo. **PT**: Quando criança, eu **vivia** em um vilarejo. **IT**: Quando ero bambino, **vivevo** in un villaggio. **FR**: Enfant, je **vivais** dans un village.	Imperfect	Habit in the past, indicated by "*used to*"
EN: *My school professor **was** tall.* **SP**: Mi profesor de la escuela **era** alto. **PT**: Meu professor da escola **era** alto. **IT**: Il mio professore di scuola **era** alto. **FR**: Mon professeur d'école **était** grand.	Imperfect	Description in the past

---

[1] Although *"the other day"* may seem vague and undefined, it is considered a defined time from a grammatical viewpoint.

EN: *When I **was** 15 years old, I used to play tennis.* **SP**: Cuando **tenía** 15 años, jugaba al tenis. **PT**: Quando eu **tinha** 15 anos, jogava tênis. **IT**: Quando **avevo** 15 anni giocavo a tennis. **FR**: Quand j'**avais** 15 ans, je jouais au tennis.	Imperfect	Time and age in the past
EN: *I **was** at work when you called me.* **SP**: **Estaba** en el trabajo cuando me llamaste. **PT**: Eu **estava** no trabalho quando você me ligou. **IT**: **Ero** al lavoro quando mi hai chiamato. **FR**: J'**étais** au travail quand tu m'as appelé.	Imperfect	Actions continuously happening in the past when another action interrupted

In general, use the preterite in Spanish and Portuguese and the present perfect in Italian and French if you are talking about actions with a defined time or period in the past. Look for expressions such as: *yesterday, last night, last week, ago, in 1994, from … to …, two times, for three hours, the other day,* etc. These expressions may not be explicitly used, but the meaning can implicitly refer to a defined time or period in the past.

The preterite is also often used in Portuguese as an equivalent to the present perfect tense in English. The present perfect in Portuguese is more like the present perfect continuous in English.

On the other hand, use the imperfect when you see phrases such as: "*when I was a child,*" "*when I was younger,*" "*when I was 15 years old,*" etc.

SP	Cuando era joven, **podía** correr mucho.	
PT	Quando eu era jovem, **podia** correr muito.	*When I was young, I **could** run a lot.*
IT	Quando ero giovane, **potevo** correre molto.	
FR	Quand j'étais jeune, je **pouvais** beaucoup courir.	

SP	De niño, me **gustaba** la fruta.	
PT	Quando criança, eu **gostava** de frutas.	*When I was a child,* I **used to like** *fruits.*
IT	Quando ero bambino, mi **piaceva** la frutta.	
FR	Quand j'étais enfant, j'**aimais** les fruits.	
SP	Cuando era un adolescente, **tomaba** café.	
PT	Quando eu era adolescente, **bebia** café.	*When I was a teenager,* I **used to drink** *coffee.*
IT	Quando ero adolescente, **bevevo** caffè.	
FR	Quand j'étais adolescente, je **buvais** du café.	

Also, use the *imperfect* when comparing the present to the past:

SP	Hoy es fácil viajar, **pero antes** era muy difícil.	
PT	Hoje é fácil viajar, **mas antes** era muito difícil.	*Today it is easy to travel,* **but before**, *it used to be difficult.*
IT	Oggi è facile viaggiare, **ma prima** era difficile.	
FR	Aujourd'hui, il est facile de voyager, **mais avant** c'était difficile.	

Another important use of the imperfect tense is to express a past intention of doing something that does not end up being done in the present. These are expressions such as *"I was going to …,"* *"I was thinking of …,"* and *"I wanted to …."*

The general formula of such expressions is as follows:

SP	*Imperfect tense* of ("**ir a**," "**pensar en**," or "**querer**") + *infinitive*
PT	*Imperfect tense* of ("**ir**," "**pensar em**," or "**querer**") + *infinitive*
IT	*Imperfect tense* of ("**stare per**," "**pensare di**," or "**volere**") + *infinitive*
FR	*Imperfect tense* of ("**aller**," "**penser**," or "**vouloir**") + *infinitive*

For example:

SP	Iba a llamarte, pero me dormí.	
PT	Ia ligar para você, mas adormeci.	*I was going to call you, but I fell asleep.*
IT	Stavo per chiamarti, ma mi sono addormentato.	
FR	J'allais t'appeler, mais je me suis endormi.	
SP	Pensaba en salir, pero ya es muy tarde.	
PT	Pensava em sair, mas já é tarde demais.	*I was thinking of going out, but it's already too late.*
IT	Pensavo di andarmene, ma è troppo tardi.	
FR	Je pensais partir, mais c'est trop tard.	
SP	Quería venir, pero tuve un accidente.	
PT	Queria vir, mas sofri um acidente.	*I wanted to come, but I had an accident.*
IT	Volevo venire, ma ho avuto un incidente.	
FR	Je voulais venir, mais j'ai eu un accident.	

3. Reflexive Pronouns & Verbs

A verb is considered reflexive if the subject and the object of the verb are the same. This means that the subject is doing the action to itself, not to something or someone else. For instance, *"I wash myself"* is reflexive, while *"I wash my car"* is not reflexive.

Some verbs in Spanish, Portuguese, Italian, and French are commonly used in the reflexive form. Let us take one example that we are familiar with, that is, the verb *"to call."*

SP	llamar		Él llama a su amigo desde muy lejos.	
PT	chamar	to call	Ele chama seu amigo de longe.	*He calls his friend from afar.*
IT	chiamare		Lui chiama il suo amico da molto lontano.	
FR	appeler		Il appelle son ami de loin.	

However, the reflexive form of the verb, which literally means *"to call oneself,"* is used to express one's name. For example:

SP	llamarse		Me llamo Marco.	
PT	chamar-se	to call oneself	Eu me chamo Marco.	*My name is Marco. (I call myself Marco.)*
IT	chiamarsi		Mi chiamo Marco.	
FR	s'appeler		Je m'appelle Marco.	

A reflexive verb is formed as follows:

SP	by attaching "**-se**" to the end of the infinitive, e.g., "**llamar**" becomes "**llamarse**"
PT	by attaching "**-se**" to the end of the infinitive separated from the verb by a hyphen, e.g., "**chamar**" becomes "**chamar-se**."
IT	by replacing final "**-e**" in the infinitive with "**-si**," e.g., "**chiamar**" becomes "**chiamar-si**"
FR	by preceding the infinitive with "**se**," or "**s'**" before a vowel or mute "**h**," e.g., "**appeler**" becomes "**s'appeler**."

There are many verbs in Spanish, Portuguese, Italian, and French that have reflexive forms. We will discuss some examples; however, let us first learn how to conjugate reflexive verbs.

- In Spanish:

	Object Personal Pron.	e.g., llamar
yo	me	me llamo
tú	te	te llamas
él/ella/usted	se	se llama
nosotros/-as	nos	nos llamamos
vosotros/-as	os	os llamáis
ellos/ellas/ustedes	se	se llaman

- In Portuguese:

	Object Personal Pron.	e.g., chamar
eu	me	me chamo
ele/ela/você	se	se chama
nós	nos	nos chamamos
eles/elas/vocês	se	se chamam

- In Italian:

	Object Personal Pron.	e.g., chiamarsi
io	mi	mi chiamo
tu	ti	ti chiami
lui/lei	si	si chiama
noi	ci	ci chiamiamo
voi	vi	vi chiamate
loro	si	si chiamano

- In French:

	Object Personal Pron.	e.g., s'appeler
je	me/m'	m'appelle
tu	te/t'	t'appelles
il/elle/on	se/s'	s'appelle
nous	nous	nous appelons
vous	vous	vous appelez
ils/elles	se/s'	s'appellent

Note that the subject and object personal pronouns are of the same gender and number because the subject and the object are essentially the same.

Here are more examples of reflexive verbs:

SP	afeitarse		aburrirse		
PT	barbear-se	to shave	aborrecer-se	to get bored	
IT	radersi		annoiarsi		
FR	se raser		s'ennuyer		
SP	bañarse		alegrarse		
PT	banhar-se	to take a bath	alegrar-se	to rejoice or be glad	
IT	farsi il bagno		rallegrarsi		
FR	se beigner		se réjouir		
SP	despertarse		cansarse		
PT	-	to wake up	cansar-se	to get tired	
IT	svegliarsi		stancarsi		
FR	se réveiller		se fatiguer		
SP	distraerse		prepararse		
PT	distrair-se	to distract oneself	preparar-se	to get ready	
IT	distrarsi		prepararsi		
FR	se distraire		se préparer		
SP	emborracharse		enamorarse		
PT	embebedar-se	to get drunk	apaixonar-se	to fall in love	
IT	ubriacarsi		innamorarsi		
FR	se saouler		-		
SP	maquillarse		levantarse		
PT	maquiar-se	to put on makeup	levantar-se	to get up	
IT	truccarsi		alzarsi		
FR	se maquiller		se lever		

SP	peinarse		divertirse	
PT	pentear-se	*to comb one's hair*	divertir-se	*to have fun*
IT	pettinarsi		divertirsi	
FR	se peigner		s'amuser	
SP	sentarse		preocuparse	
PT	sentar-se	*to sit down*	preoccuparsi	*to worry*
IT	sedersi		preocupar-se	
FR	s'asseoir		s'inquiéter	
SP	vestirse		sentirse	
PT	vestir-se	*to get dressed*	sentir-se	*to feel*
IT	vestirsi		sentirsi	
FR	s'habiller		se sentir	

Let us look at some examples:

SP	**Me aburro** rápido en casa.	
PT	Eu **me aborreço** rapidamente em casa.	*I **get bored** fast at home.*
IT	**Mi annoio** velocemente a casa.	
FR	Je **m'ennuie** vite à la maison.	
SP	Ella **se preocupa** mucho por su hijo.	
PT	Ela **se preocupa** muito com o filho.	*She **worries** a lot about her son.*
IT	Lei **si preoccupa** molto per suo figlio.	
FR	Elle **s'inquiète** beaucoup pour son fils.	
SP	Nosotros **nos divertimos** mucho juntos.	
PT	Nós **nos divertimos** muito juntos.	*We **have** a lot of **fun** together.*
IT	**Ci divertiamo** molto insieme.	
FR	Nous **nous amusons** beaucoup ensemble.	

One can add the reflexive pronoun to verbs that are not usually reflexive to make them reflexive, for example:

SP	verse	
PT	ver-se	*to see each other*
IT	vedersi	
FR	se voir	
SP	escucharse	
PT	ouvir-se	*to listen to oneself*
IT	ascoltarsi	
FR	s'écouter	

Some verbs are used *only* in reflexive form, such as:

SP	suicidarse	
PT	suicidar-se	*to commit suicide*
IT	suicidarsi	
FR	se suicider	
SP	quejarse	
PT	queixar-se	*to complain*
IT	lamentarsi[1]	
FR	se plaindre[1]	

Some verbs change their meaning when they are used in reflexive form, for example:

SP	aburrir		aburrirse	
PT	aborrecer	*to bore*	aborrecer-se	*to get bored*
IT	annoiare		annoiarsi	
FR	ennuyer		s'ennuyer	
SP	acostar		acostarse	
PT	deitar	*to lay down*	deitar-se	*to lie down or go to bed*
IT	coricare		coricarsi	
FR	coucher		se coucher	
SP	casar		casarse	
PT	casar	*to join in marriage*	casar-se	*to get married*
IT	sposare		sposarsi	
FR	marier		se marier	

Finally, keep in mind that all reflexive verbs use the auxiliary verb *"to be"* in Italian and French when conjugated in compound tenses, such as the present perfect tense, regardless of the auxiliary used by the non-reflexive form of the verb. For example:

SP	**Me aburrí** anoche.	
PT	Eu **me aborreci** ontem à noite.	*I **got bored** last night.*
IT	Ieri sera **mi <u>sono</u> annoiato**.	
FR	Je me **<u>suis</u> ennuyé** hier soir.	
SP	Ella **se despertó** temprano hoy.	
PT	Ela **acordou** cedo hoje.	*She **woke up** early today.*
IT	Lei **si <u>è</u> svegliata** presto oggi.	
FR	Elle **s'<u>est</u> réveillée** tôt aujourd'hui.	

---

[1] The verbs "**lamentarsi**" in Italian and "**se plaindre**" in French have non-reflexive forms.

SP	**Nos divertimos** mucho ayer.	
PT	**Nos divertimos** muito ontem.	*We **had** a lot of **fun** yesterday.*
IT	Ieri **ci <u>siamo</u> divertiti** molto.	
FR	Nous **nous <u>sommes</u>** beaucoup **amusés** hier.	
SP	Ellos **se vieron** por accidente.	
PT	Eles **se viram** por acidente.	*They **saw each other** by accident.*
IT	**Si <u>sono</u> visti** per caso.	
FR	Elles **se <u>sont</u> vus** par hasard.	

Remember that when the verb *"to be"* is used as an auxiliary, the past participle takes the treatment of an adjective and must agree in gender and number with the subject.

4. EXPRESSIONS USING "TO HAVE" & "TO DO"

Some expressions do not make sense if literally translated into English. For example, the expression "**dare un esame**," in Italian, meaning *"to take an exam,"* uses the verb "**dare**" *(to give)* rather than "**prendere**" *(to take)*. In this section, we will learn some expressions using *"to have"* and *"to do or to make"* that are common in Spanish, Portuguese, Italian, and French.

	"to have"	*"to do or to make"*
SP	"**tener**" or "**haber**"	"**hacer**"
PT	"**ter**" or "**haver**"	"**fazer**"
IT	"**avere**"	"**fare**"
FR	"**avoir**"	"**faire**"

1. Expressions using *"to have"*

In addition to the obvious use of *"to have"* to indicate possession, e.g., *"I have two children,"* there are some less obvious uses of the verb *"to have"* in Spanish, Portuguese, Italian, and French.

In English, we use the verb *"to be"* to describe age, as in *"how old <u>are</u> you?"* and *"I <u>am</u> 30 years old."*

In Spanish, Portuguese, Italian, and French, the verb *"to have"* is used instead; that is, we literally say, *"I have 30 years old"* rather than, *"I am 30 years old."*

Here are a few more examples:

SP	¿Cuántos años **tienes?**	
PT	Quantos anos **tem?**	*How old **are** you?*
IT	Quanti anni **hai?**	
FR	Quel âge **as**-tu?	
SP	**Tengo** 40 años.	
PT	**Tenho** 40 anos.	*I **am** 40 years old.*
IT	**Ho** 40 anni.	
FR	J'**ai** 40 ans.	
SP	Ella **tiene** 20 años.	
PT	Ele **tem** 20 anos.	*He **is** 20 years old.*
IT	Lui **ha** 20 anni.	
FR	Il **a** 20 ans.	

Some expressions describe a feeling or desire using the verb *"to have,"* while their equivalents in English use the verb *"to be."* For example, in the expression "**Tengo miedo**" in Spanish, meaning *"I am afraid,"* the word "**miedo**" means *"fear."* Thus, we literally say, *"I have fear."* Some other examples include:

SP	tener hambre		tener sed	
PT	ter fome	*to be hungry*	ter sede	*to be thirsty*
IT	avere fame		avere sete	
FR	avoir faim		avoir soif	
SP	tener frío		tener calor	
PT	ter frio	*to be cold*	ter calor	*to be hot*
IT	avere freddo		avere caldo	
FR	avoir froid		avoir chaud	
SP	tener sueño		tener miedo	
PT	ter sono	*to be sleepy*	ter medo	*to be afraid*
IT	avere sonno		avere paura	
FR	avoir sommeil		avoir peur	
SP	tener razón		tener dolor	
PT	ter razão	*to be right*	ter dor	*to have pain*
IT	avere ragione		avere dolore	
FR	avoir raison		avoir mal à	
SP	tener éxito		tener sentido	
PT	ter êxito	*to be successful*	ter sentido	*to make sense*
IT	avere successo		avere senso	
FR	avoir du succès		avoir du sens	

The verbs "**haber**" in Spanish and "**haver**" in Portuguese are used as auxiliary verbs in some compound tenses.

Another common and special use of the verb "**haber**" in Spanish and "**haver**" in Portuguese is the expression "*there is/are ...*," and is the same for singular and plural. The verbal form is considered in the present tense and does not take a personal pronoun as a subject.

SP	Hay ...	*There is/are ...*
PT	Há ...	
SP	Había/Hubo ...	*There was/were ...*
PT	Houve ...	
SP	Habrá ...	*There will be ...*
PT	Haverá ...	

Another use of the verb "**haber**" in Spanish in the form "**hay que**...(*infinitive*)" is to express obligation, meaning "*One must ...*" or "*It must be that you ....*" For example:

Hay que tener cuidado en la ciudad.	***One must*** *be careful in the city.*
Hay que hacer ejercicio frecuentemente.	***One must*** *exercise frequently.*

We can express the obligation "*have to ...*" by using "**tener que**" in Spanish and "**haver de**" or "**ter que**" in Portuguese followed by the *infinitive*, for example:

SP	Yo **tengo que** hacerlo.	*I **have to** do it.*
PT	Eu **hei de/tenho que** fazer isso.	
SP	Ellos **tienen que** pagar.	*They **have to** pay.*
PT	Eles **hão de/têm que** pagar.	
SP	Nosotros **tenemos que** ir.	*We **have to** go.*
PT	Nós **havemos de/temos que** ir.	

In Portuguese, one way to express the meaning of "*ago*" or "*for*" is by using the form "**há**" of the verb "**haver**," for example:

Ele chegou **há** duas horas.	*He arrived two hours **ago**.*
Eu não o vejo **há** muito tempo.	*I haven't seen him **for** a long time.*

Notice that the second example above uses the present tense in Portuguese, i.e., "**vejo**," whereas the equivalent sentence in English uses the present perfect tense.

2. Expressions using *"to do"*

There are many expressions that use the verb *"to do or to make"* in Spanish, Portuguese, Italian, and French, when similar expressions in English would not. We have encountered the verb *"to do or to make"* used with weather expressions in **Level III, Lesson 7**.

Let us examine some other expressions that use the verb *"to do or to make."* In general, we use the verb *"to do"* when referring to sports and hobbies. Here are some examples:

SP	hacer deporte		hacer gimnasia	
PT	fazer desporto	*to play sports*	fazer ginástica	*to go to the gym*
IT	fare sport		fare ginnastica	
FR	faire du sport		faire de la gym	
SP	-		-	
PT	-	*to go cycling*	-	*to take a walk*
IT	fare ciclismo		fare una passeggiata	
FR	faire du vélo		faire une promenade	
SP	hacer surf		hacer snowboard	
PT	fazer surf	*to do surfing*	fazer snowboard	*to snowboard*
IT	fare surf		fare snowboard	
FR	faire du surf		faire du snowboard	

The verb *"to do or to make"* is also used with many house chores and day-to-day tasks. Examples include:

SP	hacer la tarea		hacer la colada	
PT	fazer os deveres	*to do homework*	-	*to do laundry*
IT	fare i compiti		fare il bucato	
FR	faire des devoirs		faire la lessive	
SP	hacer la cama		-	
PT	fazer a cama	*to make the bed*	-	*to fill up on gas*
IT	fare il letto		fare il pieno	
FR	faire le lit		faire le plein	
SP	hacer compras		hacer la compra	
PT	fazer compras	*to buy groceries*	fazer compras	*to go shopping.*
IT	fare la spesa		fare spese	
FR	faire les courses		faire les magasins	

SP	hacer las tareas		hacer la limpieza	
PT	fazer tarefas	*to do the chores*	fazer uma limpeza	*to do the cleaning*
IT	fare le faccende		fare le pulizie	
FR	faire le ménage		faire le ménage	

There are many other idioms and expressions that use the verb *"to do or to make"* that do not fall under any of the aforementioned categories, such as:

SP	hacer cola		hacer una pausa	
PT	fazer fila	*to wait in line*	fazer uma pausa	*to take a break*
IT	fare la fila/coda		fare una pausa	
FR	faire la queue		faire une pause	
SP	-		hacer tú mismo	
PT	fazer uma sesta	*to take a nap*	faça você mesmo	*DIY*
IT	fare un pisolino		fai da te	
FR	faire une sieste		faire soi-même	

The verb **"fare"** in Italian can be used in many causative expressions meaning *"to have someone do something."* For example:

fare vedere a qualcuno	*to have someone see (to show someone)*
fare cucinare a qualcuno	*to have someone cook*

Similarly, the verb **"faire"** in French can be used meaning *"to have someone do something."* For example:

Il me **fait voir** la différence.	*He **makes** me **see** the difference.*
Je lui **fais écrire** pour moi.	*I **have** him **write** for me.*

Finally, the verb **"hacer"** in Spanish can be used to describe something that happened in the past. Depending on the context, it can mean the equivalent of *"ago,"* as shown in the following examples:

Hace tres meses **que** hablé con mi hermana.	*It was three months **ago** that I talked with my sister.*
Me desperté **hace** 15 minutos.	*I woke up 15 minutes **ago**.*

5. PRESENT SUBJUNCTIVE TENSE I

All the tenses we have encountered so far were in the indicative mood. The indicative mood is what we use to express facts. This is the mood we encounter often. There are five moods in total in Spanish, Portuguese, Italian, and French: infinitive, indicative, subjunctive, imperative, and conditional. The subjunctive mood is used to express opinion, possibility, and feelings, such as fear, doubt, hope, desire, etc. Generally speaking, the indicative describes facts, whereas the subjunctive describes non-facts.

In Spanish, Portuguese, and Italian, we begin from the *first-person singular in the present indicative*, and we extract the stem by dropping the last "-o."

SP	"yo hablo" > "habl-"	"yo como" > "com-"	"yo vivo" > "viv-"
PT	"eu falo" > "fal-"	"eu como" > "com-"	"eu parto" > "part-"
IT	"io parlo" > "parl-"	"io vendo" > "vend-"	"io parto" > "part-"

In French, to conjugate verbs in the present subjunctive, we begin from the *third-person plural in the present indicative*, that is, the "**ils/ells**" form, and we extract the stem from these verbs by dropping the last "**-ent.**"

FR	"ils parlent" > "parl-"	"ils finissent" > "finiss-"	"ils vendent" > "vend-"

Then, we add the endings shown in the following tables:

- In Spanish:

	-ar ending hablar	-er ending comer	-ir ending vivir
yo	hable	coma	viva
tú	hables	comas	vivas
él/ella/usted	hable	coma	viva
nosotros/-as	hablemos	comamos	vivamos
vosotros/-as	habléis	comáis	viváis
ellos/ellas/ustedes	hablen	coman	vivan

We use the stem from the *first-person* "**yo**" form in the present indicative by removing the final "-o." This is especially important with verbs that are irregular in the first-person "**yo**" form in the present indicative. For example, use the stem from **"yo tengo"** to use the verb **"tener"** in the present subjunctive. Below are some examples:

	tener teng-	querer quier-	jugar jueg-	dormir duerm-	conocer conozc-
yo	tenga	quiera	juegue	duerma	conozca
tú	tengas	quieras	juegues	duermas	conozcas
él/ella/usted	tenga	quiera	juegue	duerma	conozca
nosotros/-as	tengamos	queramos	juguemos	durmamos	conozcamos
vosotros/-as	tengáis	queráis	juguéis	durmáis	conozcáis
ellos/ellas/ustedes	tengan	quieran	jueguen	duerman	conozcan

Notice that, in these examples, the verbs **"querer,"** **"jugar,"** and **"dormir"** change the conjugation stem in the **"nosotros/-as"** and **"vosotros/-as"** forms.

The following verbs are irregular in the present subjunctive:

	ir	ser	estar	saber	dar	haber
yo	vaya	sea	esté	sepa	dé	haya
tú	vayas	seas	estés	sepas	des	hayas
él/ella/usted	vaya	sea	esté	sepa	dé	haya
nosotros/-as	vayamos	seamos	estemos	sepamos	demos	hayamos
vosotros/-as	vayáis	seáis	estéis	sepáis	deis	hayáis
ellos/ellas/ustedes	vayan	sean	estén	sepan	den	hayan

- In Portuguese:

	-ar ending **falar** *(to speak)*	-er ending **comer** *(to eat)*	-ir ending **partir** *(to leave)*
eu	fale	coma	parta
ele/ela/você	fale	coma	parta
nós	falemos	comamos	partamos
eles/elas/vocês	falem	comam	partam

We use the stem from the *first-person* **"eu"** form in the present indicative, not the stem from the infinitive. For example, use the stem from **"eu tenho"** to use the verb **"ter"** in the present subjunctive, i.e., **"tenh-."** Below are some examples:

	ter *(to have)* tenh-	fazer *(to do)* faç-	poder *(can)* poss-	ver *(to see)* vej-
eu	tenha	faça	possa	veja
ele/ela/você	tenha	faça	possa	veja
nós	tenhamos	façamos	possamos	vejamos
eles/elas/vocês	tenham	façam	possam	vejam

Some verbs in the present subjunctive undergo minor spelling changes like those encountered in the present indicative to maintain the proper pronunciation, for example:

	eu	ele/ela/você	nós	eles/elas/vocês
pagar *to pay*	pague	pague	paguemos	paguem
ficar *to stay*	fique	fique	fiquemos	fiquem
caçar *to hunt*	cace	cace	cacemos	cacem

The following verbs have completely irregular stems and must be memorized:

	eu	ele/ela/você	nós	eles/elas/vocês
estar *to be*	esteja	esteja	estejamos	estejam
dar *to give*	dê	dê	dêmos	dêem
ser *to be*	seja	seja	sejamos	sejam
saber *to know*	saiba	saiba	saibamos	saibam
querer *to want*	queira	queira	queiramos	queiram
haver *to have*	haja	haja	hajamos	hajam
ir *to go*	vá	vá	vamos	vão

- In Italian:

	-are ending parlare *(to speak)*	-ere ending vendere *(to sell)*	-ire ending (Type I) partire *(to leave)*	-ire ending (Type II) finire *(to finish)*
io	parli	venda	parta	finisca
tu	parli	venda	parta	finisca
lui/lei	parli	venda	parta	finisca
noi	parliamo	vendiamo	partiamo	finiamo
voi	parliate	vendiate	partiate	finiate
loro	parlino	vendano	partano	finiscano

We use the stem from the *first-person* "**io**" form in the present indicative by removing the final "**-o**."

From the examples in the table, notice that:

1. The "**noi**" and "**voi**" forms are conjugated differently. The "**noi**" form is the same as the indicative, and the "**voi**" form has "**-iate**" ending regardless of the verb group.

2. The forms "**io**," "**tu**," and "**lui/lei**" have identical conjugation. This makes them, unlike in the indicative mood, indistinguishable if the subject is omitted. Thus, we often include the subject if one of these three forms is used.

3. The "**noi**" form of regular verbs has identical conjugation in both the indicative and subjunctive moods.

4. The "**voi**" form has the same conjugation ending in all verb groups in the present subjunctive.

5. All verbs with "**-ere**" and "**-ire**" endings have the same conjugation patterns in the present subjunctive.

Again, remember to use the stem from the first-person "**io**" form in the present indicative, not the stem from the infinitive. For example, the stem from "**io bevo**" is used for the verb "**bere**" *(to drink)* in the present subjunctive. Here are some examples:

	bere bev-	dire dic-	potere poss-	uscire esc-	volere vogli-
io	beva	dica	possa	esca	voglia
tu	beva	dica	possa	esca	voglia
lui/lei	beva	dica	possa	esca	voglia
noi	beviamo	diciamo	possiamo	usciamo	vogliamo
voi	beviate	diciate	possiate	usciate	vogliate
loro	bevano	dicano	possano	escano	vogliano

There are only few irregular verbs that do not follow the aforementioned conjugation patterns. These include the following:

1. Verbs with "**-are**" ending that follow the conjugation pattern of "**-ere**" and "**-ire**" verbs. There are two common verbs in this group: "**andare**" *(to go)* and "**fare**" *(to do or to make)*. The "**noi**" form is the same as the indicative. The "**voi**" form of "**andare**" is irregular and uses the stem from the *infinitive*.

	andare vad-	fare facci-
io	vada	faccia
tu	vada	faccia
lui/lei	vada	faccia
noi	andiamo	facciamo
voi	andiate	facciate
loro	vadano	facciano

2. Verbs that use the stem from the "**noi**" form instead of the "**io**" form, by dropping the last "**-amo**." There are a few common verbs in this category. The "**noi**" form is the same as the indicative, and the "**voi**" form drops one "**i**" to avoid the double "**i**" sound.

	avere abbi-	dare di-	essere si-	sapere sappi-	stare sti-
io	abbia	dia	sia	sappia	stia
tu	abbia	dia	sia	sappia	stia
lui/lei	abbia	dia	sia	sappia	stia
noi	abbiamo	diamo	siamo	sappiamo	stiamo
voi	abbiate	diate	siate	sappiate	stiate
loro	abbiano	diano	siano	sappiano	stiano

3. Contracted infinitive verbs with "**-rre**" endings are all conjugated like "**-ere**" and "**-ire**" verbs. The "**noi**" form is the same as the indicative, and the "**voi**" form uses the stem from the *infinitive* with the "**-iate**" ending.

	trarre *(to pull)* **tragg-**	**porre** *(to put)* **pong-**	**tradurre** *(to translate)* **traduc-**
io	tra**gg**a	po**ng**a	tradu**c**a
tu	tra**gg**a	po**ng**a	tradu**c**a
lui/lei	tra**gg**a	po**ng**a	tradu**c**a
noi	tra**iamo**	po**niamo**	tradu**ciamo**
voi	tra**iate**	po**niate**	tradu**ciate**
loro	tra**gg**ano	po**ng**ano	tradu**c**ano

4. Finally, the same orthographic changes applied to verbs ending in "**-care**," "**-gare**," "**-ciare**," "**-giare**," and "**-gliare**" in the present indicative tense are applied here to maintain the proper pronunciation.

- **In French**:

	parler *(to speak)* ils <u>parl</u>ent	**finir** *(to finish)* ils <u>finiss</u>ent	**vendre** *(to sell)* ils <u>vend</u>ent
je	parl**e**	finiss**e**	vend**e**
tu	parl**es**	finiss**es**	vend**es**
il/elle/on	parl**e**	finiss**e**	vend**e**
nous	parl**ions**	finiss**ions**	vend**ions**
vous	parl**iez**	finiss**iez**	vend**iez**
ils/elles	parl**ent**	finiss**ent**	vend**ent**

We use the stem from the third-person plural "**ils/elles**" form in the present indicative by removing the final "**-ent**."

There are some irregular verbs that do not follow the above conjugation patterns. These include the following:

1. The verbs "**être**" *(to be)* and "**avoir**" *(to have)* are irregular and must be memorized.

	être	**avoir**
je	sois	aie
tu	sois	aies

il/elle/on	soit	ait
nous	soyons	ayons
vous	soyez	ayez
ils/elles	soient	aient

2. In some verbs, the "**nous**" and "**vous**" forms are conjugated differently. The stem is formed from the *first-person plural in the present indicative*, that is, the "**nous**" form, by dropping the suffix "**-ons.**" Here are some examples:

	je	tu	il/elle	nous	vous	ils/elles
appeler *to call*	appelle	appelles	appelle	appelions	appeliez	appellent
acheter *to buy*	achète	achètes	achète	achetions	achetiez	achètent
boir *to drink*	boive	boives	boive	buvions	buviez	boivent
croire *to believe*	croie	croies	croie	croyions	croyiez	croient
jeter *to throw*	jette	jettes	jette	jetions	jetiez	jettent
mourir *to die*	meure	meures	meure	mourions	mouriez	meurent
préférer *to prefer*	préfère	préfères	préfère	préférions	préfériez	préfèrent
prendre *to take*	prenne	prennes	prenne	prenions	preniez	prennent
recevoir *to receive*	reçoive	reçoives	reçoive	recevions	receviez	reçoivent
tenir *to hold*	tienne	tiennes	tienne	tenions	teniez	tiennent
venir *to come*	vienne	viennes	vienne	venions	veniez	viennent
voir *to see*	voie	voies	voie	voyions	voyiez	voient

3. Some verbs have irregular stems but regular endings. The most common ones are:

	je	tu	il/elle	nous	vous	ils/elles
aller *to go*	aille	ailles	aille	allions	alliez	aillent

faire *to do*	fasse	fasses	fasse	fassions	fassiez	fassent
pouvoir *to rain*	puisse	puisses	puisse	puissions	puissiez	puissent
savoir *to know*	sache	saches	sache	sachions	sachiez	sachent
valoir *to be worth*	vaille	vailles	vaille	valions	valiez	vaillent
vouloir *to want*	veuille	veuilles	veuille	voulions	vouliez	veuillent

In addition, the verb "**falloir**" *(to be necessary)* is impersonal and has only a third-person singular form, which is irregular in the subjunctive, i.e., "**il faille**" *(it is necessary)*.

Uses of the Subjunctive

The subjunctive is usually used in subordinate clauses that use the conjunction *"that,"* where the main clause expresses opinions and feelings such as fear, doubt, desire, etc.

	Examples
Impersonal opinion	**EN**: *It is important that you eat well.* **SP**: **Es importante que** tú comas bien. **PT**: **É importante que** você coma bem. **IT**: **È importante che** tu mangi bene. **FR**: **Il est important que** vous mangiez bien.
Happiness	**EN**: *I'm glad they are well.* **SP**: **Me alegro de que** estén bien. **PT**: **Me alegro que** estejam bem. **IT**: **Sono contento che** stiano bene. **FR**: **Je suis content qu'**ils aillent bien.
Doubt	**EN**: *I doubt that it is sunny today.* **SP**: **Dudo que** esté soleado hoy. **PT**: **Duvido que** esteja ensolarado hoje. **IT**: **Dubito che** oggi ci sia il sole. **FR**: **Je doute qu'**il y ait du soleil aujourd'hui.
Desire	**EN**: *I want him to study well.* **SP**: **Quiero que** estudie bien. **PT**: **Quero que** ele estude bem. **IT**: **Voglio che** lui studi bene. **FR**: **Je veux qu'**il étudie bien.

Expressing Opinions

Knowing when to use the indicative mood and when to use the subjunctive mood when expressing an opinion can be a little tricky. Nevertheless, these are the main guidelines:

1. Impersonal Opinions

For impersonal opinions, such as *"it is important that ...,"* *"it is good that ...,"* and *"it is bad that ...,"* we generally use the subjunctive mood, for example:

SP	**Es importante que** tú <u>visites</u> a tu familia.	
PT	**É importante que** você <u>visite</u> sua família.	*It is important that you <u>visit</u> your family.*
IT	**È importante che** tu <u>visiti</u> la tua famiglia.	
FR	**Il est important que** vous <u>visitiez</u> à votre famille.	
SP	**Es bueno que** tú <u>estés</u> aquí hoy.	
PT	**É bom que** você <u>esteja</u> aqui hoje.	*It is good that you <u>are</u> here today.*
IT	**È bello che** tu <u>sia</u> qui oggi.	
FR	**C'est bien que** tu <u>sois</u> ici aujourd'hui.	

However, if the impersonal statement expresses some sense of certainty, such as *"it is true that ..."* or *"it is obvious that ...,"* the indicative mood is used, for example:

SP	**Está claro que** ellos <u>pueden</u> ganar este partido.	
PT	**É claro que** eles <u>podem</u> vencer esta partida.	*It is clear that they <u>can</u> win this match.*
IT	**È chiaro che** <u>possono</u> vincere questa partita.	
FR	**Il est clair qu'**ils <u>peuvent</u> gagner ce match.	
SP	**Es verdad que** <u>quiero</u> salir hoy.	
PT	**É verdade que** <u>quero</u> sair hoje.	*It is true that I <u>want</u> to go out today.*
IT	**È vero che** <u>voglio</u> uscire oggi.	
FR	**C'est vrai que** je <u>veux</u> sortir aujourd'hui.	

2. Personal Opinions

In Spanish, Portuguese, and French, if the main clause expresses an opinion in the negative, the subordinate clause is in the subjunctive mood, for example:

SP	**No pienso que** esta casa <u>sea</u> muy grande.	
PT	**Não acho que** esta casa <u>seja</u> muito grande.	***I don't think that*** *this house* <u>*is*</u> *too big.*
FR	**Je ne pense pas que** cette maison <u>soit</u> trop grande.	
SP	**No creo que** <u>haya</u> gente viviendo allí.	
PT	**Não creio que** <u>haja</u> pessoas morando lá.	***I don't believe that*** <u>*there are*</u> *people living there.*
FR	**Je ne crois pas qu'**<u>il y ait</u> des gens qui vivent là-bas.	

If the main clause is in the affirmative, the subordinate clause must be in the indicative, not in the subjunctive mood, for example:

SP	**Pienso que** esta casa <u>es</u> muy grande.	
PT	**Eu acho que** esta casa <u>é</u> muito grande.	***I think that*** *this house* <u>*is*</u> *too big.*
FR	**Je pense que** cette maison <u>est</u> trop grande.	
SP	**Creo que** <u>hay</u> gente viviendo allí.	
PT	**Creio que** <u>há</u> pessoas morando lá.	***I believe that*** <u>*there are*</u> *people living there.*
FR	**Je crois qu'**<u>il y a</u> des gens qui vivent là-bas.	

In Italian, if the main clause expresses an opinion that is not asserted as a fact, the subordinate clause is in the subjunctive mood, whether the main clause is in the affirmative or the negative, for example:

Penso che questa casa <u>sia</u> molto grande.	***I think that*** *this house* <u>*is*</u> *too big.*
Non penso che questa casa <u>sia</u> molto grande.	***I don't think that*** *this house* <u>*is*</u> *too big.*

Credo che ci <u>siano</u> persone che vivono lì.	**I believe that** *there <u>are</u> people living there.*
Non credo che ci <u>siano</u> persone che vivono lì.	**I don't believe that** *there <u>are</u> people living there.*

If the main clause indicates certainty or the assertion of a fact, the subordinate clause must be in the indicative, not in the subjunctive mood, for example:

Sono sicuro che questa casa <u>è</u> troppo grande.	**I am sure that** *this house <u>is</u> too big.*
Sa che ci <u>sono</u> persone che vivono lì.	**He knows that** *there <u>are</u> people living there.*

Expressing Possibilities

Most expressions that express the possibility or probability of something being one way or the other use the subjunctive mood. For example:

SP	**Es posible que** mañana <u>esté</u> nublado.	**It is possible that** *it <u>is</u> cloudy tomorrow.*
PT	**É possível que** amanhã <u>esteja</u> nublado.	
IT	**È possibile che** domani <u>sia</u> nuvolo.	
FR	**Il est possible que** ce <u>soit</u> nuageux à l'extérieur.	
SP	**Puede ser que** Marco <u>esté</u> atrapado en el tráfico.	**It could be that** *Marco <u>is</u> stuck in traffic.*
PT	**Pode ser que** Marco <u>esteja</u> preso no trânsito.	
IT	**Può darsi che** Marco <u>sia</u> bloccato nel traffico.	
FR	**Il se pourrait que** Marco <u>soit</u> coincé dans les embouteillages.	

In Spanish, some expressions that express the possibility of something being one way or the other can use indicative or subjunctive mood without any preference, for example:

Tal vez **salgo/salga** hoy.	*Perhaps I **will go out** today.*
Quizás **hablamos/hablemos** mañana.	*Maybe we **talk** tomorrow.*
Probablemente **voy/vaya** al parque solo.	*I **will** probably **go** to the park alone.*
Posiblemente **vienes/vengas** tarde.	*Possibly you **will come** late.*

A notable exception that only uses the indicative in Spanish is "**a lo mejor**" (*maybe*), for example:

No hay nadie aquí. A lo mejor **están** en el parque.	*There is no one here. Maybe they **are** at the park.*

In Portuguese, some expressions that suggest the possibility of something being one way or the other, such as "**talvez**" and "**pode ser**," meaning *"perhaps"* or *"maybe,"* use the subjunctive mood. For example:

Talvez **possamos** sair hoje.	*Perhaps we **can** go out today.*
Pode ser que não **haja** ninguém aqui.	*It could be that **there is** no one here.*

Note that some equivalent expressions exclusively use the indicative, such as "**provavelmente**" *(probably)*, "**possivelmente**" *(possibly)*, and "**se calhar**" *(maybe)*. For example:

Provavelmente **podemos** sair hoje.	*Probably we **can** go out today.*
Possivelmente não **há** ninguém aqui.	*Possibly **there is** no one here.*
Se calhar **é** melhor ir embora.	*Maybe it **is** better to leave.*

In Italian, some notable exceptions that use the indicative are "**forse**" and "**magari**." Both words mean *"perhaps"* or *"maybe,"* but "**magari**" indicates more excitement or hope. For example:

Forse Anna dorme presto.	***Maybe** Anna sleeps early.*
Magari domani c'è il sole.	***Maybe** it is sunny tomorrow.*

In French, a notable exception that uses the indicative is "**peut-être**," meaning *"perhaps"* or *"maybe,"* for example:

Peut-être que c'<u>est</u> nuageux dehors.	***Maybe** it <u>is</u> cloudy outside.*

Expressing Desires, Wishes, Feelings, and Requests

In general, desires, wishes, feelings, and requests are expressed in the subjunctive mood, for example:

SP	**Quiero que** <u>comas</u> con nosotros.	
PT	**Quero que** você <u>coma</u> conosco.	***I want you** to <u>eat</u> with us.*
IT	**Voglio che** <u>mangi</u> con noi.	
FR	**Je veux que** tu <u>manges</u> avec nous.	

SP	**Espero que** nos <u>veamos</u> pronto.	
PT	**Espero que** nos <u>vejamos</u> em breve.	***I hope that*** *we <u>see</u> each*
IT	**Spero che** ci <u>vedremo</u> presto.	*other soon.*
FR	**J'espère que** nous nous <u>reverrons</u> bientôt.	
SP	**Me alegro que** tu <u>estés</u> aquí.	
PT	**Fico feliz que** você <u>esteja</u> aqui.	***I'm glad*** *you <u>are</u> here.*
IT	**Sono contento che** tu <u>sia</u> qui.	
FR	**Je suis content que** tu <u>sois</u> là.	

Note that when the verb in the main clause is used to express desire, the subjunctive mood is only used if the subject and the performer of the action are not the same. For example:

SP	Quiero que **estudies** bien.	
PT	Eu quero que você **estude** bem.	*I want you to **study** well.*
IT	Voglio che tu **studi** bene.	
FR	Je veux que tu **étudies** bien.	

If the subject and the performer of the action are the same, we use the infinitive following the verb. For example:

SP	Quiero **estudiar** bien.	
PT	Eu quero **estudar** bem.	*I want to **study** well.*
IT	Voglio **studiare** bene.	
FR	Je veux bien **étudier**.	

In Italian, when the verb in the main clause expresses an opinion, feeling, demand, or doubt, and the subject and the performer of the action are the same, we use the infinitive preceded by "**di**." For example:

Penso che tu **guidi** molto.	*I think that <u>you</u> **drive** a lot.*
Penso **di guidare** molto.	*I think that <u>I</u> **drive** a lot.*

Crede che lei **corra** veloce.	*He believes that <u>she</u> **runs** fast.*
Crede **di correre** veloce.	*He believes that <u>he</u> **runs** fast.*

6. PRESENT PROGRESSIVE TENSE

In Spanish, Portuguese, and Italian, the present progressive tense, similar to its use in English, describes an event that continues to take place in the present, e.g., *"I am speaking."*

In Spanish, the present progressive tense is formed by adding the auxiliary verb "**estar**" to the present participle, also known as the *gerund*. The gerund is formed by attaching "-**ando**" to the stem of "-**ar**" ending verbs and "-**iendo**" to the stem of "-**er**" and "-**ir**" ending verbs.

"-**ar**" verbs	subject pronoun + "**estar**" in present tense + (verb stem+ **ando**)
"-**er**" verbs	subject pronoun + "**estar**" in present tense + (verb stem+ **iendo**)
"-**ir**" verbs	subject pronoun + "**estar**" in present tense + (verb stem+ **iendo**)

		-ar ending e.g., hablar	-er ending e.g., comer	-ir ending e.g., vivir
yo	estoy			
tú	estás			
él/ella/usted	está	hab**lando**	com**iendo**	viv**iendo**
nosotros/-as	estamos			
vosotros/-as	estáis			
ellos/ellas/ustedes	están			

In Portuguese, the present progressive tense is formed by adding the auxiliary verb "**estar**" to the gerund. The gerund is formed by attaching "-**ando**" to the stem of "-**ar**" ending verbs, "-**endo**" to the stem of "-**er**" ending verbs, and "-**indo**" to the stem of "-**ir**" ending verbs.

"-**ar**" verbs	subject pronoun + "**estar**" in present tense + (verb stem+ **ando**)
"-**er**" verbs	subject pronoun + "**estar**" in present tense + (verb stem+ **endo**)
"-**ir**" verbs	subject pronoun + "**estar**" in present tense + (verb stem+ **indo**)

		-ar ending e.g., falar	-er ending e.g., comer	-ir ending e.g., partir
eu	estou			
ele/ela/você	está	fa**lando**	com**endo**	part**indo**
nós	estamos			
eles/elas/vocês	estão			

In Italian, the present progressive tense uses the auxiliary verb "**stare**" in the present indicative tense, followed by the *gerund*. The gerund is formed by attaching "-**ando**" to the stem of "-**are**" ending verbs and "**-endo**" to the stem of "**-ere**" and "**-ire**" ending verbs.

"**-are**" verbs	subject pronoun + "**stare**" in present tense + (verb stem+ **ando**)
"**-ere**" verbs	subject pronoun + "**stare**" in present tense + (verb stem+ **endo**)
"**-ire**" verbs	subject pronoun + "**stare**" in present tense + (verb stem+ **endo**)

		-ar ending e.g., parlare	-er ending e.g., vivere	-ir ending e.g., finire
io	sto			
tu	stai			
lui/lei	sta	parl**ando**	viv**endo**	fin**endo**
noi	stiamo			
voi	state			
loro	stanno			

Unlike in English, it is possible to use the present simple tense to describe something happening continuously at the moment to convey the same meaning as the present progressive tense. For example:

SP	¿Qué **haces**? (or) ¿Qué **estás haciendo**?	
PT	O que você **faz**? (or) O que você **está fazendo**?	*What **are** you **doing**?*
IT	Cosa **fai**? (or) Cosa **stai facendo**?	

In French, there is no equivalent to the present progressive tense in English. It is common to use the simple present tense in French to talk about actions that are happening right now, e.g., "**Je <u>parle</u>**" *(I am talking)*, "**Qu'est-ce que tu <u>fais</u>?**" *(What <u>are</u> you <u>doing</u>?)*, etc.

To emphasize the continuous state of an action, one could use the expression "**être en train de**" *(to be in the process of)*. Here are some examples:

Je **suis en train de parler**.	*I **am speaking**.*
Il **est en train de manger**.	*He **is eating**.*
Nous **sommes en train de jouer**.	*We **are playing**.*

Irregular Gerunds

In Spanish, we have mentioned that a gerund can be easily constructed by attaching "**-ando**" to an "**-ar**" ending verb and "**-iendo**" to an "**-er**" or "**-ir**" ending verb. Nevertheless, there are a few irregular verbs that require some practice:

❖ The gerund of the verb "**ir**" (*to go*), which is a very common verb in Spanish, is "**yendo**," e.g., "**Yo estoy yendo al aeropuerto**" (*I am going to the airport*). To say *"I'm coming"* in Spanish, you could use "**Estoy yendo**" or "**Ya voy**" because in Spanish we use the verb "**ir**" based on the point of reference of the speaker rather than that of the destination.

❖ In verbs ending in "**-er**" or "**-ir**," if the stem (the remaining part of the verb after removing the "**-er**" or "**-ir**" ending) ends in a vowel, "**-iendo**" becomes "**-yendo**," e.g., the gerund of "**leer**" *(to read)* is "**leyendo**," the gerund of "**atraer**" *(to attract)* is "**atrayendo**," the gerund of "**destruir**" (*to destroy*) is "**destruyendo**," and that of "**huir**" (*to run away*) is "**huyendo**."

❖ Many verbs ending in "**-ir**" that change stem in third-person forms of the present tense conjugation from "**e**" to "**i**" or from "**o**" to "**u**" maintain the same stem change in the gerund form, e.g., "**decir**" *(to say)* becomes "**diciendo**," "**pedir**" *(to ask for)* becomes "**pidiendo**," "**dormir**" *(to sleep)* becomes "**durmiendo**," and "**morir**" *(to die)* becomes "**muriendo**."

❖ In the verbs ending in "**-er**" or "**-ir**," if the stem ends in "**-ll**" or "**-ñ**," "**-iendo**" becomes "**-endo**." There are few verbs in this group, most of which are not very common, e.g., "**bullir**" *(to boil)* becomes "**bullendo**," "**mullir**" *(to fluff)* becomes "**mullendo**," and "**teñir**" *(to dye)* becomes "**tiñendo**," where the latter changes the first "**e**" to "**i**" as an exception to the rule.

In Italian, there are only a few irregular gerunds. The most common ones are: "**bere**" *(to drink)*, "**dare**" *(to give)*, "**dire**" *(to say)*, "**fare**" *(to do or to make)*, and "**stare**" *(to stay or to be)*. Notice that, with these irregular verbs, the gerund is often formed from the stem of the first-person "**io**" form in the present indicative.

	bere	**dare**	**dire**	**fare**	**stare**
"**io**" Form	be<u>v</u>o	<u>d</u>o	<u>dic</u>o	<u>facc</u>io	<u>st</u>o
Gerund	bev**endo**	dand**o**	dic**endo**	fac**endo**	stand**o**

More on the present participle and gerund in French was discussed in **Level III, Lesson 9**.

Examples

Here are some more examples in context:

SP	Yo **estoy comiendo** ahora.	
PT	Eu **estou comendo** agora.	*I **am eating** now.*
IT	Io **sto mangiando** adesso.	
SP	Tú **estás tomando** café.	
PT	Você **está tomando** café.	*You **are drinking** coffee.*
IT	Tu **stai bevendo** un caffè.	
SP	Ella **está hablando** con su madre.	
PT	Ela **está falando** com a mãe.	*She **is speaking** to her mother.*
IT	Lei **sta parlando** con sua madre.	
SP	Nosotros **estamos durmiendo**	
PT	Nós **estamos dormindo**.	*We **are sleeping**.*
IT	Noi **stiamo dormendo**.	
SP	Ellos **estan nadando** aqui	
PT	Eles **estão nadando** aqui.	*They **are swimming** here.*
IT	Loro **stanno nuotando** qui.	

7. FUTURE PERFECT TENSE

The future perfect tense, similar to its use in English, describes events that will happen and be completed in the future by a certain time or happen after another event is completed in the future.

The future perfect is formed as follows:

SP	"**haber**" in the *simple future* tense	
PT	"**ter**" or "**haver**" in the *simple future* tense	+ past participle
IT	"**avere**" or "**essere**" in the *simple future* tense	
FR	"**avoir**" or "**être**" in the *simple future* tense	

The auxiliary verb in future tense serves a similar function to the auxiliary *"will have"* in English, e.g., *"I will have done my homework by the time they come."*

In Spanish, the verb **"haber"** in the future form is used:

		-ar ending e.g., hablar	-er ending e.g., comer	-ir ending e.g., vivir
yo	habré			
tú	habrás			
él/ella/usted	habrá	hablado	comido	vivido
nosotros/-as	habremos			
vosotros/-as	habréis			
ellos/ellas/ustedes	habrán			

In Portuguese, both **"ter"** and **"haver"** are grammatically correct and can be used interchangeably. However, the use of **"haver"** is usually limited to writing. In everyday language, the verb **"ter"** is often used.

The future perfect tense is structured as follows:

		-ar ending e.g., falar	-er ending e.g., comer	-ir ending e.g., partir
eu	terei/haverei			
ele/ela/você	terá/haverá	falado	comido	partido
nós	teremos/haveremos			
eles/elas/vocês	terão/haverão			

In Italian, the verb **"avere"** in the future form is conjugated as follows:

		-are ending e.g., parlare	-ere ending e.g., vendere	-ire ending e.g., dormire
io	avrò			
tu	avrai			
lui/lei	avrà	parlato	venduto	dormito
noi	avremo			
voi	avrete			
loro	avranno			

On the other hand, the verb **"essere"** in the future form is conjugated as follows:

		-are ending e.g., andare	-ere ending e.g., cadere	-ire ending e.g., partire
io	sarò	and**ato**/-**a**	cad**uto**/-**a**	part**ito**/-**a**
tu	sarai	and**ato**/-**a**	cad**uto**/-**a**	part**ito**/-**a**
lui	sarà	and**ato**	cad**uto**	part**ito**
lei	sarà	and**ata**	cad**uta**	part**ita**
noi	saremo	and**ati**/-**e**	cad**uti**/-**e**	part**iti**/-**e**
voi	sarete	and**ati**/-**e**	cad**uti**/-**e**	part**iti**/-**e**
loro	saranno	and**ati**/-**e**	cad**uti**/-**e**	part**iti**/-**e**

In French, the verb **"avoir"** in the future form is conjugated as follows:

		-er ending e.g., parlare	-ir ending e.g., finir	-re ending e.g., vendre
j'	aurai			
tu	auras			
il/elle/on	aura			
nous	aurons	par**lé**	fi**ni**	ven**du**
vous	aurez			
ils/elles	auront			

On the other hand, the verb **"être"** in the future form is conjugated as follows:

		-er ending e.g., aller	-ir ending e.g., partir	-re ending e.g., descendre
je	serai	all**é**(**e**)	part**i**(**e**)	descend**u**(**e**)
tu	seras	all**é**(**e**)	part**i**(**e**)	descend**u**(**e**)
il/on	sera	all**é**	part**i**	descend**u**
elle	sera	all**ée**	part**ie**	descend**ue**
nous	serons	all**é**(**e**)**s**	part**i**(**e**)**s**	descend**u**(**e**)**s**
vous	serez	all**é**(**e**)**s**	part**i**(**e**)**s**	descend**u**(**e**)**s**
ils	seront	all**és**	part**is**	descend**us**
elles	seront	all**ées**	part**ies**	descend**ues**

Let us look at some examples of the future perfect tense:

SP	Yo **habré visitado** Egipto en enero.	*I **will have visited** Egypt in January.*
PT	**Terei visitado** o Egito em janeiro.	
IT	**Avrò visitato** l'Egitto a gennaio.	
FR	J'**aurai visité** l'Egypte en janvier.	

SP	Tú **habrás bebido** el café.	*You **will have drunk** the coffee.*
PT	Você **terá bebido** o café.	
IT	**Avrai bevuto** il caffè.	
FR	Tu **auras bu** le café.	
SP	Ella habrá hablado con su madre.	*She **will have spoken** to her mother.*
PT	Ela **terá falado** com a mãe.	
IT	**Avrà parlato** con sua madre.	
FR	Elle **aura parlé** à sa mère.	
SP	Nosotros **habremos comido**.	*We **will have eaten**.*
PT	Nós **teremos comido**.	
IT	Noi **avremo mangiato**.	
FR	Nous **aurons mangé**.	

8. PERSONAL "A" IN SPANISH

The use of the personal "**a**" is unique to the Spanish language and does not appear in Portuguese, Italian, or French. The preposition "**a**" is used frequently in Spanish, e.g., "**Voy a la escuela**" *(I go to school).*

A special use of the preposition "**a**" is to precede the direct object when it is a defined person or a group of defined persons. In this case, the preposition "**a**" is known as personal "**a**," for example:

Yo vi **a** mi mamá ayer.	*I saw my mom yesterday.*
Él llama **a** su amigo frecuentemente.	*He calls his friend frequently.*
Ella visitó **a** sus padres anoche.	*She visited her parents last night.*
Comprendo **a** mi profesor fácilmente.	*I understand my professor easily.*

Notice that the English translation of the above sentences has no direct equivalent of the personal "**a**" in Spanish.

If we refer generally, and not specifically to a person, we do not use the personal "**a**," for example:

| Yo vi dos mujeres charlando ayer. | *I saw two women chatting yesterday.* |
| Él necesita un médico inmediatamente. | *He needs a doctor immediately.* |

Generally, a pet is treated as a person in Spanish. The personal "**a**" is used when referring to a pet, but not with ordinary animals, for example:

| Le doy un baño **a** mi gato todos los meses. | *I give my cat a bath every month.* |
| Vi un conejo en el zoológico. | *I saw a rabbit in the zoo.* |

In the first sentence above, the *"cat"* is a pet. Thus, the personal "**a**" is used. On the other hand, the *"rabbit"* in the second sentence is an ordinary animal that does not require the use of the personal "**a**."

Pronouns referring to a person or persons are also treated in the same way as a specific person or persons. Thus, the personal "**a**" is used. This includes each of the following pronouns when used as a direct object referring to people: "**alguien**" (*somebody*), "**nadie**" (*nobody*), "**quien**" (*whom*), "**alguno**" (*some*), and "**ninguno**" (*none*), for example:

| No vi **a** nadie ayer. | *I didn't see anybody yesterday.* |
| Tengo que llamar **a** alguien. | *I have to call someone.* |

If a direct object is personified to express emotion or attachment, the personal "**a**" can be used to imply such emotion, for example:

| Extraño mucho **a** mi país. | *I miss my country a lot.* |
| Abrazaría **a** la almohada como si fuera mi amiga. | *I'd hug my pillow as if it were my friend.* |

The only verbs that generally do not use the personal "**a**," even when referring to a specific person or persons, are "**haber**" and "**tener**," for example:

| Hay 15 estudiantes en la clase. | *There are 15 students in the class.* |
| Tengo cinco primos. | *I have five cousins.* |

The only exception to the verb "**tener**" is when it is used to mean holding someone physically or emotionally close to you. In this case, the personal "**a**" is used, for example:

| Cuando hay un problema, tengo **a** mi familia. | *When there is a problem, I have my family.* |
| Tendré **a** mi hermano en los brazos. | *I will have my brother in my arms.* |

LEVEL V: ADVANCED

As you plow through the languages to reach this advanced level, take your time to go over the new topics, which will become a little more challenging but much more interesting. You can Anki cards to reinforce these topics in your memory with reviews and exercises.

1. THE PRONOUNS "CI" & "NE" IN ITALIAN AND "Y" & "EN" IN FRENCH

The pronouns "**ci**" and "**ne**" in Italian and the pronouns "**y**" and "**en**" in French are a constant source of confusion to many learners of these two languages. We will look at the most common uses of these pronominal particles in different contexts.

Uses of "Ci" in Italian and "Y" in French

Here we discuss some important uses of the pronouns "**ci**" in Italian and "**y**" in French:

1. Meaning *"there"* when referring to a place.

- In Italian:

For example, in the sentence: "**Vado <u>in quella caffetteria</u> tutte le mattine**" *(I go <u>to that coffee shop</u> every morning)*, we can eliminate "**in quella caffetteria**" *(to that coffee shop)* and say: "**<u>Ci</u> vado tutte le mattine**" *(I go <u>there</u> every morning)*.

Notice that "**ci**" is placed before the verb. Here are more examples:

Vado sempre **al mare** d'estate.	I always go **to the beach** in summer.
Ci vado sempre d'estate.	I always go **there** in summer.
Vivremo **a Napoli** per due anni.	We will live **in Naples** for two years.
Ci vivremo per due anni.	We will live **there** for two years.

| Sei stato **a Roma**? | *Have you been **to Rome**?* |
| **Ci** sei stato? | *Have you been **there**?* |

- In French:

For example, in the sentence: "**Je vais à ce café tous les matins**" *(I go to that coffee shop every morning)*, we can eliminate "**à ce café**" *(to that coffee shop)* and say: "**J'y vais tous les matins**" *(I go there every morning)*.

Notice that "**y**" is placed before the verb. Here are more examples:

Je vais toujours **à la plage** en été.	*I always go **to the beach** in summer.*
J'**y** vais toujours en été.	*I always go **there** in summer.*
Nous habiterons **à Paris** pendant deux ans.	*We will live **in Paris** for two years.*
Nous **y** habiterons pendant deux ans.	*We will live **there** for two years.*
Êtes-vous allé **à Rome**?	*Have you been **to Rome**?*
Y êtes-vous allé?	*Have you been **there**?*

2. Use with some verbs that are usually followed by a preposition.

- In Italian:

Some verbs are usually followed by the preposition "**a**," "**in**," or "**su**," such as: "**pensare a**" *(to think about)*, "**credere in**" *(to believe in)*, "**contare su**" *(to count on)*, etc.

For example, in the sentence "**Stai pensando al lavoro?**" *(Are you thinking about work?)*, we can replace "**al lavoro**" *(about work)* with "**ci**" and place it before the verb, that is, "**Ci stai pensando?**" *(Are you thinking about it?)*. Notice that "**ci**" here is placed before the verb and is translated as *"about it."*

Here are some more examples:

Penserò **a questo problema**.	*I will think **about that problem**.*
Ci penserò.	*I will think **about it**.*
Puoi contare **sul loro aiuto**.	*You can count **on their help**.*
Ci puoi contare.	*You can count **on it**.*

| Credo **in ciò di cui è capace**. | *I believe in **what he is capable of**.* |
| **Ci** credo. | *I believe **in it**.* |

Notice that "**ci**" is always placed before the verb, unless the verb is in the infinitive or the imperative. For example:

È importante pensare **al futuro**.	*It is important to think **about the future**.*
È importante pensar**ci**.	*It is important to think **about it**.*
Non contare **sul loro aiuto**.	*Don't count **on their help**.*
Non contar**ci**.	*Don't count **on it**.*
Pensa **all'offerta**.	*Think **about the offer**.*
Pensa**ci**.	*Think **about it**.*

- In French:

Some verbs are usually followed by the preposition "**à**," "**en**," or "**sur**," such as: "**penser à**" *(to think about)*, "**croire en**" *(to believe in)*, "**compter sur**" *(to count on)*, etc. In this case, the pronoun "**y**" can replace the preposition and the following noun.

For example, in the sentence "**Vous pensez au travail?**" *(Are you thinking about work?)*, we can replace "**au travail**" *(about work)* with "**y**" before the verb, that is, "**Vous y pensez?**" *(Are you thinking about it?)*.

Notice that "**y**" here is placed before the verb and is translated as *"about it."* The inanimate noun (thing or idea) that "**y**" replaces is considered an indirect object because it is preceded by a preposition.

Here are some more examples:

Je vais penser **à ce problème**.	*I will think **about that problem**.*
Je vais **y** penser.	*I will think **about it**.*
Vous pouvez compter **sur leur aide**.	*You can count **on their help**.*
Vous pouvez **y** compter.	*You can count **on it**.*
Je crois en **ce dont il est capable**.	*I believe in **what he is capable of**.*
J'**y** crois.	*I believe **in it**.*

Notice that "**y**" is always placed before the verb. The only exception is if the verb is in the affirmative imperative. In this case, the "**y**" is attached to the end of the verb. For example:

Pensez **à l'offre**.	*Think **about the offer**.*
Pensez-**y**.	*Think **about it**.*
Ne comptez pas **sur leur aide**.	*Don't count **on their help**.*
N'**y** comptez pas.	*Don't count **on it**.*

3. The pronouns "**ci**" and "**y**" are used in expressions meaning *"there is/are …"*

- In Italian:

The pronoun "**ci**" is used in the expressions "**c'è**" *(there is)* and "**ci sono**" *(there are)*, as we have encountered in **Level III, Lesson 7**. For example:

C'è solo un modo per risolvere questo problema.	***There is*** *only one way to solve this problem.*
Ci sono molti modi per risolvere questo problema.	***There are*** *many ways to solve this problem.*
Non **c'è** nessuno qui.	***There is*** *no one here.*
Non **ci sono** abbastanza sedie nella stanza.	***There aren't*** *enough chairs in the room.*

- In French:

The pronoun "**y**" is used in the expression "**il y a**" which can mean *"there is/are."* For example:

Il y a une façon de résoudre ce problème.	***There is*** *a way to solve this problem.*
Il y a beaucoup de monde ici.	***There are*** *many people here.*
Il n'**y a** personne ici.	***There is*** *no one here.*
Il n'**y a** pas assez de chaises dans la salle.	***There aren't*** *enough chairs in the room.*

The expression **"il y a"** in French has the equivalent meaning of *"ago"* when referring to events that happened in the past, for example:

Le colis est arrivé **il y a** 30 minutes.	*The package arrived 30 minutes **ago**.*
Le problème a commencé **il y a** deux ans.	*The problem started two years **ago**.*
Il y a deux heures qu'ils ont appelé.	*They called two hours **ago**.*
J'ai déménagé ici **il y a** 3 mois.	*I moved here 3 months **ago**.*

Uses of "Ne" in Italian and "En" in French

The pronouns **"ne"** in Italian and **"en"** in French often precede the verb unless the verb is in the infinitive or the imperative. The pronouns **"ne"** and **"en"** have the following uses:

1. Use with some verbs and expressions that are followed by a preposition.

- In Italian:

Some verbs and expressions that are followed by the preposition. **"di,"** such as: **"parlare di"** *(to talk about)*, **"avere bisogno di"** *(to need)*, **"felice di"** *(happy about)*, **"sicuro di"** *(sure of)*, etc. In these expressions, **"ne"** can replace *"of it"* or *"about it."*

For example, in the sentence **"Sono felice del risultato"** *(I am happy about the result)*, we can replace **"del risultato"** *(about the result)* with **"ne"** and place it before the verb, that is, **"Ne sono felice"** *(I am happy about it)*. Notice that **"ne"** here is placed before the verb and is translated as *"about it."*

Here are some more examples:

Sta parlando **del nuovo progetto**. **Ne** sta parlando.	*He is talking **about the new project**. He is talking **about it**.*
Ho bisogno **di soldi** per uscire. **Ne** ho bisogno per uscire.	*I need **the money** to go out. I need **it** to go out.*

Sei sicuro **della risposta**?	*Are you sure **of the answer**?*
Ne sei sicuro?	*Are you sure **of it**?*

There are also some idiomatic expressions that use the pronoun "**ne**," even though it may sometimes seem redundant. For example:

Ne vale la pena.	*It is worth **it**.*
Chi se **ne** importa di …?	*Who cares **about** …?*
Non me **ne** importa niente.	*I don't care at all (**about it**).*
Non **ne** posso più.	*I can't stand **it** anymore.*

- In French:

Some verbs and expressions are followed by the preposition "**de**," such as: "**parler de**" *(to talk about)*, "**avoir besoin de**" *(to need)*, "**content de**" *(happy about)*, "**sûr de**" *(sure of)*, etc. In these expressions, "**en**" can replace the preposition and the following noun.

For example, in the sentence "**Je suis content du résultat**" *(I am happy about the result)*, we can replace "**du résultat**" *(about the result)* with "**en**" and place it before the verb, that is, "**J'en suis content**" *(I am happy about it)*.

Notice that "**en**" here is placed before the verb and is translated as *"about it."* The inanimate noun (thing or idea) that "**en**" replaces is also considered an indirect object.

Here are some more examples:

Il parle **du nouveau projet**.	*He is talking **about the new project**.*
Il **en** parle.	*He is talking **about it**.*
J'ai besoin **d'argent** pour sortir.	*I need **the money** to go out.*
J'**en** ai besoin pour sortir.	*I need **it** to go out.*
Es-tu sûr **de la réponse**?	*Are you sure **of the answer**?*
En es-tu sûr?	*Are you sure **of it**?*

There are also some idiomatic expressions that use the pronoun "**en**," even though it may sometimes seem redundant. For example:

Ça **en** vaut la peine.	*It is worth **it**.*

Qui s'**en** soucie de ...?	*Who cares **about** ...?*
Je **en** m'en soucie pas du tout.	*I don't care at all (**about it**).*
Je n'**en** peux plus.	*I can't stand **it** anymore.*

2. The pronouns "**ne**" in Italian and "**en**" in French are used with quantities and amounts, and are often translated as *"of it"* or *"of them."* They usually replace a number or a partitive such as *"some"* or *"a little."*

- In Italian:

For example, in the sentence "**Voglio del latte**" *(I want some milk)*, we can replace "**del latte**" *(some milk)* with "**ne**" and place it before the verb, that is, "**Ne voglio**" *(I want some of it)*. Notice that "**ne**" here is placed before the verb and is translated as *"some of it."*

Similarly, in the sentence "**Ho due biscotti**" *(I have two cookies)*, we can replace "**biscotti**" *(cookies)* with "**ne**" and place it before the verb, that is, "**Ne ho due**" *(I have two "of them")*. Notice that "**ne**" here is placed before the verb and is translated as *"of them."*

Here are some more examples:

Vuoi **un po' d'acqua**?	*Do you want **some water**?*
Ne vuoi?	*Do you want **some**?*
Ho preso la metà **dello zucchero**.	*I took half **the sugar**.*
Ne ho preso la metà.	*I took half **of it**.*
Ci sono tre **mele** sul tavolo.	*There are three **apples** on the table.*
Ce **ne** sono tre sul tavolo.	*There are three **of them** on the table.*

Notice that in the last example "**ci sono**" *(there are)* is changed to "**ce ne sono**" *(there are "of them")* because "**ci**" is often changed to "**ce**" when followed by another pronoun. Also, notice that the noun that "**ne**" replaces can be countable or uncountable.

In case there is a reflexive or indirect pronoun in the sentence, the reflexive or indirect pronoun is placed before "**ne**." For example:

Ti darò due **libri**.	*I will give you two **books**.*
Ti **ne** darò due.	*I will give you two (**of them**).*

| Gli darò due libri. | I will give _him_ two **books**. |
| Glie**ne** darò due. | I will give _him_ two (**of them**). |

Notice that, in the last example, the indirect pronoun "**gli**" is combined with "**ne**" to form the contraction "**gliene**."

| gli | + | ne | = | gliene |

The pronoun "**ne**" can also attach to the verb in the infinitive or the imperative. This is more common with pronominal verbs which we will cover in **Level VI, Lesson 6**.

- In French:

For example, in the sentence "**Je veux du lait**" (I want _some milk_), we can replace "**du lait**" (some milk) with "**en**" and place it before the verb, that is, "**J'en veux**" (I want _some of it_). Notice that "**en**" here is placed before the verb and is translated as "some of it."

Similarly, in the sentence "**J'ai deux biscuits**" (I have two _cookies_), we can replace "**biscuits**" (cookies) with "**en**" and place it before the verb, that is, "**J'en ai deux**" (I have two "_of them_"). Notice that "**en**" here is placed before the verb and is translated as "of them."

Here are some more examples:

Veux-tu **de l'eau**?	Do you want **some water**?
En veux-tu?	Do you want **some**?
J'ai pris la moitié **du sucre**.	I took half **the sugar**.
J'**en** ai pris la moitié.	I took half **of it**.
Il y a trois **pommes** sur la table.	There are three **apples** on the table.
Il y **en** a trois sur la table.	There are three **of them** on the table.

Notice that the noun that "**en**" replaces can be countable or uncountable.

In case there is a reflexive or indirect pronoun in the sentence, the reflexive or indirect pronoun is placed before "**en**." For example:

| Je _te_ donnerai deux **livres**. | I will give _you_ two **books**. |
| Je _t'_**en** donnerai deux. | I will give _you_ two (**of them**). |

| Je <u>lui</u> donnerai deux **livres**. | *I will give <u>him</u> two **books**.* |
| Je <u>lui</u> **en** donnerai deux. | *I will give <u>him</u> two (**of them**).* |

The pronoun "**en**" is placed after the verb in the case of the affirmative imperative, for example:

Donnez-<u>moi</u> deux **livres**.	*Give <u>me</u> two **books**.*
Donnez-<u>m'</u>**en** deux.	*Give <u>me</u> two (**of them**).*
Donnez-<u>nous</u> **du pain**.	*Give <u>us</u> some **bread**.*
Donnez-<u>nous</u> **en**.	*Give <u>us</u> some (**of it**).*

The pronoun "**en**" is also used in some pronominal verbs, which we will cover in **Level VI, Lesson 6**.

3. Meaning *"from here"* or *"from there"* when referring to a place in Italian.

For example, in the sentence: "**È appena arrivato <u>da Milano</u>**" *(He has just arrived <u>from Milan</u>)*, we can eliminate "**da Milano**" *(from Milan)* and say: "**<u>Ne</u> è appena arrivato**" *(He has just arrived <u>from there</u>)*.

Notice that "**ne**" is placed before the verb. It is also common to use "**ne**" with the verb "**andare**." Here are more examples:

Me **ne** vado domani.	*I am leaving (**from here**) tomorrow.*
Se **n'**è andato.	*He's gone (**from here**).*
Devo andarme**ne**.	*I must get out (**of here**).*
È uscito salvo **dall'incidente**.	*He got out **of the accident** safely.*
Ne è uscito salvo.	*He got out (**of there**) safely.*

2. PAST ABSOLUTE TENSE IN ITALIAN & SIMPLE PAST TENSE IN FRENCH

The past absolute tense in Italian and the simple past tense in French are equivalent to the preterite tense in Spanish and Portuguese. However, they are considered more formal and are less used in common-day language. The present perfect tense is often used instead in daily life in Italian and French. We will cover the most important aspects of the past absolute tense in Italian and the simple past tense in French.

Past Absolute Tense in Italian

In Italian, the past absolute tense is often used to refer to the distant or remote past. It is often used in reference to past events or narrations. However, since defining a certain past event as distant is something relative, one can use both the present perfect and the past absolute to refer to events that have been completed in the past. Nevertheless, the past absolute cannot be used to refer to past events that have not been completed at the present moment. In this case, only the present perfect can be used. Thus, words such as **"già"** *(already)* and **"appena"** *(just)* are often not seen in the past absolute tense, but only in the present perfect tense.

In general, the past absolute tense finds more use in the southern part of Italy, whereas the present perfect tense is more common in other parts of Italy in daily spoken language.

Conjugation

The stem is formed by removing the final "-**are**," "-**ere**," or "-**ire**," and attaching the conjugation suffix according to the personal pronoun, as shown in the following table:

	-are ending par<u>lare</u> *(to speak)*	-ere ending <u>vend</u>ere *(to sell)*	-ire ending <u>part</u>ire *(to leave)*
io	par**lai**	vend**ei** (or) vend**etti**	part**ii**
tu	par**lasti**	vend**esti**	part**isti**
lui/lei	par**lò**	vend**é** (or) vend**ette**	part**ì**
noi	par**lammo**	vend**emmo**	part**immo**
voi	par**laste**	vend**este**	part**iste**
loro	par**larono**	vend**erono** (or) vend**ettero**	part**irono**

Many, but not all, regular verbs in the "-**ere**" group have an alternative form in the "**io**," "**lui/lei**," and "**loro**" forms. These have the endings: "-**etti**," "-**ette**," and "-**ettero**," respectively.

There are many irregular verbs in the past absolute, especially verbs with the "-**ere**" ending. Note that most of these irregular verbs have regular "**tu**," "**noi**," and "**voi**" forms. Here, we list the most common ones:

	io	tu	lui/lei	noi	voi	loro
avere *to have*	ebbi	avesti	ebbe	avemmo	aveste	ebbero
bere *to drink*	bevvi	bevesti	bevve	bevemmo	beveste	bevvero
cadere *to fall*	caddi	cadesti	cadde	cademmo	cadeste	caddero
chiedere *to ask*	chiesi	chiedesti	chiese	chiedemmo	chiedeste	chiesero
chiudere *to close*	chiusi	chiudesti	chiuse	chiudemmo	chiudeste	chiusero
conoscere *to know*	conobbi	conoscesti	conobbe	conoscemmo	conosceste	conobbero
correggere *to correct*	corressi	correggesti	corresse	correggemmo	correggeste	corressero
dare *to give*	diedi	desti	diede	demmo	deste	diedero
decidere *to decide*	decisi	decidesti	decise	decidemmo	decideste	decisero
dire *to say or tell*	dissi	dicesti	disse	dicemmo	diceste	dissero
discutere *to discuss*	discussi	discutesti	discusse	discutemmo	discuteste	discussero
essere *to be*	fui	fosti	fu	fummo	foste	furono
fare *to do or make*	feci	facesti	fece	facemmo	faceste	fecero
leggere *to read*	lessi	leggesti	lesse	leggemmo	leggeste	lessero
mettere *to put*	misi	mettesti	mise	mettemmo	metteste	misero
nascere *to be born*	nacqui	nacesti	nacque	nascemmo	naceste	nacquero
perdere *to lose*	persi	perdesti	perse	perdemmo	perdeste	persero
piacere *to please*	piacqui	piacesti	piacque	piacemmo	piaceste	piacquero
prendere *to take*	presi	prendesti	prese	prendemmo	prendeste	presero
ridere *to laugh*	risi	ridesti	rise	ridemmo	rideste	risero

sapere *to know*	seppi	sapesti	seppe	sapemmo	sapeste	seppero
scegliere *to choose*	scelsi	scegliesti	scelse	scegliemmo	sceglieste	scelsero
scendere *to descend*	scesi	scendesti	scese	scendemmo	scendeste	scesero
scrivere *to write*	scrissi	scrivesti	scrisse	scrivemmo	scriveste	scrissero
stare *to stay or be*	stetti	stesti	stette	stemmo	steste	stettero
vedere *to see*	vidi	vedesti	vide	vedemmo	vedeste	videro
venire *to come*	venni	venisti	venne	venimmo	veniste	vennero
vincere *to win*	vinsi	vincesti	vinse	vincemmo	vinceste	vinsero
volere *to want*	volli	volesti	volle	volemmo	voleste	vollero

Notice that the verbs in the list above are all "-**ere**" verbs except for "**dare**," "**dire**," "**fare**," and "**stare**." [1]

Examples

Let us examine some examples that use the past absolute tense:

Servirono pasti deliziosi in questo ristorante.	*They **served** delicious meals in this restaurant.*
Perse le chiavi qui molto tempo fa.	*He **lost** his keys here a long time ago.*
Comprammo questa casa prima dell'ultima recessione.	*We **bought** this house before the last recession.*
Scrivesti molti bei libri.	*You **wrote** many great books.*
Lei **lesse** molti articoli sull'argomento.	*She **read** many articles on the topic.*
Vinsi molti premi per le mie ricerche in questo campo	*I **won** many awards for my research in this field.*

---

[1] The treatment of the verbs "**fare**" and "**dire**" as "-**ere**" verbs can be attributed to the fact that both verbs are derived from the Latin verbs "facere" and "dicere," respectively.

Simple Past Tense in French

The simple past tense is often used in literary French to relate past or historical events. It is often used in reference to past events or narrations. In general, the simple past is not used in daily spoken language except in formal speech. Nevertheless, it is important to recognize this special tense, especially in writing.

Conjugation

To conjugate a verb, we use the stem from the *infinitive*. We remove the final "-er," "-ir," or "-re," and attach the conjugation suffix. The suffixes are the same for "-ir" and "-re" verbs.

	-er ending parler *(to speak)*	-ir ending finir *(to finish)*	-re ending vendre *(to sell)*
je	parlai	finis	vendis
tu	parlas	finis	vendis
il/elle/on	parla	finit	vendit
nous	parlâmes	finîmes	vendîmes
vous	parlâtes	finîtes	vendîtes
ils/elles	parlèrent	finirent	vendirent

Irregular Verbs

The verbs "**être**" *(to be)* and "**avoir**" *(to have)* are irregular in the simple past:

	être	avoir
je/j'	fus	eus
tu	fus	eus
il/elle/on	fut	eut
nous	fûmes	eûmes
vous	fûtes	eûtes
ils/elles	furent	eurent

Other irregular verbs include the following:

	je	tu	il/elle	nous	vous	ils/elles
boire *to drink*	bus	bus	but	bûmes	bûtes	burent

conduire *to drive*	conduisis	conduisis	conduisit	conduisîmes	conduisîtes	conduisirent
connaître *to know*	connus	connus	connut	connûmes	connûtes	connurent
courir *to run*	courus	courus	courut	courûmes	courûtes	coururent
couvrir *to cover*	couvris	couvris	couvrit	couvrîmes	couvrîtes	couvrirent
craindre *to fear*	craignis	craignis	craignit	craignîmes	craignîtes	craignirent
croire *to believe*	crus	crus	crut	crûmes	crûtes	crurent
devoir *must*	dus	dus	dut	dûmes	dûtes	durent
écrire *to write*	écrivis	écrivis	écrivit	écrivîmes	écrivîtes	écrivirent
éteindre *to turn off*	éteignis	éteignis	éteignit	éteignîmes	éteignîtes	éteignirent
faire *to do*	fis	fis	fit	fîmes	fîtes	firent
falloir *to have to*	-	-	fallut	-	-	-
introduire *to introduce*	introdusis	introdusis	introdusit	introdusîmes	introdusîtes	introdusirent
lire *to read*	lus	lus	lut	lûmes	lûtes	lurent
mettre *to put*	mis	mis	mit	mîmes	mîtes	mirent
mourir *to die*	mourus	mourus	mourut	mourûmes	mourûtes	moururent
naître *to be born*	naquis	naquis	naquit	naquîmes	naquîtes	naquirent
obtenir *to obtain*	obtins	obtins	obtint	obtînmes	obtîntes	obtinrent
offrir *to offer*	offris	offris	offrit	offrîmes	offrîtes	offrirent
peindre *to paint*	peignis	peignis	peignit	peignîmes	peignîtes	peignirent
plaire *to please*	plus	plus	plut	plûmes	plûtes	plurent
pleuvoir *to rain*	-	-	plut	-	-	-
pouvoir *can*	pus	pus	put	pûmes	pûtes	purent
prendre *to take*	pris	pris	prit	prîmes	prîtes	prirent

recevoir *to receive*	reçus	reçus	reçut	reçûmes	reçûtes	reçurent
rire *to laugh*	ris	ris	rit	rîmes	rîtes	rirent
savoir *to know*	sus	sus	sut	sûmes	sûtes	surent
sourire *to smile*	souris	souris	sourit	sourîmes	sourîtes	sourirent
tenir *to hold*	tins	tins	tint	tînmes	tîntes	tinrent
valoir *to be worth*	valus	valus	valut	valûmes	valûtes	valurent
venir *to come*	vins	vins	vint	vînmes	vîntes	vinrent
vivre *to live*	vécus	vécus	vécut	vécûmes	vécûtes	vécurent
vouloir *to want*	voulus	voulus	voulut	voulûmes	voulûtes	voulurent

Examples

Let us look at some examples:

La guerre **se termina** par une victoire nette.	*The war **ended** with a clear victory.*
Cette invention **eut** un grand impact sur la vie des gens.	*That invention **had** a great impact on people's lives.*
Il **remporta** de nombreux prix pour ses recherches sur le sujet.	*He **won** many awards for his research on the topic.*
Les événements de cette année **changèrent** notre mode de vie.	*The events of that year **changed** our way of life.*
Il **parla** de ce qu'il avait appris lors de sa dernière visite en Afrique.	*He **spoke** about what he had learned in his last visit to Africa.*

3. IMPERATIVE MOOD & GIVING COMMANDS

The imperative mood is generally used to give commands or instructions in the affirmative or the negative. We have so far encountered the indicative and the subjunctive moods. The imperative is considered a separate mood.

The imperative mood can be used in the singular or plural form and can be formal or informal. Thus, we have four cases:

1. Singular informal
2. Singular formal
3. Plural informal
4. Plural formal

Each of the above can be used in the affirmative or the negative. In addition to these four cases of imperative commands, we will study commands using the first-person plural.

1. Singular Informal Imperative

To give commands to a single person in an informal way, we use:

	Affirmative	Negative
SP	*present indicative* in the **third-person** singular form	*present subjunctive* in the **second-person** singular form
PT	*present indicative* in the **third-person** singular form	*present subjunctive* in the **third-person** singular form
IT	*present indicative* in **second-person** singular form	*infinitive*
FR	*present indicative* in **second-person** singular form	

In Italian, the only exception is the "**-are**" verbs in the affirmative, which use the *present indicative* in the *third-person* singular form, i.e., "**lui/lei/Lei**."

In French, a minor change is the dropping of the final "**-s**" in the "**-er**" verbs in both the affirmative and negative.

Here are some examples:

SP	**Camina** despacio.	**Walk** *slowly.*
PT	**Caminha** lentamente.	
IT	**Cammina** piano.	
FR	**Marche** doucement.	
SP	**Láva**te las manos.	**Wash** *your hands.*
PT	**Lava** as mãos.	
IT	**Lavati** le mani.	
FR	**Lave**-toi les mains.	

SP	No me **mientas**.	
PT	**Não minta** para mim.	***Don't lie*** *to me.*
IT	**Non mentir**mi.	
FR	Ne me **mens pas**.	
SP	**No hables** rápido.	
PT	**Não fale** rápido.	***Don't speak*** *fast.*
IT	**Non parlare** velocemente.	
FR	**Ne parle pas** vite.	

Notice that if there is a pronoun related to the verb, e.g., reflexive or indirect object pronoun, it is attached to the affirmative imperative or the infinitive in case of the negative imperative.

Irregular Verbs

In Spanish, there are eight common irregular verbs in the affirmative singular informal command form:

Infinitive	Command	Example	
ser	sé	**Sé** cortés.	***Be*** *polite.*
ir	ve	**Ve** a la escuela.	***Go*** *to school.*
venir	ven	**Ven** aquí.	***Come*** *here.*
tener	ten	**Ten** cuidado.	***Take*** *caution.*
decir	di	**Di** la verdad.	***Tell*** *the truth.*
hacer	haz	**Haz** la tarea.	***Do*** *the homework.*
poner	pon	**Pon** el lápiz aquí.	***Put*** *the pencil here.*
salir	sal	**Sal** con tus amigos.	***Go out*** *with your friends.*

In Portuguese, there are only two irregular verbs in the affirmative singular informal command form. These are "**ser**" and "**estar**" which only have formal imperative forms using the subjunctive:

Infinitive	Command	Example	
ser	seja	**Seja** educado.	***Be*** *polite.*
estar	esteja	**Esteja** à vontade.	***Be*** *my guest.*

In Italian, there are a few common irregular verbs in the affirmative singular informal command form:

Infinitive	Command	Example	
essere	sii	**Sii** educato.	***Be*** *polite.*
andare	vai (or) va'	**Vai** a scuola.	***Go*** *to school.*

avere	abbi	**Abbi** tutto.	*Have it all.*
dire	di'	**Di'** la verità.	*Tell the truth.*
fare	fai (or) fa'	**Fai** i tuoi compiti.	*Do your homework.*
stare	stai (or) sta'	**Stai** tranquillo!	*Calm down!*
dare	dai (or) da'	**Dai** il meglio.	*Give your best.*
sapere	sappi	**Sappi** questo!	*Know this!*

In French, there are only four irregular verbs in the singular informal command form:

Infinitive	Command	Example	
être	sois	**Sois** poli.	*Be polite.*
avoir	aie	**Aie** tout.	*Have it all.*
savoir	sache	**Sache** la vérité.	*Know the truth.*
vouloir	veuille	**Veuille** patienter.	*Please wait.*

Notice that the imperative of the verb "**vouloir**" *(to want)* is an invitation to do something and is often roughly translated into English as *"please."*

2. Singular Formal Imperative

To give commands to a single person in a formal way, we use:

	Affirmative	Negative
SP	*present subjunctive* in the **third-person** singular form	
PT	*present subjunctive* in the **third-person** singular form	
IT	*present subjunctive* in **third-person** singular form	
FR	*present indicative* in **second-person** plural form	

Here are some examples:

SP	Señora, **entre** desde aquí, por favor.	*Ma'am, enter from here, please.*
PT	Senhora, **entre** daqui, por favor.	
IT	Signora, **entri** da qui, per favore.	
FR	Madame, **entrez** par ici, s'il vous plaît.	
SP	Señor, **no fume** aquí, por favor.	*Sir, don't smoke here, please.*
PT	Senhor, **não fume** aqui, por favor.	
IT	Signore, **non fumi** qui, per favore.	
FR	Monsieur, **ne fumez pas** ici, s'il vous plaît.	

Irregular Verbs

In Spanish, Portuguese, and Italian, there are no irregular verbs in the singular formal imperative.

In French, the irregular verbs are the same as the singular informal imperative:

Infinitive	Command	Example	
être	soyez	**Soyez** poli.	*Be polite.*
avoir	ayez	**Ayez** tout.	*Have it all.*
savoir	sachez	**Sachez** la vérité.	*Know the truth.*
vouloir	veuillez	**Veuillez** trouver ci-joint.	*Please find attached.*

3. Plural Informal Imperative

To give commands to a group of people, we use:

	Affirmative	Negative
SP	*present subjunctive* in the **third-person** plural form	
PT	*present subjunctive* in the **third-person** plural form	
IT	*present indicative* in **second-person** *informal* plural form (i.e., "voi")	
FR	*present indicative* in **second-person** plural form	

Here are some examples:

SP	Chicos, **hagan** la tarea.	
PT	Meninos, **façam** sua lição de casa.	*Boys, do the homework.*
IT	Ragazzi, **fate** i compiti.	
FR	Les garçons, **faites** vos devoirs.	
SP	**No fumen** aquí.	
PT	**Não fumem** aqui.	*Don't smoke here.*
IT	**Non fumate** qui.	
FR	**Ne fumez** pas ici.	

4. Plural Formal Imperative

In Latin American Spanish, Portuguese, and French, there is no distinction between formal and informal imperative. This distinction only exists in Italian.

In Italian, to formally give commands to a group of people, we use the *present subjunctive* in the third-person plural formal form in both the affirmative and the negative; that is, the form used with **"loro"** (which is the same as the polite second-person **"Loro"** plural formal), for example:

Signore, **seguano** le istruzioni.	*Ladies, **follow** the instructions.*
Signori, **non fumino** qui, per favore.	*Gentlemen, **don't smoke** here, please.*

5. Commands using the First-Person Plural

Similar to the expression *"let's do something"* in English, commands using the fist-person plural express the same idea and can be affirmative or negative. Both use the *present subjunctive* in Spanish, Portuguese, and French, and the *present indicative* in Italian. Here are some examples:

SP	**Hagamos** nuestra tarea.	
PT	**Façamos** nossa lição de casa.	***Let's do** our homework.*
IT	**Facciamo** i compiti.	
FR	**Faisons** nos devoirs.	
SP	**No fumemos.**	
PT	**Não fumemos.**	***Let's not smoke.***
IT	**Non fumiamo.**	
FR	**Ne fumons pas.**	
SP	**Vamos!**	
PT	**Vamos!**	***Let's go!***
IT	**Andiamo!**	
FR	**Allons-y!**	

In Spanish, the only exception is **"vamos,"** which is in the *indicative* and is used to mean *"let's go"* instead of **"vayamos"** in the affirmative.

In the negative, however, "**no vayamos**" is how you say *"let's not go"* in Spanish.

In French, the following three verbs are irregular:

Infinitive	Command	Example	
être	soyons	**Soyons** poli.	*Let's be polite.*
avoir	ayons	**Ayons** tout.	*Let's have it all.*
savoir	sachons	**Sachons** la vérité.	*Let's know the truth.*

4. THE CONDITIONAL TENSES

The simple conditional tense is used to describe a hypothetical situation, express wishes, give advice, or make a polite request. It is similar in its use to the simple conditional tense in English, for example, *"I would do the laundry if I had time."*

Conjugation

In Spanish and Portuguese, the regular verb conjugation is the same for all verb endings and is formed by adding the conjugation ending to the *infinitive* rather than to the stem.

In Italian, we begin with the *infinitive* as a stem and drop the final "**e**" of the verb and change the final "-**ar**" to "-**er**" in the case of "-**are**" verbs.

In French, we use the *infinitive* as a stem and drop the final "-**e**" in the case of "-**re**" verbs.

The endings are the same for the three types of verbs:

- In Spanish:

	-ar ending e.g., hablar	-er ending e.g., comer	-ir ending e.g., vivir
yo	hablaría	comería	viviría
tú	hablarías	comerías	vivirías
él/ella/usted	hablaría	comería	viviría
nosotros/-as	hablaríamos	comeríamos	viviríamos
vosotros/-as	hablaríais	comeríais	viviríais
ellos/ellas/ustedes	hablarían	comerían	vivirían

- In Portuguese:

	-ar ending e.g., falar	-er ending e.g., comer	-ir ending e.g., partir
eu	falaria	comeria	partiria
ele/ela/você	falaria	comeria	partiria
nós	falaríamos	comeríamos	partiríamos
eles/elas/vocês	falariam	comeriam	partiriam

- In Italian:

	-are ending e.g., parlare	-ere ending e.g., vendere	-ire ending e.g., partire
io	parlerei	venderei	partirei
tu	parleresti	venderesti	partiresti
lui/lei	parlerebbe	venderebbe	partirebbe
noi	parleremmo	venderemmo	partiremmo
voi	parlereste	vendereste	partireste
loro	parlerebbero	venderebbero	partirebbero

- In French:

	-er ending e.g., parler	-ir ending e.g., finir	-re ending e.g., vendre
je	parlerais	finirais	vendrais
tu	parlerais	finirais	vendrais
il/elle/on	parlerait	finirait	vendrait
nous	parlerions	finirions	vendrions
vous	parleriez	finiriez	vendriez
ils/elles	parleraient	finiraient	vendraient

Irregular Verbs in Spanish

In Spanish, there are a few irregular verbs in the simple conditional tense; twelve are commonly used and will be discussed here.

Some verbs ending in "-er" and "-ir" drop the "e" or "i" from the infinitive ending and replace it with a "d." There are five common verbs in this category: "tener" *(to have)*, "poner" *(to put)*, "valer" *(to value or to be worth)*, "venir" *(to come)*, and "salir" *(to go out or to exit)*.

	tener tendr-	poner pondr-	venir vendr-	salir sladr-
yo	tendría	pondría	vendría	saldría
tú	tendrías	pondrías	vendrías	saldrías
él/ella/usted	tendría	pondría	vendría	saldría
nosotros/-as	tendríamos	pondríamos	vendríamos	saldríamos
vosotros/-as	tendríais	pondríais	vendríais	saldríais
ellos/ellas/ustedes	tendrían	pondrían	vendrían	saldrían

Some verbs ending in "-**er**" simply drop the "**e**" from the infinitive ending. There are also five common verbs in this category: "**saber**" (*to know*), "**poder**" (*can*), "**caber**" (*to fit*), "**querer**" (*to want*), and "**haber**," which is an auxiliary verb equivalent to the English auxiliary verb *"have."*

	saber sabr-	poder podr-	querer querr-	haber habr-
yo	sabría	podría	querría	habría
tú	sabrías	podrías	querrías	habrías
él/ella/usted	sabría	podría	querría	habría
nosotros/-as	sabríamos	podríamos	querríamos	habríamos
vosotros/-as	sabríais	podríais	querríais	habríais
ellos/ellas/ustedes	sabrían	podrían	querrían	habrían

The verbs "**decir**" (*to say*) and "**hacer**" (*to do*) change their stem to "**dir-**" and "**har-**" to form the simple conditional tense conjugation. These two verbs are irregular and must be memorized.

	decir dir-	hacer har-
yo	diría	haría
tú	dirías	harías
él/ella/usted	diría	haría
nosotros/-as	diríamos	haríamos
vosotros/-as	diríais	haríais
ellos/ellas/ustedes	dirían	harían

Irregular Verbs in Portuguese

In Portuguese, the verbs "**dizer**" (*to say*), "**fazer**" (*to do*), and "**trazer**" (*to bring*) change their stem to "**dir-**," "**far-**," and "**trar-**," respectively, to form the simple conditional tense conjugation. These three verbs are irregular and must be memorized.

	dizer dir-	fazer far-	trazer trar-
eu	diria	faria	traria
ele/ela/você	diria	faria	traria
nós	diríamos	faríamos	traríamos
eles/elas/vocês	diriam	fariam	trariam

Irregular Verbs in Italian

In Italian, the same verbs that are irregular in the simple future tense are also irregular in the simple conditional tense. We summarize these verbs here in a similar fashion:

1. Some verbs, in addition to dropping the final "**e**," drop the vowel before the final "**r**" from the infinitive to form the stem. For example, the stem from the verb "**andare**" becomes "**andr-**" instead of "**andar-**." Other examples from this group are: "**avere**" *(to have)*, "**cadere**" *(to fall)*, "**dovere**" *(must)*, "**potere**" *(can)*, "**sapere**" *(to know)*, "**vedere**" *(to see)*, and "**vivere**" *(to live)*.

	andare andr-	avere avr-	cadere cadr-	dovere dovr-	potere potr-
io	andrei	avrei	cadrei	dovrei	potrei
tu	andresti	avresti	cadresti	dovresti	potresti
lui/lei	andrebbe	avrebbe	cadrebbe	dovrebbe	potrebbe
noi	andremmo	avremmo	cadremmo	dovremmo	potremmo
voi	andreste	avreste	cadreste	dovreste	potreste
loro	andrebbero	avrebbero	cadrebbero	dovrebbero	potrebbero

2. Some short verbs with the "**-are**" ending do not change the "**-ar**" to "**-er**" after dropping the final "**e**" to form the stem. The

most common verbs in this group are: "**dare**" *(to give)*, "**fare**" *(to do or to make)*, and "**stare**" *(to stay or to be)*.

	dare dar-	fare far-	stare star-
io	darei	farei	starei
tu	daresti	faresti	staresti
lui/lei	darebbe	farebbe	starebbe
noi	daremmo	faremmo	staremmo
voi	dareste	fareste	stareste
loro	darebbero	farebbero	starebbero

3. Some verbs, in addition to dropping the final "**e**," replace both the consonant and the vowel preceding the final "**r**" of the infinitive with an extra "**r**" to form the stem. For example, the stem from "**tenere**" *(to hold)* is "**terr-**" instead of "**tener-**." The most common verbs in this group are: "**tenere**" *(to hold)*, "**volere**" *(to want)*, and "**venire**" *(to come)*.

	tenere terr-	volere vorr-	venire verr-
io	terrei	vorrei	verrei
tu	terresti	vorresti	verresti
lui/lei	terrebbe	vorrebbe	verrebbe
noi	terremmo	vorremmo	verremmo
voi	terreste	vorreste	verreste
loro	terrebbero	vorrebbero	verrebbero

4. Some verbs are completely irregular, such as "**essere**" *(to be)* and "**bere**" *(to drink)*, whose stems are "**sar-**" and "**berr-**," respectively.

	essere sar-	bere berr-
io	sarei	berrei
tu	saresti	berresti
lui/lei	sarebbe	berrebbe
noi	saremmo	berremmo
voi	sareste	berreste
loro	sarebbero	berrebbero

5. Finally, the same orthographic changes applied to verbs ending in "**-care**," "**-gare**," "**-ciare**," "**-giare**," and "**-gliare**" in the present indicative tense and the simple future tense are applied here to maintain the proper pronunciation.

Irregular Verbs in French

In French, the The same verbs that are irregular in the simple future tense are also irregular in the simple conditional tense and use the same stem. Here is a list of irregular verbs in the simple conditional tense:

	je	tu	il/elle	nous	vous	ils/elles
aller *to go*	irais	irais	irait	irions	iriez	iraient
avoir *to have*	aurais	aurais	aurait	aurions	auriez	auraient
courir *to run*	courrais	courrais	courrait	courrions	courriez	courraient
devenir *to become*	deviendrais	deviendrais	deviendrait	deviendrions	deviendriez	deviendraient
devoir *must*	devrais	devrais	devrait	devrions	devriez	devraient
envoyer *to send*	enverrais	enverrais	enverrait	enverrions	enverriez	enverraient
être *to be*	serais	serais	serait	serions	seriez	seraient
faire *to do*	ferais	ferais	ferait	ferions	feriez	feraient
falloir *to have to*	-	-	faudrait	-	-	-
mourir *to die*	mourrais	mourrais	mourrait	mourrions	mourriez	mourraient
pleuvoir *to rain*	-	-	pleuvrait	-	-	-
recevoir *to receive*	recevrais	recevrais	recevrait	recevrions	recevriez	recevraient
revenir *to return*	reviendrais	reviendrais	reviendrait	reviendrions	reviendriez	reviendraient
savoir *to know*	saurais	saurais	saurait	saurions	sauriez	sauraient
tenir *to hold*	tiendrais	tiendrais	tiendrait	tiendrions	tiendriez	tiendraient

valoir *to be worth*	-	-	vaudrait	-	-	-
venir *to come*	viendrais	viendrais	viendrait	viendrions	viendriez	viendraient
voir *to see*	verrais	verrais	verrait	verrions	verriez	verraient
vouloir *to want*	voudrais	voudrais	voudrait	voudrions	voudriez	voudraient

There are some verbs that undergo minor spelling changes. Here are some common examples:

	je	tu	il/elle	nous	vous	ils/elles
employer *to hire*	emploierais	emploierais	emploierait	emploierions	emploieriez	emploieraient
essuyer *to wipe*	essuierais	essuierais	essuierait	essuierions	essuieriez	essuieraient
nettoyer *to clean*	nettoierais	nettoierais	nettoierait	nettoierions	nettoieriez	nettoieraient
acheter *to buy*	achèterais	achèterais	achèterait	achèterions	achèteriez	achèteraient
appeler *to call*	appellerais	appellerais	appellerait	appellerions	appelleriez	appelleraient
jeter *to throw*	jetterais	jetterais	jetterait	jetterions	jetteriez	jetteraient

Examples

Here are some examples that use the simple conditional tense:

SP	**Viajaría** cada año si tuviera dinero.	*I **would travel** every year if I had money.*
PT	Eu **viajaria** todos os anos se tivesse dinheiro.	
IT	**Viaggerei** ogni anno se avessi soldi.	
FR	Je **voyagerais** chaque année si j'avais de l'argent.	
SP	Si yo fuera tú, no **iría** al gimnasio hoy.	*If I were you, I **wouldn't go** to the gym today.*
PT	Se eu fosse você, não **iria** para a academia hoje.	
IT	Se fossi in te, oggi non **andrei** in palestra.	
FR	Si j'étais toi, je n'**irais** pas à la gym aujourd'hui.	

SP	Si tuviera mucho dinero, **compraría** un palacio.	*If I had a lot of money, I **would buy** a palace.*
PT	Se eu tivesse muito dinheiro, **compraria** um palácio.	
IT	Se avessi molti soldi, **comprerei** un palazzo.	
FR	Si j'avais beaucoup d'argent, j'**achèterais** un palais.	
SP	**Podrías** estudiar más horas para el examen.	*You **could** study more hours for the exam.*
PT	Você **poderia** estudar mais horas para o exame.	
IT	**Potresti** studiare più ore per l'esame.	
FR	Vous **pourriez** étudier plus d'heures pour l'examen.	
SP	¿**Podrías** pasarme la pimienta?	***Could** you pass me the pepper?*
PT	Você **poderia** me passar a pimenta?	
IT	**Potresti** passarmi il pepe?	
FR	**Pourriez**-vous me passer le poivre?	
SP	¿**Viviríamos** en una ciudad pequeña?	***Would** we **live** in a small city?*
PT	**Viveríamos** em uma cidade pequena?	
IT	**Vivremmo** in una piccola città?	
FR	**Vivrions**-nous dans une petite ville?	
SP	**Dormirían** todo el día si no tuvieran trabajo.	*They **would sleep** all day if they didn't have work.*
PT	Eles **dormiriam** o dia todo se não tivessem trabalho.	
IT	**Dormirebbero** tutto il giorno se non avessero un lavoro.	
FR	Ils **dormiraient** toute la journée s'ils n'avaient pas de travail.	
SP	**Diría** la verdad si le preguntaran.	*He **would tell** the truth if they asked him.*
PT	Ele **diria** a verdade se lhe perguntassem.	
IT	**Direbbe** la verità se glielo chiedessero.	
FR	Il **dirait** la vérité s'ils le lui demandaient.	

The Conditional Perfect: "Would/Could/Should have"

To convey the meaning of *"would/could/should have ...,"* we resort to the conditional perfect tense.

❖ *"Would have"* + past participle =

SP	"haber" in the *simple conditional*	
PT	"ter" or "haver" in the *simple conditional*	+ past participle
IT	"avere" or "essere" in the *simple conditional*	
FR	"avoir" or "être" in the *simple conditional*	

Here are some examples:

SP	Yo lo **habría hecho.**	
PT	Eu o **teria feito.**	*I **would have done** it.*
IT	Io l'**avrei fatto.**	
FR	Je l'**aurais fait.**	
SP	Ellos **habrían pagado.**	
PT	Eles **teriam pago.**	*They **would have paid**.*
IT	Loro **avrebbero pagato.**	
FR	Ils **auraient payé.**	
SP	Nosotros **habríamos venido.**	
PT	Nós **teríamos vindo.**	*We **would have come**.*
IT	Noi **saremmo venuti.**	
FR	Nous **serions venus.**	

❖ *"Could have"* + past participle =

SP	"poder" in the *simple conditional* + "haber" + *past participle*
PT	"poder" in the *simple conditional* + "ter" + *past participle*
IT	"avere" or "essere" in *simple conditional* + "potere" in *past participle* + *infinitive*
FR	"avoir" in *simple conditional* + "pouvoir" in *past participle* + *infinitive*

Here are some examples:

SP	Yo lo **podría haber hecho.**	
PT	Eu o **poderia ter feito.**	*I **could have done** it.*
IT	Io **avrei potuto farlo.**	
FR	J'**aurais pu le faire.**	
SP	Ellos **podrían haber pagado.**	
PT	Eles **poderiam ter pago.**	*They **could have paid**.*
IT	Loro **avrebbero potuto pagare.**	
FR	Ils **auraient pu payer.**	

SP	Nosotros **podríamos haber venido**.	
PT	Nós **poderíamos ter vindo**.	*We could have come.*
IT	Noi **saremmo potuti venire**.	
FR	Nous **aurions pu venir**.	

❖ *"Should have"* + past participle =

SP	**"deber"** in the *simple conditional* + **"haber"** + *past participle*
PT	**"dever"** in the *simple conditional* + **"ter"** + *past participle*
IT	**"avere"** or **"essere"** in *simple conditional* + **"dovere"** in *past participle* + *infinitive*
FR	**"avoir"** in *simple conditional* + **"devoir"** in *past participle* + *infinitive*

Here are some examples:

SP	Yo lo **debería haber hecho**.	
PT	Eu o **deveria ter feito**.	*I should have done it.*
IT	Io **avrei dovuto farlo**.	
FR	J'**aurais dû le faire**.	
SP	Ellos **deberían haber pagado**.	
PT	Eles **deveriam ter pago**.	*They should have paid.*
IT	Loro **avrebbero dovuto pagare**.	
FR	Ils **auraient dû payer**.	
SP	Nosotros **deberíamos haber venido**.	
PT	Nós **deveríamos ter vindo**.	*We should have come.*
IT	Noi **saremmo dovuti venire**.	
FR	Nous **aurions dû venir**.	

Another way to express *"should have …"* in Spanish is by using **"tener"** in the conditional tense:

"Should have" … + past participle =

"tener" in the *simple conditional* + **"que haber"** + *past participle*

Here are some examples:

Yo **tendría que haberlo hecho**.	*I should have done it.*
Ellos **tendrían que haber pagado**.	*They should have paid.*
Nosotros **tendríamos que haber venido**.	*We should have come.*

5. PRESENT SUBJUNCTIVE TENSE II & FUTURE SUBJUNCTIVE TENSE

We discussed some of the uses of the subjunctive mood in **Level IV, Lesson 5**, mainly expressing opinions, possibilities, desires, wishes, feelings, and requests. Here, we will cover other cases in which the subjunctive mood ought to be used. We will also cover two cases in which Portuguese uniquely uses the *future subjunctive* tense, whereas Spanish, Italian, and French use the *present subjunctive* tense.

The Expressions "Ojalá" in Spanish & "Oxalá" in Portuguese

The expressions "**ojalá**" in Spanish and "**oxalá**" in Portuguese are derived from the Arabic influence on both languages and are used to express hope that something would happen or would have happened. We will cover the use of these two expressions in the present subjunctive, which can be translated roughly as *"hopefully"* to express hope for something to happen in the present or the future, for example:

SP	Ojalá (que) **no llueva** esta noche.	*Hopefully, it **won't rain** tonight.*
PT	Oxalá (que) **não chova** esta noite.	
SP	Ojalá (que) mi hermano **venga** hoy.	*Hopefully, my brother **will come** today.*
PT	Oxalá (que) meu irmão **venha** hoje.	

"**Ojalá**" and "**oxalá**" can also be used to express hope that something has happened or would have happened in the past. We will cover that in the lessons to come with the imperfect and perfect subjunctive.

An alternative to "**oxalá**" that is more common in Brazilian Portuguese is "**tomara**." For example:

Tomara que **não chova** esta noite.	*Hopefully, it **won't rain** tonight.*
Tomara que meu irmão **venha** hoje.	*Hopefully, my brother **will come** today.*

More Expressions that use the Subjunctive

It is really hard to include all expressions that use the subjunctive in this limited space. However, a few expressions are still worth mentioning as we are likely to encounter them more frequently. Notice that most of these expressions end with "**que**" in Spanish, Portuguese, and French, and "**che**" in Italian.

Here are some expressions that often use the subjective:

SP	PT	IT	FR	EN
para que a fin de que	para que a fim de que	affinché perché in modo che	afin que pour que	*so that, in order that*
mientras que siempre que con tal de que	contanto que desde que	purché a patto che sempre che	pourvu que	*provided (that), as long as*
a menos que	a menos que	a meno che	à moins que	*unless*
sin que	sem que	senza che	sans que	*without (that)*
antes de que	antes de que	prima che	avant que	*before (that)*

Notice that, in Portuguese, time expressions like *"before"* or *"as soon as"* that describe an action in the future, especially one that is plausible and likely to happen, use the future subjunctive, which will be covered at the end of this lesson.

Here are some examples:

SP	Dame la llave <u>para que</u> **pueda** entrar.	*Give me the key <u>so that</u> he* ***can*** *get in.*
PT	Dê-me a chave <u>para que</u> ele **possa** entrar.	
IT	Dammi la chiave <u>in modo che</u> **possa** entrare.	
FR	Donnez-moi la clé <u>pour qu'il</u> **puisse** entrer.	
SP	<u>Mientras que</u> el café **sea** bueno, lo tomaré.	*<u>As long as</u> the coffee* ***is*** *good, I'll drink it.*
PT	<u>Contanto que</u> o café **seja** bom, eu beberei.	
IT	<u>Purché</u> il caffè **sia** buono, lo berrò.	
FR	<u>Pourvu que</u> le café **soit** bon, je le boirai.	

SP	A menos que **tengas** bastante dinero, será difícil vivir aquí.	*Unless you **have** enough money, it will be difficult to live here.*
PT	A menos que você **tenha** muito dinheiro, será difícil morar aqui.	
IT	A meno che tu (non) **abbia** molti soldi, sarà difficile vivere qui.	
FR	À moins que vous **ayez** assez d'argent, il sera difficile de vivre ici.	
SP	Dejaré la llave sin que él la **vea**.	*I will leave the key without him **seeing**.*
PT	Vou deixar a chave sem que ele **veja**.	
IT	Lascerò la chiave senza che lui **veda**.	
FR	Je laisserai la clé sans qu'il la **voie**.	

Notice that, in Italian, the "**non**" after "**a meno che**" is redundant and does not affect the meaning of *"unless."*

Expressions with Some Conjunctions ending in "-que"

Some conjunctions as *"whatever," "whenever," "wherever," "whoever,"* etc., convey the meaning of *"any"* and require the use of the present subjunctive in Spanish, Italian, and French. In Portuguese, these expressions require the use of the future subjunctive as we will discuss later in this lesson. Examples of these conjunctions include:

SP	cualquiera que (sea)	*any, whatever, whichever (it is)*
PT	qualquer que (seja)	
IT	qualsiasi (sia), qualunque (sia)	
FR	quel que (soit)	
SP	quienquiera que (sea)	*whoever (it is)*
PT	quem quer que (seja)	
IT	chiunque (sia)	
FR	qui que (ce soit)	
SP	dondequiera que (estés)	*wherever (you are)*
PT	onde quer que (esteja)	
IT	dovunque (tu sia)	
FR	où que (tu sois)	

Let us take examples with these conjunctions:

SP	Cualquiera que **prefieran**, pueden tomarlo.	*Whichever they **prefer**, they can take.*
IT	Qualunque cosa **preferiscano**, possono prenderla.	
FR	Quel que **soit** leur choix *(whatever their choice **is**)*, ils peuvent le prendre.	
SP	Te encontraré dondequiera que **estés** ahora mismo.	*I will meet you wherever you **are** right now.*
IT	Ti incontrerò dovunque tu **sia** in questo momento.	
FR	Je vous rencontrerai où que vous **soyez** en ce moment.	

Superlative Expressions with *"that"* followed by a Verb

In Italian and French, if a superlative expression has a verb in the subordinate clause that follows *"that,"* the verb should be in the subjunctive. For example:

IT	È la persona più onesta che **conosca**.	*He is the most honest person that I **know**.*
FR	C'est la personne la plus honnête que je **connaisse**.	
IT	Questo è il massimo che tu **possa** fare.	*This is the best that you **can** do.*
FR	C'est le maximum que vous **puissiez** faire.	

Expressions meaning "Although" or "Despite (that)"

All the following conjunctions mean *"although," "even though,"* or *"despite (that)."* Take this example *"He travels a lot although he **is** not rich"*:

SP	aunque	Viaja mucho aunque no **es** rico.
	si bien	Viaja mucho si bien no **es** rico.
PT	embora	Ele viaja muito embora não **seja** rico.
	ainda que	Ele viaja muito ainda que não **seja** rico.
	mesmo que	Ele viaja muito mesmo que não **seja** rico.
	se bem que	Ele viaja muito se bem que não **é** rico.

IT	benché	Viaggia molto <u>benché</u> non **sia** ricco.
	sebbene	Viaggia molto <u>sebbene</u> non **sia** ricco.
	malgrado	Viaggia molto <u>malgrado</u> non **sia** ricco.
	nonostante	Viaggia molto <u>nonostante</u> non **sia** ricco.
	anche se	Viaggia molto <u>anche se</u> non **è** ricco.
FR	bien que	Il voyage beaucoup <u>bien qu</u>'il ne **soit** pas riche.
	malgré que	Il voyage beaucoup <u>malgré qu</u>'il ne **soit** pas riche.
	quoique	Il voyage beaucoup <u>quoiqu</u>'il ne **soit** pas riche.
	encore que	Il voyage beaucoup <u>encore qu</u>'il ne **soit** pas riche.
	même si	Il voyage beaucoup <u>même s</u>'il n'**est** pas riche.

Notice that, in Spanish, we use the *indicative* mood. In Portuguese, Italian, and French, we use the *subjunctive* except when "**se bem que**" in Portuguese, "**anche se**" in Italian, or "**même si**" in French, is used, which require the use of the *indicative*.

In Spanish, "**aunque**" conveys the meaning of *"even if"* when followed by the *subjunctive*, for example:

Aunque no quiera comer, iré al café contigo.	***Even if*** *I don't want to eat, I will go to the café with you.*
Aunque haga mucho ejercicio, no bajo de peso.	***Even if*** *I exercise a lot, I don't lose weight.*

Notice that only "**aunque**," and not "**si bien**," can be used in these examples, followed by the *subjunctive*.

In Portuguese, although not very common, "**se bem que**" is used sometimes in the subjunctive in formal writing only.

The conjunctions "**a pesar de**" in Spanish and "**apesar de**" in Portuguese mean *"despite"* or *"in spite of,"* which can be used in one of three formulas:

1. A pesar de/Apesar de + Infinitive, for example:

SP	**A pesar de** estar cansado, quiero salir con mis amigos.	***In spite of*** *being tired, I want to go out with my friends.*
PT	**Apesar de** estar cansado, quero sair com meus amigos.	

2. A pesar de/Apesar de + Noun, for example:

SP	**A pesar de** las advertencias, Ana sigue fumando.	***Despite*** *the warnings, Ana continues to smoke.*
PT	**Apesar d**os avisos, Ana continua fumando.	

3. A pesar de que/Apesar de que + Indicative Tense, for example:

SP	**A pesar de que** estoy triste, voy a celebrar mi cumpleaños.	***Despite the fact that*** *I am sad, I will celebrate my birthday.*
PT	**Apesar de** que estou triste, vou comemorar meu aniversário.	

In Italian, another possible conjunction that conveys the same meaning is **"pur"** which is often followed by the *gerund*. For example:

Viaggia molto <u>pur</u> non **essendo** ricco.	*He travels a lot <u>despite</u> not **being** rich.*

Future Subjunctive in Portuguese

Here, we cover cases in which the future tense in the subjunctive mood ought to be used in Portuguese. The future subjunctive is used mainly in time clauses that indicate a likely scenario in the future. Similar sentences often use the present subjunctive in Spanish, Italian, and French.

Before we dive into use cases, let us first learn how to conjugate verbs in the future subjunctive.

The stem used to form the future subjunctive conjugation comes from the *third-person plural form* of the *preterite* rather than the infinitive, that is, the preterite that follows "**eles**" or "**elas**" minus the final "**-am**," for example:

Infinitive	Third-person plural preterite	Future subjunctive stem
falar	eles/elas falaram	falar-
comer	eles/elas comeram	comer-
partir	eles/elas partiram	partir-

Next, the ending "**-mos**" is attached to the stem in the "**nós**" form, and the ending "**-em**" is attached to the stem in the third-person plural forms. Notice that all single forms do not have any endings. All verbs follow these conjugation rules, and there are no irregular verbs in the future subjunctive.

	-ar ending e.g., **falar**	-er ending e.g., **comer**	-ir ending e.g., **partir**
eu	falar	comer	partir
ele/ela/você	falar	comer	partir
nós	falar**mos**	comer**mos**	partir**mos**
eles/elas/vocês	falar**em**	comer**em**	partir**em**

You may notice that the conjugation of all the single forms in the examples above are equivalent to the infinitive. This is true as long as the verb is regular in the preterite tense. If the verb is irregular in the preterite, the conjugation of the single forms is different from the infinitive. Here are some examples:

	ir, ser "eles **for**am"	estar "eles **estiver**am"	fazer "eles **fizer**am"
eu	for	estiver	fizer
ele/ela/você	for	estiver	fizer
nós	for**mos**	estiver**mos**	fizer**mos**
eles/elas/vocês	for**em**	estiver**em**	fizer**em**

#1: Time Expressions in the Future

Let us examine the following time expressions:

se	*if*
quando	*when*
assim que, logo que, tão logo	*as soon as*
até que	*until*
antes de que	*before*
depois de que	*after*

When one of the above expressions is used in the *present* or the *past*, we use the *indicative*, for example:

Vi meu irmão quando **cheguei** em casa.	*I saw my brother when I **arrived** home.*
Eu leio o e-mail assim que o **recebo**.	*I read the email as soon as I **receive** it.*
Enviei o pacote depois que eles me **pagaram**.	*I sent the parcel after they **paid** me.*

However, if used to describe an action in the *future*, especially one that is plausible and likely to happen, the sentence after the above time expressions shall be in the *future subjunctive*:

Verei meu irmão quando **chegar** em casa.	*I will see my brother when I **arrive** home.*
Lerei o e-mail assim que o **receber**.	*I will read the email as soon as I **receive** it.*
Enviarei o pacote depois que eles me **pagarem**.	*I will send the parcel after they **pay** me.*

Notice that clauses after the conditional "**if**" can fall under this category if the meaning implies likely action in the future. For example:

Ficarei em casa se **chover** hoje.	*I will stay home if it **rains** today.*
Se **tivermos** tempo, iremos à praia.	*If we **have** time, we will go to the beach.*

#2: Relative Pronouns Hinting at Possibility in the Future

Some conjunctions such as *"whatever," "whenever," "wherever," "whoever,"* etc., hint at the possibility of an event in the future. In

Portuguese, relative pronouns are often used in this context. The clause following the relative pronoun in such sentences is often in the future subjunctive. Examples of these relative pronouns and conjunctions that can be used to convey meaning include:

que	*whatever*
qualquer que	*whatever, whichever*
quem	*whoever*
onde	*wherever*
como	*no matter how*

Here are some examples in context:

Qualquer que eles **preferirem**, eles podem pegar.	*Whichever they **prefer**, they can take.*
Eu poderia convidar <u>quem</u> você **quiser** para a reunião.	*I could invite <u>whoever</u> you **want** to the meeting.*
Eu te encontrarei <u>onde</u> você **estiver** agora.	*I will meet you <u>wherever</u> you **are** right now.*
Faça o <u>que</u> **fizermos**, não será suficiente.	*Whatever we **do**, it won't be enough.*

6. PERFECT SUBJUNCTIVE TENSE

We have previously studied the subjunctive mood and the present subjunctive tense. The subjunctive mood is used to express opinion, possibility, and feelings, such as fear, doubt, hope, desire, etc.

Now, we will study the case when we want to express opinions, possibilities, and feelings, such as fear, doubt, hope, desire, etc., about something that happened in the past. In other words, we want to describe the past tense but in the subjunctive mood, i.e., the perfect subjunctive.

The perfect subjunctive, similar to the present perfect in the indicative, uses the past participle. However, the only difference is that the auxiliary verb is conjugated in the present subjunctive:

SP	"haber" in the present subjunctive	
PT	"ter" or "haver" in the present subjunctive	+ past participle
IT	"avere" or "essere" in the present subjunctive	
FR	"avoir" or "être" in the present subjunctive	

Here are some more examples in context:

SP	Es bueno que **hayas descansado** después del partido.	
PT	É bom que você **tenha descansado** depois do jogo.	*It is good that you **have relaxed** after the match.*
IT	È importante che tu **ti sia riposato** dopo la partita.	
FR	C'est bien que vous **vous soyez détendu** après le match.	
SP	Espero que **hayas disfrutado** tu viaje.	
PT	Espero que você **tenha gostado** da sua viagem.	*I hope that you **have enjoyed** your trip.*
IT	Spero **ti sia piaciuto** il tuo viaggio.	
FR	Je suis content que tu **aies apprécié** ton voyage.	
SP	Me pone triste que no me **haya llamado**.	
PT	Fico triste que ele não **tenha** me **ligado**.	*It makes me sad that he **hasn't called** me.*
IT	Mi rattrista che non mi **abbia chiamato**.	
FR	Ça me rend triste qu'il ne m'**ait** pas **appelé**.	
SP	Dudo que **hayamos visto** tu casa antes de hoy.	
PT	Duvido que **tenhamos visto** sua casa antes de hoje.	*I doubt that we **have seen** your house before today.*
IT	Dubito che **abbiamo visto** casa tua prima di oggi.	
FR	Je doute que nous **ayons vu** votre maison avant aujourd'hui.	
SP	Estoy feliz de que **hayas llegado**.	
PT	Estou feliz que você **tenha chegado**.	*I am happy that you **have arrived**.*
IT	Sono felice che tu **sia arrivato**.	
FR	Je suis content que tu **sois arrivé**.	

SP	No creo que **hayan vivido** aquí.	
PT	Não acredito que eles **tenham vivido** aqui.	*I don't believe they **have lived** here.*
IT	Non credo che **abbiano vissuto** qui.	
FR	Je ne crois pas qu'ils **aient vécu** ici.	

7. PARTITIVES

To refer to an unidentified quantity of something in English, we often use words or phrases like *"some," "a few,"* and *"a little bit of."* These are called *partitives* because they refer to a part of something, whether it is countable, e.g., *"some trees,"* or uncountable, e.g., *"some water."*

In Spanish and Portuguese, the indefinite articles in plural form can be used to mean *"some."* Here are some examples:

SP	un	un hombre (*a man*)	unos	unos hombres (*some men*)
	una	una casa (*a house*)	unas	unas casas (*some houses*)
PT	um	um homem (*a man*)	uns	uns homens (*some men*)
	uma	uma casa (*a house*)	umas	umas casas (*some houses*)

In addition, one can use other partitive words meaning *"some"* or *"a bit of,"* for example:

SP	algunos	*some*	un poco de	*a bit of*
	pocos	*few*	ciertos	*certain*
PT	alguns	*some*	um pouco de	*a bit of*
	poucos	few	certos	*certain*

In Italian and French, the most common way to form a partitive is using the preposition **"di"** in Italian or **"de"** in French followed by a definite article, also known as a *partitive article*. This would literally translate to *"of the."* However, it serves more as an equivalent to the partitive *"some"* in English.

Countable Nouns

In Italian, because countable nouns have a plural form, we use the preposition **"di"** followed by the plural definite article **"i"** or **"gli"** for masculine and "**le**" for feminine. This results in the three following partitive articles:

di +	gli	=	degli	Before a plural *masculine* noun that begins with a vowel, "**z**," "**gn**," "**ps**," or "**s**" + consonant
	i	=	dei	Before any other plural *masculine* noun
	le	=	delle	Before any plural *feminine* noun

Let us take some examples with countable nouns:

un ragazzo	*a boy*	dei ragazzi	*some boys*
un albero	*a tree*	degli alberi	*some trees*
una casa	*a house*	delle case	*some houses*
un porto	*a port*	dei porti	*some ports*
uno zio	*an uncle*	degli zii	*some uncles*
una stanza	*a room*	delle stanze	*some rooms*
uno sbaglio	*a mistake*	degli sbagli	*some mistakes*
un libro	*a book*	dei libri	*some books*
uno schermo	*a screen*	degli schermi	*some screens*

Remember that using partitive articles is not the only way to describe an undefined quantity of countable nouns in Italian. Other partitive words include "**alcuni/-e**" and "**qualche**," both meaning *"some."* The more specific partitive "**certi/-e**" *(certain)* can also be used depending on the context.

Let us take some examples:

una casa	*a house*	alcune case	qualche <u>casa</u>	certe case	*some houses*
un porto	*a port*	alcuni porti	qualche <u>porto</u>	certi porti	*some ports*
uno zio	*an uncle*	alcuni zii	qualche <u>zio</u>	certi zii	*some uncles*

Notice that "**qualche**" is invariable and always followed by a *singular* noun although the meaning is plural.

In French, we use the partitive article "**des**," which comes from the contraction of the preposition "**de**" and the plural definite article "**les**."

Let us look at some examples with countable nouns:

un garçon	*a boy*	des garçons	*some boys*
un arbre	*a tree*	des arbres	*some trees*
une maison	*a house*	des maisons	*some houses*
une erreur	*a mistake*	des erreurs	*some mistakes*

Similarly, other partitive words like "**quelques**" *(some)* and "**certain(e)s**" *(certain)* can be used in French. For example:

| un livre | *a book* | quelques livres | certains livres | *some books* |
| une fille | *a girl* | quelques filles | certaines filles | *some houses* |

Uncountable Nouns

By uncountable nouns, we refer to nouns that are not often used in plural form, even if a plural form can be used in some contexts. For example, in English, we could say *"three fruits"* referring to three pieces of fruit. However, the word *"fruit"* is often used as an uncountable noun. Here, we discuss how to refer to an undefined quantity of such nouns when used in their uncountable form.

In Italian, to refer to an uncountable noun using a partitive article, we treat it as a singular noun. Thus, we use the preposition "**di**" followed by the singular definite article "**l'**," "**il**," or "**lo**" for masculine and "**l'**" or "**la**" for feminine. This results in the three following partitive articles:

	l'	=	dell'	Before a *masculine* or *feminine* uncountable noun that begins with a vowel
di +	lo	=	dello	Before a *masculine* uncountable noun that begins with "**z**," "**gn**," "**ps**," or "**s**" + consonant
	il	=	del	Before any other *masculine* uncountable noun
	la	=	della	Before any other *feminine* uncountable noun

Let us take some examples with uncountable nouns:

l'acqua	*the water*	dell'acqua	*some water*
lo zucchero	*the sugar*	dello zucchero	*some sugar*
il pane	*the bread*	del pane	*some bread*
la pasta	*the pasta*	della pasta	*some pasta*
l'orzo	*the barley*	dell'orzo	*some barley*

| il latte | *the milk* | del latte | *some milk* |
| la frutta | *the fruit* | della frutta | *some fruit* |

As an alternative to partitive articles, one can, depending on the context, use the partitive word "**un po' di**" *(a bit of)* to refer to an undefined quantity of an uncountable noun.

Here are some examples:

l'acqua	*the water*	**un po' d'acqua**	*a bit of water*
lo zucchero	*the sugar*	**un po' di zucchero**	*a bit of sugar*
il pane	*the bread*	**un po' di pane**	*a bit of bread*
la pasta	*the pasta*	**un po' di pasta**	*a bit of pasta*

In French, we use the preposition "**de**" followed by the singular definite article "**le**," "**la**," or "**l'**." This results in the three following partitive articles:

de +	l'	=	de l'	Before a **masculine** or a **feminine** noun that begins with a vowel or a mute "**h**"
	le	=	du	Before a **masculine** noun that does not begin with a vowel or a mute "**h**"
	la	=	de la	Before a **feminine** noun that does not begin with a vowel or a mute "**h**"

Let us look at some examples with uncountable nouns:

l'eau	*the water*	**de l'eau**	*some water*
le sucre	*the sugar*	**du sucre**	*some sugar*
la viande	*the meat*	**de la viande**	*some meat*
le pain	*the bread*	**du pain**	*some bread*
la pluie	*the rain*	**de la pluie**	*some rain*
le lait	*the milk*	**du lait**	*some milk*

As an alternative to partitive articles, one can use the partitive word "**un peu de**" *(a bit of)* to refer to an undefined quantity of an uncountable noun. For example:

l'eau	*the water*	**un peu d'eau**	*a bit of water*
le sucre	*the sugar*	**un peu de sucre**	*a bit of sugar*
la viande	*the meat*	**un peu de viande**	*a bit of meat*

Further Notes on Partitive Articles

❖ Remember that if an adjective precedes the noun, the definite article, and thus the partitive article, must change according to the beginning of the adjective, for example:

IT	dell'orzo	*some barley*	del nuovo orzo	*some new barley*
FR	d'orge		de la nouvelle orge	

❖ In Italian, the partitive article is often dropped in the following cases:

1. When listing two or more items. The partitive article is often dropped rather than repeated before each item, e.g., "**Vorrei pane e zucchero**" *(I would like bread and sugar)*, "**Abbiamo finito il riso, la pasta, la carne e l'acqua**" *(We ran out of rice, pasta, meat and water)*, etc.

2. In negative sentences. The partitive is omitted in negative sentences whether the noun is countable or uncountable, e.g., "**Non ho zii**" *(I don't have uncles)*, "**Non voglio zucchero**" *(I don't want sugar)*, "**Non c'è pane**" *(There isn't bread)*, etc.

❖ In French, if the sentence is in the negative, the partitive is omitted and replaced with "**de**," whether the noun is countable or uncountable, e.g., "**Je n'ai pas <u>d</u>'oncles**" *(I don't have uncles)*, "**Je ne veux pas <u>de</u> sucre**" *(I don't want sugar)*, "**Il n'y a pas <u>de</u> pain**" *(There isn't bread)*, etc. The only exception is when the verb "**être**" *(to be)* is used. In this case, the partitive article is used, e.g., "**Ce n'est pas <u>de l</u>'eau**" *(This is not water)*, "**Ce n'est pas <u>de la</u> viande**" *(This is not meat)*, etc.

❖ In negative sentences with countable nouns, the negative meaning of *"any,"* as in *"There isn't any bread,"* can be rendered by the use of "**nessuno**" and its variants in Italian or "**aucun(e)**" in French. Both words are treated like an indefinite article. They convey the meaning of *"not one"* or *"not any,"* and are always followed by a singular noun even if the meaning is plural. Here are some examples:

IT	Non c'è **nessun** albero nel deserto.	*There aren't **any** trees in the desert.*
FR	Il n'y a **aucun** arbre dans le désert.	
IT	Non c'è **nessuna** casa in questa zona.	*There aren't **any** houses in this area.*
FR	Il n'y a **aucune** maison dans cette zone.	

8. PAST & CONDITIONAL PROGRESSIVE TENSES

The past progressive tense, similar to its use in English, describes an event that continued to take place in the past, e.g., *"I was speaking."* It is formed as follows:

SP	"**estar**" in imperfect tense	
PT	"**estar**" in imperfect tense	*+ gerund*
IT	"**stare**" in imperfect tense	
FR	"**être**" in imperfect tense+ "**en train de**" + *infinitive*	

Here are some examples:

SP	Mi mamá **estaba cocinando** cuando mi papá entró a la casa.	
PT	Minha mãe **estava cozinhando** quando meu pai entrou em casa.	*My mom **was cooking** when my dad entered the house.*
IT	Mia madre **stava cucinando** quando mio padre è entrato in casa.	
FR	Ma mère **était en train de cuisiner** lorsque mon père est entré dans la maison.	
SP	**Estábamos nadando** mientras estabas estudiando.	
PT	**Estávamos nadando** enquanto você estudava.	*We **were swimming** while you were studying.*
IT	**Stavamo nuotando** mentre tu studiavi.	
FR	Nous **était en train de nager** pendant que tu étudiais.	

Remember that the imperfect indicative tense can also correspond to the past progressive tense in English when describing continuous actions in the past. For example, *"I was cooking"* can be translated in two ways:

SP	Cocinaba.	Estaba cocinando.
PT	Cozinhava.	Estava cozinhando
IT	Cucinavo.	Stavo cucinando.
FR	Je cuisinais.	J'étais en train de cuisine.

The past progressive tense may be interpreted as giving more focus on the action than the imperfect. However, in most contexts, both are valid options to express continuous actions in the past.

On the other hand, the conditional progressive tense is used to describe an event that would be happening now had another event happened earlier. It is constructed from the conditional form of the auxiliary verb followed by the gerund.

SP	"**estar**" in conditional tense	
PT	"**estar**" in conditional tense	*+ gerund*
IT	"**stare**" in conditional tense	
FR	"**être**" in conditional tense+ "**en train de**" + *infinitive*	

Here are some examples:

SP	**Estaría hablando** con mi hermano si hubiera ido a su casa ayer.	
PT	**Estaria falando** com meu irmão se tivesse ido à casa dele ontem.	*I **would be talking** to my brother had I gone to his house.*
IT	**Starei parlando** con mio fratello se fossi andato a casa sua.	
FR	Je **serais en train de parler** à mon frère si j'étais allé chez lui.	
SP	No **estaría comiendo** mucho si estuviera a dieta.	
PT	Eu não **estaria comendo** muito se estivesse de dieta.	*I **wouldn't be eating** much if I were on a diet.*
IT	Non **starei mangiando** molto se fossi a dieta.	
FR	Je ne **serais** pas **en train de manger** beaucoup si j'étais au régime.	

9. The Verb "Acabar" in Spanish & Portuguese

The verb "**acabar**" is an important verb in Spanish and Portuguese that expresses the timing of an action.

1. "acabar" & "acabarse"

If used on its own, the verb **"acabar"** often means *"to finish or complete"* or *"to reach an end"* or *"to run out of something."* In Spanish, the verb can also be in the reflexive form **"acabarse,"** which means *"to reach an end"* or *"to run out or run its course before dying off."* For example:

SP	**Acabamos** el proyecto el año pasado.	*We* **finished** *the project last year.*
PT	**Acabamos** o projeto no ano passado.	
SP	El partido **se acabó**.	*The match* **ended.**
PT	A partida **acabou**.	
SP	**Se acabó** la leche de la nevera.	*The milk in the fridge* **ran out.**
PT	O leite na geladeira **acabou**.	
SP	Si **se acaba** todo eso, me iré de vacaciones.	*If all this* **ends***, I'll go on vacation.*
PT	Se tudo isso **acaba**, sairei de férias.	

2. "acabar de"

In Spanish, the verbal expression **"acabar de"** in the *present* tense followed by the infinitive is used to describe an event that has just finished in the present, for example:

Acabo de llegar a casa.	*I* **have just arrived** *home.*
Ella **acaba de** comer.	*She* **has just finished** *eating.*

If the expression **"acabar de"** is used to describe something in the distant past that had just finished when another event took place, the *imperfect* tense of the verb **"acabar"** is used, for example:

Acababa de llegar a la casa cuando él me llamó.	*I* **had just arrived** *home when he called me.*
Ellos **acababan de comer** cuando llegamos.	*They* **had just finished eating** *when we arrived.*

In Portuguese, the verbal expression **"acabar de"** in the *preterite* followed by the *infinitive* is used to describe an event that has just finished in the present. For example:

Acabei de chegar em casa.	*I* **have just arrived** *home.*
Ela **acabou de** comer.	*She* **has just finished** *eating.*

3. "acabar" + *Gerund*

In Portuguese, the verbal "**acabar**" in the *preterite* followed by the *gerund* is used to describe the meaning of finally doing something or ending up doing something unexpectedly. For example:

Acabei indo para a Itália.	*I **ended up** going to Italy.*
Você **acabou** fazendo a lição de casa.	*You **ended up** doing the homework.*
Acabamos viajando sozinhos.	*We **ended up** traveling alone.*

4. "acabar por"

In Spanish, the verbal expression "**acabar por**" in the *preterite* followed by the infinitive is used to describe the meaning of finally doing something or ending up doing something unexpectedly, for example:

Yo **acabé por** ir a Italia.	*I **ended up** going to Italy.*
Tú **acabaste por** hacer la tarea.	*You **finally** did the task.*
Acabamos por viajar solos.	*We **ended up** traveling alone.*

5. "acabar con/com"

Finally, the verbal expression "**acabar con**" (in Spanish) or "**acabar com**" (in Portuguese) followed by the infinitive means *"to finish off,"* *"to put an end to,"* or *"to ruin."* For example:

SP	Tú **acabaste con** nuestra amistad.	*You **ruined** our friendship.*
PT	Você **acabou com** nossa amizade.	
SP	La guerra **acabó con** nuestros planes.	*The war **ruined** our plans.*
PT	A guerra **acabou com** nossos planos.	
SP	La lluvia **acabó con** el partido.	*The rain **finished off** the match.*
PT	A chuva **acabou com** o jogo.	

LEVEL VI: FLUENT

Congratulations on reaching the fluent level. It must feel great to have achieved this accomplishment. All you need now is to perfect a few concepts that are preventing you from achieving full fluency.

1. ORDINAL NUMBERS II

Ordinal numbers beyond 10 are less often used. Ordinal numbers between 11 and 19 are as follows:

11	SP	once	undécimo/-a	11.º / 11.ª
	PT	onze	décimo primeiro/-a	11.º / 11.ª
	IT	undici	undicesimo/-a	11.º / 11.ª
	FR	onze	onzième	11ᵉ
12	SP	doce	duodécimo/-a	12.º / 12.ª
	PT	doze	décimo segundo/-a	12.º / 12.ª
	IT	dodici	dodicesimo/-a	12.º / 12.ª
	FR	douze	douzième	12ᵉ
13	SP	trece	decimotercero/-a	13.º / 13.ª
	PT	treze	décimo terceiro/-a	13.º / 13.ª
	IT	tredici	tredicesimo/-a	13.º / 13.ª
	FR	treize	treizième	13ᵉ
14	SP	catorce	decimocuarto/-a	14.º / 14.ª
	PT	quatorze	décimo quarto/-a	14.º / 14.ª
	IT	quattordici	quattordicesimo/-a	14.º / 14.ª
	FR	quatorze	quatorzième	14ᵉ
15	SP	quince	decimoquinto/-a	15.º / 15.ª
	PT	quinze	décimo quinto/-a	15.º / 15.ª
	IT	quindici	quindicesimo/-a	15.º / 15.ª
	FR	quinze	quinzième	15ᵉ
16	SP	dieciséis	decimosexto/-a	16.º / 16.ª
	PT	dezesseis	décimo sexto/-a	16.º / 16.ª
	IT	sedici	sedicesimo/-a	16.º / 16.ª
	FR	seize	seizième	16ᵉ
17	SP	diecisiete	decimoséptimo/-a	17.º / 17.ª
	PT	dezessete	décimo sétimo/-a	17.º / 17.ª
	IT	diciassette	diciassettesimo/-a	17.º / 17.ª
	FR	dix-sept	dix-septième	17ᵉ

18	**SP**	dieciocho	decimoctavo/-a	18.º / 18.ª
	PT	dezoito	décimo oitavo/-a	18.º / 18.ª
	IT	diciotto	diciottesimo/-a	18.º / 18.ª
	FR	dix-huit	dix-huitième	18ᵉ
19	**SP**	diecinueve	decimonoveno/-a	19.º / 19.ª
	PT	dezenove	décimo nono/-a	19.º / 19.ª
	IT	diciannove	diciannovesimo/-a	19.º / 19.ª
	FR	dix-neuf	dix-neuvième	19ᵉ

Note that ordinal numbers are adjectives and must agree in gender and number with the noun. Here are some higher ordinal numbers:

20	**SP**	veinte	vigésimo/-a	20.º / 20.ª
	PT	vinte	vigésimo/-a	20.º / 20.ª
	IT	venti	ventesimo/-a	20.º / 20.ª
	FR	vingt	vingtième	20.ᵉ
30	**SP**	treinta	trigésimo/-a	30.º / 30.ª
	PT	trinta	trigésimo/-a	30.º / 30.ª
	IT	trenta	trentesimo/-a	30.º / 30.ª
	FR	trente	trentième	30.ᵉ
40	**SP**	cuarenta	cuadragésimo/-a	40.º / 40.ª
	PT	quarenta	quadragésimo/-a	40.º / 40.ª
	IT	quaranta	quarantesimo/-a	40.º / 40.ª
	FR	quarante	quarantième	40.ᵉ
50	**SP**	cincuenta	quincuagésimo/-a	50.º / 50.ª
	PT	cinquenta	quinquagésimo/-a	50.º / 50.ª
	IT	cinquanta	cinquantesimo/-a	50.º / 50.ª
	FR	cinquante	cinquantième	50.ᵉ
60	**SP**	sesenta	sexagésimo/-a	60.º / 60.ª
	PT	sessenta	sexagésimo/-a	60.º / 60.ª
	IT	sessanta	sessantesimo/-a	60.º / 60.ª
	FR	soixante	soixantième	60.ᵉ
70	**SP**	setenta	septuagésimo/-a	70.º / 70.ª
	PT	setenta	septuagésimo/-a	70.º / 70.ª
	IT	settanta	settantesimo/-a	70.º / 70.ª
	FR	soixante-dix	soixante-dixième	70.ᵉ
80	**SP**	ochenta	octogésimo/-a	80.º / 80.ª
	PT	oitenta	octogésimo/-a	80.º / 80.ª
	IT	ottanta	ottantesimo/-a	80.º / 80.ª
	FR	quatre-vingts	quatre-vingtième	80.ᵉ

90	SP	noventa	nonagésimo/-a	90.º / 90.ª
	PT	noventa	nonagésimo/-a	90.º / 90.ª
	IT	novanta	novantesimo/-a	90.º / 90.ª
	FR	quatre-vingt-dix	quatre-vingt-dixième	90.ᵉ
100	SP	cien	centésimo/-a	100.º / 100.ª
	PT	centenas	centésimo/-a	100.º / 100.ª
	IT	cento	centesimo/-a	100.º / 100.ª
	FR	cent	centième	100.ᵉ
200	SP	doscientos	ducentésimo/-a	200.º / 200.ª
	PT	duzentos	ducentésimo/-a	200.º / 200.ª
	IT	duecento	duecentesimo/-a	200.º / 200.ª
	FR	deux cents	deux centième	200.ᵉ
300	SP	trescientos	tricentésimo/-a	300.º / 300.ª
	PT	trezentos	tricentésimo/-a	300.º / 300.ª
	IT	trecento	trecentesimo/-a	300.º / 300.ª
	FR	trois cents	trois centième	300.ᵉ
400	SP	cuatrocientos	cuadrigentésimo/-a	400.º / 400.ª
	PT	quatrocentos	quadricentésimo/-a	400.º / 400.ª
	IT	quattrocento	quattrocentesimo/-a	400.º / 400.ª
	FR	quatre cents	quatre centième	400.ᵉ
500	SP	quinientos	quingentésimo/-a	500.º / 500.ª
	PT	quinhentos	quingentésimo/-a	500.º / 500.ª
	IT	cinquecento	cinquecentesimo/-a	500.º / 500.ª
	FR	cinq cents	cinq centième	500.ᵉ
600	SP	seiscientos	sexcentésimo/-a	600.º / 600.ª
	PT	seiscentos	sexcentésimo/-a	600.º / 600.ª
	IT	seicento	seicentesimo/-a	600.º / 600.ª
	FR	six cents	six centième	600.ᵉ
700	SP	setecientos	septingentésimo/-a	700.º / 700.ª
	PT	setecentos	setecentésimo/-a	700.º / 700.ª
	IT	settecento	settecentesimo/-a	700.º / 700.ª
	FR	sept cents	sept centième	700.ᵉ
800	SP	ochocientos	octingentésimo/-a	800.º / 800.ª
	PT	oitocentos	oitocentésimo/-a	800.º / 800.ª
	IT	ottocento	ottocentesimo/-a	800.º / 800.ª
	FR	huit cent	huit centième	800.ᵉ
900	SP	novecientos	noningentésimo/-a	900.º / 900.ª
	PT	novecentos	novecentésimo/-a	900.º / 900.ª
	IT	novecento	novecentesimo/-a	900.º / 900.ª
	FR	neuf cent	neuf centième	900.ᵉ

1.000	**SP**	mil	milésimo/-a	1000.º/1000.ª
	PT	mil	milésimo/-a	1000.º/1000.ª
	IT	mille	millesimo/-a	1000.º/1000.ª
	FR	mille	millième	1000.ᶜ
1.000.000	**SP**	un millón	millonésimo/-a	1000000.º / 1000000.ª
	PT	um milhão	milionésimo/-a	1000000.º / 1000000.ª
	IT	un milione	milionesimo/-a	1000000.º / 1000000.ª
	FR	un million	millionième	1000000.ᶜ

❖ In Spanish and Portuguese, numbers following the names of kings and queens are *ordinal* from first to tenth, and *cardinal* above that. In Italian, these numbers are always *ordinal*. In French, all these numbers are *cardinal*, except for "**premier**" and "**première**," which are *ordinal*. Here are some examples:

SP	Isabel Segunda (2.ª)	
PT	Isabel Segunda (2.ª)	*Elizabeth the Second*
IT	Elisabetta Seconda (2.ª)	
FR	Elizabeth Deux (2)	
SP	Isabel Primera(1.ª)	
PT	Isabel Primeira (1.ª)	*Elizabeth the First*
IT	Elisabetta Prima (1.ª)	
FR	Elizabeth Première (1ᵉʳᵉ)	
SP	Eduardo Tercero (3.º)	
PT	Eduardo Terceiro (3.º)	*Edward the Third*
IT	Edoardo Terzo (3.º)	
FR	Edouard Trois (3)	
SP	Luis Catorce (14)	
PT	Louis Quatorze (14)	*Louis the Fourteenth*
IT	Luigi Quattordicesimo (14.º)	
FR	Louis Quatorze (14)	

❖ Fractional numbers in Spanish, Portuguese, Italian, and French are as follows:

	1/2	1/3	1/4	1/5 ... 1/10	1/11 ...
SP	medio	tercio	*Same as ordinal number*		*Add "-avo" to the end of the cardinal number*, e.g., 1/16 = **un dieciseisavo**.
PT	meio	terço	*Same as ordinal number*		
IT	mezzo		*Same as ordinal number*		
FR	demi	tiers	quart	*Same as ordinal number*	

Here are some examples:

SP	un **tercio** de la población	*a **third** of the population*
PT	um **terço** da população	
IT	un **terzo** della popolazione	
FR	un **tiers** de la population	
SP	un **cuarto** de los jugadores	*a **fourth** of the players*
PT	um **quarto** dos jogadores	
IT	un **quarto** dei giocatori	
FR	un **quart** des joueurs	
SP	un **quinto** de los recursos	*a **fifth** of the resources*
PT	um **quinto** dos recursos	
IT	un **quinto** delle risorse	
FR	un **cinquième** des ressources	
SP	un **dieciseisavo** del agua	*a **1/16**th of the water*
PT	um **décimo sexto** da água	
IT	un **sedicesimo** dell'acqua	
FR	un **seizième** de l'eau	

❖ If the numerator is larger than one, the denominator is expressed in plural, for example:

SP	tres cuarto<u>s</u>	*3/4*
PT	três quarto<u>s</u>	
IT	tre quart<u>i</u>	
FR	trois quart<u>s</u>	

❖ Here are some useful collective numbers and number adjectives in Spanish, Portuguese, Italian, and French:

SP	un par	*a pair*
PT	um par	
IT	un paio	
FR	une paire	

SP	doble	
PT	duplo	*double*
IT	doppio	
FR	double	
SP	triple	
PT	triplo	*triple*
IT	triplo	
FR	triple	
SP	una docena	
PT	uma dúzia	*a dozen*
IT	una dozzina	
FR	une douzaine	

2. IMPERFECT SUBJUNCTIVE TENSE

The imperfect subjunctive, similar to the present perfect in the subjunctive, is used to express desires and wishes. However, these desires and wishes are often in the past or refer to unlikely events or possibilities.

In French, the imperfect subjunctive tense exists only in formal writing and remains mostly a literary tense. The present subjunctive or the imperfect indicative tense is often used instead, as shown in the following example.

SP	Si yo **fuera**/**fuese** tú, no iría.	
PT	Se eu **fosse** você, não iria.	*If I **were** you, I wouldn't go.*
IT	Se **fossi** in te, non andrei.	
FR	Si j'**étais** toi, je n'irais pas.	

Conjugation

In Spanish and Portuguese, the stem used to form the imperfect subjunctive conjugation comes from the *third-person plural form* of the *preterite* rather than the infinitive, that is:

1. In Spanish: the preterite that follows "**ellos**" or "**ellas**" minus the final "**-ron**."
2. In Portuguese: the preterite that follows "**eles**" or "**elas**" minus the final "**-ram**."

	Infinitive	Third-person plural preterite	Imp. Subj. Stem
SP	hablar *(to speak)*	ellos/ellas hablaron	habla-
PT	falar *(to speak)*	eles/elas falaram	fala-
SP	ir *(to go)*	ellos/ellas fueron	fue-
PT	ir *(to go)*	eles/elas foram	fo-
SP	comer *(to eat)*	ellos/ellas comieron	comie-
PT	comer *(to eat)*	eles/elas comeram	come-

Next, one of the following two endings is attached to the stem in Spanish:

yo	-ra	-se	e.g., hablara/hablase
tú	-ras	-ses	e.g., hablaras/hablases
él/ella/usted	-ra	-se	e.g., hablara/hablase
nosotros/-as	-ramos	-semos	e.g., habláramos/hablásemos
vosotros/-as	-rais	-seis	e.g., hablarais/hablaseis
ellos/ellas/ustedes	-ran	-sen	e.g., hablaran/hablasen

In Portuguese, there is only one set of endings that can be added:

eu	-sse	e.g., eu falasse
ele/ela/você	-sse	e.g., ele falasse
nós	-ssemos	e.g., nós falássemos
eles/elas/vocês	-ssem	e.g., eles falassem

All verbs follow these conjugation rules, and there are no irregular verbs.

In Italian, to form the stem of the verb needed for regular verb conjugation, we drop the final "**-re**" of the verb and attach the conjugation suffix. The suffixes are the same for the three types of verbs.

	-are ending parlare *(to speak)*	-ere ending vendere *(to sell)*	-ire ending partire *(to leave)*
io	parla**ssi**	vende**ssi**	parti**ssi**
tu	parla**ssi**	vende**ssi**	parti**ssi**
lui/lei	parla**sse**	vende**sse**	parti**sse**
noi	parla**ssimo**	vende**ssimo**	parti**ssimo**
voi	parla**ste**	vende**ste**	parti**ste**
loro	parla**ssero**	vende**ssero**	parti**ssero**

There are a few irregular verbs in Italian. Verbs that are irregular in the imperfect indicative are also irregular in the imperfect subjunctive. Here are the most common irregular verbs:

	io	tu	lui/lei	noi	voi	loro
bere *(to drink)*	bevessi	bevessi	bevesse	bevessimo	beveste	bevessero
dare *(to give)*	dessi	dessi	desse	dessimo	deste	dessero
dire *(to say/tell)*	dicessi	dicessi	dicesse	dicessimo	diceste	dicessero
essere *(to be)*	fossi	fossi	fosse	fossimo	foste	fossero
fare *(to do/make)*	facessi	facessi	facesse	facessimo	faceste	facessero
stare *(to stay/be)*	stessi	stessi	stesse	stessimo	steste	stessero

Uses of the Imperfect Subjunctive

Let us discuss the common uses of the imperfect subjunctive and check some examples:

1. Expressing Past Desires, Wishes, Feelings, Requests, and Recommendations.

Whereas the present subjunctive is used to express opinion, possibility, and feelings such as fear, doubt, hope, desire, etc., about something in the present or the future, the imperfect subjunctive can be used similarly, but when the hope, desire, feeling, etc. itself is in the past.

For example, using the present subjunctive, we can say:

SP	Quiero que **vengas** a mi casa.	
PT	Quero que você **venha** à minha casa.	*I want you to **come** to my house.*
IT	Voglio che tu **venga** a casa mia.	
FR	Je veux que tu **viennes** chez moi.	
SP	Sugiero que **se queden** con nosotros.	
PT	Sugiro que eles **fiquem** conosco.	*I suggest that they **stay** with us.*
IT	Suggerisco che **restino** con noi.	
FR	Je suggère qu'ils **restent** avec nous.	

If that hope or desire occurred in the past, the imperfect subjunctive should be used in Spanish, Portuguese, and Italian, whereas the present subjunctive is often used instead in French:

SP	Quería que **vinieras/vinieses** a mi casa.	
PT	Queria que você **viesse** à minha casa.	*I wanted you to **come** to my house.*
IT	Volevo che tu **venissi** a casa mia.	
FR	Je voulais que tu **viennes** chez moi.	
SP	Sugerí que **se quedaran/qudesen** con nosotros.	
PT	Sugeri que **ficassem** conosco.	*I suggested that they **stay** with us.*
IT	Ho suggerito che **restassero** con noi.	
FR	Je suggère qu'ils **restent** avec nous.	

2. Unlikely or Hypothetical Conditional Statements.

As discussed previously, conditional statements that contain hypothetical or unlikely assumptions, such as *"if I were you," "if I were the president,"* and *"if I had a lot of money,"* the imperfect subjunctive should be used in Spanish, Portuguese, and Italian, whereas the imperfect indicative is often used instead in French:

SP	Si yo **fuera/fuese** tú, no iría al gimnasio hoy.	
PT	Se eu **fosse** você, não iria para a academia hoje.	*If I **were** you, I wouldn't go to the gym today.*
IT	Se **fossi** in te, oggi non andrei in palestra.	
FR	Si j'**étais** toi, je n'irais pas à la salle de sport aujourd'hui.	
SP	Si **tuviera/tuviese** mucho dinero, compraría un palacio.	
PT	Se eu **tivesse** muito dinheiro, compraria um palácio.	*If I **had** a lot of money, I would buy a palace.*
IT	Se **avessi** molti soldi, comprerei un palazzo.	
FR	Si j'**avais** beaucoup d'argent, j'achèterais un palais.	

3. Expressions that contain unlikely or hypothetical events in the present or the future.

We have previously discussed the use of **"ojalá"** in Spanish, and **"oxalá"** and **"tomara"** in Portuguese, in the present subjunctive to express hope for something to happen in the present or the future, for example:

SP	Ojalá que **no llueva** esta noche.	*Hopefully, it **won't rain** tonight.*
PT	Tomara que **não chova** esta noite.	
SP	Ojalá que **venga** mi hermano hoy.	*Hopefully, my brother **will come** today.*
PT	Oxalá que meu irmão **venha** hoje.	

"**Ojalá**" in Spanish, and "**oxalá**" and "**tomara**" in Portuguese, can also be used along with the imperfect subjunctive to express hope that something, which is *unlikely* or *improbable*, would happen in the present or the future, for example:

SP	Ojalá que **pudiéramos/pudiésemos** ganar mucho dinero en un año.	*I wish we **could** make a lot of money in one year.*
PT	Tomara que **pudéssemos** ganhar muito dinheiro em um ano.	
SP	Ojalá que **viniera/viniese** mi hermano hoy, pero siempre está ocupado.	*I wish my brother **would come** today, but he is always busy.*
PT	Oxalá que meu irmão **viesse** hoje, mas ele está sempre ocupado.	

In Italian, if "**anche se**" is followed by the *imperfect subjunctive*, the meaning would change to *"even if"* and the preceding phrase is often in the *conditional tense*, that is, for example:

Viaggerebbe molto <u>anche se</u> non **fosse** ricco.	*He would travel a lot <u>even if</u> he **were** not rich.*

Similarly, in French, if "**même si**" is followed by the *imperfect indicative*, the meaning changes to *"even if,"* and the preceding phrase is often in the *conditional tense*, for example:

Il voyagerait beaucoup <u>même s</u>'il n'**était** pas riche.	*He would travel a lot <u>even if</u> he **were** not rich.*

4. Polite Requests in Spanish

It is also very common to use the imperfect subjunctive in Spanish to make polite requests, for example:

SP	**Quisiera** un café, por favor.	*I would like a coffee, please.*
SP	**Quisiera** que vinieras mañana.	*I would like you to come tomorrow.*

3. PLUPERFECT INDICATIVE TENSE

The pluperfect tense, literally *the more than perfect*, describes the past before the simple past. If two actions took place in the past, the one that occurred before is often described in the pluperfect.

The pluperfect indicative is formed as follows:

SP	"haber" in the imperfect indicative	
PT	"ter" or "haver" in the imperfect indicative	+ past participle
IT	"avere" or "essere" in the imperfect indicative	
FR	"avoir" or "être" in the imperfect indicative	

In Spanish, "haber" is conjugated in the imperfect indicative as follows:

		-ar ending hablar	-er ending comer	-ir ending vivir
yo	había			
tú	habías			
él/ella/usted	había	hablado	comido	vivido
nosotros/-as	habíamos			
vosotros/-as	habíais			
ellos/ellas/ustedes	habían			

In Portuguese, both "ter" and "haver" are grammatically correct and can be used interchangeably. However, the use of "haver" is usually limited to writing. In everyday language, the verb "ter" is often used, which is conjugated in the imperfect indicative as follows:

		-ar ending falar	-er ending comer	-ir ending partir
eu	tinha			
ele/ela/você	tinha	falado	comido	partido
nós	tínhamos			
eles/elas/vocês	tinham			

In Italian, depending on the verb, the pluperfect indicative uses the auxiliary "avere" or "essere" in the imperfect, which are conjugated as follows:

	"avere" in the imperfect indicative	"essere" in the imperfect indicative
io	avevo	ero
tu	avevi	eri
lui/lei	aveva	era
noi	avevamo	eravamo
voi	avevate	eravate
loro	avevano	erano

In French, depending on the verb, the pluperfect indicative uses the auxiliary "**avoir**" or "**être**" in the imperfect, which are conjugated as follows:

	"avoir" in the imperfect indicative	"être" in the imperfect indicative
j'	avais	étais
tu	avais	étais
il/elle/on	avait	était
nous	avions	étions
vous	aviez	étiez
ils/elles	avaient	étaient

For example:

SP	Antes de conocernos, nunca **había ido** a España.	
PT	Antes de nos conhecermos, eu nunca **tinha ido** na Espanha.	*Before we met, I **had** never **been** to Spain.*
IT	Prima che ci conoscessimo, non **ero** mai **stato** in Spagna.	
FR	Avant notre rencontre, je n'**étais** jamais **allé** en Espagne.	
SP	Cuando visité a mi mamá, mi hermana ya **había llegado**.	
PT	Quando fui visitar minha mãe, minha irmã já **tinha chegado**.	*When I visited my mom, my sister **had** already **arrived**.*
IT	Quando sono andato a trovare mia madre, mia sorella **era** già **arrivata**.	
FR	Quand je suis allé voir ma mère, ma sœur **était** déjà **arrivée**.	

SP	Después de que la seguridad **había cerrado** la puerta, la multitud se fue a casa.	*After the security **had closed** the door, the crowd went home.*
PT	Depois que a segurança **tinha fechado** a porta, a multidão foi para casa.	
IT	Dopo che la sicurezza **aveva chiuso** la porta, la folla è tornata a casa.	
FR	Après que la sécurité **avait fermé** la porte, la foule est rentrée chez elle.	

4. PLUPERFECT SUBJUNCTIVE TENSE

The pluperfect subjunctive is formed as follows:

SP	"**haber**" in the imperfect subjunctive	+ past participle
PT	"**ter**" or "**haver**" in the imperfect subjunctive	
IT	"**avere**" or "**essere**" in the imperfect subjunctive	
FR	"**avoir**" or "**être**" in the imperfect subjunctive	

In Spanish, "**haber**" is conjugated in the imperfect subjunctive as follows:

		-ar ending hablar	-er ending comer	-ir ending vivir
yo	hubiera			
tú	hubieras			
él/ella/usted	hubiera	habl**ado**	com**ido**	viv**ido**
nosotros/-as	hubiéramos			
vosotros/-as	hubierais			
ellos/ellas/ustedes	hubieran			

Remember that there is another accepted but less common conjugation of "**haber**" in the imperfect subjunctive:

		-ar ending hablar	-er ending comer	-ir ending vivir
yo	hubiese			
tú	hubieses			
él/ella/usted	hubiese	habl**ado**	com**ido**	viv**ido**
nosotros/-as	hubiésemos			
vosotros/-as	hubieseis			
ellos/ellas/ustedes	hubiesen			

In Portuguese, both "**ter**" and "**haver**" are grammatically correct and can be used interchangeably. However, the use of "**haver**" is usually limited to writing. In everyday language, the verb "**ter**" is often used, which is conjugated in the imperfect subjunctive as follows:

		-ar ending falar	**-er ending** comer	**-ir ending** partir
eu	tivesse			
ele/ela/você	tivesse	fal**ado**	com**ido**	part**ido**
nós	tivéssemos			
eles/elas/vocês	tivessem			

In Italian, depending on the verb, the pluperfect subjunctive uses the auxiliary "**avere**" or "**essere**" in the imperfect subjunctive, which are conjugated as follows:

	"**avere**" in the imperfect subjunctive	"**essere**" in the imperfect subjunctive
io	avessi	fossi
tu	avessi	fossi
lui/lei	avesse	fosse
noi	avessimo	fossimo
voi	aveste	foste
loro	avessero	fossero

In French, the pluperfect subjunctive tense remains mostly a literary tense and is rarely used. Instead, the pluperfect indicative tense is often used.

In Spanish, Portuguese, and Italian, the pluperfect subjunctive tense is mostly used to describe an event that already happened in the past, but we wish it did not happen or happened differently, or we want to discuss what would happen if we hypothetically changed that past event.

We will discuss two examples in which the pluperfect subjunctive is used:

1. The pluperfect subjunctive can be used in conditional statements to convey the meaning of the impossible past, for example:

SP	Si **hubiera estudiado** medicina, …	*If I **had studied** medicine, …*
PT	Se eu **tivesse** estudado medicina, …	
IT	Se **avessi studiato** medicina, …	
FR	Si j'**avais étudié** la médecine, …	
SP	Si mi abuelo no **hubiera muerto**, …	*If my grandfather **hadn't** **died**, …*
PT	Se meu avô não **tivesse morrido**, …	
IT	Se mio nonno non **fosse morto**, …	
FR	Si mon grand-père n'**était** pas **mort**, …	

Notice that the French examples use the pluperfect indicative tense.

The conditional statements above are usually followed by:

❖ a verb in simple conditional, or

❖ *"would have"* + past participle

SP	Si **hubiera estudiado** medicina, **sería** rico hoy.	*If I **had studied** medicine, I **would be** rich today.*
PT	Se eu **tivesse estudado** medicina, **estaria** rico hoje.	
IT	Se **avesse studiato** medicina, oggi **sarebbe** ricco.	
FR	Si j'**avais étudié** la médecine, je **serais** riche aujourd'hui.	
SP	Si mi abuelo no **hubiera muerto**, **habría pasado** tiempo con él. [1]	*If my grandfather **hadn't died**, I **would have spent** time with him.*
PT	Se meu avô não **tivesse morrido**, eu **teria passado** um tempo com ele.	
IT	Se mio nonno non **fosse morto**, avrei **passato** del tempo con lui.	
FR	Si mon grand-père n'**était** pas **mort**, j'**aurais passé** du temps avec lui.	

---

[1] It is not uncommon to hear "**habría**" replaced with "**hubiera**" in informal conversation, e.g., "**Si mi abuelo no hubiera muerto, hubiera pasado tiempo con él.**" According to the RAE, this sentence is considered grammatically acceptable.

Another way to describe a hypothetical or impossible past is using the expression *"as if,"* for example:

SP	Habla <u>como si</u> **hubiera estudiado** medicina.	
PT	Ele fala <u>como se</u> **tivesse estudado** medicina.	*He talks <u>as if</u> he **had**
IT	Parla <u>come se</u> **avesse studiato** medicina.	**studied** medicine.*
FR	Il parle <u>comme s</u>'il **avait étudié** la médecine.	
SP	Lloró <u>como si</u> su abuelo **hubiera muerto**.	
PT	Ele chorou <u>como se</u> seu avô **tivesse morrido**.	*He cried <u>as if</u> his
IT	Pianse <u>come se</u> suo nonno **fosse morto**.	grandfather **had died**.*
FR	Il a pleuré <u>comme si</u> son grand-père **était mort**.	

2. The other use of the pluperfect in the subjunctive is similar to that in the indicative mood. As studied earlier, the pluperfect in the indicative mood is used to describe the past before the simple past. If a feeling, doubt, or hope is added to the action described in the pluperfect, the subjunctive mood should be used. Let us look at the following examples for comparison:

a) Pluperfect in the indicative mood:

SP	**Habías ido** a España antes de conocernos.	
PT	Você **tinha ido** na Espanha antes de nos conhecermos.	*You **had been** to Spain before we met.*
IT	**Eri andato** in Spagna prima che ci conoscessimo.	
FR	Vous **étiez allé** en Espagne avant notre rencontre.	
SP	Cuando visité a mi mamá, mi hermana ya **había llegado**.	
PT	Quando fui visitar minha mãe, minha irmã já **tinha chegado**.	*When I visited my mom, my sister **had** already **arrived**.*
IT	Quando sono andato a trovare mia madre, mia sorella **era** già **arrivata**.	
FR	Lorsque j'ai rendu visite à ma mère, ma sœur **était** déjà **arrivée**.	

b) Pluperfect in the subjunctive mood:

SP	Me gustó que ya **hubieras ido** a España antes de conocernos.	*I was delighted that you **had** already **been** to Spain before we met.*
PT	Fiquei encantado que você já **tivesso ido** na Espanha antes de nos conhecermos.	

IT	Mi piaceva che tu **fossi** già **andato** in Spagna prima che ci conoscessimo.	
FR	J'étais ravi que vous **étiez allé** allé en Espagne avant notre rencontre.	
SP	Cuando visité a mi mamá, dudé que mi hermana **hubiera llegado**.	*When I visited my mom, I doubted that my sister **had arrived**.*
PT	Quando visitei minha mãe, duvidei que minha irmã já **tivesse chegado**.	
IT	Quando sono andato a trovare mia madre, dubitavo che mia sorella **fosse arrivata**.	
FR	Lorsque j'ai rendu visite à ma mère, je doutais que ma sœur **était arrivée**.	

5. Passive Voice

One way to describe something in the passive voice is by moving the noun acted upon to the beginning of the sentence to emphasize it and using a *"to be"* verb followed by the adjective or the past participle. For example:

SP	El tejido fue **hecho** de material reciclado (por la fábrica).	*The textile was **made** from recycled material (by the factory).*
PT	O tecido foi **feito** com material reciclado (pela fábrica).	
IT	Il tessuto è stato **realizzato** con materiale riciclato (dalla fabbrica).	
FR	Le tissu a été **fabriqué** à partir de matériaux recyclés (par l'usine).	
SP	El contrato será **firmado** (por la empresa).	*The contract will be **signed** (by the company).*
PT	O contrato será **assinado** (pela empresa).	
IT	Il contratto sarà **firmato** (dalla società).	
FR	Le contrat sera **signé** (par l'entreprise).	

The performer of the action in the above two examples, denoted by **"por ..."** in Spanish and Portuguese, **"da ..."** in Italian, and **"par**

..." in French, all meaning *"by ...,"* can be omitted because it is deemed not to be of great significance.

In French, the preposition "**de**" is used to denote the agent if the agent plays a less active role, for example:

| Le bâtiment est encerclé **d'**un mur. | *The building is surrounded **by** a wall.* |
| Le bâtiment est encerclé **par** des soldats. | *The building is surrounded **by** soldiers.* |

In the two examples above, notice that the agent plays a less active role in the first example. Thus, we use the proposition "**de**." On the other hand, we use "**par**" in the second example to highlight the active role of the agent.

The preposition "**de**" is commonly used in French to denote the agent with verbs that express emotion or opinion.

| Il est <u>aimé</u> **de** tous ses voisins. | *He is <u>liked</u> **by** all his neighbors.* |
| Cette idée est <u>appréciée</u> **d**es élèves. | *This idea is <u>appreciated</u> **by** the students.* |

Reflexive Passive Constructions

Another way to construct the passive voice in Spanish, Portuguese, and Italian is by using the reflexive passive pronoun "**se**" in Spanish and Portuguese or "**si**" in Italian with *transitive* verbs. The transitive verb is in the third-person singular or plural form, depending on the noun which follows the verb.

SP	"**Se**" + third-person *transitive* verb (sing. or pl.) + noun (sing. or pl.)
PT	Third-person *transitive* verb (sing. or pl.)-"**se**" + noun (sing. or pl.)
IT	"**Si**" + third-person *transitive* verb (sing. or pl.) + noun (sing. or pl.)

This is the passive construction you are likely to encounter in ads, commercials, or when the performer of the action is unknown or not as important. For example:

SP	**Se buscan** personas con experiencia.	***Wanted*** *people with experience.*
PT	**Procuram-se** pessoas com experiência.	
IT	**Si ricercano** persone con esperienza.	

SP	**Se venden** celulares aquí.	
PT	**Vendem-se** telemóveis aqui.	*Cell phones **are sold** here.*
IT	Qui **si vendono** i cellulari.	
SP	En Egipto, **se habla** árabe.	
PT	No Egito, **fala-se** o árabe.	*In Egypt, they **speak** Arabic.*
IT	In Egitto, **si parla** l'arabo.	

Notice that only transitive verbs can be used to construct sentences using the reflexive passive pronoun, and the noun that follows the third-person verb can represent thing(s) or person(s).

In French, some pronominal verbs are used in a manner similar to reflexive verbs to convey the passive voice. The following are some examples:

Ça **se voit**.	*It **shows**.*
Ça ne **se fait** pas.	*That is not **done** (We don't do that).*
Ça ne **se dit** pas.	*That is not **said** (We don't say that).*
La porte **s'ouvre** facilement.	*The door is easy to **open**.*
Comment ça **se répare**?	*How is this **repaired**?*

Impersonal Constructions

In English, we sometimes make general statements, such as:

We *work better as a team.*

They *sleep early in the village.*

It *feels better without social pressure.*

One *is happier alone than in bad company.*

One *must follow the rules.*

Notice that in the above sentences, we used the subject pronouns *(we, they, it,* and *one)* to convey a general meaning. For instance, the subject *"we"* in the sentence *"We work better as a team"* does not necessarily refer to the speaker(s) but rather refers to the general fact that humans work better as a team rather than individually. In other words, work is better done as a team.

Notice also that the verbs *"to work"* and *"to sleep"* are *intransitive*, meaning that they do not need an object for the meaning to be complete. On the other hand, *"to feel," "must,"* and *"to be"* are *copular* verbs, meaning they connect a subject to an adjective, adverb, noun, or phrase. Examples of copular verbs include: *seem, feel, appear, look, become, taste, get, sound, turn, grow,* and *find*.

In Spanish, Portuguese, and Italian, there is a special way to express such observations or statements using the third-person conjugation of the verb and the pronoun "**se**" in Spanish and Portuguese or "**si**" in Italian. Because the subject is undefined, we call this construction *impersonal*. The construction is made as follows:

SP	"**Se**" + third-person *intransitive* or *copular* verb (always singular)
PT	Third-person *intransitive* or *copular* verb (always singular)-"**se**"
IT	"**Si**" + third-person *intransitive* verb (singular) "**Si**" + third-person *copular* verb (singular) + adjective (plural)

Here are some examples:

SP	**Se trabaja** mejor en equipo.	
PT	**Trabalha-se** melhor em equipe.	*We **work** better as a team.*
IT	**Si lavora** meglio in una squadra.	
SP	**Se duerme** temprano en el pueblo.	
PT	**Dorme-se** cedo na cidade pequena.	*They **sleep** early in the village.*
IT	**Si dorme** presto al villaggio.	
SP	No **se viaja** solo lejos.	
PT	Não **se viaja** muito sozinho.	*One does not **travel** far alone.*
IT	Non **si viaggia** lontano da soli.	
SP	**Se debe** seguir las reglas.	
PT	**Deve-se** seguir as regras.	*One **must** follow the traffic.*
IT	**Si devono** seguire le regole.	
SP	**Se está** más feliz solo que mal acompañado.	
PT	**Está-se** mais feliz sozinho que mal acompanhado.	*One **is** happier alone than in bad company.*
IT	**Si è** più <u>felici</u> da soli che in cattiva compagnia.	

In Spanish and Portuguese, notice that the verb is always singular regardless of any implicit assumptions about the subject, which is grammatically absent.

In Italian, notice that if a copular verb falls between the impersonal "**si**" and an adjective, the adjective must be in plural form.

Passive Voice Using the Pronoun "On" in French

It is common to use the third-person singular pronoun "**on**" to construct the passive voice in French, especially in daily speech. In this context, the subject pronoun "**on**" can mean *"we," "one,"* or *"they,"* e.g., "**On parle francais ici**" *(We/They speak French here)* means *"French is spoken here."*

6. IDIOMATIC PRONOMINAL VERBS

A pronominal verb is a verb that is accompanied by at least one pronoun. An example of pronominal verbs is reflexive verbs indicating that the action is performed on oneself.

Not all pronominal verbs are reflexive. Some verbs simply change their meaning when attached to pronouns to form new idiomatic meanings that do not often make complete sense if translated literally into English.

Take, for example, the Italian verb "**andare**" *(to go)*. If we attach the pronouns "**si**" and "**ne**" to the verb "**andare**," we obtain the pronominal verb "**andarsene**," which means *"to go away,"* often encountered in the command form "**Vattene!**" *(Go away!)*, that is: "**va**" + "**ti**" + "**ne**," or "**Andiamocene!**" *(Let's go!)*, that is: "**andiamo**" + "**ci**" + "**ne**."

Similarly, if we attach the pronouns "**ci**" and "**la**" to the Italian verb "**avere**" *(to have)*, we obtain the pronominal verb "**avercela**," which means *"to be mad or angry."*

Most Common Pronominal Verbs in Italian

There are many similar idiomatic pronominal verbs in Italian. Some are formed by attaching one pronoun, while others are formed by attaching two pronouns. The pronouns attached can be reflexive such as "**si**," direct object such as "**le**" *(it)* and "**la**" *(them)*, or the special pronouns "**ci**" and "**ne**." Remember that the pronoun "**mi**," "**ti**," "**ci**," or "**vi**" is changed to "**me**," "**te**," "**ce**," or "**ve**," respectively, when followed by a second pronoun attached to it. One notable exception is when "**ci**" and "**si**" are used together to form "**-cisi**" at the end of a pronominal verb.

Unless the pronominal verb is in the infinitive or the imperative, the pronouns are placed in the same order before the conjugated verb. If the conjugation needs a past participle, as in the present perfect tense, the past participle takes the treatment of an adjective and must follow the ending pronoun in gender and number. Here is the conjugation of the pronominal verb "**farcela**" *(to make it or to succeed)* and "**prenderle**" *(to get it or to give a beating)* in the present perfect:

	farcela	prenderle
io	ce l'ho fatta	le ho prese
tu	ce l'hai fatta	le hai prese
lui/lei	ce l'ha fatta	le ha prese
noi	ce l'abbiamo fatta	le abbiamo prese
voi	ce l'avete fatta	le avete prese
loro	ce l'hanno fatta	le hanno prese

The following table lists some of the most common idiomatic pronominal verbs in Italian:

Verb	Meaning	Example
andarsene	*to leave a place or to go away*	**Andatevene!** Non voglio parlare. *Go away! I do not want to talk.*
avercela	*to be mad or angry*	Non **avercela** con me! *Don't be angry with me!*
cavarsela	*to manage a difficult situation*	**Se la** sono **cavata** da soli. *They managed on their own.*
cercarsela	*to look for trouble*	**Ce la** siamo **cercata** da soli. *We brought this on ourselves.*

farcela	to make it or to succeed	Sono rimasto sorpreso ma **ce l'ha fatta**. *I was surprised but he **made it**.*
godersela	*to enjoy something*	**Se la gode** in questa atmosfera. *He **enjoys it** in this atmosphere.*
intendersene	*to know a lot about something*	Lo lasci dire a chi **se ne intende**! *Leave it to those who **know best**!*
mettercela	*to put all effort into something*	**Ce l'hanno messa** tutta in campo. *They **gave it their all** on the field.*
piantarla	*to quit something*	Per favore! Ti ho detto di **piantarla**. *Please! I told you to **knock it off**.*
prendersela	*to get angry*	Mio fratello sempre **se la prende** con me. *My brother always **gets angry** with me.*
sbrigarsela	*to manage or to deal with*	La prossima volta, **se la sbrigherà** da solo. *Next time, he'll **handle it** himself.*
sentirsela	*to feel like or have desire to*	Può partecipare quando **se la sente**. *He can participate when he **feels like it**.*
smetterla	*to stop or quit something*	Devi **smetterla** di metterti in mostra. *You need to **stop** showing off.*
spassarsela	*to have a blast*	**Me la** sono **spassata** in quel periodo. *I **had a blast** during that period.*
tirarsela	*to show off*	**Se la tira** sempre tanto. *He always **shows off** too much.*
trovarcisi	*to find oneself in*	**Mi ci** sono **trovato** per caso. *I **found myself there** by accident.*
vedercisi	*to see oneself in*	Non **mi ci vedo** con loro. *I don't **see myself** with them.*
vederne	*to see something of*	Non **ne vedo** il motivo. *I don't **see** the reason **of** it.*
venirne	*to get to the bottom of*	Alla fine, **ne sono venuto** a conoscenza. *Eventually, I **came to** know about it.*

Most Common Pronominal Verbs in French

There are many idiomatic pronominal verbs in French. Some are formed using one pronoun, while others are formed by using two pronouns. In general, a pronominal verb uses a reflexive pronoun and/or one of the special pronouns "**y**" and "**en**."

To conjugate a pronominal verb, the pronouns are placed in the same order before the conjugated verb. If the conjugation needs a past participle, as in the present perfect tense, the auxiliary "**être**" is used, and the past participle takes the treatment of an adjective, meaning it must follow the subject in gender and number. Here is the conjugation of the pronominal verbs "**s'en aller**" *(to go away)* and "**s'y prendre**" *(to set about doing something)* in the present perfect:

	s'en aller	s'y prendre
je	m'en suis allé(e)	m'y suis pris(e)
tu	t'en es allé(e)	t'y es pris(e)
il/ on	s'en est allé	s'y est pris
elle	s'en est allée	s'y est prise
nous	nous en sommes allé(e)s	nous y sommes pris(es)
vous	vous en êtes allé(e)s	vous y êtes pris(e)(s)
il	s'en sont allés	s'y sont pris
elles	s'en sont allées	s'y sont prises

The following table lists some of the most common idiomatic pronominal verbs in French:

Verb	Meaning	Example
s'en aller	*to go away*	**Va-t'en**! Je ne veux pas parler. **Go away**! I do not want to talk.
s'amuser	*to have a good time*	Ils **se sont amusés** sur la plage. They **had a good time** on the beach.
s'apercevoir	*to notice*	Je **me suis aperçu** que le travail était difficile. I **noticed** that the work was difficult.
s'attendre	*to expect*	Ils **s'attendent** à ce que l'économie s'améliore. They **expect** the economy to improve.
se demander	*to wonder*	Je **me demandais** ce qui s'était passé. I **was wondering** what had happened.
se dépêcher	*to hurry*	**Dépêche-toi**! Nous sommes en retard. **Hurry up**! We are late.
se dérouler	*to unfold or happen*	Les événements **se sont déroulés** si vite. The events **unfolded** so fast.
se douter	*to suspect*	Je crois qu'il **se doute** de quelque chose. I think he **suspects** something.
s'éclater	*to have a blast*	Ils **se sont éclatés** pendant leurs vacances. They **had a blast** during their vacation.
s'enfuir	*to run away*	Il **s'est enfui** des lieux en quelques minutes. He **ran away** from the scene within minutes.
s'ennuyer	*to be bored*	Je **me suis ennuyé** devant la télé hier soir. I **was bored** watching TV last night.
s'entendre	*to get along*	Les deux voisins ne **s'entendent** pas. The two neighbors don't **get along**.
s'évanouir	*to faint*	Elle **s'est évanouie** quand elle a vu le sang. She **fainted** when she saw the blood.

se figurer	*to imagine*	Je peux **me figurer** la beauté du paysage. *I can **imagine** the beauty of the landscape.*
s'habituer à	*to get used to*	Je **me suis habitué à** la vie en ville. *I **got used to** life in the city.*
s'installer	*to settle in*	J'ai besoin de temps pour **m'installer** ici. *I need some time to **settle in** here.*
se mettre à	*to begin to*	Je rentrerai chez moi si la pluie **se met à** tomber. *I will go home if the rain **begins to** fall.*
se moquer de	*to make fun of*	Ne **te moque** pas **de** ton amie. *Don't **make fun of** your friend.*
se passer	*to happen*	Que **s'est**-il **passé** hier soir? *What **happened** last night?*
se perdre	*to get lost*	Nous **nous sommes perdus** au parc hier. *We **got lost** at the park yesterday.*
se plaindre	*to complain*	Ils **se plaignent** toujours des règles. *They always **complain** about the rules.*
s'y prendre	*to set about or do something*	Comment on **s'y prend** n'est pas important. *How we **do** it is not important.*
se refuser à	*to deny oneself*	Il **s'est refusé** à accepter le pot-de-vin. *He **refused to** take the bribe.*
se rendre à	*to go to*	Il **se rendra à** Paris le mois prochain. *He will **go to** Paris next month.*
se rendre compte de	*to realize*	Il **s'est rendu compte** qu'il avait tort. *He **realized** that he was wrong.*
s'en retourner	*to go back*	Il sauva ses hommes avant de **s'en retourner** en Espagne. *He saved his men before **going back** to Spain.*
se réunir	*to meet or get together*	Nous **nous réunirons** demain matin. *We will **get together** tomorrow morning.*
se saisir de	*to take up*	Il **s'est saisi** du pouvoir il y a 20 ans. *He **took up** power 20 years ago.*
se servir de	*to make use of*	Ce site **se sert de** cookies. *This site **makes use of** cookies.*
se tromper	*to be mistaken*	Elle **s'est trompée** l'autre jour. *She **was wrong** the other day.*
se trouver	*to be located*	L'entrée **se trouve** de l'autre côté. *The entrance **is located** on the other side.*

7. DIMINUTIVES & AUGMENTATIVES

Diminutives and augmentatives are sometimes used to exaggerate descriptions or show certain emotions such as endearment or affection. Understanding some rules and familiarity with some vocabulary in this category will help you enhance your understanding of the language.

1. Diminutives

In the English language, we sometimes form the diminutive by suffixing *"-ie"* or *"-y,"* as in *"doggie"* for *"dog"* and *"kitty"* for *"kitten,"* indicating small size and sometimes the state or quality of being familiarly known, lovable, pitiable, or contemptible. Sometimes other suffixes are used, such as *"-ette"* in *"kitchenette"* and *"novelette,"* *"-let"* in *"booklet"* and *"droplet,"* and *"-ling"* in *"duckling"* and *"gosling"* *(a young goose)*.

In Spanish, Portuguese, Italian, and French, the purpose of using the diminutive is often similar to that in English, although in a few cases, the diminutive may be used to express sarcasm or negativity.

Unfortunately, there are not always specific rules on which suffix to use for a particular word. However, we discuss the most common examples and hope that with practice you can continue to enrich your vocabulary in this area.

Spanish Diminutive Suffixes:

There are two general rules to form the diminutive in Spanish. However, there are a few exceptions that we will cover as well as some orthographic changes and regional variations. Let us start with the two general rules:

Rule # 1: Diminutives with the "-**ito**/-**ita**" Suffix

For words that end in "**o**," "**a**," or a consonant other than "**n**" or "**r**," add the ending "-**ito**" for masculine and "-**ita**" for feminine at the end of the word.

In the case of words ending with "**o**" or "**a**," remove the "**o**" or "**a**" to avoid the double vowel. For example:

pollo^m *(chicken)*	poll~~o~~ + -ito	=	pollito *(chick)*	

pato[m] *(duck)*	pato	+	-ito	=	patito *(duckling)*
casa[f] *(house)*	casa	+	-ita	=	casita *(small house)*
mesa[f] *(table)*	mesa	+	-ita	=	mesita *(small table)*
mano[f] *(hand)*	mano	+	-ita	=	manita[1] *(little hand)*
pastel[m] *(cake)*	pastel	+	-ito	=	pastelito *(small cake)*
reloj[m] *(clock)*	reloj	+	-ito	=	relojito *(small clock)*

[1] Notice that "**mano**" takes the suffix "**-ita**" because it is a feminine noun, even though it ends with an "**o**."

Rule # 2: Diminutives with the "-**cito**/-**cita**" Suffix

For words that end in "**e**," "**n**," or "**r**," add the ending "-**cito**" for masculine and "-**cita**" for feminine at the end of the word. For example:

café[m] *(coffee)*	café	+	-cito	=	cafecito *(little coffee)*
calle[f] *(street)*	calle	+	-cita	=	callecita *(little street)*
suave[m,f] *(soft)*	suave	+	-cito -cita	=	suavecito *(very soft)* suavecita *(very soft)*
favor[m] *(favor)*	favor	+	-cito	=	favorcito *(little favor)*
amor[m] *(love)*	amor	+	-cito	=	amorcito *(sweetie)*
camión *(truck)*	camión	+	-cito	=	camioncito *(little truck)*
rincón *(corner)*	rincón	+	-cito	=	rinconcito *(little corner)*

In some words, especially the ones ending in "**c**" or "**z**," an extra "**e**" is added before the suffix "-**cito**" or "-**cita**." For example:

| flor[f] *(flower)* | flor | + | -ecita | = | florecita[2] *(small flower)* |

[2] The diminutive "**florcita**" is also used in some parts of Latin America.

In addition to the aforementioned suffixes, there are three less common suffixes used to form the diminutive: "-**illo**/-**illa**," "-**ico**/-**ica**," "-**zuelo**/-**zuela**." There are very few words that use these three suffixes, the most common of which are: "**bolsillo**" *(pouch or pocket)*, which is diminutive of "**bolso**" *(bag)*, "**barbilla**" *(chin)*, which is diminutive of "**barba**" *(beard)*, "**mantequilla**" *(butter)*, which is diminutive of "**manteca**" *(lard)*, and "**Venezuela**" *(Little Venice)*, which is diminutive of "**Venecia**" *(Venice)*. The "-**ico**" suffix is used in some regions of Spain and the Caribbean to form some uncommon diminutives, such as "**perrico**," which is a diminutive of "**perro**" *(dog)* instead of the more common "**perrito**."

The variation of diminutives across regions is not uncommon. For example, while the standard diminutive of the word "**sol**" *(sun)* is "**solecito**" *(little sun)*, "**solcito**" is the diminutive used in Argentina.

To highlight the regional aspect of the use of diminutives, consider the term "**ticos**," the name the Costa Ricans are called and proudly call themselves due to their ubiquitous use of the "-**tico**" ending to form diminutives, e.g., "**momentico**," "**pizzatica**," "**perritico**," "**chiquitico**," etc.

While the aforementioned rules cover most diminutives, some words remain difficult to categorize, such as "**nuevo**" *(new)*, the diminutive of which is "**nuevecito**" *(brand-new)*, and "**pez**" *(fish)*, the diminutive of which is "**pececito**" *(small fish)*. Note also that the meaning sometimes changes when the word is in the diminutive form.

Finally, when necessary, orthographic changes are applied to maintain the correct pronunciation sounds and spelling rules. These are similar to the rules we encountered in verb conjugation rules throughout the book. For example:

	poco^m *(little)*	poc**o**	+	-ito	=	poq**u**ito *(very little)*
"c" to "**qu**"	chico^m *(small, boy)*	chic**o**	+	-ito	=	chiq**u**ito *(tiny, little boy)*
	chica^f *(girl)*	chic**a**	+	-ita	=	chiq**u**ita *(little girl)*
"**g**" to "**gu**"	amigo^m *(friend)*	amig**o**	+	-ito	=	amig**u**ito *(little friend)*
	trago^m *(sip)*	trag**o**	+	-ito	=	trag**u**ito *(little sip)*
"**z**" to "**c**"	lápiz^m *(pencil)*	lápiz	+	-ito	=	lapi**c**ito *(small pencil)*
	luz^f *(light)*	luz	+	-ecita	=	lu**c**ecita[1] *(little light)*

---

[1] The diminutive "**lucita**" is also used in some regions.

Portuguese Diminutive Suffixes:

The most common suffixes to form diminutives in Brazilian Portuguese are "**-inho**" for the masculine and "**-inha**" for the feminine. We will classify the diminutives based on the ending of the noun or adjective:

1. Nouns and adjectives that end with "**-s**," "**-z**," unstressed "**-a**," "**-e**," or "**-o**" (except "**-io**" and "**-ia**")

These words drop the final unstressed vowel, then add "**-inho**" if the word is masculine and "**-inha**" if the word is feminine.

Some examples in this category include:

carro[m] *(car)*	carre	+	-inho	=	carr**inho**[m] *(small car)*
casa[f] *(house)*	casa	+	-inha	=	cas**inha**[f] *(little house)*
voz[f] *(voice)*	voz	+	-inha	=	voz**inha**[f] *(little voice)*
rapaz[m] *(boy)*	rapaz	+	-inho	=	rapaz**inho**[m] *(little boy)*
bonito[m] *(pretty)*	bonite	+	-inho	=	bonit**inho**[m] *(cute)*
			-inha	=	bonit**inha**[f] *(cute)*

2. Nouns and adjectives with other endings (including "**-io**," "**-ia**", and stressed "**-a**," "**-e**," or "**-o**")

Most words in this group add a "**z**" before "**-inho**" if the word is masculine and "**-inha**" if the word is feminine.

Here are some examples:

papel[m] *(sun)*	papel	+	-zinho	=	papel**zinho**[m] *(little paper)*
flor[f] *(flower)*	flor	+	-zinha	=	flor**zinha**[f] *(little flower)*
café[m] *(coffee)*	café	+	-zinho	=	cafe**zinho**[m] *(small coffee)*
mão[f] *(hand)*	mão	+	-zinha	=	mão**zinha**[f] *(little hand)*
viagem[f] *(trip)*	viagem	+	-zinha	=	viagen**zinha**[f] *(small trip)*

Notice also that the stress is always on the diminutive ending. Thus, any written accent is dropped except accents that denote nasal sound, e.g., "**caf_e_zinho**" *(small coffee)*.

In addition, if a word ends with an "m," it is changed into "n" before adding the diminutive ending, e.g., "**viagenzinha**" *(little trip)*.

In some cases, the word can acquire a new meaning in the diminutive form. For example, the diminutive "**carrinho**" means a *"small car,"* but it can also mean a *"toy car."*

Not all diminutives follow these rules. Some use less common suffixes, such as "**livrete**ᵐ" *(carnet)*, "**ruela**ᶠ" *(small street)*, and "**riacho**ᵐ" *(creek or brook)*, the diminutive forms of "**livro**ᵐ" *(book)*, "**rua**ᶠ" *(street)*, and "**rio**ᵐ" *(river)*, respectively.

Italian Diminutive Suffixes:

1. "-ino"

The suffix "**-ino**" is commonly used to form diminutives from masculine singular nouns and adjectives. Regular end-changes often apply for feminine and plural forms.

Let us take some examples of diminutives ending in "**-ino**":

ragazzoᵐ *(boy)*	ragazzo	+	-ino	=	ragazzinoᵐ *(young or little boy)*
ragazzaᶠ *(girl)*	ragazza	+	-ina	=	ragazzinaᶠ *(young or little girl)*
gattoᵐ *(cat)*	gatto	+	-ino	=	gattinoᵐ *(kitten)*
tazzaᶠ *(cup)*	tazza	+	-ina	=	tazzinaᶠ *(small cup)*
manoᶠ *(hand)*	mano	+	-ina	=	maninaᶠ [1] *(little hand)*
belloᵐ *(beautiful)*	bello	+	-ino	=	bellinoᵐ *(cute)*

---

[1] Remember that "**mano**" *(hand)* is a feminine noun although it ends with an "-**o**." Thus, it takes the suffix "-**ina**" instead of "-**ino**."

The above examples include nouns and adjectives. Some adverbs can also be used in diminutive forms. These usually use the "**-ino**" suffix. For example:

bene *(well)*	bene	+	-ino	=	benino *(goodish)*
male *(badly)*	male	+	-ino	=	malino *(a little badly)*
presto *(soon)*	presto	+	-ino	=	prestino *(a little soon)*
tanto *(much)*	tanto	+	-ino	=	tantino *(a little much)*
poco *(little)*	poco	+	-ino	=	pochino *(a tiny bit)*
tardi *(late)*	tardi	+	-ino	=	tardinoᵐ *(a bit late)*

Sometimes "-ic-" or "-ol-" is inserted before the suffix, forming the modified suffixes "-icino" or "-olino," respectively. Here are some examples:

posto[m] (place)	post<del>o</del>	+	-ino	=	posticino[m] (small place)
libro[m] (book)	libr<del>o</del>	+	-ino	=	libriccino[m] (booklet)
topo[m] (mouse)	top<del>o</del>	+	-ino	=	topolino[m] (little mouse)
magro[m] (thin)	magr<del>o</del>	+	-ino	=	magrolino[f] (skinny)
cane[m] (dog)	can<del>e</del>	+	-ino	=	cagnolino[m] (small dog)

The suffix "-ino" is widely used when affectionately describing or talking about babies, e.g., "**faccino**" (little face), "**manina**" (little hand), etc.

2. "-etto"

Another common suffix used to form diminutives is "-**etto**." This suffix is often applied affectionately to names, especially female names, using the suffix feminine form "-**etta**," e.g., "**Lauretta**" (diminutive for "**Laura**"), "**Paoletta**" (diminutive for "**Paola**"). Let us take a look at some examples:

casa[f] (house)	cas<del>a</del>	+	-etta	=	casetta[f] (small house)
povero[m] (poor)	pover<del>o</del>	+	-etto	=	poveretto[m] (poor little guy)
cane[m] (dog)	can<del>e</del>	+	-etto	=	cagnetto[m] (small dog)
borsa[f] (purse)	bors<del>a</del>	+	-etta	=	borsetta[f] (small purse)
piccolo[m] (small)	piccol<del>o</del>	+	-etto	=	piccoletto[m] (shorty)

3. "-ello"

The suffix "-**ello**" can also be used to form diminutives. Here are some examples:

albero[m] (tree)	alber<del>o</del>	+	-ello	=	alberello[m] (small tree)
finestra[f] (window)	finestr<del>a</del>	+	-ella	=	finestrella[m] (little window)
cattivo[m] (bad)	cattiv<del>o</del>	+	-ello	=	cattivello[m] (naughty)

Sometimes "-ic-" or "-er-" is inserted before the suffix, forming the modified suffixes "-**icello**" or "-**erello**," respectively. Here are some examples:

| campo[m] (field) | camp<del>o</del> | + | -icello | = | campicello[m] (small field) |
| fatto[m] (fact) | fatt<del>o</del> | + | -erello | = | fatterello[m] (anecdote or minor event) |

4. "-uccio"

The suffix "-uccio" is sometimes used to form diminutives showing affection or endearment when used with proper nouns, e.g., "Micheluccio" (diminutive for "Michele"), "Guiduccio" (diminutive for "Guido"), "Mariuccia" (diminutive for "Maria"), etc. In other contexts, it may be used as a pejorative. Here are some examples of diminutives using the suffix "-uccio":

avvocato^m *(lawyer)*	avvocato	+ -uccio =	avvocatuccio^m *(inferior lawyer)*
caldo^m *(hot)*	caldo	+ -uccio =	calduccio^m *(cozy)*
cappello^m *(hat)*	cappello	+ -uccio =	cappelluccio^m *(worn-out hat)*
casa^f *(house)*	casa	+ -uccia =	casuccia^f *(small cozy house)*
zio^m *(uncle)*	zio	+ -uccio =	ziuccio^m *(dear uncle)*

5. "-otto"

The suffix "-otto" is used to form diminutives. It is sometimes used to refer to baby animals. Here are some examples of diminutives that take the suffix "-otto":

giovane^m *(young)*	giovane	+ -otto	=	giovanotto^m *(young lad)*
aquila^f *(eagle)*	aquila	+ -otto	=	aquilotto^m *(eaglet)*
tigre^f *(tiger)*	tigre	+ -otto	=	tigrotto^m *(tiger cub)*

Sometimes "-acchi-" is inserted before the suffix, forming the modified suffix "-acchiotto." Here are some examples:

lupo^m *(wolf)*	lupo	+ -acchiotto	=	lupacchiotto^m *(wolf cub)*
orso^m *(bear)*	orso	+ -acchiotto	=	orsacchiotto^m *(bear cub or teddy bear)*
tigre^f *(tiger)*	tigre	+ -acchiotto	=	tigracchiotto^m *(tiger cub)*

6. "-uzzo"

Another less common suffix is "-uzzo," although is more common in some Southern regions of Italy. Examples include:

pietra^f *(stone)*	pietra	+ -uzza	=	pietruzza^f *(pebble)*
paglia^f *(straw)*	paglia	+ -uzza	=	pagliuzza^f *(little straw)*

We can also sometimes combine two diminutive suffixes, e.g., **"casettina"** *(very small house)*, **"giovanottino"** *(young lad)*.

Although these are not all the suffixes used to form diminutives in Italian, most other suffixes are either of mainly regional use or rarely encountered in daily life.

French Diminutive Suffixes:

The most common diminutive suffixes in French are "**-et**" for masculine and "**-ette**" for feminine. If the word ends with a vowel, the final vowel is dropped before adding the suffix. Here are some nouns in diminutive forms:

livre^m *(boy)*	livre	+	-et	=	livret^m *(booklet)*
jardin^m *(garden)*	jardin	+	-et	=	jardinet^m *(little garden)*
fille^f *(girl)*	fille	+	-ette	=	fillette^f *(little girl)*
cigare^m *(cigar)*	cigare	+	-ette	=	cigarette^f *(cigarette)*
maison^f *(house)*	maison	+	-ette	=	maisonette^f *(little house)*

The suffixes "**-et**" and "**-ette**" can also be used with adjectives. In this context, the suffix has a similar function to the "**-ish**" suffix in English. The suffix is usually added to the feminine form of the adjective, for example:

gentille^f *(nice)*	gentille	+	-et / -ette	=	gentillet^m / gentillette^f	*(somewhat nice)*
jaune^{m,f} *(yellow)*	jaune	+	-et / -ette	=	jaunet^m / jaunette^f	*(yellowish)*
molle^f *(soft)*	molle	+	-et / -ette	=	mollet^m / mollette^f	*(somewhat soft)*

In addition, some verbs take on the suffix "**-et**" or "**-ette**" to form a noun that is related to the verb, for example:

jouer *(to play)*	jouer	+	-et	=	jouet^m *(toy)*
sonner *(to ring)*	sonner	+	-ette	=	sonnette^m *(bell)*
fumer *(to smoke)*	fumer	+	-et	=	fumet^m *(aroma)*

Finally, some given names, especially female names, take the suffix "**-et**" or "**-ette**" to form diminutive forms, for example:

Marie	Marie	+	-ette	=	Mariette
Anne	Anne	+	-ette	=	Annette
Jeanne	Jeanne	+	-ette	=	Jeannette

Other less common diminutives in French include: "-ot," "-otte," and "-on." Here are some examples:

Pierre	Pierre	+	-ot	=	Pierrot
chat^m (cat)	chat	+	-on	=	chaton^m (kitten)
ours^m (bear)	ours	+	-on	=	ourson^m (cub)

2. Augmentatives

Augmentatives are the opposite of diminutives. They indicate that something is large or intense, sometimes in an undesirable way. Augmentatives can apply to nouns and adjectives. In the English language, although not as versatile and common, augmentatives are formed by using prefixes rather than suffixes. You can think of the prefix *"super-"* in *"superpower"* and *"supernatural,"* the prefix *"mega-"* in *"megaphone"* and *"megastore,"* the prefix *"grand-"* in *"grandmaster"* and *"grandfather,"* the prefix *"over-"* in *"overgrown"* and *"overqualified,"* and the prefix *"arch-"* in *"archrival"* and *"archenemy."*

Spanish Augmentative Suffixes:

In Spanish, we use suffixes, such as: "-**ón**/-**ona**," "-**azo**/-**aza**," "-**ote**/-**ota**," "-**udo**/-**uda**," and "-**achón**/-**achona**," to form augmentatives. Unfortunately, there are no rules to guess which suffix to use. Practice is the only way. Thus, we will classify the augmentatives based on the meaning they convey rather than the suffix they use.

1. Augmentatives that indicate a large size

Some examples in this category include:

perro^m (dog)	perro	+	-ote	=	perrote^m (big or mean dog)
			-azo	=	perrazo^m (big or mean dog)
hombre^m (man)	hombre	+	-ón	=	hombrón^m (big strong man)

| casa[f] *(house)* | casa | + | -ona | = | casona[f] *(big house)* |
| animal[m] *(animal)* | animal | + | -ote | = | animalote[m] *(big or nasty animal)* |

2. Augmentatives that indicate intensity

Some examples in this category include:

bueno[m] *(good)*	bueno	+	-azo	=	buenazo[m] *(good-natured)*
éxito[m] *(success)*	éxito	+	-azo	=	exitazo[m] *(great success)*
coche[m] *(car)*	coche	+	-azo	=	cochazo[m] *(amazing car)*
película[f] *(movie)*	película	+	-ón	=	peliculón[m] *(blockbuster)*

3. Augmentatives that indicate a strike or blow

The suffix "**-azo**" is often used to form masculine words that refer to a specific type of strike, hit, or blow. Examples in this category include:

codo[m] *(elbow)*	codo	+	-azo	=	codazo[m] *(elbow jab)*
cabeza[f] *(head)*	cabeza	+	-azo	=	cabezazo[m] *(headbutt)*
martillo[m] *(hammer)*	martillo	+	-azo	=	martillazo[m] *(hammer blow)*
misil[m] *(missile)*	misil	+	-azo	=	misilazo[m] *(missile strike)*

4. Augmentatives that form new words

In some cases, new words with their own meanings can be formed using augmentatives. Examples in this category include:

silla[f] *(chair)*	silla	+ -ón	=	sillón[m] *(armchair)*
cintura[f] *(waist)*	cintura	+ -ón	=	cinturón[m] *(belt)*
rata[f] *(rat)*	rata	+ -ón	=	ratón[m] *(mouse)*
caja[f] *(box)*	caja	+ -ón	=	cajón[m] *(drawer)*
papel[m] *(paper)*	papel	+ -ote	=	papelote[m] *(worthless[1] paper)*

---

[1] This can be literal or figurative.

Notice that in some cases, the augmentative word changes gender, often from feminine to masculine, as in the feminine words "**película**," "**silla**," and "**rata**," the augmentatives of which are masculine: "**peliculón**," "**sillón**," and "**ratón**," respectively.

Some words have multiple augmentative forms. These forms may convey the same meaning or a different meaning. For example, the augmentatives "**cabezón**," "**cabezote**," and "**cabezudo**" all mean *stubborn* or *big-headed*, literally or figuratively, formed from the word "**cabeza**" *(head)*. On the other hand, the augmentative "**cabezazo**," also formed from the word "**cabeza**," has a different meaning, that is, a *headbutt* or a *header* (in sports).

In addition to the dropping of "**o**" or "**a**" to avoid the double vowel, some words undergo some minor changes, such as the "**ue**" change to "**o**" in "**cordón**" *(shoelace)*, "**portazo**" *(door slam)*, and "**fortachón**" *(beefy)*, augmentatives of "**cuerda**" *(rope or string)*, "**puerta**" *(door)*, and "**fuerte**" *(strong)*, respectively.

Finally, some words remain hard to guess and must be learned by practice, such as "**grandullón**" *(overgrown)* and "**favorzote**" *(huge favor)*, augmentatives of "**grande**" *(big)* and "**favor**" *(favor)*, respectively.

Portuguese Augmentative Suffixes:

In Portuguese, the most common suffix to form augmentatives is "**-ão**" for the masculine and "**-ona**" for the feminine. We will classify the augmentatives based on the ending of the noun or adjective:

1. Nouns and adjectives that end with unstressed "**-a**," "**-e**," or "**-o**" (except "**-io**" and "**-ia**")

These words drop the final unstressed vowel, then add "**-ão**" if the word is masculine or "**-ona**" if the word is feminine.

Some examples in this category include:

livro^m *(book)*	livr~~o~~	+	-ão	=	livrão^m *(large book)*
mesa^f *(table)*	mes~~a~~	+	-ona	=	mesona^f *(large table)*
peixe^m *(fish)*	peix~~e~~	+	-ão	=	peixão^m *(big fish)*
bonito^m *(pretty)*	bonit~~o~~	+	-ão	=	bonitão^m *(very handsome)*
			-ona	=	bonitona^f *(very pretty)*

2. Nouns and adjectives with other endings (including "-**io**," "-**ia**", and stressed "-**a**," "-**e**," or "-**o**")

Most words in this group simply add "-**zão**" if the word is masculine or "-**zona**" if the word is feminine.

Some examples in this category include:

sol^m *(sun)*	sol	+	-zão	=	sol**zão**^m *(very hot or bright son)*
pai^m *(father)*	pai	+	-zão	=	pai**zão**^m *(dedicated father)*
mãe^f *(mother)*	mãe		-zona		mãe**zona**^f *(dedicated mother)*
tio^m *(uncle)*	tio	+	-zão	=	tio**zão**^m *(dedicated uncle)*
pé^m *(foot)*	pé	+	-zão	=	pe**zão**^m *(big foot)*

Notice also that the stress is always on the augmentative ending. Thus, any written accent is dropped except accents that denote nasal sound, e.g., "**pẹzão**" *(big foot)*.

As an exception to words in this category, some nouns and adjectives ending in "-**l**" or "-**r**" add a final "-**ão/-ona**" to form the augmentative instead of "-**zão/-zona**," e.g., "**colherona**^f" *(large spoon)*, i.e., the augmentative of "**colher**^f" *(spoon)*.

In some cases, feminine nouns have masculine gender in the augmentatives. For example:

cabeça^f *(head)*	cabeça	+ -ão	=	cabeç**ão**^m *(big head)*
mão^f *(hand)*	mão	+ -zão	=	mão**zão**^m *(big hand)*

Some words do not follow the above rules and must be learned by practice, such as "**casarão**" *(big house)* and "**vozeirão**" *(powerful voice)*, augmentatives of "**casa**" *(house)* and "**voz**" *(voice)*, respectively.

Another less common suffix in the augmentative is "-**aço**." The most common examples are:

gol^m *(goal)*	gol	+	-aço	=	gol**aço**^m *(great goal)*
jogo^m *(game)*	jogo	+	-aço	=	jog**aço**^f *(great game)*

Italian Augmentative Suffixes:

In Italian, we mainly use the suffix "-**one**," and in less common cases "-**ona**," to form augmentatives. It is common for many feminine nouns to change their gender to masculine and take the suffix "-**one**" to form the augmentative. To form the augmentative, the final vowel is dropped, and the suffix is added.

Let us take some examples:

ragazzo^m *(boy)*	ragazzo	+	-one	=	ragazzone^m *(very tall boy)*
casa^f *(house)*	casa	+	-one	=	casone^m *(big house)*
libro^m *(book)*	libro	+	-one	=	librone^m *(very large book)*
porta^f *(door)*	porta	+	-one	=	portone^m *(main gate or entrance)*
donna^f *(woman)*	donna	+	-one	=	donnone^m *(very tall woman)*
sorella^f *(sister)*	sorella	+	-ona	=	sorellona^f *(big sister)*

While these are the most common suffixes, there are some less-common suffixes, some of which may also have a pejorative or sarcastic connotation, such as "-**accione**" and "-**acchione**." For example:

buono^m *(good)*	buono	+	-accione	=	bonaccione^m *(good-natured)*
matto^m *(mad)*	matto	+	-acchione	=	mattacchione^m *(joker)*
furbo^m *(cunning)*	furbo	+	-acchione	=	furbacchione^m *(slick)*

Notice that the above examples are of singular nouns. The plural is often regular and formed by changing the ending to "-**i**" for masculine plural, e.g., "**casoni**" *(big houses)* and "-**e**" for feminine plural, e.g., "**sorellone**" *(big sisters)*.

French Augmentative Suffixes:

In French, it is uncommon to use augmentative suffixes. Instead, similar prefixes to the ones used in English are sometimes used with some words, such as: "**supermarché**" *(supermarket)*, "**surhumain**" *(superhuman)*, "**hyperactif**" *(hyperactive)*, etc.

8. THE PAST INFINITIVE

The past infinitive is formed as follows:

SP	"**haber**" in the infinitive	
PT	"**ter**" or "**haver**" in the infinitive	+ past participle
IT	"**avere**" or "**essere**" in the infinitive	
FR	"**avoir**" or "**être**" in the infinitive	

It is equivalent to the English combination of *"having"* followed by the past participle, e.g., *"having finished," "having eaten,"* etc.

One common use of the past infinitive is when there are two actions in the past and the subject is the same. For example:

SP	Después de **haber terminado** su trabajo, se tomó una semana de descanso.	*After **having finished** his work, he took a week off.*
PT	Depois de **ter terminado** o trabalho, ele tirou uma semana de folga.	
IT	Dopo **aver terminato** il suo lavoro, si è preso una settimana di ferie.	
FR	Après **avoir terminé** son travail, il a pris une semaine de repos.	
SP	Le dijeron que abandonara el lugar por **haber violado** las normas.	*He was told to leave the place for **having violated** the rules.*
PT	Ele foi orientado a deixar o local por **ter violado** as regras.	
IT	Gli è stato detto di lasciare il posto per **aver violato** le regole.	
FR	On lui a demandé de quitter les lieux pour **avoir violé** les règles.	
SP	Después de **haberme ido** anoche, tuve que caminar a casa.	*After **having left** late last night, I had to walk home.*
PT	Depois de **ter saído** tarde ontem à noite, tive que voltar para casa a pé.	
IT	Dopo **essere uscito** tardi ieri sera, sono dovuto tornare a casa a piedi.	
FR	Après **être parti** tard hier soir, j'ai dû rentrer à pied.	

Notice that the infinitive forms **"avere"** and **"essere"** in Italian are often shortened to **"aver"** and **"esser,"** respectively, when used in the past infinitive in daily informal speech.

In addition to this common use of the past infinitive, there is another special use in Italian in the subordinate clause when the verb in the main clause is in the past.

Let us consider the following two examples:

| Penso di **guidare** molto. | *I think that I **drive** a lot.* |
| Crede di **cambiare** velocemente. | *He believes that he **changes** fast.* |

Notice that both examples are in the present tense, and that the subject is the same in the main clause and the subordinate clause. In Italian, unlike in English where the subject is repeated, we use the infinitive preceded by **"di"** to avoid repeating the subject.

Now, consider the case when the subordinate clause in the two examples is in the past instead of the present. In this case, the past infinitive is used instead of the infinitive. For example:

| Pensavo di **aver guidato** molto. | *I thought that I **had driven** a lot.* |
| Crede di **essere cambiato** velocemente. | *He believes that he **changed** fast.* |

Notice that only the verb in the subordinate clause must be in the past to use the past infinitive, whereas the verb in the main clause can be in the present or in the past.

We can also use the past infinitive in cases where we would normally use the infinitive in English, if the action referred to by the infinitive is in the past. Here are some examples in Italian:

| Grazie per **aver**mi **invitato.** | *Thank you for **inviting** me.* |
| Mi dispiace di **essere andato** via prima ieri sera. | *I'm sorry for **leaving** early last night.* |

Notice that the actions that the past infinitive refers to in both examples are understood to be in the past. Notice also that a pronoun can be attached to the end of **"avere"** or **"essere."**

REFERENCES

The following is a list of references that we found useful in writing this book:

Sagar-Fenton, Beth & McNeill, Lizzy (2018). How many words do you need to speak a language? Retrieved from
https://www.bbc.com/news/world-44569277

Nation, Paul & Waring, Robert (1997). Vocabulary Size, Text Coverage, and Word Lists, by Paul Nation and Robert Waring. Retrieved from
https://www.lextutor.ca/research/nation_waring_97.html

Francis, W. N., Kucera, H., Kučera, H., & Mackie, A. W. (1982). Frequency analysis of English usage: Lexicon and grammar. Houghton Mifflin.

Nation, Paul. (2019). 4000 Essential English Words 1-6. Compass Publishing.

Foreign Service Institute (FSI)
https://www.state.gov/foreign-language-training/

Anki Webpage
https://apps.ankiweb.net/

Vermeer, Alex. (2017). Anki Essentials v1.1: The complete guide to remembering anything with Anki [Kindle edition].

Real Academia Española (RAE)
https://www.rae.es/

Toledano, C. A. (2005). Pitman's Commercial Spanish Grammar (2nd edition). Project Gutenberg.

Madrigal, Margarita (1989). Madrigal's Magic Key to Spanish: A Creative and Proven Approach. Broadway Books.

Bregstein, Barbara (2020). Easy Spanish Step-by-Step (2nd edition). McGraw Hill.

Vilaplana, Cynthia (2017). Argentine Spanish: A Guide to Speaking Like an Argentine: The Complete Lessons [Kindle edition].

Whitlam, John. (2011). Modern Brazilian Portuguese Grammar: A Practical Guide. Routledge.

Hutchinson, Amélia and Lloyd, Janet. (2003). Portuguese: An Essential Grammar (2nd edition). Routledge.

Danesi, Marcel. (2016). Complete Italian Grammar (2nd edition). McGraw Hill.

Battista, J. L. (2014). Essentials of Italian Grammar. Harvard University Press.

Petrunin, Mikhail. (2018). Comparative Grammar of Spanish, Portuguese, Italian, and French. McGraw Hill.

Heminway, Annie. (2008). Complete French Grammar. McGraw Hill.

APPENDIX

Appendix A. Coupon Code for Free Flashcards

The Anki flashcards that accompany this book are available for free until December 31, 2024. Once you download the cards and back them up with the Anki account you create, the cards do not expire.

To download the free flashcards that accompany this book:

1. Visit the ADROS VERSE EDUCATION website at: https://www.adrosverse.com/books-and-flashcards/
2. Add the product "**Spanish/Portuguese/Italian/French: Level I - Basic**" Anki Flashcards to the *Shopping Cart*.
3. Go to the *Shopping Cart* and use the following Coupon Code:

AMZNAVERL4Q

4. Proceed to *Checkout* and place your order.
5. Download the flashcards in ".zip" format and extract the ".apkg" files.

Appendix B. Verb Tenses and Conjugation Charts

For each language, we provide two useful cheat sheets that give you an overall perspective of most moods and verb tenses.

The two sheets are available **in color** in pdf format on the resources page of our website at https://www.adrosverse.com/resources/

The first cheat sheet is the Verb Conjugation Chart, which is structured as a comprehensive reference for the reader.

The second sheet dives into the irregular verbs of each tense, where applicable.

We recommend that you keep these two sheets handy by printing them out or having them available separately on your desk or electronic device.

VERB CONJUGATION CHART

SP

CONDITIONAL

CONDITIONAL PERFECT

Yo habría hablado (I would have spoken)

Same past participle irregulars discussed in the indicative present perfect.	**Irregular** **Regular**	habría habrías había + past participle habríamos habríais habrían

SIMPLE CONDITIONAL

Yo hablaría (I would speak)

Same irregular verbs in the simple future: decir, haber, hacer, poder, poner, querer, saber, salir, caber, tener, venir, valer.	**Irregular** **Regular**	-ía -ías -ía -íamos -íais -ían

*Add one of the above endings to the infinitive

INDICATIVE

FUTURE PERFECT

Yo habré hablado (I will have spoken)

habré habrás habrá + past participle habremos habréis habrán	**Regular** **Irregular**	Same past participle irregulars discussed in the indicative present perfect.

SIMPLE FUTURE

Yo hablaré (I will speak)

-é -ás -á -emos -éis -án	**Regular** **Irregular**	decir, haber, hacer, poder, poner, querer, saber, salir, caber, tener, venir, valer. One can use conjugated "ir" + "a" + infinitive to express the future in informal speech.

*Add one of the above endings to the infinitive

SUBJUNCTIVE

PRESENT

que yo hable (that I speak)						Yo hablo (I speak)				
Irregular verbs: ir dar ser estar saber haber as well some verbs with orthographic-only changes	**Irregular** **Regular**	-ar -e -es -e -emos -éis -en	-er/-ir -a -as -a -amos -áis -an			-ar -o -as -a -amos -áis -an	-er -o -es -e -emos -éis -en	-ir -o -es -e -imos -ís -en	**Regular** **Irregular**	e → ie, e.g. pensar (pienso) o → ue, e.g. poder (puedo) e → i, e.g. pedir (pido) i → ie, e.g. adquirir (adquiero) u → ue, e.g. jugar (juego) irregular yo form, e.g. dar (doy) others: ir, ser, oler, oír

*Stem formed from third-person singular by dropping "-o"

PRESENT PERFECT

que yo haya hablado (that I have spoken)			Yo he hablado (I have spoken)		
Same past participle irregulars discussed in the indicative present perfect	**Irregular** **Regular**	haya hayas haya + past participle hayamos hayáis hayan	he has ha + past participle hemos habéis han	**Regular** **Irregular**	Regular past participle: -ado (-ar verbs), -ido (-er/-ir verbs). Irregular verbs: abrir, cubrir, decir, escribir, hacer, imprimir, morir, poner, resolver, romper, ver, volver.

PROGRESSIVE TENSES

Progressive tenses are formed by adding the proper conjugation of the verb "estar" to the gerund:

Present Progressive: Yo estoy hablando (I am speaking)
Past Progressive: Yo estaba hablando (I was speaking)
Future Progressive: Yo estaré hablando (I will be speaking)
Conditional Progressive: Yo estaría hablando (I would be speaking)

PRETERITE

Yo hablé (I spoke)

-ar -é -aste -ó -amos -asteis -aron	-er/-ir -í -iste -ió -imos -isteis -ieron	**Regular** **Irregular**	andar, conducir, dar, decir, estar, hacer, ir, poder, poner, querer, saber, ser, tener, traer, venir, ver, as well as some other verbs with orthographic changes.

IMPERFECT

que yo hablara (that I spoke) or que yo hablase				Yo hablaba (I spoke)			
No irregular verbs: Either set of verb endings can be used for conjugation.	**Irregular** **Regular**	-ra -ras -ra -ramos -rais -ran	-se -ses -se -semos -seis -sen	-ar -aba -abas -aba -ábamos -abais -aban	-er/-ir -ía -ías -ía -íamos -íais -ían	**Regular** **Irregular**	Only three irregular verbs: ir ser ver

*Stem formed from third-person plural by dropping "-ron"

PLUPERFECT

que yo hubiera hablado (that I had spoken) or que yo hubiese hablado				Yo había hablado (I had spoken)		
Same past participle irregulars in the indicative present perfect.	**Irregular** **Regular**	hubiera hubieras hubiera or hubiéramos hubierais hubieran	hubiese hubieses hubiese + past participle hubiésemos hubieseis hubiesen	había habías había + past participle habíamos habíais habían	**Regular** **Irregular**	Same past participle irregulars discussed in the indicative present perfect.

FUTURE

PRESENT

PAST

IRREGULAR VERBS

PRESENT INDICATIVE TENSE

1. Irregular in the "yo" form only
"-oy": estar (estoy), dar (doy)
"-go": hacer (hago), poner (pongo), valer (valgo), salir (salgo), traer (traigo), caer (caigo)
"-cer"/"-cir": conocer (conozco), ofrecer (ofrezco), conducir (conduzco), traducir (traduzco)
Completely irregular in the "yo" form:
saber (sé), caber (quepo), ver (veo)

2. Stem change except "nosotros/-as" & "vosotros/-as"
e → ie: corregir, elegir, medir, pedir, reir, repetir, seguir, servir
e → i: advertir, atender, atravesar, calentar, cerrar, comenzar, confesar, convertir, defender, divertir, empezar, encender, entender, enterrar, fregar, herir, hervir, mentir, negar, pensar, perder, preferir, querer, regar, sugerir, temblar, tropezar, verter
o → ue: acordar, almorzar, aprobar, contar, costar, dormir, encontrar, forzar, morder, mostrar, poder, probar, volar, volver
u → ue: jugar
i → ie: adquirir, inquirir

3. Irregular in the "yo" form with "-go" ending + Stem change in all other forms except "nosotros/-as" & "vosotros/-as":
decir (digo, dice), venir (vengo, viene), tener (tengo, tiene)

4. Completely irregular verbs: ser, ir, oler, oír

5. Orthographic changes only:
"-guir" → "-go": e.g., extenguir (extingo), seguir (sigo)
"-ger"/"-gir" → "-jo": e.g., proteger (protejo), exigir (exijo)
"-quir" → "-co": e.g., delinquir (delinco)
"-uir" (excluding "-guir") add "y" between stem & suffix in all forms except "nosotros/-as" & "vosotros/-as":
atribuir (atribuyo, atribuye), construir (construyo, construye), contribuir (contribuyo, contribuye), disminuir (disminuyo, disminuye), distribuir (distribuyo, distribuye), huir (huyo, huye), incluir (incluyo, incluye), sustituir (sutituyo, sustituye)
Some "-iar" & "-uar" ending verbs add an accent to "i" or "u" before conjugation suffix in all forms except "nosotros/-as" & "vosotros/-as":
enviar (envío, envía), fiar (fío, fía), liar (lio, lía), variar (vario, varia), actuar (actúo, actúa), continuar (continúo, continúa), habituar (habitúo, habitúa), situar (sitúo, sitúa)

PRESENT SUBJUNCTIVE TENSE

Only 6 irregular verbs:
ser: sea, seas, sea, seamos, seáis, sean
estar: esté, estés, esté, estemos, estéis, estén
ir: vaya, vayas, vaya, vayamos, vayáis, vayan
haber: haya, hayas, haya, hayamos, hayáis, hayan
saber: sepa, sepas, sepa, sepamos, sepáis, sepan
dar: dé, des, dé, demos, deis, den

GERUND

1. ir → yendo

2. "-iendo" → "-yendo"
"-er" or "-ir" with stem the ending in a vowel
leer → leyendo, atraer → atrayendo, destruir → destruyendo, huir → huyendo

3. e → i: decir → diciendo, pedir → pidiendo

4. o → u: dormir → durmiendo, morir → muriendo

5. "-iendo" → "-endo"
"-er" or "-ir" with stem the ending in "-ll" or "-ñ"
bullir → bullendo, mullir → mullendo, tenir → tiñendo

PRETERITE TENSE

1. Verbs ending in "-ducir" + "decir" & "traer"

"-ducir" → "-duj-": conducir (conduj-), traducir (traduj-), producir (produj-), reducir (reduj-), introducir (introduj-), deducir (deduj-), seducir (seduj-)
"decir" → "dij-" & "traer" → "traj-"

2. Verbs "estar", "tener" & "andar"
"estar" → "estuv-", "tener" → "tuv-", "andar" → "anduv-"
e → ie: corregir, elegir, medir, pedir, reir, repetir, seguir, servir

3. Verbs that change first vowel from "a" or "o" to "u"
a → u: haber (hub-), poder (pud-)
o → u: poner (pus-), saber (sup-), caber (cup-)

4. Verbs that change the stem in the 3rd person
e → i: pedir (pidió), mentir (mintió), sentir (sintió), seguir (siguió), servir (sirvió), hervir (hirvió), preferir (prefirió), convertir (convirtió), despedir (despidió), impedir (impidió), divertir (divirtió), sugerir (sugirió), vestir (vistió), repetir (repitió), reir (rió)
o → u: dormir (durmió), morir (murió)
"final stem vowel" → "y": caer (cayó), leer (leyó), roer (royó), oír (oyó), influir (influyó), concluir (concluyó)

5. Verbs "venir" & "querer"
irregular: "venir" → "vin-", "querer" → "quis-"

6. Verbs "ser", "ir", "dar" & "ver"
Irregular and do not follow a specific rule.
ser/ir (for both verbs): fui, fuiste, fue, fuimos, fuisteis, fueron
dar: di, diste, dio, dimos, disteis, dieron
ver: vi, viste, vio, vimos, visteis, vieron

IMPERFECT TENSE

Only 3 completely irregular verbs:
ser: era, eras, era, éramos, erais, eran
ir: iba, ibas, iba, íbamos, ibais, iban
ver: veía, veías, veía, veíamos, veíais, veían

FUTURE INDICATIVE TENSE

1. Some verbs ending in "-er" and "-ir" drop the "e" or the "i" and add a "d" to the stem:
tener → tendr-, poner → pondr-, valer → valdr-, venir → vendr-, salir → saldr-

2. Some verbs ending in "-er" drop the "e" from the stem:
saber → sabr-, poder → podr-, caber → cabr-, querer → querr-, haber → habr-

3. Verbs "decir" & "hacer"
decir → dir-, hacer → har-

IMPERATIVE

Only 8 completely irregular verbs:
ser (sé), ir (ve), venir (ven), tener (ten), decir (di), hacer (haz), poner (pon), salir (sal)

PAST PARTICIPLE

abrir (abierto), absolver (absuelto), cubrir (cubierto), decir (dicho), escribir (escrito), freir (frito), hacer (hecho), imprimir (impreso), morir (muerto), poner (puesto), proveer (provisto), resolver (resuelto), romper (roto), satisfacer (satisfecho), ver (visto), volver (vuelto)

VERB CONJUGATION CHART

FUTURE → PRESENT → PAST

CONDITIONAL

SIMPLE
Eu falaria (I would speak)

-ia	Same irregular verbs in the
-ia	simple future: dizer → dir-,
-íamos	fazer → far-, trazaer → trar-
-iam	

*Add one of these endings to the infinitive

PERFECT
Eu teria falado (I would've spoken)

teria
teria
teríamos + past participle
teriam

INDICATIVE

FUTURE PERFECT
Eu terei falado (I will have spoken)

	Regular	Irregular
terei		Same past participle
terá		irregulars discussed in the
teremos + past participle		present perfect.
terão		

SUBJUNCTIVE

FUTURE

que eu falar (that I will speak)

No irregular verbs.

	Irregular	Regular	
		-	
		-mos	
		-em	

"Stem formed from third-person plural preterite by dropping final "-am"

Eu falarei (I will speak)

	Regular	Irregular
-ei		Irregular verbs are:
-á		dizer → dir-
-emos		fazer → far-
-ão		trazaer → trar-

*Add one of these endings to the infinitive

PRESENT

que eu fale (that I speak)

7 Completely Irregular verbs:
estar: esteja, esteja, estejamos, estejam
dar: dê, dê, dêmos, dêem
ser: seja, seja, sejamos, sejam
saber: saiba, saiba, saibamos, saibam
querer: queira, queira, queiramos, queiram
haver: haja, haja, hajamos, hajam
ir: vá, vá, vamos, vão

		-ar	-er/-ir
		e	a
		e	a
		emos	amos
		em	am

*Stem formed from first-person singular by dropping "-o"

Eu falo (I speak)

-ar	-er	-ir
-o	-o	-o
-a	-e	-e
-amos	-emos	-imos
-am	-em	-em

Completely Irregular Verbs:
-ar: estar, dar
-er: ser, ter, ver, poder, dizer, trazer, fazer, caber, saber, querer, haver, ler, vrer, perder, valer.
-ir: ir, vir, rir, sourir, sair, cair, ouvrir. as well as some other verbs with orthographic changes.

PRESENT PERFECT

que eu tenha falado (that I have spoken)

Same past participle irregulars discussed in the present perfect

	Irregular	Regular	
		tenha	
		tenha	
		tenhamos + past participle	
		tenham	

Eu tenho falado (I have spoken)

	Regular	Irregular
tenho		
tem		
temos + past participle		
têm		

Past participles that have only irregular forms:
abrir, cobrir, dizer, escrever, fazer, pôr, ver, vir.

Past participles that have both regular and irregular forms: aceitar, acender, dispersar, eleger, entregar, expressar, exprimir, expulsar, extinguir, fritar, ganhar, gastar, impergir, limpar, matar, pagar, pegar, prender, salvar, soltar, submerger, suprimir, suspender.

PROGRESSIVE TENSES

Progressive tenses are formed by adding the proper conjugation of the verb "estar" to the gerund:

Present Progressive: Eu estou falando (I am speaking)
Past Progressive: Eu estava falando (I was speaking)
Future Progressive: Eu estarei falando (I will be speaking)
Conditional Progressive: Eu estaria falando (I would be speaking)

PRETERITE

Eu falei (I spoke)

-ar	-er	-ir
-ei	-i	-i
-ou	-eu	-iu
-ámos	-emos	-imos
-aram	-eram	-iram

Irregular verbs:
-ar: estar, dar
-ir: ir, vir
-er: ser, ter, ver, poder, dizer, trazer, fazer, caber, saber, querer, haver, pôr

IMPERFECT

que eu falasse (that I spoke)

No irregular verbs.

	Irregular	Regular	
		-sse	
		-sse	
		-ssemos	
		-ssem	

"Stem formed from third-person plural preterite by dropping final "-ram"

Eu falava (I spoke)

-ar	-er/-ir
-ava	-ia
-ava	-ia
-ávamos	-íamos
-avam	-iam

Only 4 irregular verbs.

vir: vinha, vinha, vinhamos, vinham
ter: tinha, tinha, tinhamos, tinham
ser: era, era, éramos, eram
pôr: punha, punha, púnhamos, punham

PLUPERFECT

que eu tivesse falado (that I had spoken)

Same past participle irregulars discussed in the present perfect.

	Irregular	Regular	
		tivesse	
		tivesse	
		tivéssemos + past participle	
		tivessem	

Eu tinha falado (I had spoken)

	Regular	Irregular
tinha		
tinha		Same past participle irregulars
tinhamos + past participle		discussed in the present perfect.
tinham		

PRESENT INDICATIVE TENSE

Completely Irregular Verbs	Minor Stem & Spelling Changes

"-ar" Verbs

estar: estou, está, estamos, estão
dar: dou, dá, damos, dão

In some "-iar" verbs:
e → ie in all forms except "nós"
odiar, ansiar, incendiar, mediar
e.g., odeio, odeia, odiamos, odeiam

"-er" Verbs

ser: sou, é, somos, são
ter: tenho, tem, temos, têm
ver: vejo, vê, vemos, veem
poder: posso, pode, podemos, podem
dizer: digo, diz, dizemos, dizem
trazer: trago, traz, trazemos, trazem
fazer: faço, faz, fazemos, fazem
caber: caibo, cabe, cabemos, cabem
saber: sei, sabe, sabemos, sabem
querer: quero, quer, queremos, querem
haver: hei, há, hemos, hão
ler: leio, lê, lemos, leem
crer: creio, crê, cremos, crêem
perder: perco, perde, perdemos, perdem
valer: valho, vale, valemos, valem

Spelling changes in the "eu" form:
c → ç : vencer, parecer
e.g., venço, vence, vencemos, vencem
g → j : eleger, proteger
e.g., elejo, elege, elegemos, elegem
gu → g : erguer
e.g., ergo, ergue, erguemos, erguem

"-ir" Verbs

ir: vou, vai, vamos, vão
vir: venho, vem, vimos, vêm
rir: rio, ri, rimos, riem
sourir: sourio, souri, sourimos, souriem
sair: saio, sai, saímos, saem
cair: caio, cai, caímos, caem
ouvrir: ouço, ouve, ouvimos, ouvem

1. Stem Changes
e → i : mentir, servir, repetir, prevenir
o → u : vencer, parecer, dormir, cobrir
u → o : subir, fugir, cuspir, sacudir
2. Spelling Changes
c → ç : e.g., ressarcir → eu ressarço
g → j : e.g., dirigir → eu dirijo
gu → g : e.g., seguir → eu sigo
3. Some "-dir" verbs change d → ç :
pedir, medir, despedir
4. Many "-zir" verbs have no ending in
third-person singular, e.g., conduzir,
deduzir, introduzir, produzir, traduzir.
5. Some "-buir" & "-truir" verbs are
irregular, e.g, construir, destruir.

PRESENT SUBJUNCTIVE TENSE

7 completely irregular verbs:
estar: esteja, esteja, estejamos, estejam
dar: dê, dê, dêmos, dêem
ser: seja, seja, sejamos, sejam
saber: saiba, saiba, saibamos, saibam
querer: queira, queira, queiramos, queiram
haver: haja, haja, hajamos, hajam
ir: vá, vá, vamos, vão

* Remember to use the stem from the first-person "eu" form in the
present indicative, not the stem from the infinitive, e.g., "ter" → "tenh-"

IMPERATIVE

Only 2 irregular verbs in the affirmative informal singular:
ser: seja
estar: esteja

PRETERITE TENSE

"-ar" Verbs

estar: estive, esteve, estivemos, estiveram
dar: dei, deu, demos, deram

"-er" Verbs

ser: fui, foi, fomos, foram
ter: tive, teve, tivemos, tiveram
ver: vi, viu, vimos, viram
poder: pude, pôde, pudemos, puderam
dizer: disse, disse, dissemos, disseram
trazer: trouxe, trouxe, trouxemos, trouxeram
fazer: fiz, fez, fizemos, fizeram
caber: coube, coube, coubemos, couberam
saber: soube, soube, soubemos, souberam
querer: quis, quis, quisemos, quiseram
haver: houve, houve, houvemos, houveram
pôr: pus, pôs, pusemos, puseram

"-ir" Verbs

ir: fui, foi, fomos, foram
vir: vim, veio, viemos, vieram

IMPERFECT TENSE

Only 4 irregular verbs:
vir: vinha, vinha, vínhamos, vinham
ter: tinha, tinha, tínhamos, tinham
ser: era, era, éramos, eram
pôr: punha, punha, púnhamos, punham

SIMPLE FUTURE TENSE

Only 3 irregular verbs:
dizer (dir-): direi, dirá, diremos, dirão
fazer (far-): farei, fará, faremos, farão
trazer (trar-): trarei, trará, traremos, trarão

SIMPLE CONDITIONAL TENSE

Only 3 irregular verbs:
dizer (dir-): diria, diria, diríamos, diriam
fazer (far-): faria, faria, faríamos, fariam
trazer (trar-): traria, traria, traríamos, trariam

PAST PARTICIPLE

Past participles that have only irregular forms:
abrir (aberto), cobrir (coberto), dizer (dito), escrever (escrito), fazer
(feito), pôr (posto), ver (visto), vir (vindo).

Past participles that have both regular and irregular forms:
aceitar (aceito), acender (aceso), dispersar (disperso), eleger
(eleito), entregar (entregue), expressar (expresso), exprimir
(expresso), expulsar (expulso), extinguir (extinto), fritar (frito),
ganhar (ganho), gastar (gasto), impergir (imerso), limpar (limpo),
matar (morto), pagar (pago), pegar (pego), prender (preso), salvar
(salvo), soltar (solto), submerger (submerso), suprimir (supresso),
suspender (suspenso).

FUTURE

CONDITIONAL

CONDITIONAL PERFECT

Io avrei parlato (I would have spoken)

Depending on the verb, the auxiliary "avere" or "essere" is used

	"avere"	"essere"	
io	avrei	sarei	
tu	avresti	saresti	
lui/lei	avrebbe	sarebbe	(or) + past participle
noi	avremmo	saremmo	
voi	avreste	sareste	
loro	avrebbero	sarebbero	

SIMPLE CONDITIONAL

Io parlerei (I would speak)

The stem is formed by dropping the final "e" of the verb and change the final "-ar" to "-er" in the case of "-are" verbs., i.e., "parlere"

	-are	-ere	-ire (I)	-ire (II)
io	-ei	-ei	-ei	-ei
tu	-esti	-esti	-esti	-esti
lui/lei	-ebbe	-ebbe	-ebbe	-ebbe
noi	-emmo	-emmo	-emmo	-emmo
voi	-este	-este	-este	-este
loro	-ebbero	-ebbero	-ebbero	-ebbero

INDICATIVE

FUTURE PERFECT

Io avrò parlato (I will have spoken)

Depending on the verb, the auxiliary "avere" or "essere" is used

	"avere"	"essere"	
io	avrò	sarò	
tu	avrai	sarai	
lui/lei	avrà	sarà	(or) + past participle
noi	avremo	saremo	
voi	avrete	sarete	
loro	avranno	saranno	

SIMPLE FUTURE

Io parlerò (I will speak)

The stem is formed by dropping the final "e" of the verb and change the final "-ar" to "-er" in the case of "-are" verbs., i.e., "parlere"

	-are	-ere	-ire (I)	-ire (II)
io	-ò	-ò	-ò	-ò
tu	-ai	-ai	-ai	-ai
lui/lei	-à	-à	-à	-à
noi	-emo	-emo	-emo	-emo
voi	-ete	-ete	-ete	-ete
loro	-anno	-anno	-anno	-anno

SUBJUNCTIVE

PRESENT

che io parli (that I speak)

The stem is formed from the present ind. "io" form, i.e., "io parlare" for all forms except "noi" and "voi"

	-are	-ere	-ire (I)	-ire (II)
io	-i	-a	-a	-a
tu	-i	-a	-a	-a
lui/lei	-i	-a	-a	-a
noi	-iamo	-iamo	-iamo	-iamo
voi	-iate	-iate	-iate	-iate
loro	-ino	-ano	-ano	-ano

Io parlo (I speak)

The stem is formed from the infinitive, i.e., "parlare"

	-are	-ere	-ire (I)	-ire (II)
io	-o	-o	-o	-isco
tu	-i	-i	-i	-isci
lui/lei	-a	-e	-e	-isce
noi	-iamo	-iamo	-iamo	-iamo
voi	-ate	-ete	-ite	-ite
loro	-ano	-ono	-ono	-iscono

PRESENT

PRESENT PERFECT

che io abbia parlato (that I have spoken)

Depending on the verb, the auxiliary "avere" or "essere" is used

	"avere"	"essere"	
io	abbia	sia	
tu	abbia	sia	
lui/lei	abbia	sia	(or) + past participle
noi	abbiamo	siamo	
voi	abbiate	siate	
loro	abbiano	siano	

Io ho parlato (I have spoken)

Depending on the verb, the auxiliary "avere" or "essere" is used

	"avere"	"essere"	
io	ho	sono	
tu	hai	sei	
lui/lei	ha	è	(or) + past participle
noi	abbiamo	siamo	
voi	avete	siete	
loro	hanno	sono	

PROGRESSIVE TENSES

Progressive tenses are formed by adding the proper conjugation of the verb "stare" to the gerund:

Present Progressive:	Io sto parlando (I am speaking)
Past Progressive:	Io stavo parlando (I was speaking)
Future Progressive:	Io starò parlando (I will be speaking)
Conditional Progressive:	Io starei parlando (I would be speaking)

ABSOLUTE PAST

Io parlai (I spoke)

The stem is formed from the infinitive, i.e., "parlare"

	-are	-ere	-ire (I)	-ire (II)
io	-ai	-ei/-etti	-ii	-ii
tu	-asti	-esti	-isti	-isti
lui/lei	-ò	-é/-ette	-ì	-ì
noi	-ammo	-emmo	-immo	-immo
voi	-aste	-este	-iste	-iste
loro	-arono	-erono/-ettero	-irono	-irono

IMPERFECT

che io parlassi (that I spoke)

The stem is formed by dropping the final "-re", i.e., "parlare"

	-are	-ere	-ire (I)	-ire (II)
io	-ssi	-ssi	-ssi	-ssi
tu	-ssi	-ssi	-ssi	-ssi
lui/lei	-sseva	-sseva	-sseva	-sseva
noi	-ssimo	-ssimo	-ssimo	-ssimo
voi	-ste	-ste	-ste	-ste
loro	-ssero	-ssero	-ssero	-ssero

Io parlavo (I spoke)

The stem is formed by dropping the final "-re", i.e., "parlare"

	-are	-ere	-ire (I)	-ire (II)
io	-vo	-vo	-vo	-vo
tu	-vi	-vi	-vi	-vi
lui/lei	-va	-va	-va	-va
noi	-vamo	-vamo	-vamo	-vamo
voi	-vate	-vate	-vate	-vate
loro	-vano	-vano	-vano	-vano

PLUPERFECT

che io avessi parlato (that I had spoken)

Depending on the verb, the auxiliary "avere" or "essere" is used

	"avere"	"essere"	
io	avessi	fossi	
tu	avessi	fossi	
lui/lei	avesse	fosse	(or) + past participle
noi	avessimo	fossimo	
voi	aveste	foste	
loro	avessero	fossero	

Io avevo parlato (I had spoken)

Depending on the verb, the auxiliary "avere" or "essere" is used

	"avere"	"essere"	
io	avevo	ero	
tu	avevi	eri	
lui/lei	aveva	era	(or) + past participle
noi	avevamo	eravamo	
voi	avevate	eravate	
loro	avevano	erano	

PAST

IRREGULAR VERBS

PRESENT INDICATIVE TENSE

1. Completely Irregular Verbs
andare: vado, vai, va, andiamo, andate, vanno
avere: ho, hai, ha, abbiamo, avete, hanno
bere: bevo, bevi, beve, beviamo, bevete, bevono
essere: sono, sei, è, siamo, siete, sono
dare: do, dai, dà, diamo, date, danno
dire: dico, dici, dice, diciamo, dite, dicono
dovere: devo/debbo, devi, deve, dobbiamo, dovete, devono/debbono
fare: faccio, fai, fa, facciamo, fate, fanno
potere: posso, puoi, può, possiamo, potete, possono
sapere: so, sai, sa, sappiamo, sapete, sanno
stare: sto, stai, sta, stiamo, state, stanno
scegliere: scelgo, scegli, sceglie, scegliamo, scegliete, scelgono
uscire: esco, esci, esce, usciamo, uscite, escono
volere: voglio, vuoi, vuole, vogliamo, volete, vogliono

2. Add a "g" to the stem of the verb in the "io" and "loro" forms
salire: salgo, sali, sale, saliamo, salite, salgono
rimanere: rimango, rimani, rimane, rimaniamo, rimanete, rimangono
venire: vengo, vieni, viene*, veniamo, venite, vengono
tenere: tengo, tieni*, tiene*, teniamo, tenete, tengono
Note that the "venire" and "tenere" also change the stem in the "tu" and "lui/lei" forms from "ven-" and "ten-" to "vien-" and "tien-," respectively.

3. Minor Stem Changes
appaire: appaio, appari, appare, appariamo, apparite, appaiono
morire: muoio, muori, muore, moriamo, morite, muoiono
sedere: siedo, siedi, siede, sediamo, sedete, siedono
udire: odo, odi, ode, udiamo, udite, odono

4. Orthographic Changes
Add an "h" in "tu" & "noi" forms: "-care": e.g., cerchi/cerchiamo, "-gare": e.g., paghi/paghiamo
Drop one "i" in "tu" & "noi" forms: "-ciare": e.g., baci/baciamo, "-giare": e.g., mangi/mangiamo, "-gliare": e.g., tagli/tagliamo

5. Contracted Infinitive Verbs ("-rre" Ending)
"-arre":
trarre (tra-), contrarre (contra-), disttrarre (distra-), sottrarre (sottra-)
e.g., trarre (tra-): traggo, trai, trae, traiamo, traete, traggono
"-orre":
porre (pon-), comporre (compon-), esporre (espon-), imporre (impon-)
e.g., porre (pon-): pongo, poni, pone, poniamo, ponete, pongono
"-urre":
tradurre (traduc-), condurre (conduc-), produrre (produc-)
e.g., tradurre (traduc-): traduco, traduci, traduce, traduciamo, traducete, traducono

PRESENT SUBJUNCTIVE TENSE

1. "-are" verbs conjugated like "-ere" & "-ire" verbs
andare: vada, vada, vada, andiamo, andiate*, vadano
fare: faccia, faccia, faccia, facciamo, facciate, facciano
*The "voi" form "andiate" is irregular

2. "-are" verbs conjugated like "-ere" & "-ire" verbs
avere (abbi-): abbia, abbia, abbia, abbiamo, abbiate, abbiano
dare (di-): dia, dia, dia, diamo, diate, diano
essere (si-): sia, sia, sia, siamo, siate, siano
sapere (sappi-): sappia, sappia, sappia, sappiamo, sappiate, sappiano
stare (sti-): stia, stia, stia, stiamo, stiate, stiano
Note that the "voi" form drops an "i" to avoid the double "i" sound

3. Contracted Inf. verbs are conjugated like "-ere" & "-ire" verbs
trarre: tragga, tragga, tragga, traiamo, traiate, traggano
porre: ponga, ponga, ponga, poniamo, poniate, pongano
tradurre: traduca, traduca, traduca, traduciamo, traduciate, traducano
Note that the "voi" form uses stem from infinitive with "-iate" ending

4. Same orthographic changes applied to verbs ending in "-care," "-gare," "-ciare," "-giare," and "-gliare" in the present indicative tense are applied here to maintain the proper pronunciation.

ABSOLUTE PAST

Many irregular verbs, most of which are "-ere" verbs:
avere, bere, cadere, chiedere, chiudere, conoscere, correggere, dare, decidere, dire, discutere, essere, fare, leggere, mettere, nascere, perdere, piacere, prendere, ridere, sapere, scegliere, scendere, scrivere, stare, vedere, venire, vincere, volere

FUTURE INDICATIVE TENSE

1. Stem formed by dropping final "e" & the vowel before final "r"
andare (andr-): andrò, andrai, andrà, andremo, andrete, andranno
avere (avr-): avrò, avrai, avrà, avremo, avrete, avranno
cadere (cadr-): cadrò, cadrai, cadrà, cadremo, cadrete, cadranno
dovere (dovr-): dovrò, dovrai, dovrà, dovremo, dovrete, dovranno
potere (potr-): potrò, potrai, potrà, potremo, potrete, potranno
2. Stem of some short "-are" verbs does not chnage "-ar" to "-er"
dare (dar-): darò, darai, darà, daremo, darete, daranno
fare (far-): farò, farai, farà, faremo, farete, faranno
stare (star-): cadrò, cadrai, cadrà, cadremo, cadrete, cadranno
3. Stem replaces the consonant & vowel preceding the final "r" with an extra "r" to form "rr-" ending stem
tenere (terr-): terrò, terrai, terrà, terremo, terrete, terranno
volere (vorr-): vorrò, vorrai, vorrà, vorremo, vorrete, vorranno
venire (verr-): verrò, verrai, verrà, verremo, verrete, verranno
4. Completely Irregular Verbs
essere (sar-): sarò, sarai, sarà, saremo, sarete, saranno
bere (berr-): berrò, berrai, berrà, berremo, berrete, berranno
5. Same orthographic changes applied to verbs ending in "-care," "-gare," "-ciare," "-giare," and "-gliare" in the present indicative tense are applied here to maintain the proper pronunciation.

SIMPLE CONDITIONAL TENSE

Same irregular verbs as in the future indicative tense.

IMPERATIVE INDICATIVE TENSE

Most common irregular verbs:
bere: bevevo, bevevi, beveva, bevevamo, bevevate, bevevano
dare: davo, davi, dava, davamo, davate, davano
dire: dicevo, dicevi, diceva, dicevamo, dicevate, dicevano
essere: ero, eri, era, eravamo, eravate, erano
fare: facevo, facevi, faceva, facevamo, facevate, facevano
stare: stavo, stavi, stava, stavamo, stavate, stavano

IMPERATIVE SUBJUNCTIVE TENSE

Most common irregular verbs:
bere: bevessi, bevessi, bevesse, bevessimo, beveste, bevessero
dare: dessi, dessi, desse, dessimo, deste, dessero
dire: dicessi, dicess, dicesse, dicessimo, diceste, dicessero
essere: fossi, fossi, fosse, fossimo, foste, fossero
fare: facessi, facessi, facesse, facessimo, faceste, facessero
stare: stessi, stessi, stesse, stessimo, steste, stessero

IMPERATIVE

1. Singular Informal (i.e., "tu" form)
essere (sii), andare (vai/va'), avere (abbi), dire (di'), fare (fai/fa'), stare (stai/sta')
2. Singular Formal (i.e., "Lei" form)
essere (sia), andare (vada), avere (abbia), dare (dia), dire (dica), fare (faccia), stare (stia), uscire (esca), venire (venga)
3. Plural Informal (i.e., "voi" form)
essere (siate), avere (abbiate)
4. Plural Formal (i.e., "Loro" form)
essere (siano), avere (abbiano)

PAST PARTICIPLE

accendere (acceso), aprire (aperto), bere (bevuto), chiedere (chiesto), chiudere (chiuso), coprire (coperto), correre (corso), cuocere (cotto), decidere (deciso), dire (detto), discutere (discusso), dividere (diviso), fare (fatto), friggere (fritto), leggere (letto), mettere (messo), morire (morto), nascere (nato), offendere (offeso), perdere (perso/perduto), piangere (pianto), porre (posto), ridere (riso), rimanere (rimasto), risolvere (risolto), rompere (rotto), soddisfare (soddisfatto), scegliere (scelto), scendere (sceso), scrivere (scritto), soffrire (sofferto), spegnere (spento), stare (stato), tradurre (tradotto), vedere (visto/veduto), venire (venuto), vincere (vinto), vivere (vissuto)

VERB CONJUGATION CHART

CONDITIONAL

CONDITIONAL PERFECT

J'aurais parlé (I would have spoken)

The regular past participle is formed from the infinitive stem. In case of "être" conjugation, the past participle must agree in gender and number with the subject.

		-er	-ir	-re
je	aurais/serais	-é	-i	-u
tu	aurais/serais	-é	-i	-u
il/elle/on	aurait/serait	-é	-i	-u
nous	aurions/serions	-é	-i	-u
vous	auriez/seriez	-é	-i	-u
ils/elles	auraient/seraient	-é	-i	-u

SIMPLE CONDITIONAL

Je parlerais (I would speak)

The infinitive is used as a stem. In case of "-re" verbs, the final "-e" is dropped. The same suffixes are used for the three verb groups:

	-er	-ir	-re
je	-ais	-ais	-ais
tu	-ais	-ais	-ais
il/elle/on	-ait	-ait	-ait
nous	-ions	-ions	-ions
vous	-iez	-iez	-iez
ils/elles	-aient	-aient	-aient

INDICATIVE

FUTURE PERFECT

J'aurai parlé (I will have spoken)

The regular past participle is formed from the infinitive stem. In case of "être" conjugation, the past participle must agree in gender and number with the subject.

		-er	-ir	-re
je	aurai/serai	-é	-i	-u
tu	auras/seras	-é	-i	-u
il/elle/on	aura/sera	-é	-i	-u
nous	aurons/serons	-é	-i	-u
vous	aurez/serez	-é	-i	-u
ils/elles	auront/seront	-é	-i	-u

SIMPLE FUTURE

Je parlerai (I will speak)

The infinitive is used as a stem. In case of "-re" verbs, the final "-e" is dropped. The same suffixes are used for the three verb groups:

	-er	-ir	-re
je	-ai	-ai	-ai
tu	-as	-as	-as
il/elle/on	-a	-a	-a
nous	-ons	-ons	-ons
vous	-ez	-ez	-ez
ils/elles	-ont	-ont	-ont

SUBJUNCTIVE

PRESENT

que je parle (that I speak)

The stem is formed from the "ils/elles" form, by removing the final "-ent." For the "nous" & "vous" conjugations, the stem is formed from "nous" form by removing the final "-ons." The same suffixes are used for the three verb groups:

	-er	-ir	-re
je	-e	-e	-e
tu	-es	-es	-es
il/elle/on	-e	-e	-e
nous	-ions	-ions	-ions
vous	-iez	-iez	-iez
ils/elles	-ent	-ent	-ent

Je parle (I speak)

The stem is formed from the infinitive, by removing the final "-er," "-ir," or "-re." Regular verbs take the following suffixes:

	-er	-ir	-re
je	-e	-is	-s
tu	-es	-is	-s
il/elle/on	-e	-it	
nous	-ons	-issons	-ons
vous	-ez	-issez	-ez
ils/elles	-ent	-issent	-ent

COMPOUND PAST

que j'aie parlé (that I spoke/ have spoken)

The regular past participle is formed from the infinitive stem. In case of "être" conjugation, the past participle must agree in gender and number with the subject.

		-er	-ir	-re
je	aie/sois	-é	-i	-u
tu	aies/sois	-é	-i	-u
il/elle/on	ait/soit	-é	-i	-u
nous	ayons/soyons	-é	-i	-u
vous	ayez/soyez	-é	-i	-u
ils/elles	aient/soient	-é	-i	-u

J'ai parlé (I spoke/ have spoken)

The regular past participle is formed from the infinitive stem. In case of "être" conjugation, the past participle must agree in gender and number with the subject.

		-er	-ir	-re
je	ai/suis	-é	-i	-u
tu	as/es	-é	-i	-u
il/elle/on	a/est	-é	-i	-u
nous	avons/sommes	-é	-i	-u
vous	avez/êtes	-é	-i	-u
ils/elles	ont/sont	-é	-i	-u

PROGRESSIVE TENSES

The French language does not have a present or past continuous tense equivalent to that in English, e.g., "I am/was speaking." It is common to use the simple present tense in French to talk about actions that are happening right now, e.g., "**Je parle**" (I am talking).

To emphasize the continuous state of an action, one could use the expression "**être en train de**" (to be in the process of), e.g., "**Je suis en train de parler**" (I am speaking).

SIMPLE PAST

Je parlai (I spoke)

The stem is formed from the infinitive, by removing the final "-er," "-ir," or "-re." Regular verbs take the following suffixes:

	-er	-ir	-re
je	-ai	-is	-is
tu	-as	-is	-is
il/elle/on	-a	-it	-it
nous	-âmes	-îmes	-îmes
vous	-âtes	-îtes	-îtes
ils/elles	-èrent	-irent	-irent

IMPERFECT

Je parlais (I spoke)

The stem is formed from the "nous" form, by removing the final "-ons." The same suffixes are used for the three verb groups:

	-er	-ir	-re
je	-ais	-ais	-ais
tu	-ais	-ais	-ais
il/elle/on	-ait	-ait	-ait
nous	-ions	-ions	-ions
vous	-iez	-iez	-iez
ils/elles	-aient	-aient	-aient

PLUPERFECT

J'avait parlé (I had spoken)

The regular past participle is formed from the infinitive stem. In case of "être" conjugation, the past participle must agree in gender and number with the subject.

		-er	-ir	-re
je	avais/étais	-é	-i	-u
tu	avais/étais	-é	-i	-u
il/elle/on	avait/était	-é	-i	-u
nous	avions/étions	-é	-i	-u
vous	aviez/étiez	-é	-i	-u
ils/elles	avaient/étaient	-é	-i	-u

The Imperfect Subjunctive & the Pluperfect Subjunctive tense are mostly a literary tenses, and rarely used in daily spoken language.

IRREGULAR VERBS

PRESENT INDICATIVE TENSE

******-er Verbs******

1. Only one completely irregular "-er" verb
aller: vais, vas, va, allons, allez, vont

2. Minor spelling changes in some conjugation forms:
"-cer" verbs: e.g., "commencer" (nous commençons)
"-ger" verbs: e.g., "manger" (nous mangeons)
"-yer" verbs: e.g., "envoyer" (j'/il envoie, tu envoies, ils envoient)
"-eler" verbs: e.g., "appeler" (j'/il appelle, tu appelles, ils appellent)
"e" + consonant + "-er": e.g., "lever" (je/il lève, tu lèves, ils lèvent)

******-ir Verbs******

1. "-tir," "-mir," & "-vir" Verbs
dormir: dors, dors, dort, dormons, dormez, dorment
other examples: partir, servir

2. "-vrir," "-frir," & "-llir" Verbs
ouvrir: ouvre, ouvres, ouvre, ouvrons, ouvrez, ouvrent
other examples: ofrir, cueillir, couvrir, souffrir, découvrir, accueillir

3. "venir," "tenir," & their derivatives
venir: viens, viens, vient, venons, venez, viennent
other examples: tenir, devenir, obtenir, advenir, revenir, conevenir, provenir, prévenir, survenir, intervenir, détenir, retenir, abstenir, contenir, soutenir, maintenir, appartenir, entretenir

4. Irregular verbs ending in "-oir"
Verbs ending in "-oir" do not follow a single conjugation pattern.
avoir: ai, as, a, avons, avez, ont
savoir: sais, sais, sait, savons, savez, savent
devoir: dois, dois, doit, devons, devez, doivent
pouvoir: peux, peux, peut, pouvons, pouvez, peuvent
vouloir: veux, veux, veut, voulons, voulez, veulent
voir: vois, vois, voit, voyons, voyez, voient
asseoir: assieds, assieds, assied, asseyons, asseyez, asseyent
décevoir: deçois, deçois, deçoit, decevons, decevez, deçoivent
recevoir: reçois, reçois, reçoit, reçevons, reçevez, reçoivent
falloir: il faut, pleuvoir: il pleut, valoir: il vaut

5. Other irregular "-ir" verbs
A few verbs are completely irregular and do not follow any pattern:
acquérir: acquiers, acquiers, acquiert, acquérons, acquérez, acquièrent
bouillir: bous, bous, bout, bouillons, bouillez, bouillent
courir: cours, cours, court, courons, courez, courent
parcourir: parcours, parcours, parcourt, parcourons, parcourez, parcourent
secourir: secours, secours, secourt, secourons, secourez, secourent
mourir: meurs, meurs, meurt, mourons, mourez, meurent

******-re Verbs******

1. "prendre" & its derivations
prendre: prends, prends, prend, prenons, prenez, prennent
other examples: enreprendre, surprendre, reprendre, méprendre

2. "mettre," "-battre," & their derivations
mettre: mets, mets, met, mettons, mettez, mettent
battre: bats, bats, bat, battons, battez, battent
other examples: promettre, débattre, admettre, commettre, abattre, combattre, trasmettre, soumettre, permettre, compromettre

3. "rompre" & its derivations
rompre: romps, romps, rompt, rompons, rompez, rompent
other examples: corrompre, interrompre

4. "-aindre," "-eindre," & "-oindre"
peindre: peins, peins, peint, peignons, peignez, peignent
other examples: craindre, joindre, adjoindre, astreindre, atteindre, ceindre, contraindre, dépeindre, disjoindre, empreindre, éteindre, feindre, geindre, plaindre, rejoindre, restreindre, teindre

5. "-uire," "-dire," "-fire," & "-lire"
cuire: cuis, cuis, cuit, cuisons, cuisez, cuisent
lire: lis, lis, lit, lisons, lisez, lisent
other examples: dire, confire, conduire, construire, contredire, déduire, détruire, élire, induire, instruire, interdire, induire, introduire, luire, médire, nuire, prédire, produire, reconduire, reconstuire, réduire, séduire, suffire, traduire
One exception is the second-person plural of the verb "dire" (and its derivatives), which is conjugated as "vous dites."

6. "-crire" verbs
écrire: écris, écris, écrit, écrivons, écrivez, écrivent
other examples: inscrire, prescrire, proscrire, récrire, transcrire

7. "-aître" verbs (except "naître")
connaître: connais, connais, connaît, connaissons, connaissez, connaissent
other examples: apparaître, paraître, comparaître, disparaître, méconnaître, reconnaître, reapparaître, transparaître

8. Other completely irregular "-re" verbs
clore, conclure, coudre, croire, dissoudre, distraire, exclure, inclure, moudre, plaire, résoudre, rire, sourire, suivre, vivre

PRESENT SUBJUNCTIVE TENSE

1. The verbs "être" & "avoir" are completely irregular:
être: sois, sois, soit, soyons, soyez, soient
avoir: aie, aies, ait, ayons, ayez, aient

2. The following verbs have irregular stems but regular endings:
aller (aill-/all-): aille, ailles, aille, allions, alliez, aillent
faire (fass-): fasse, fasses, fasse, fassions, fassiez, fassent
pouvoir (puiss-): puisse, puisses, puisse, puissions, puissiez, puissent
savoir (sach-): sache, saches, sache, sachions, sachiez, sachent
valoir (vaill-/val-): vaille, vailles, vaille, valions, valiez, vaillent
vouloir (veuill-/voul-): veuille, veuilles, veuille, voulions, vouliez, veuillent

3. The verb "falloir"
The verb "falloir" is impersonal and has only a third-person singular form, which is irregular, i.e., "il faille" *(it is necessary)*.

SIMPLE FUTURE TENSE

The following verbs have irregular stem:
aller (ir-), avoir (aur-), courir (courr-), devenir (deviendr-), devoir (devr-), envoyer (enverr-), être (ser-), faire (fer-), falloir (faudr-), mourir (mourr-), pleuvoir (pleuvr-), recevoir (recevr-), savoir (saur-), tenir (tiendr-), valoir (vaudr-), venir (viendr-), voir (verr-), vouloir (voudr-)

Some verbs that undergo minor spelling changes, for example:
employer (emploier-), essuyer (essuier-), nettoyer (nettoier-), acheter (achèter-), appeler (appeller-), jeter (jetter-)

SIMPLE CONDITIONAL TENSE

Same irregular verbs as in the future indicative tense.

IMPERFECT INDICATIVE TENSE

Only one irregular verb:
être: étais, étais, était, étions, étiez, étaient
Some verbs undergo minor spelling changes similar to those in other tenses to maintain the proper pronunciation.

IMPERATIVE

1. Singular Informal (i.e., "tu" form)
être (sois), avoir (aie), savoir (sache), vouloir (veuille)

2. Plural and Singular Formal (i.e., "vous" form)
être (soyez), avoir (ayez), savoir (sachez), vouloir (veuillez)

3. Commands using "nous" form
être (soyon), avoir (ayon), savoir (sachon)

PAST PARTICIPLE

acquérir (acquis), apprendre (appris), avoir (eu), boire (bu), comprendre (compris), conduire (conduit), craindre (craint), devoir (dû), dire (dit), écrire (écrit), être (été), faire (fait), falloir (fallu), lire (lu), mettre (mis), mourir (mort), naître (né), offrir (offert), ouvrir (ouvert), peindre (peint), plaire (plu), pleuvoir (plu), pouvoir (pu), prendre (pris), recevoir (reçu), rire (ri), savoir (su), suivre (suivi), vivre (veçu), voir (vu), vouloir (volu)

SIMPLE PAST

avoir, être, boire, conduire, connaître, courir, couvrir, craindre, croire, devoir, écrire, éteindre, faire, falloir, introduire, lire, mettre, mourir, naître, obtenir, offrir, peindre, plaire, pleuvoir, pouvoir, prendre, recevoir, rire, savoir, tenir, valoir, venir, vivre, vouloir

Made in the USA
Coppell, TX
12 January 2025

44308902R00227